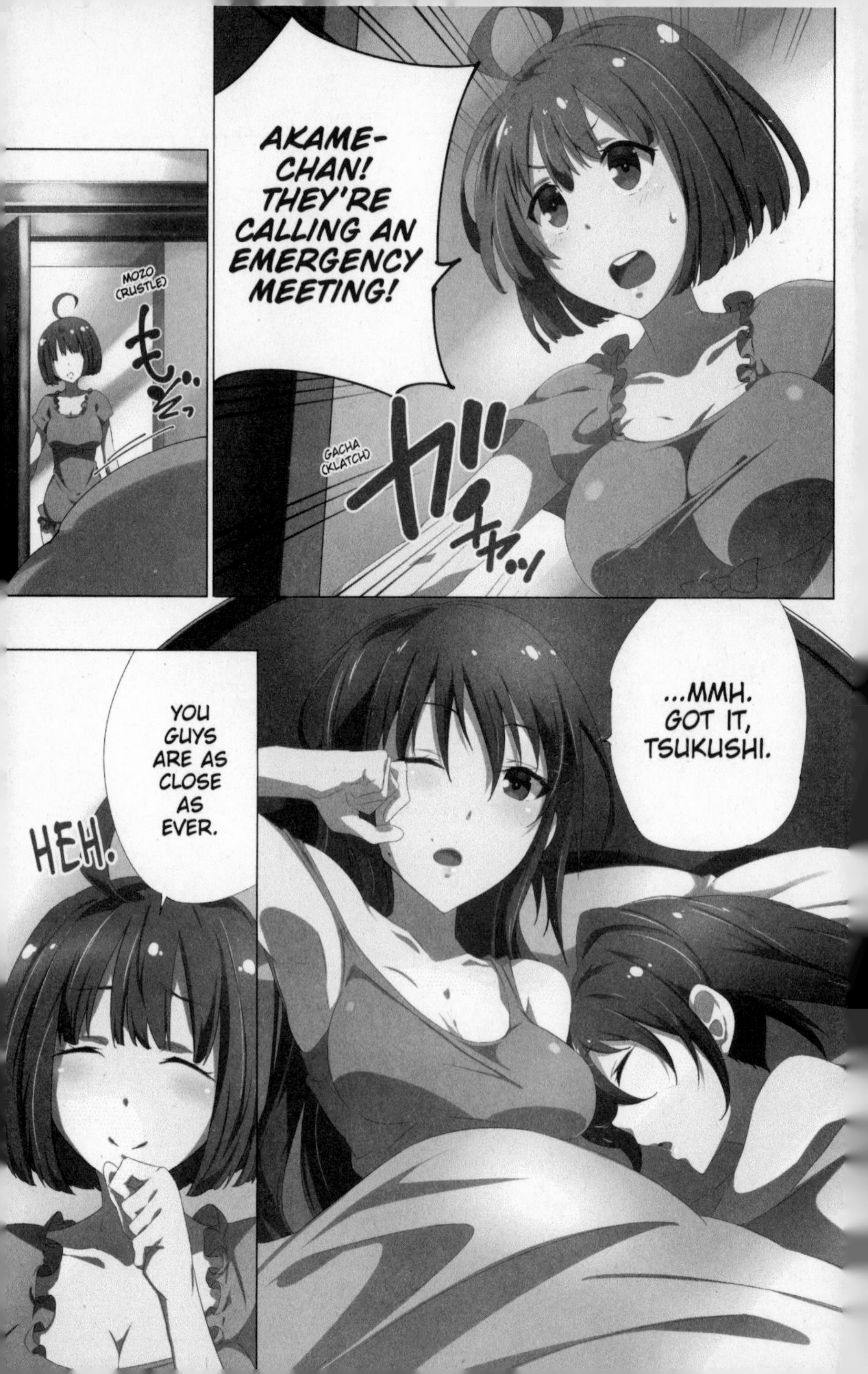
AKAME-CHAN! THEY'RE CALLING AN EMERGENCY MEETING!
GACHA (KLATCH)
ガチャッ
MOZO (RUSTLE)
もぞっ
...MMH. GOT IT, TSUKUSHI.
YOU GUYS ARE AS CLOSE AS EVER.
HEH.

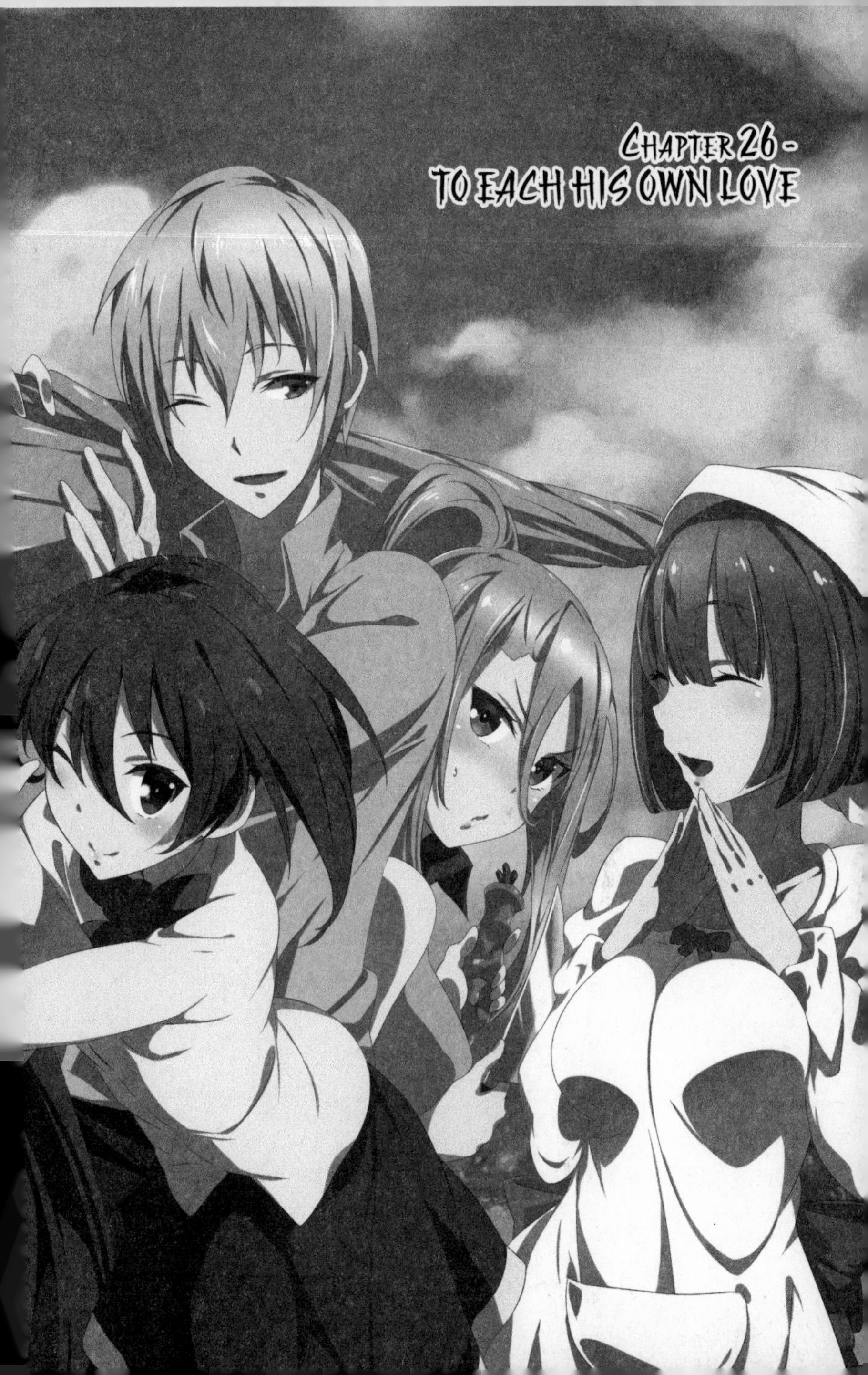
Chapter 26 -
To Each His Own Love

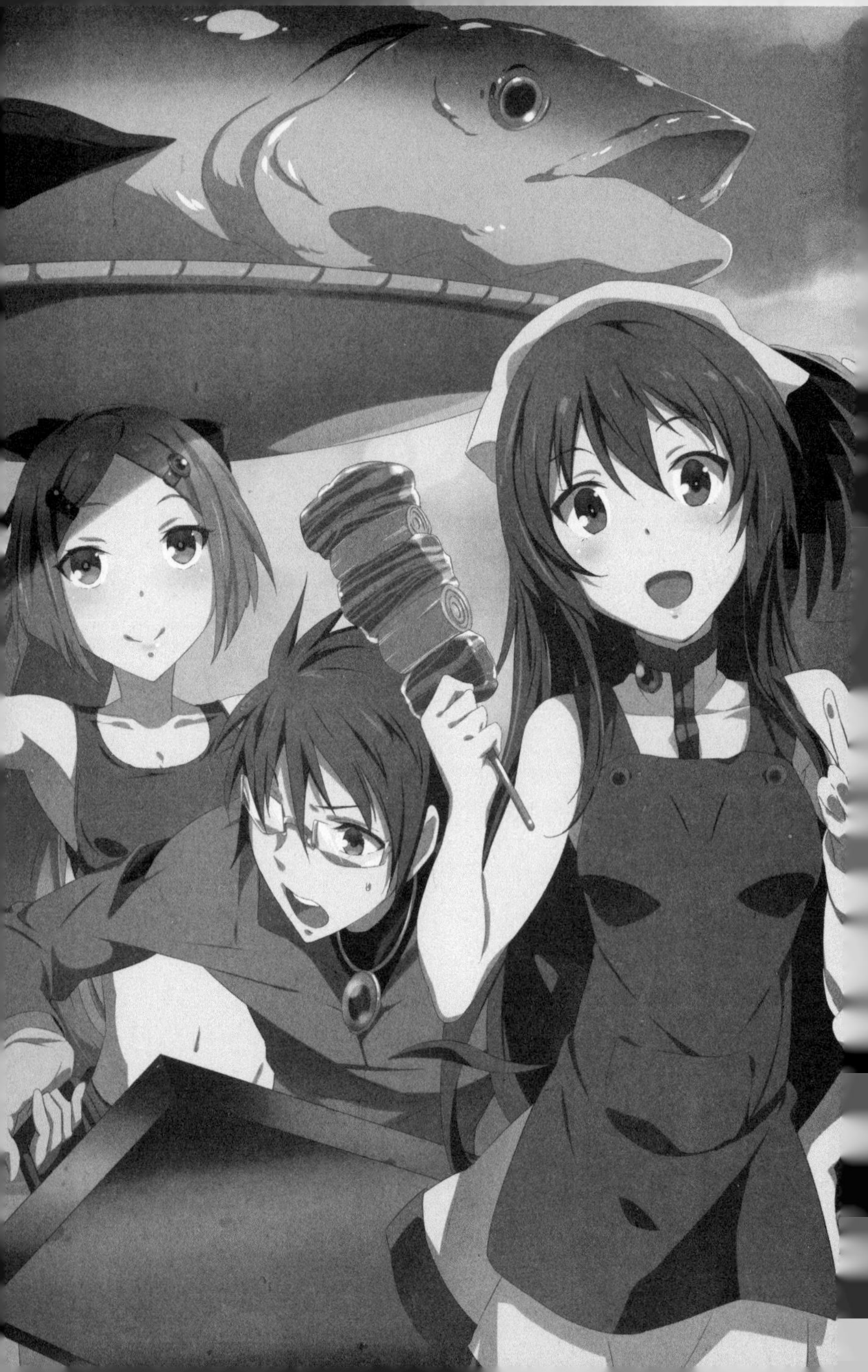

Akame ga KILL! ZERO

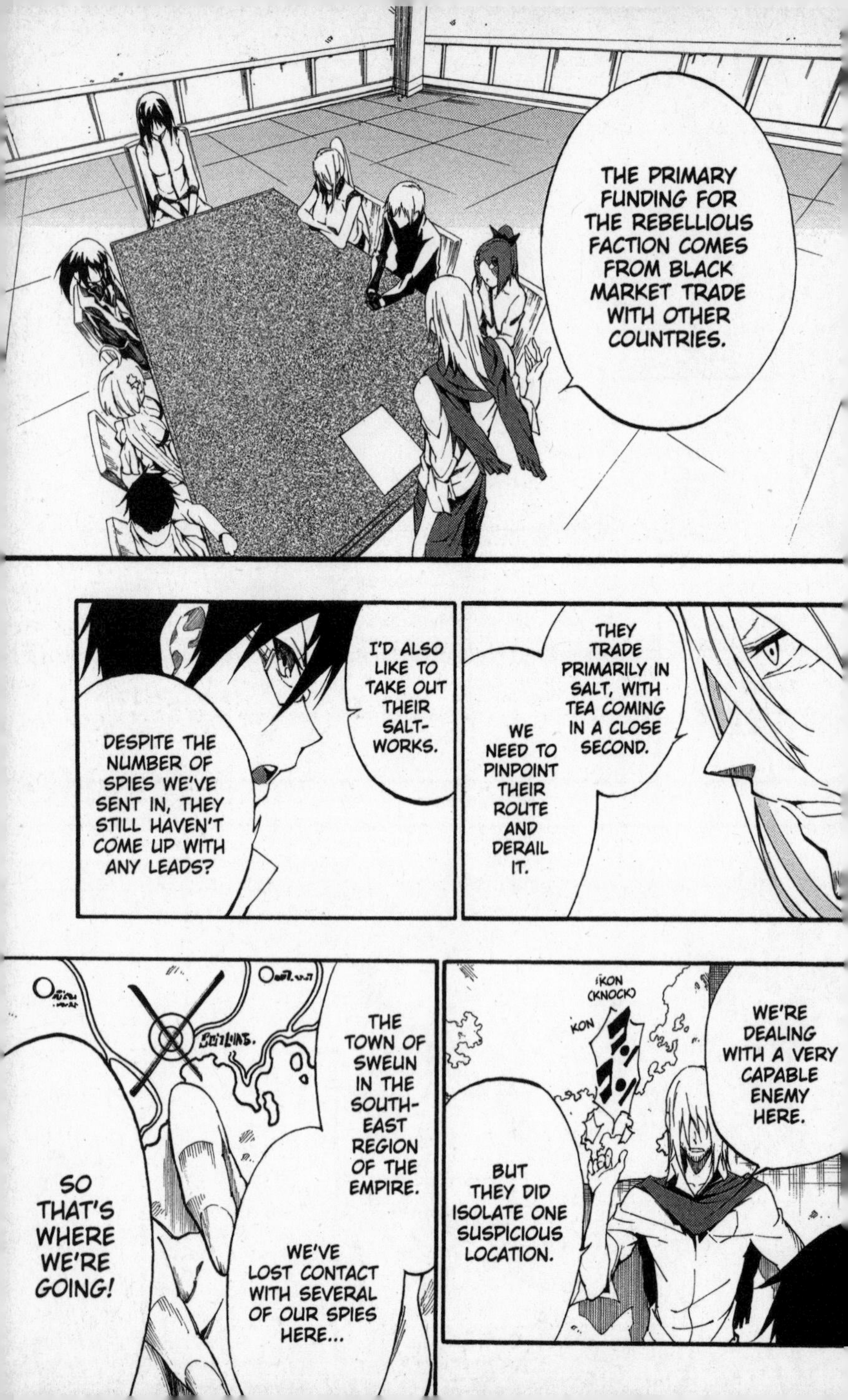
THE PRIMARY FUNDING FOR THE REBELLIOUS FACTION COMES FROM BLACK MARKET TRADE WITH OTHER COUNTRIES.
THEY TRADE PRIMARILY IN SALT, WITH TEA COMING IN A CLOSE SECOND.
WE NEED TO PINPOINT THEIR ROUTE AND DERAIL IT.
I'D ALSO LIKE TO TAKE OUT THEIR SALT-WORKS.
DESPITE THE NUMBER OF SPIES WE'VE SENT IN, THEY STILL HAVEN'T COME UP WITH ANY LEADS?
WE'RE DEALING WITH A VERY CAPABLE ENEMY HERE.
KON KON (KNOCK)
BUT THEY DID ISOLATE ONE SUSPICIOUS LOCATION.
THE TOWN OF SWELIN IN THE SOUTH-EAST REGION OF THE EMPIRE.
WE'VE LOST CONTACT WITH SEVERAL OF OUR SPIES HERE...
SO THAT'S WHERE WE'RE GOING!

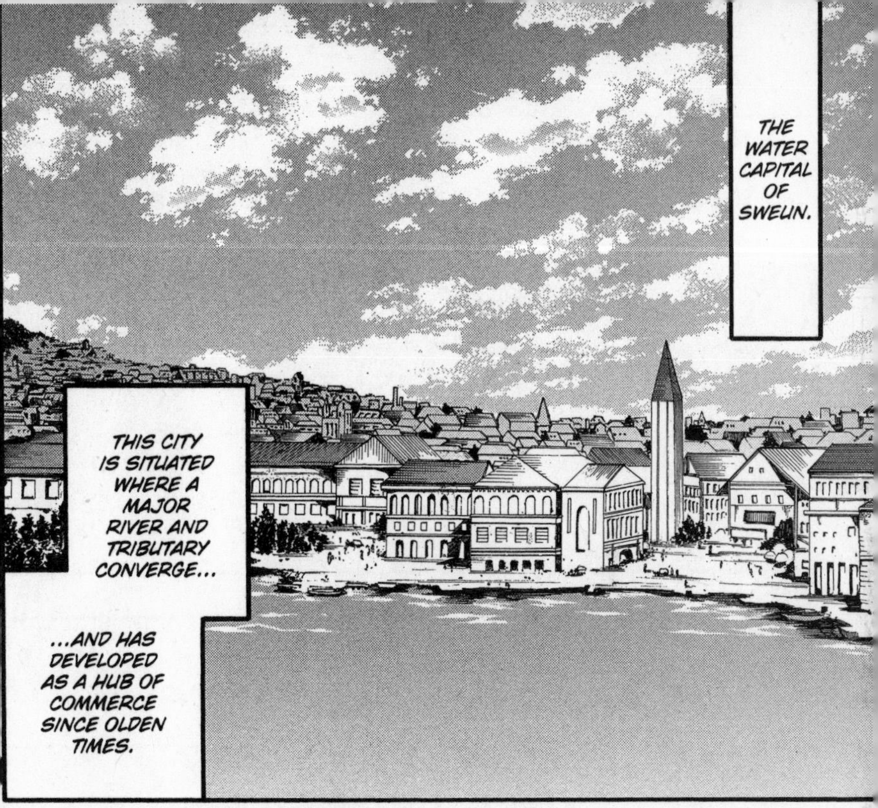
THE WATER CAPITAL OF SWEUN.
THIS CITY IS SITUATED WHERE A MAJOR RIVER AND TRIBUTARY CONVERGE...
...AND HAS DEVELOPED AS A HUB OF COMMERCE SINCE OLDEN TIMES.

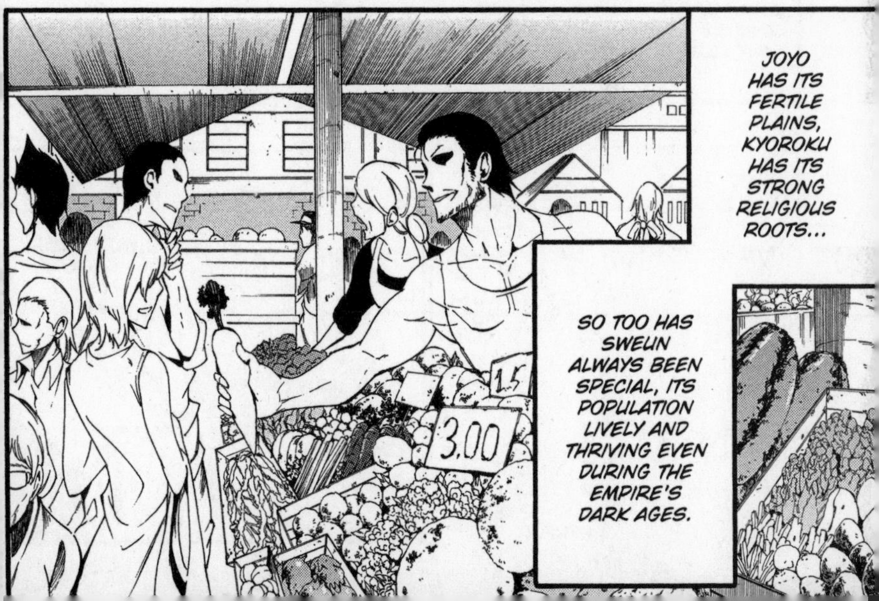
JOYO HAS ITS FERTILE PLAINS, KYOROKU HAS ITS STRONG RELIGIOUS ROOTS...
1.5
3.00
SO TOO HAS SWEUN ALWAYS BEEN SPECIAL, ITS POPULATION LIVELY AND THRIVING EVEN DURING THE EMPIRE'S DARK AGES.

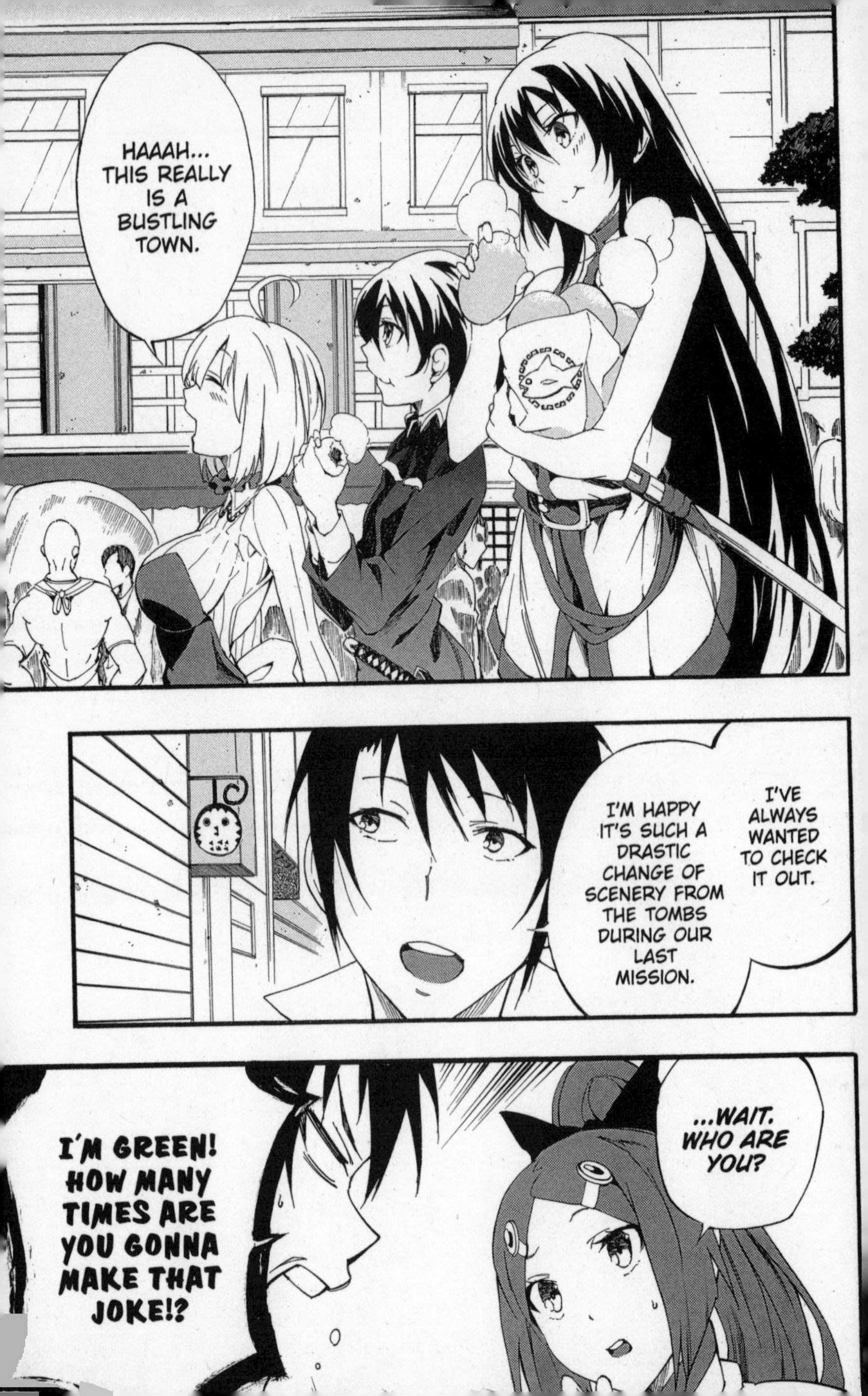
HAAAH... THIS REALLY IS A BUSTLING TOWN.
I'VE ALWAYS WANTED TO CHECK IT OUT.
I'M HAPPY IT'S SUCH A DRASTIC CHANGE OF SCENERY FROM THE TOMBS DURING OUR LAST MISSION.
...WAIT. WHO ARE YOU?
I'M GREEN! HOW MANY TIMES ARE YOU GONNA MAKE THAT JOKE!?

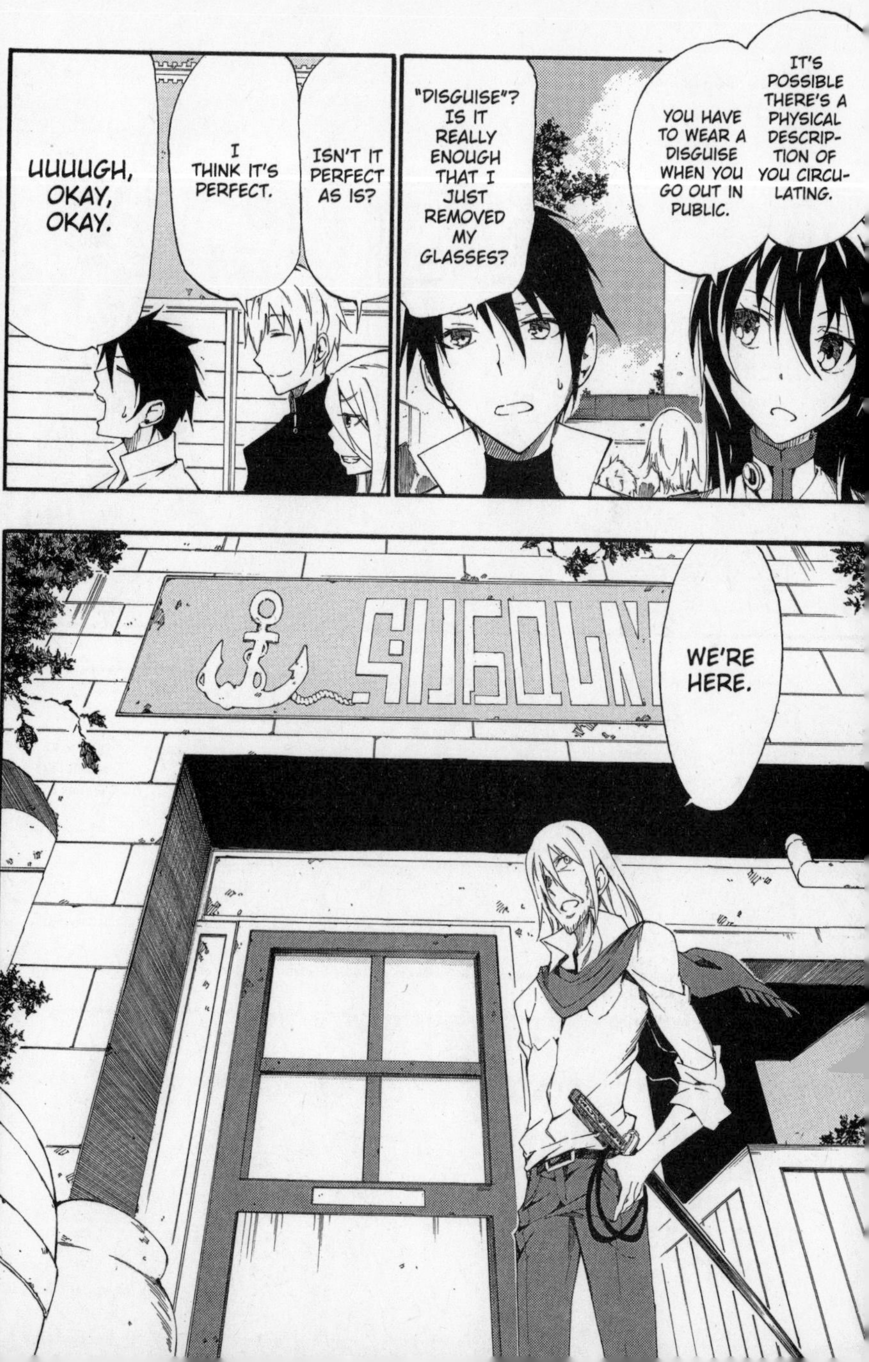
IT'S POSSIBLE THERE'S A PHYSICAL DESCRIPTION OF YOU CIRCULATING.
YOU HAVE TO WEAR A DISGUISE WHEN YOU GO OUT IN PUBLIC.
"DISGUISE"? IS IT REALLY ENOUGH THAT I JUST REMOVED MY GLASSES?
ISN'T IT PERFECT AS IS?
I THINK IT'S PERFECT.
UUUUGH, OKAY, OKAY.
WE'RE HERE.

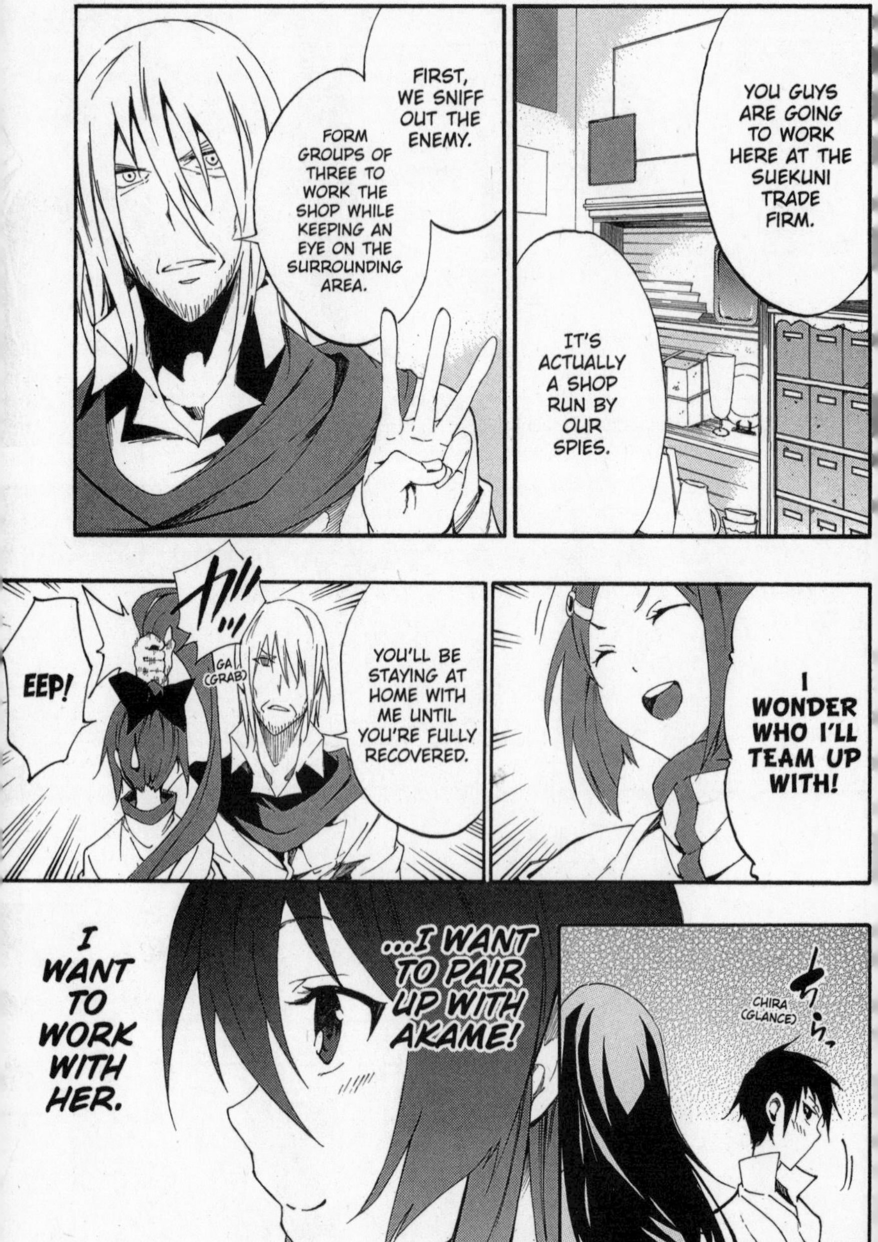
YOU GUYS ARE GOING TO WORK HERE AT THE SUEKUNI TRADE FIRM.
IT'S ACTUALLY A SHOP RUN BY OUR SPIES.
FIRST, WE SNIFF OUT THE ENEMY.
FORM GROUPS OF THREE TO WORK THE SHOP WHILE KEEPING AN EYE ON THE SURROUNDING AREA.
I WONDER WHO I'LL TEAM UP WITH!
YOU'LL BE STAYING AT HOME WITH ME UNTIL YOU'RE FULLY RECOVERED.
GA (GRAB)
EEP!
CHIRA (GLANCE)
...I WANT TO PAIR UP WITH AKAME!
I WANT TO WORK WITH HER.

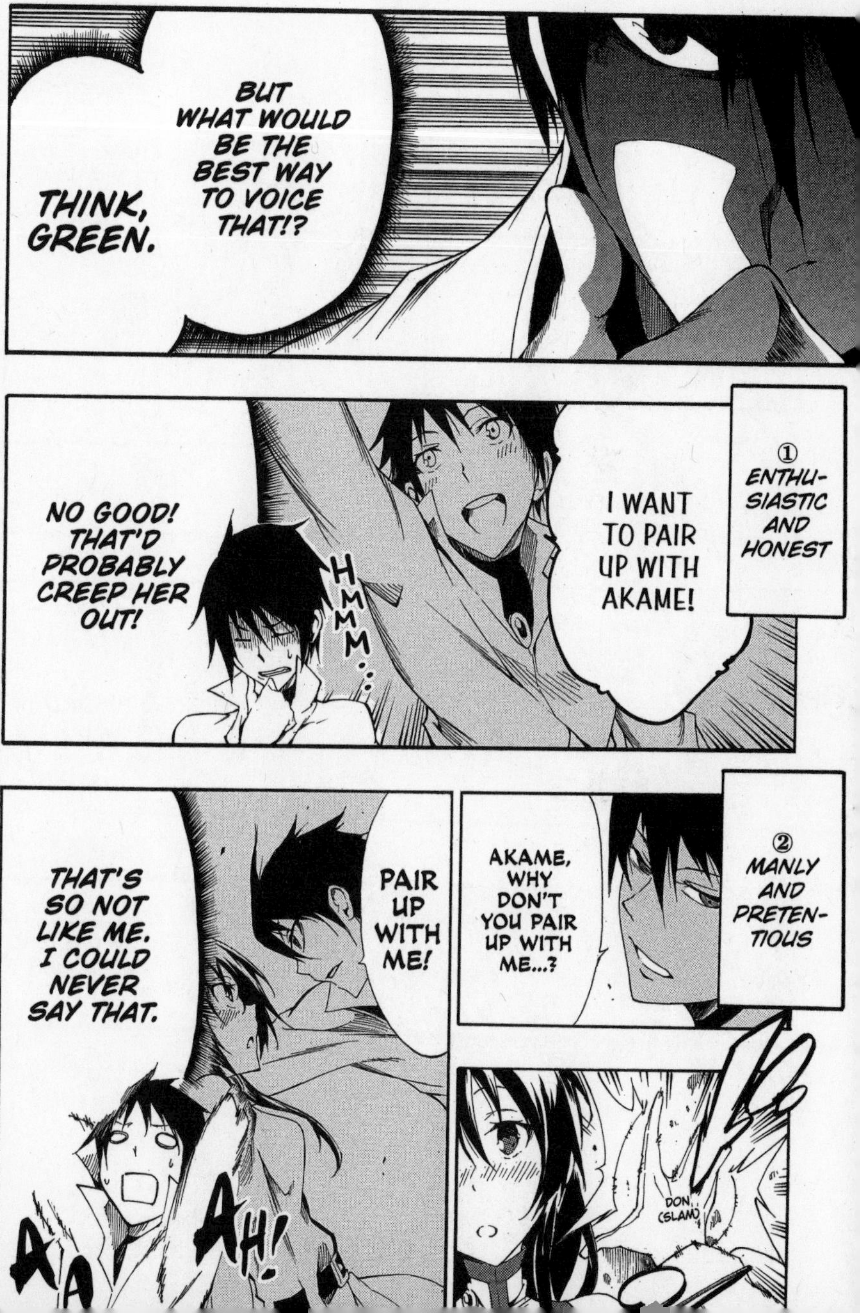
BUT WHAT WOULD BE THE BEST WAY TO VOICE THAT!?
THINK, GREEN.
① ENTHUSIASTIC AND HONEST
I WANT TO PAIR UP WITH AKAME!
HMMM...
NO GOOD! THAT'D PROBABLY CREEP HER OUT!
② MANLY AND PRETENTIOUS
AKAME, WHY DON'T YOU PAIR UP WITH ME...?
DON (SLAM)
PAIR UP WITH ME!
THAT'S SO NOT LIKE ME. I COULD NEVER SAY THAT.
AAAH!

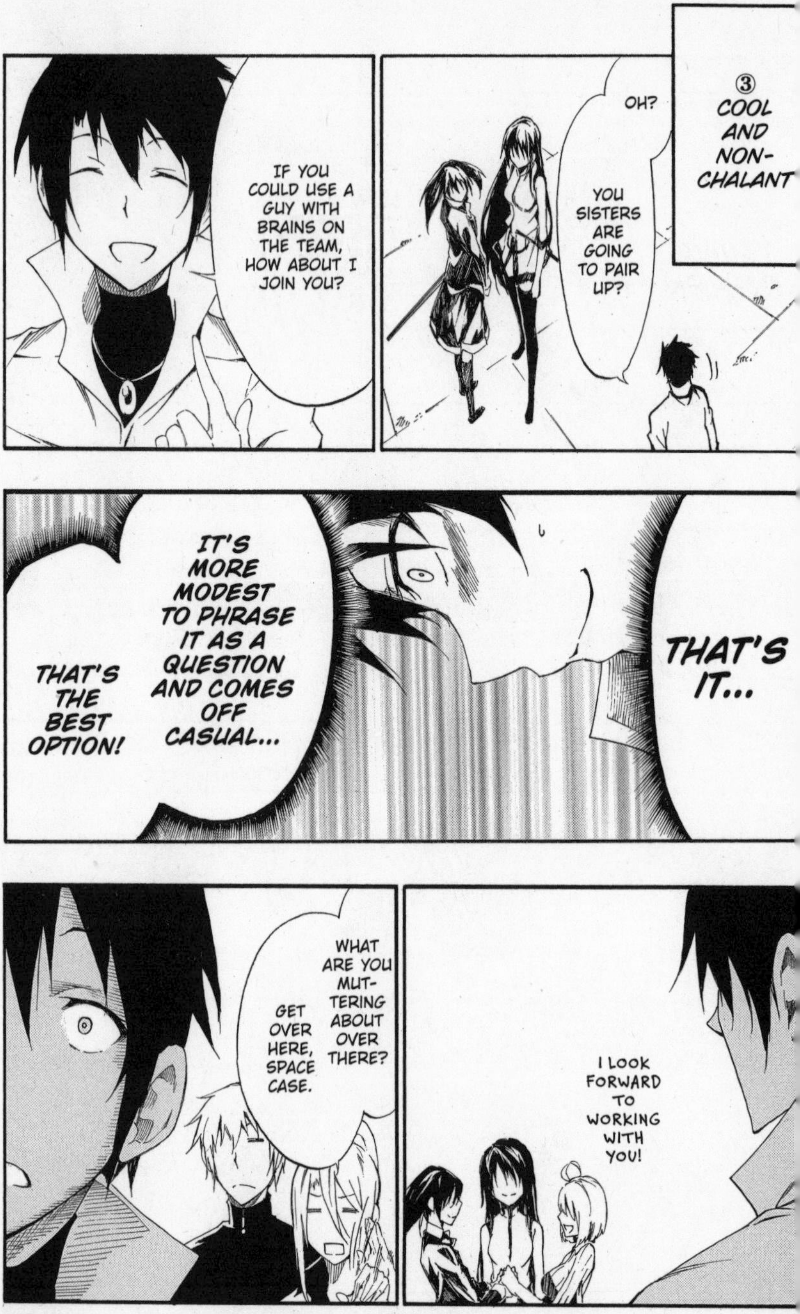
③ COOL AND NON-CHALANT
OH?
YOU SISTERS ARE GOING TO PAIR UP?
IF YOU COULD USE A GUY WITH BRAINS ON THE TEAM, HOW ABOUT I JOIN YOU?
THAT'S IT...
IT'S MORE MODEST TO PHRASE IT AS A QUESTION AND COMES OFF CASUAL...
THAT'S THE BEST OPTION!
I LOOK FORWARD TO WORKING WITH YOU!
WHAT ARE YOU MUT-TERING ABOUT OVER THERE?
GET OVER HERE, SPACE CASE.

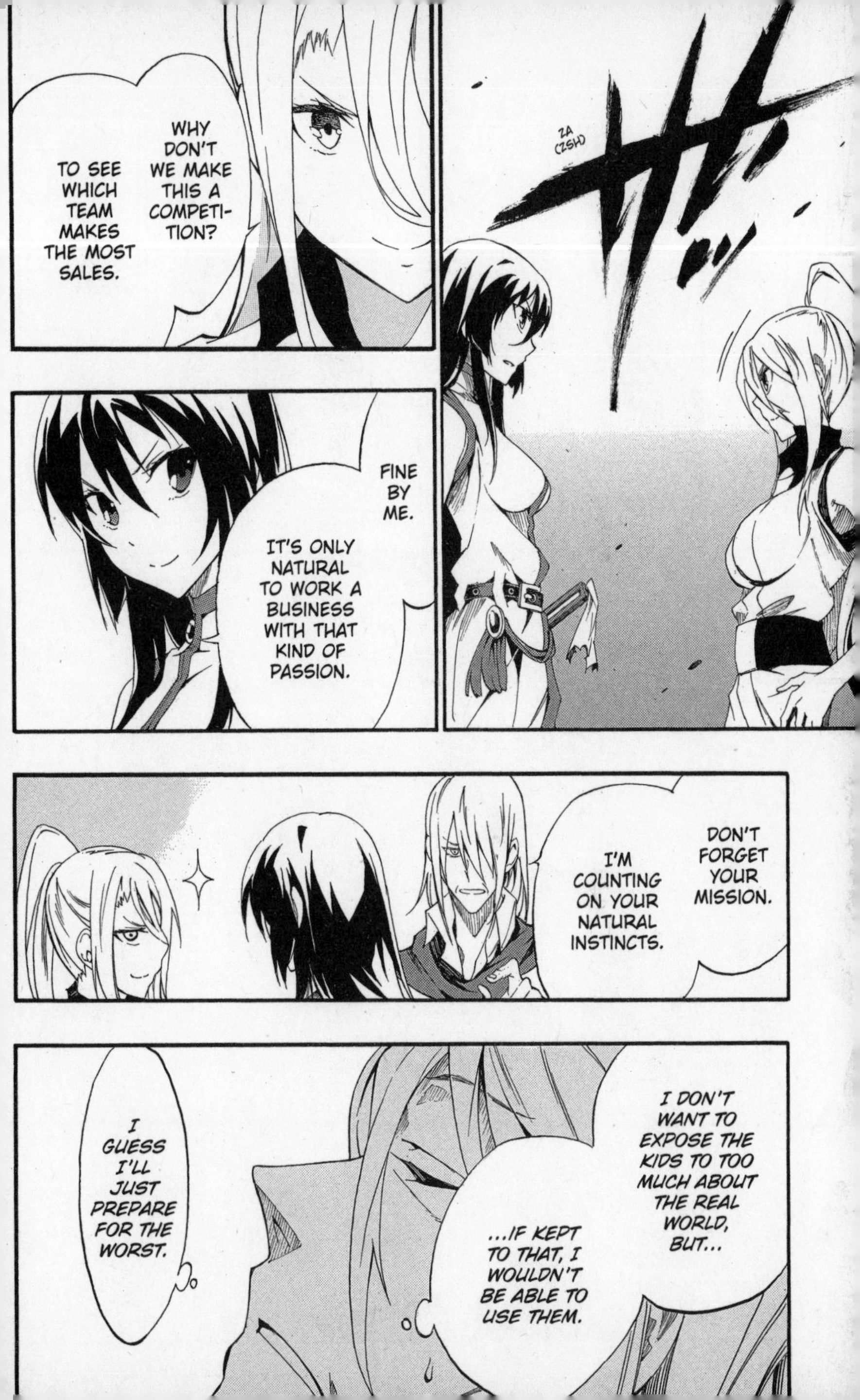
ZA (ZSH)
WHY DON'T WE MAKE THIS A COMPETITION?
TO SEE WHICH TEAM MAKES THE MOST SALES.
FINE BY ME.
IT'S ONLY NATURAL TO WORK A BUSINESS WITH THAT KIND OF PASSION.
DON'T FORGET YOUR MISSION.
I'M COUNTING ON YOUR NATURAL INSTINCTS.
I DON'T WANT TO EXPOSE THE KIDS TO TOO MUCH ABOUT THE REAL WORLD, BUT...
...IF KEPT TO THAT, I WOULDN'T BE ABLE TO USE THEM.
I GUESS I'LL JUST PREPARE FOR THE WORST.

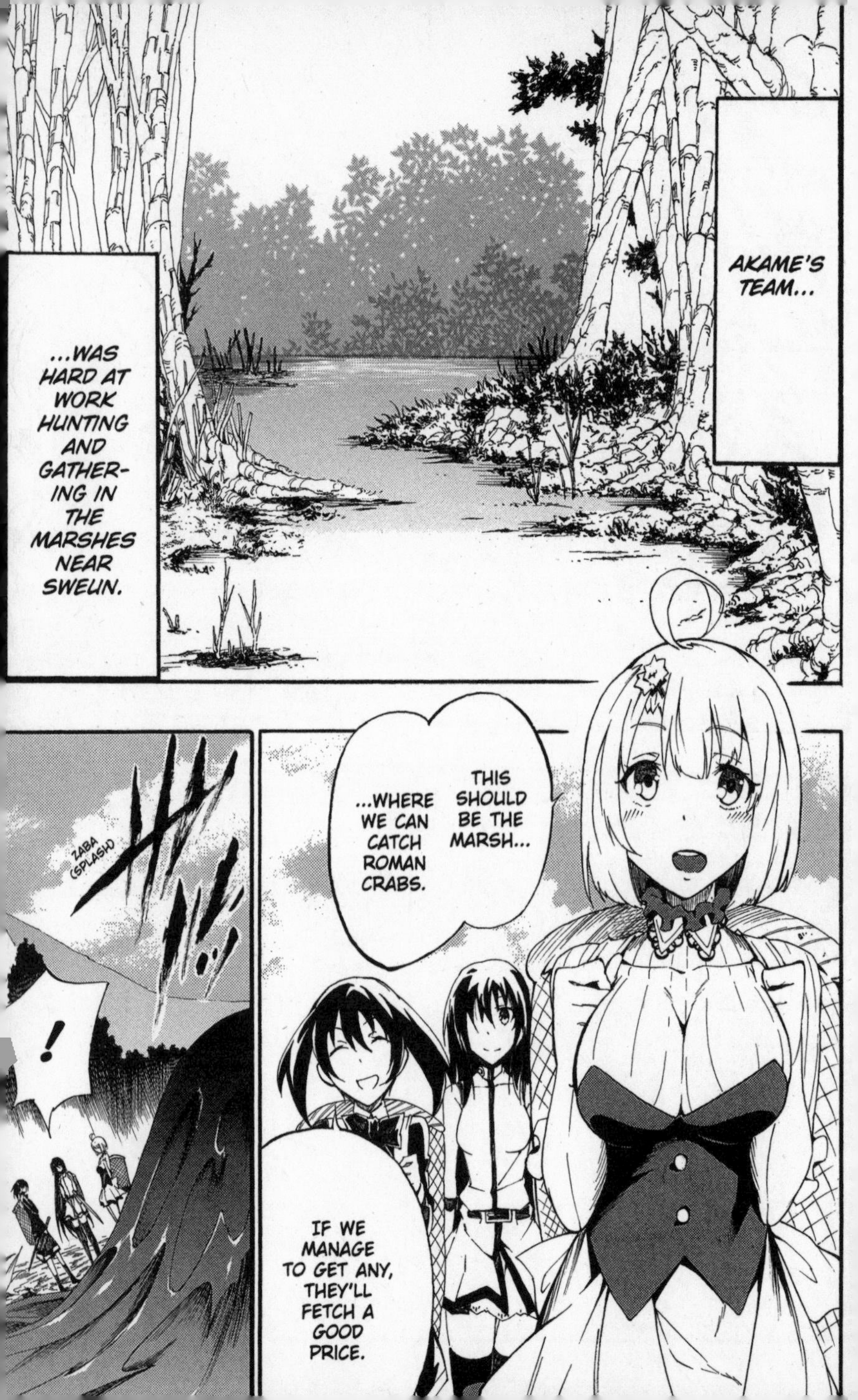
AKAME'S TEAM...
...WAS HARD AT WORK HUNTING AND GATHERING IN THE MARSHES NEAR SWEUN.
THIS SHOULD BE THE MARSH...
...WHERE WE CAN CATCH ROMAN CRABS.
IF WE MANAGE TO GET ANY, THEY'LL FETCH A GOOD PRICE.
ZABA (SPLASH)
!

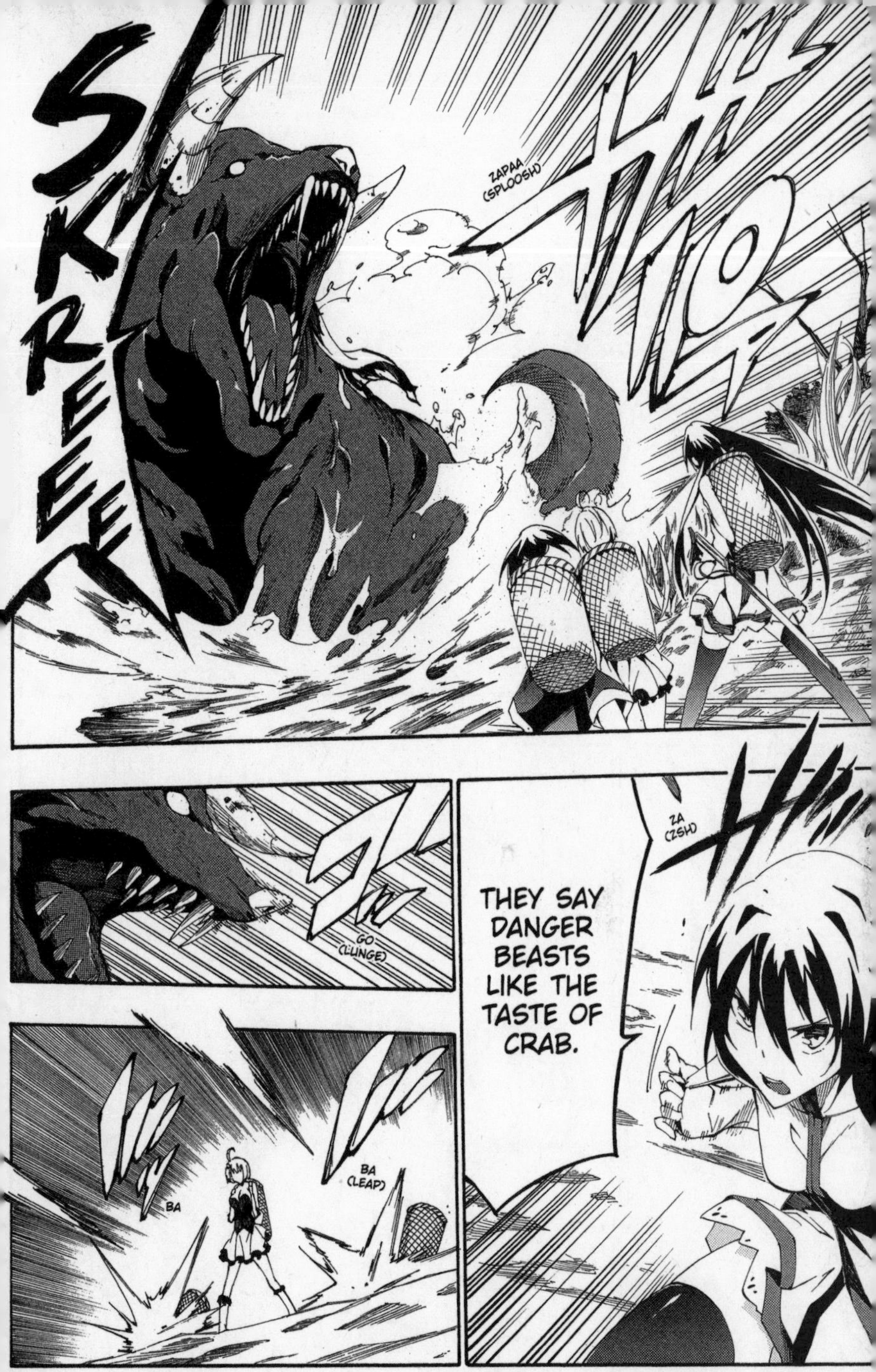
ZAPAA (SPLOOSH)
SKREEEE
ZA (ZSH)
THEY SAY DANGER BEASTS LIKE THE TASTE OF CRAB.
GO (LUNGE)
BA (LEAP)
BA

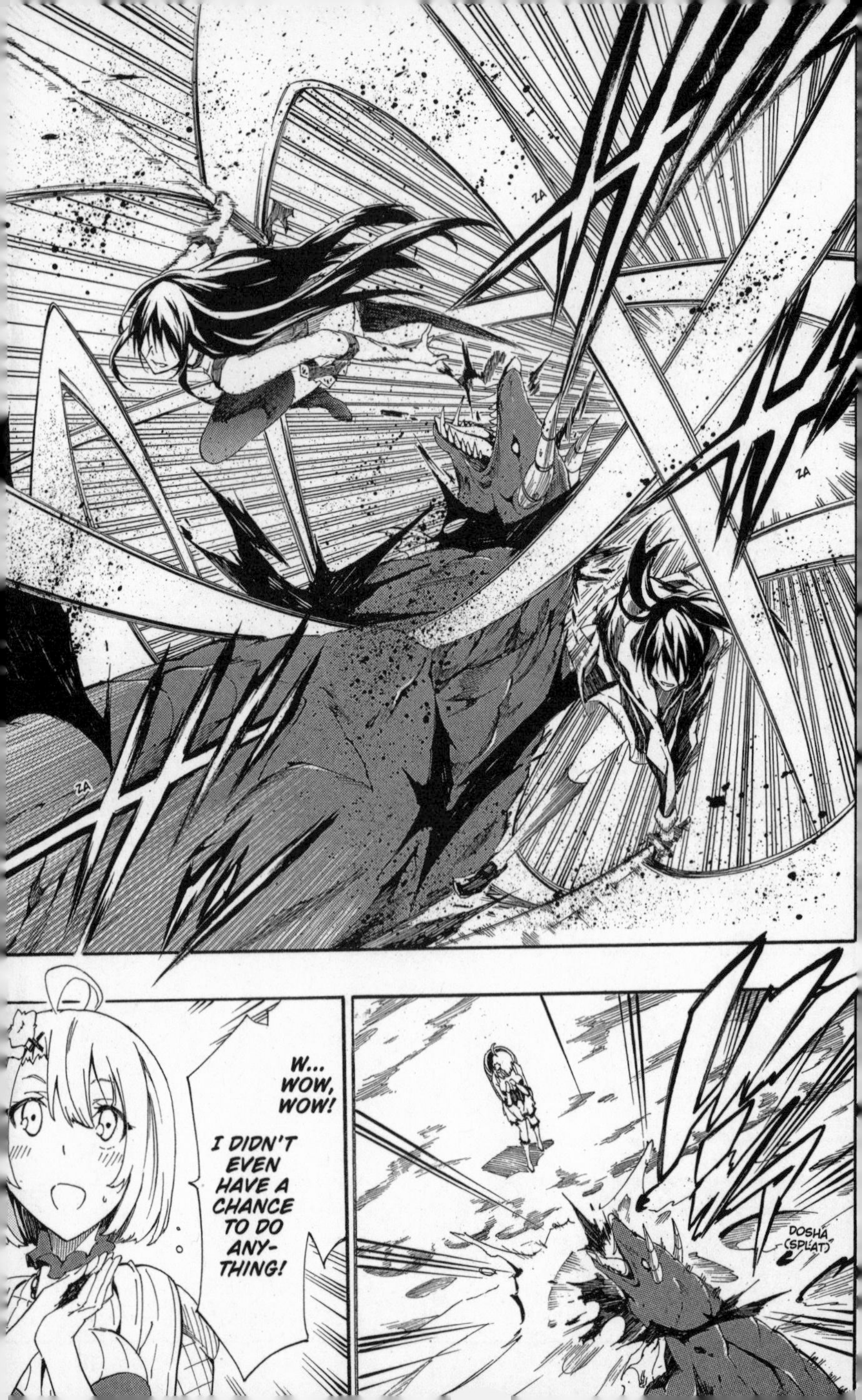
ZA
ZA
ZA
DOSHA (SPLAT)
W... WOW, WOW!
I DIDN'T EVEN HAVE A CHANCE TO DO ANY-THING!

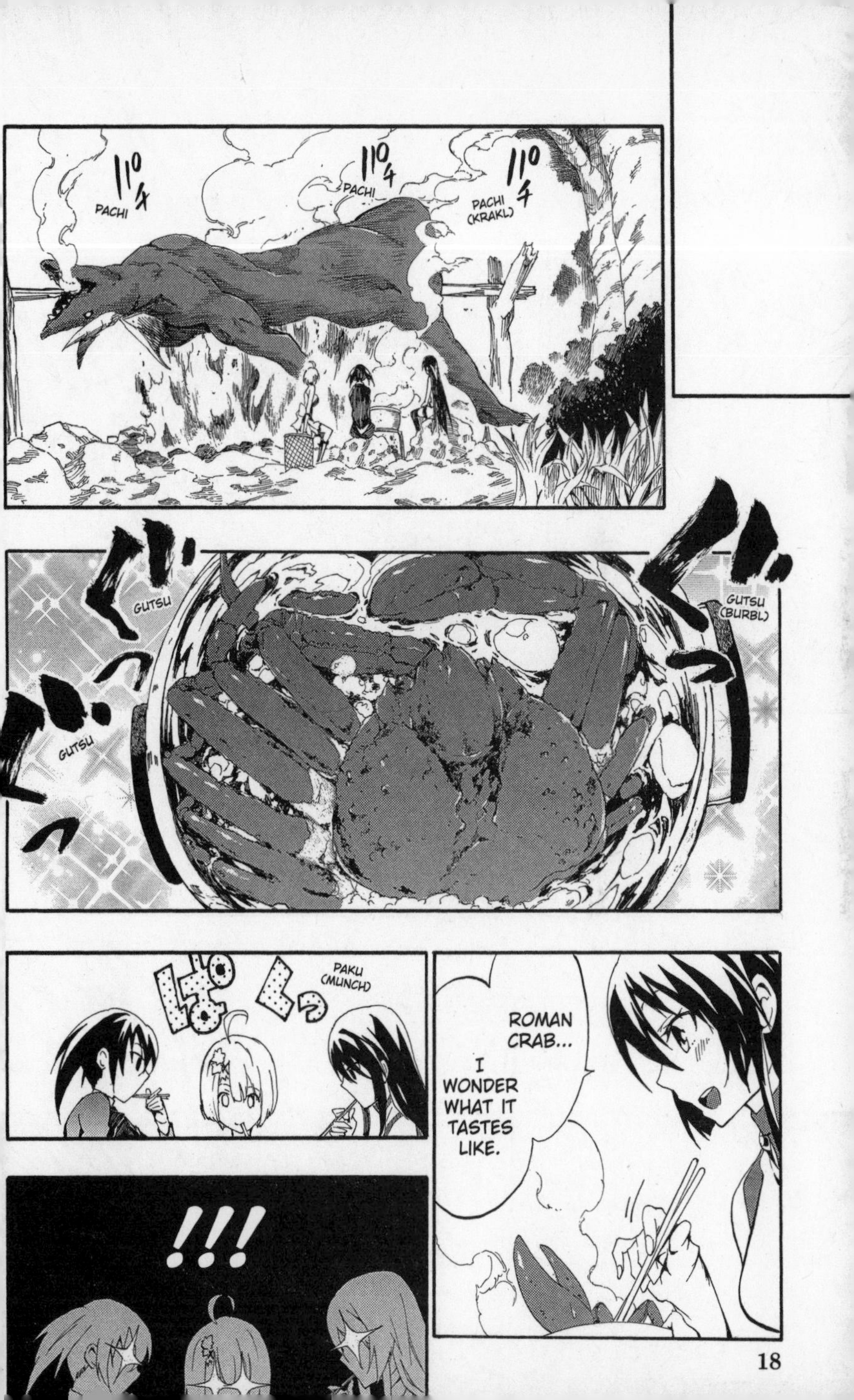

PACHI (KRAKL)
PACHI
PACHI
GUTSU (BURBL)
GUTSU
GUTSU
ROMAN CRAB... I WONDER WHAT IT TASTES LIKE.
PAKU (MUNCH)
!!!

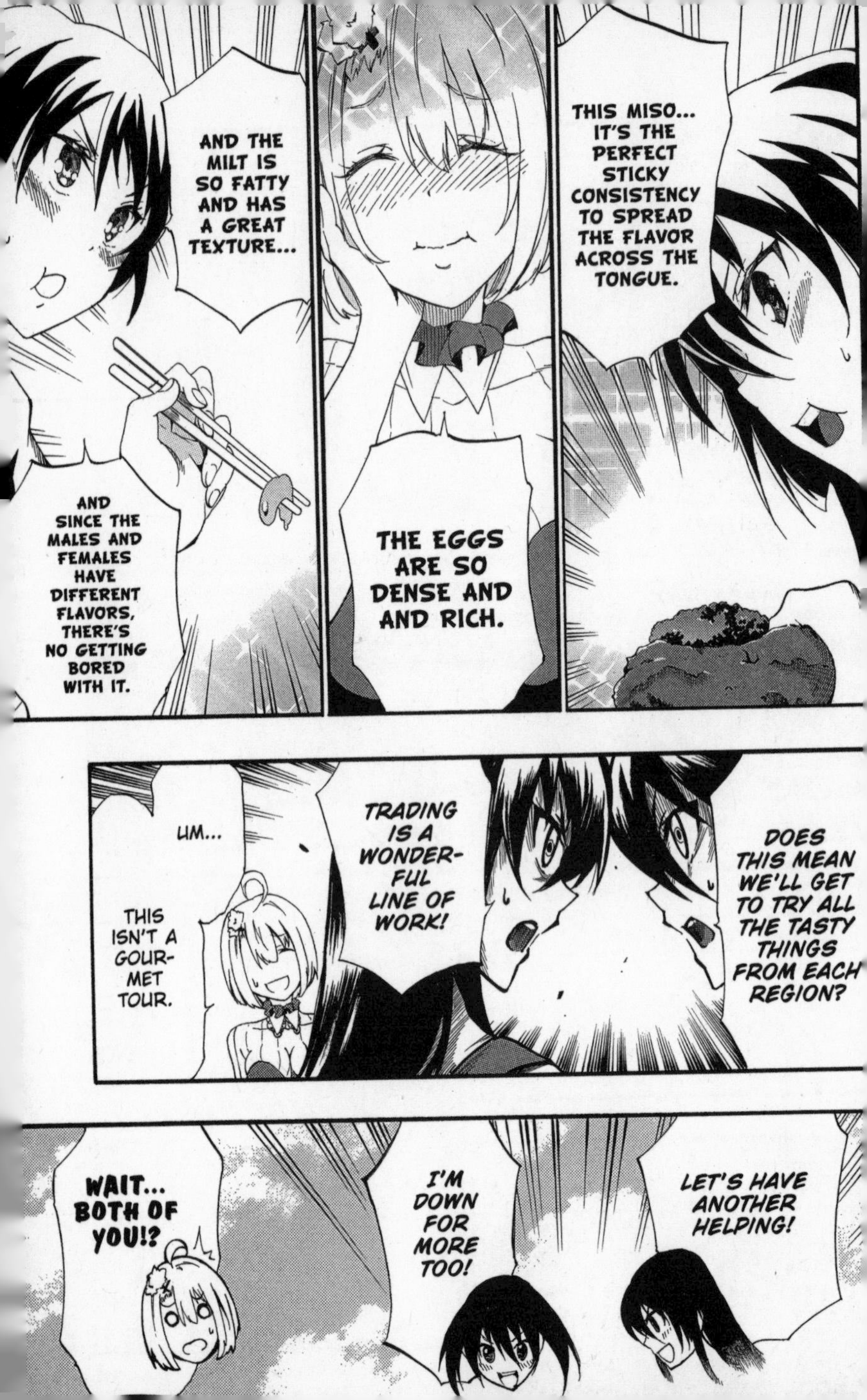
THIS MISO... IT'S THE PERFECT STICKY CONSISTENCY TO SPREAD THE FLAVOR ACROSS THE TONGUE.
THE EGGS ARE SO DENSE AND AND RICH.
AND THE MILT IS SO FATTY AND HAS A GREAT TEXTURE...
AND SINCE THE MALES AND FEMALES HAVE DIFFERENT FLAVORS, THERE'S NO GETTING BORED WITH IT.
DOES THIS MEAN WE'LL GET TO TRY ALL THE TASTY THINGS FROM EACH REGION?
TRADING IS A WONDER-FUL LINE OF WORK!
UM...
THIS ISN'T A GOUR-MET TOUR.
LET'S HAVE ANOTHER HELPING!
I'M DOWN FOR MORE TOO!
WAIT... BOTH OF YOU!?

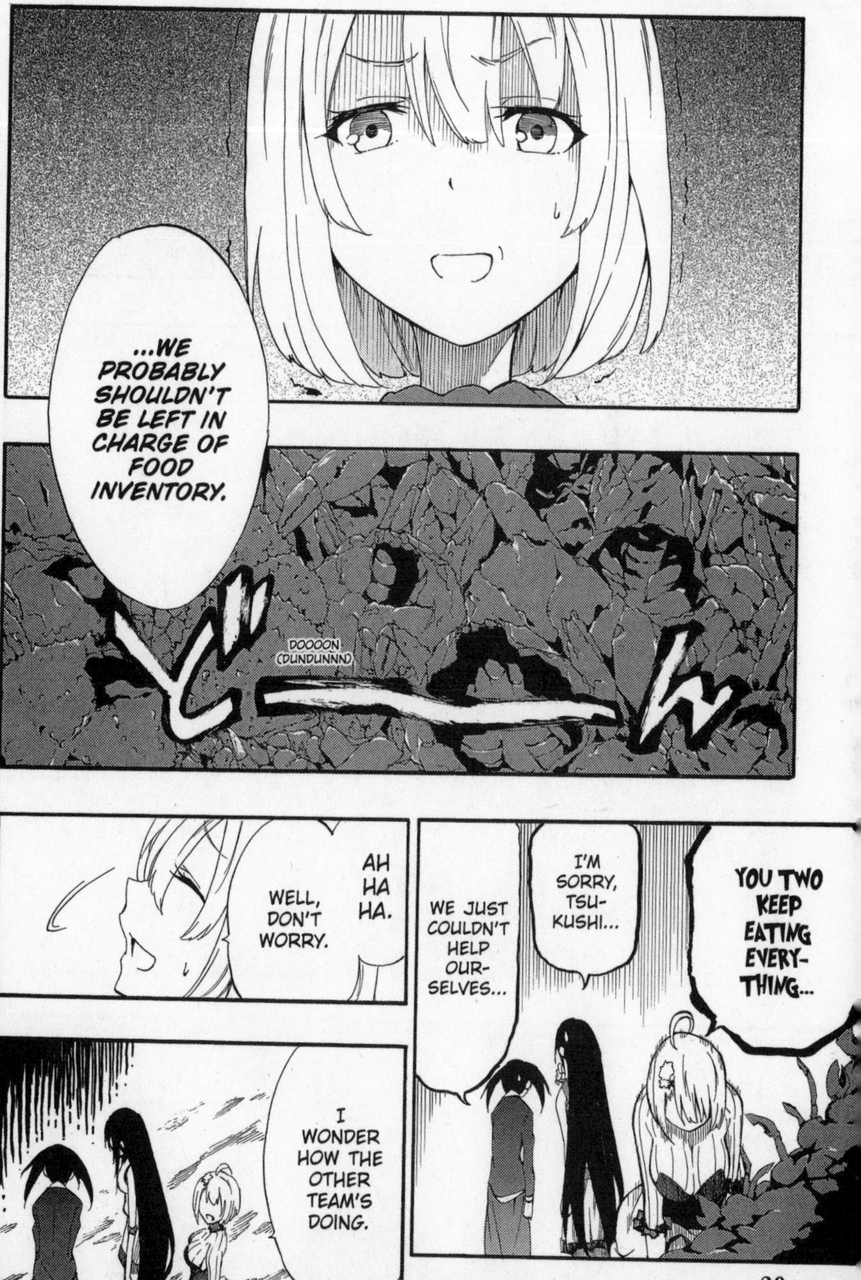
...WE PROBABLY SHOULDN'T BE LEFT IN CHARGE OF FOOD INVENTORY.
DOOOON (DUNDUNNN)
YOU TWO KEEP EATING EVERY-THING...
I'M SORRY, TSU-KUSHI...
WE JUST COULDN'T HELP OUR-SELVES...
AH HA HA.
WELL, DON'T WORRY.
I WONDER HOW THE OTHER TEAM'S DOING.

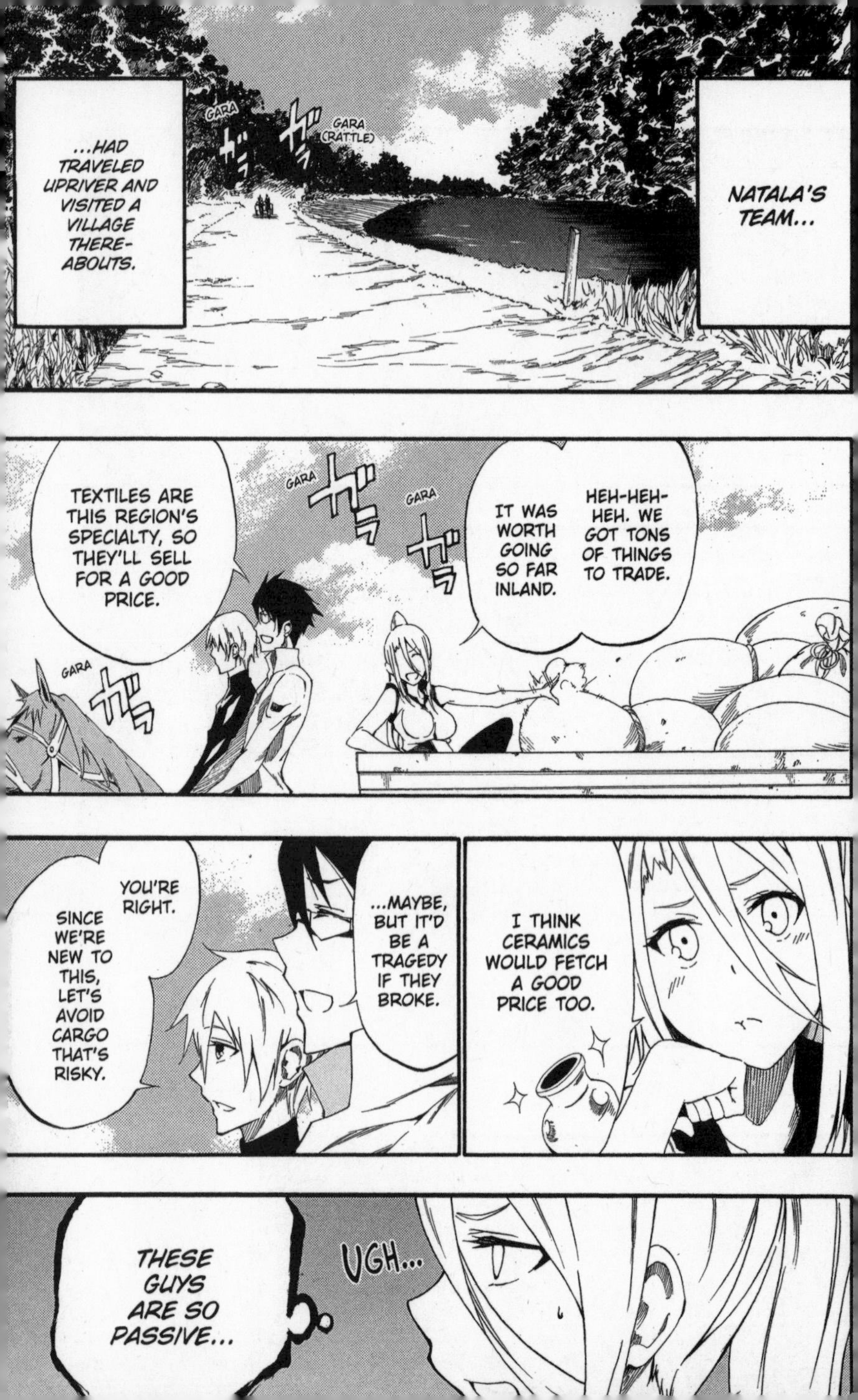
NATALA'S TEAM...
GARA (RATTLE)
GARA
...HAD TRAVELED UPRIVER AND VISITED A VILLAGE THEREABOUTS.
HEH-HEH-HEH. WE GOT TONS OF THINGS TO TRADE.
IT WAS WORTH GOING SO FAR INLAND.
GARA
GARA
TEXTILES ARE THIS REGION'S SPECIALTY, SO THEY'LL SELL FOR A GOOD PRICE.
GARA
I THINK CERAMICS WOULD FETCH A GOOD PRICE TOO.
...MAYBE, BUT IT'D BE A TRAGEDY IF THEY BROKE.
YOU'RE RIGHT.
SINCE WE'RE NEW TO THIS, LET'S AVOID CARGO THAT'S RISKY.
UGH...
THESE GUYS ARE SO PASSIVE...

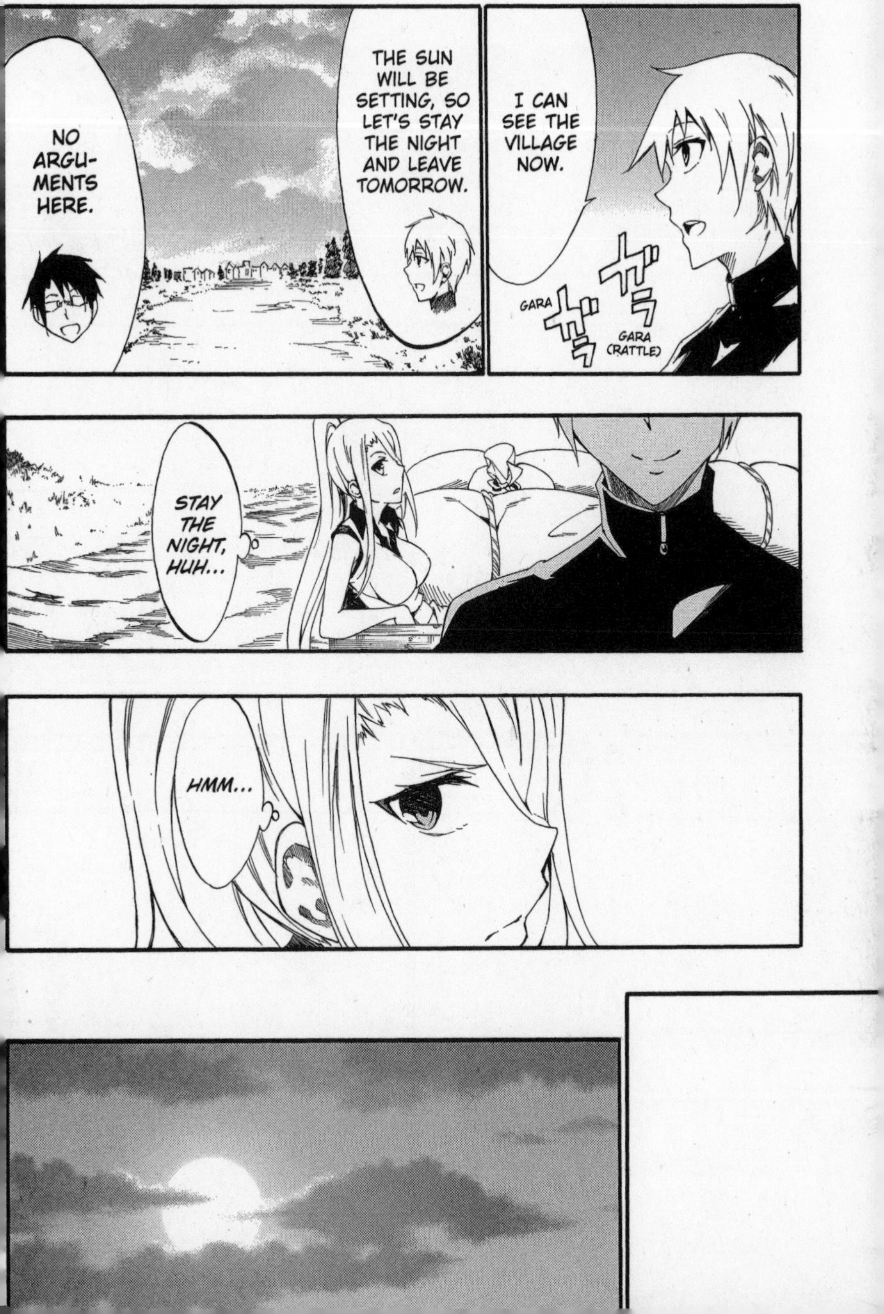
I CAN SEE THE VILLAGE NOW.
GARA
GARA (RATTLE)
THE SUN WILL BE SETTING, SO LET'S STAY THE NIGHT AND LEAVE TOMORROW.
NO ARGUMENTS HERE.
STAY THE NIGHT, HUH...
HMM...

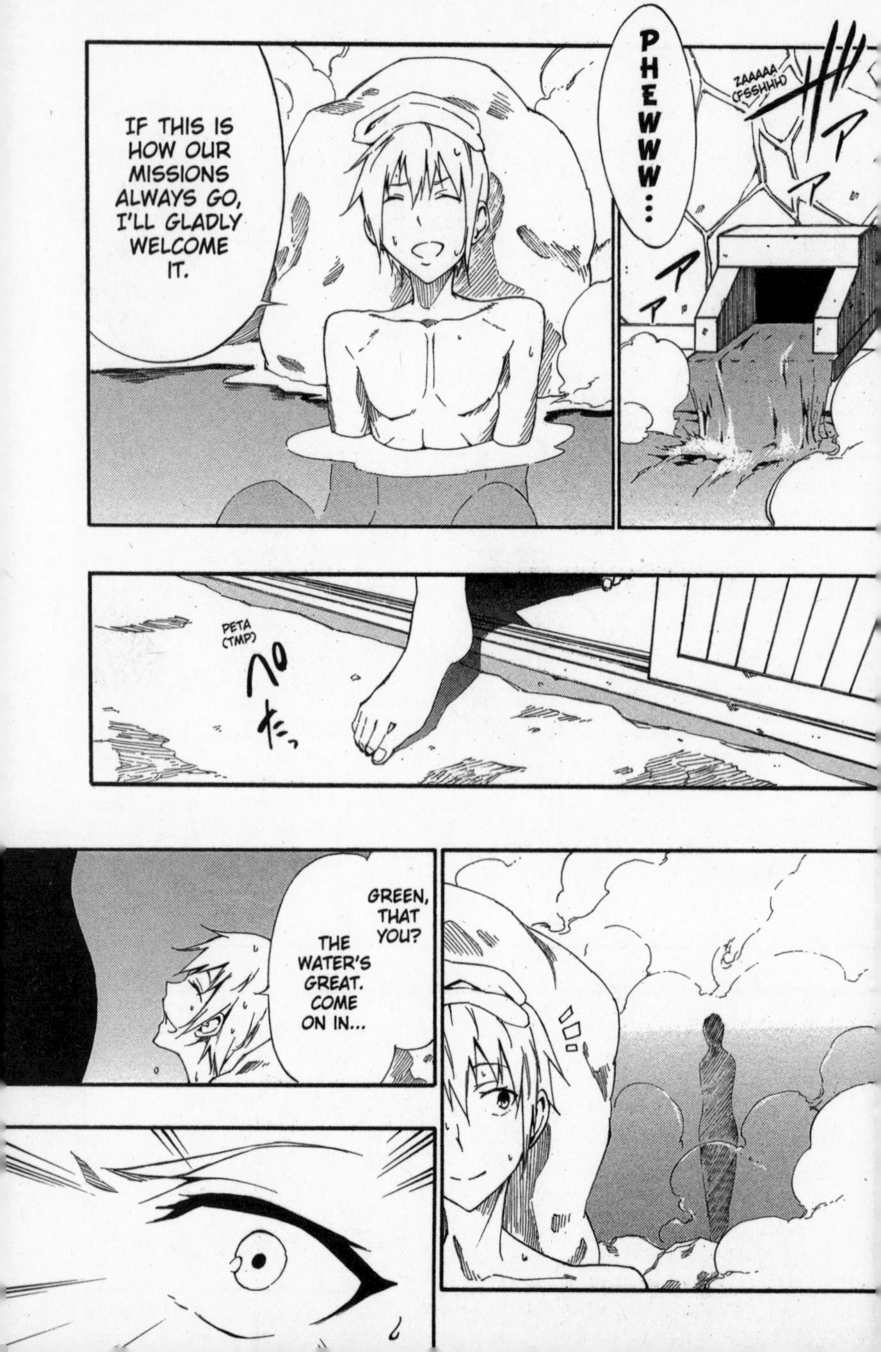
ZAAAAA (FSSHHH)
PHEWWW...
IF THIS IS HOW OUR MISSIONS ALWAYS GO, I'LL GLADLY WELCOME IT.
PETA (TMP)
GREEN, THAT YOU?
THE WATER'S GREAT. COME ON IN...

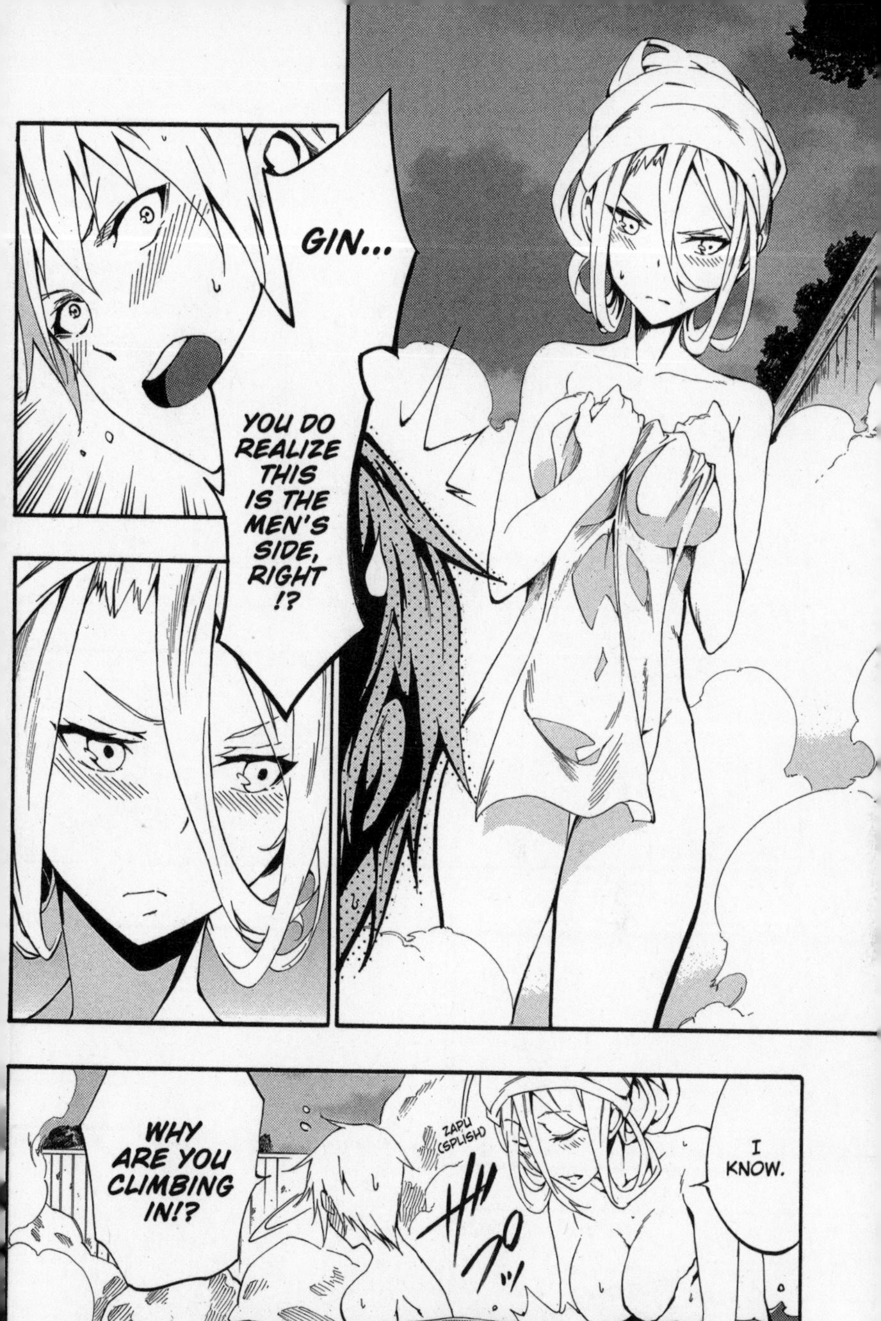
GIN...
YOU DO REALIZE THIS IS THE MEN'S SIDE, RIGHT!?
I KNOW.
ZAPU (SPLISH)
WHY ARE YOU CLIMBING IN!?

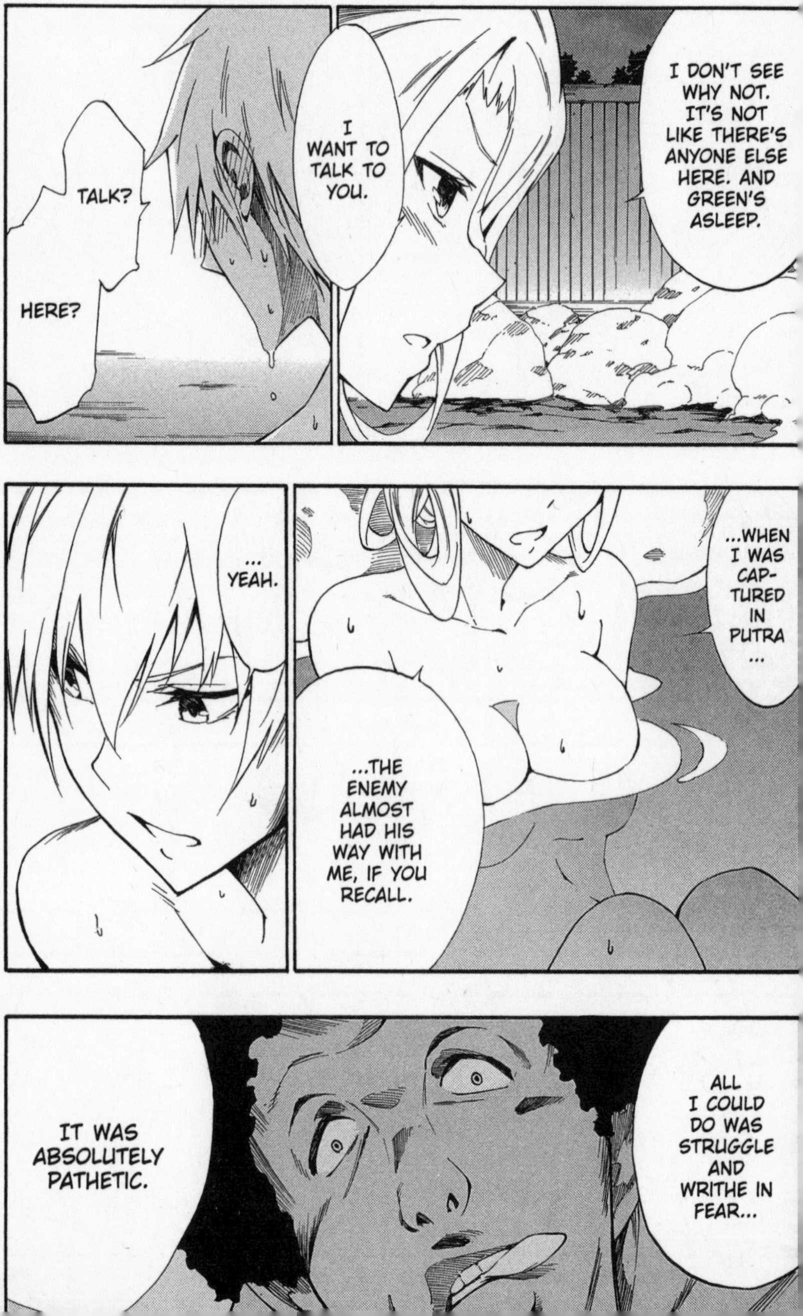
I DON'T SEE WHY NOT. IT'S NOT LIKE THERE'S ANYONE ELSE HERE. AND GREEN'S ASLEEP.
I WANT TO TALK TO YOU.
TALK?
HERE?
...WHEN I WAS CAP-TURED IN PUTRA...
...THE ENEMY ALMOST HAD HIS WAY WITH ME, IF YOU RECALL.
... YEAH.
ALL I COULD DO WAS STRUGGLE AND WRITHE IN FEAR...
IT WAS ABSOLUTELY PATHETIC.

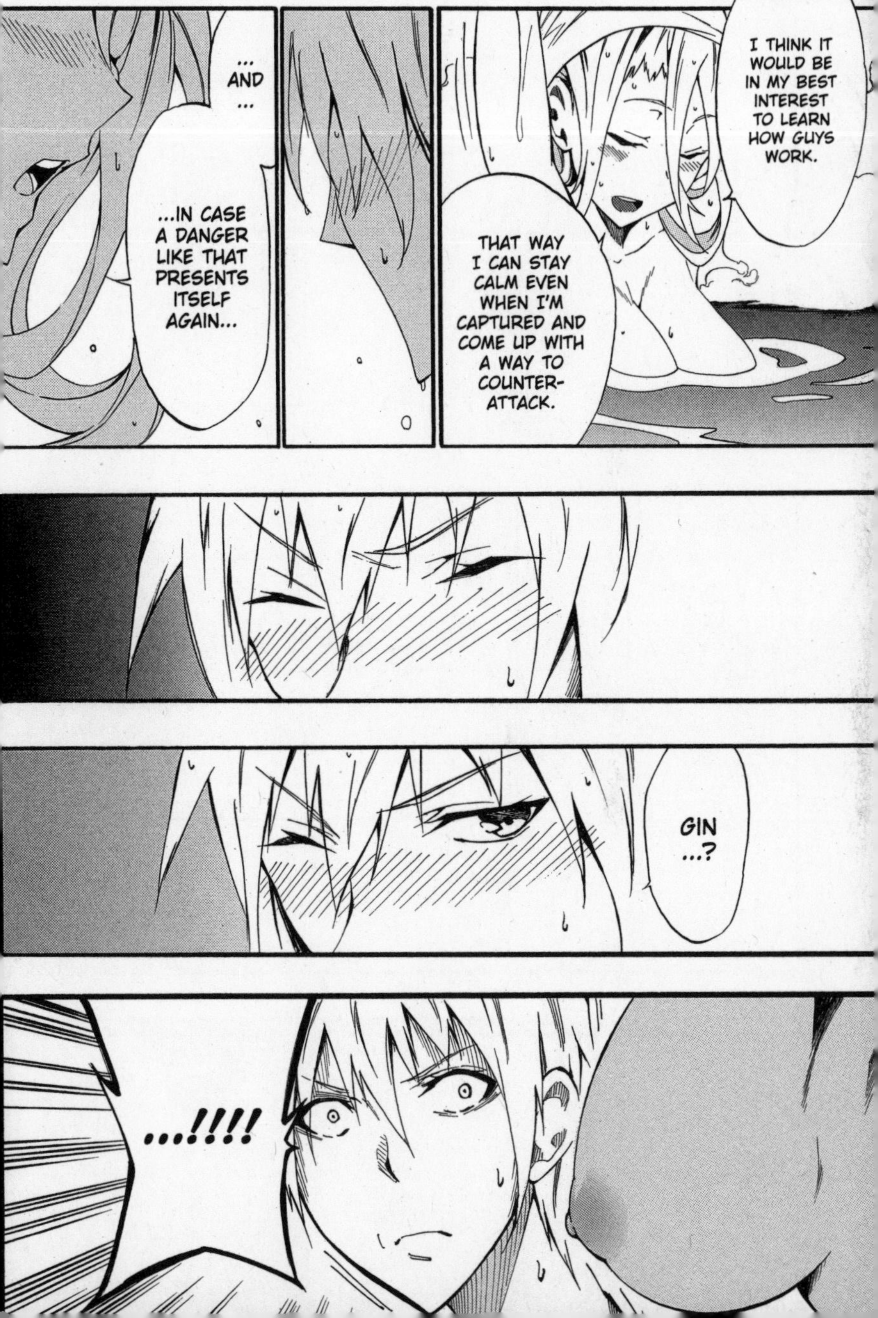
I THINK IT WOULD BE IN MY BEST INTEREST TO LEARN HOW GUYS WORK.
THAT WAY I CAN STAY CALM EVEN WHEN I'M CAPTURED AND COME UP WITH A WAY TO COUNTER-ATTACK.
... AND ...
...IN CASE A DANGER LIKE THAT PRESENTS ITSELF AGAIN...
GIN ...?
...!!!!

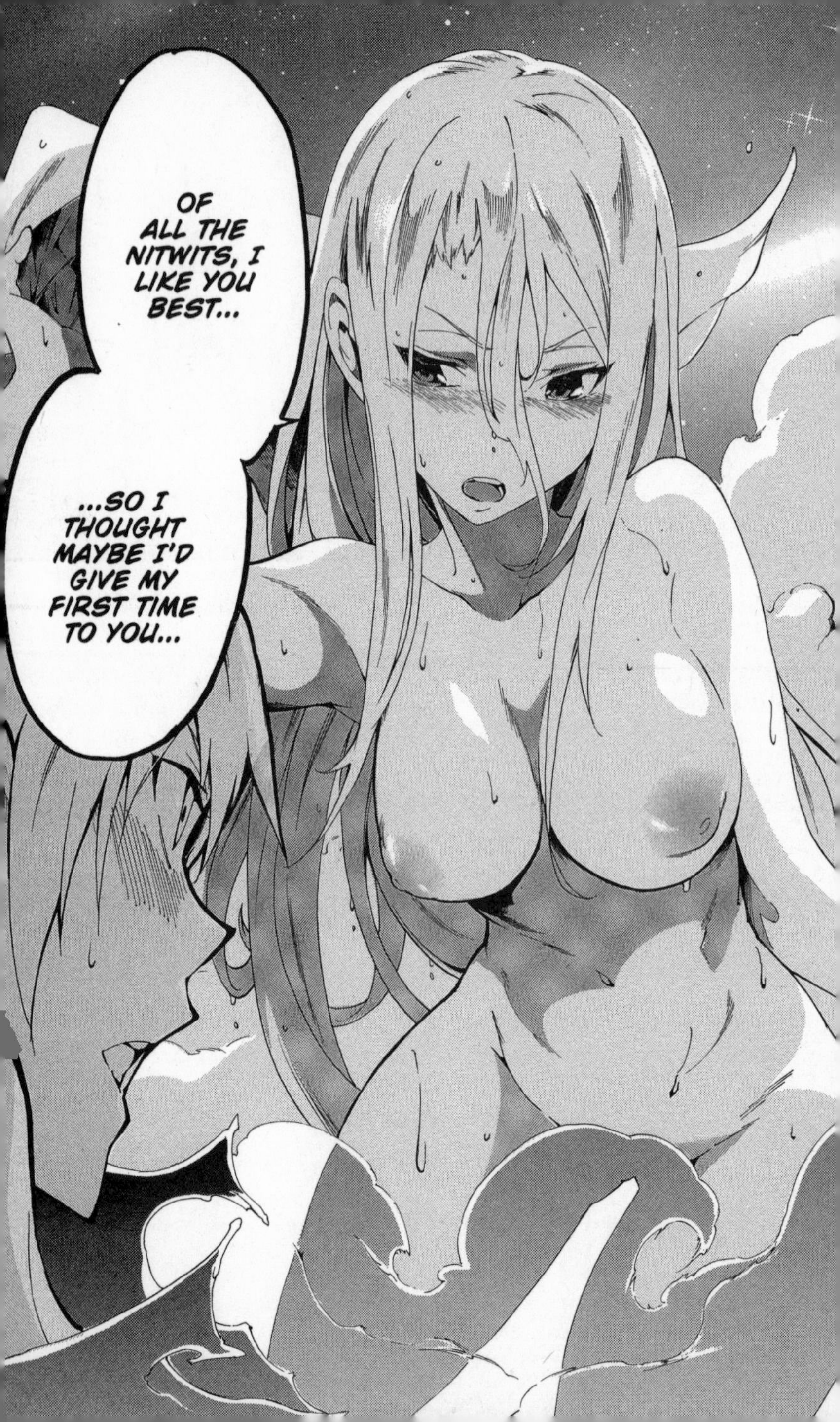
OF ALL THE NITWITS, I LIKE YOU BEST...
...SO I THOUGHT MAYBE I'D GIVE MY FIRST TIME TO YOU...

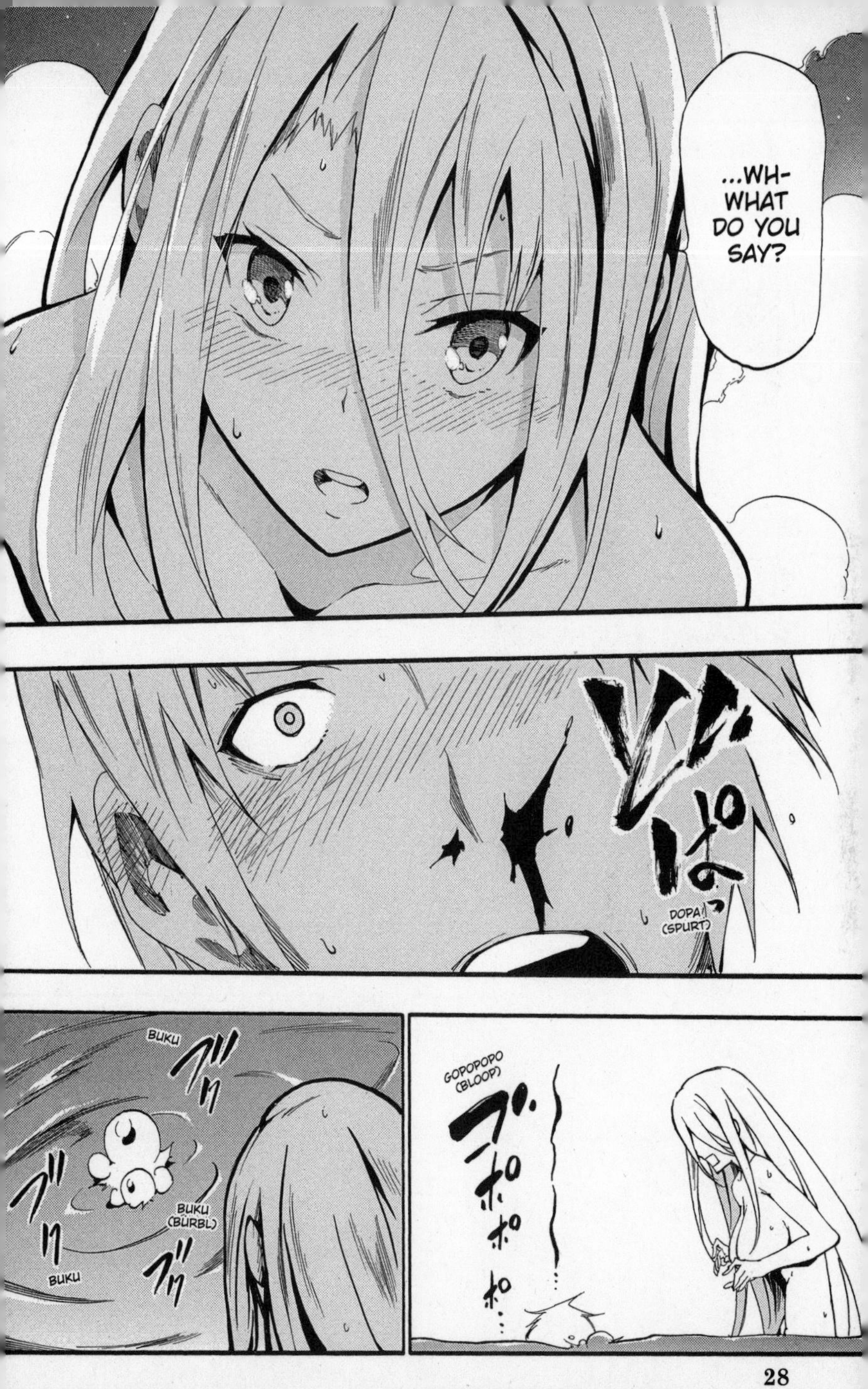
...WH-
WHAT
DO YOU
SAY?
ドパっ
DOPA!
(SPURT)
ゴポポポ...
GOPOPOPO
(BLOOP)
ブク
BUKU
ブク
BUKU
(BÜRBL)
ブク
BUKU

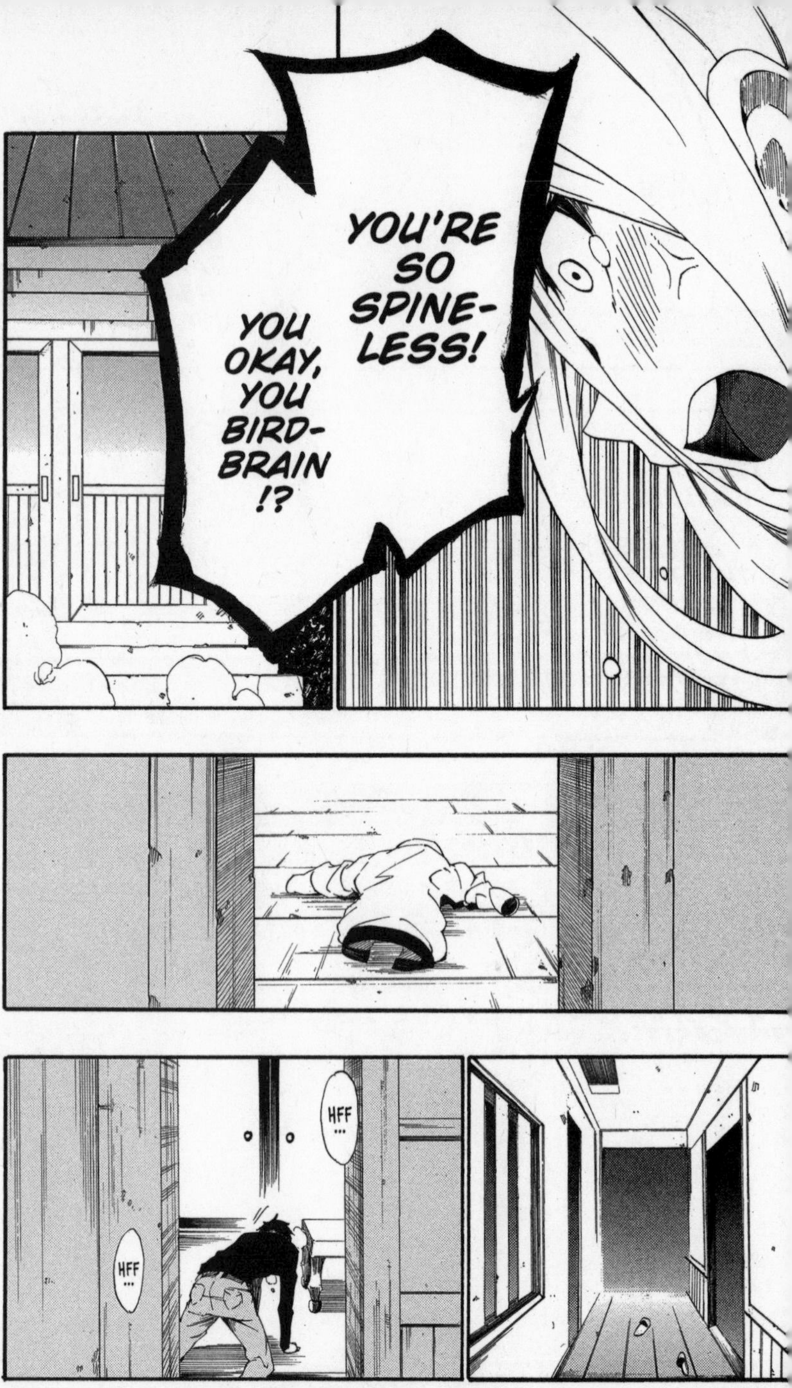
YOU'RE SO SPINE-LESS!
YOU OKAY, YOU BIRD-BRAIN!?
HFF...
HFF...

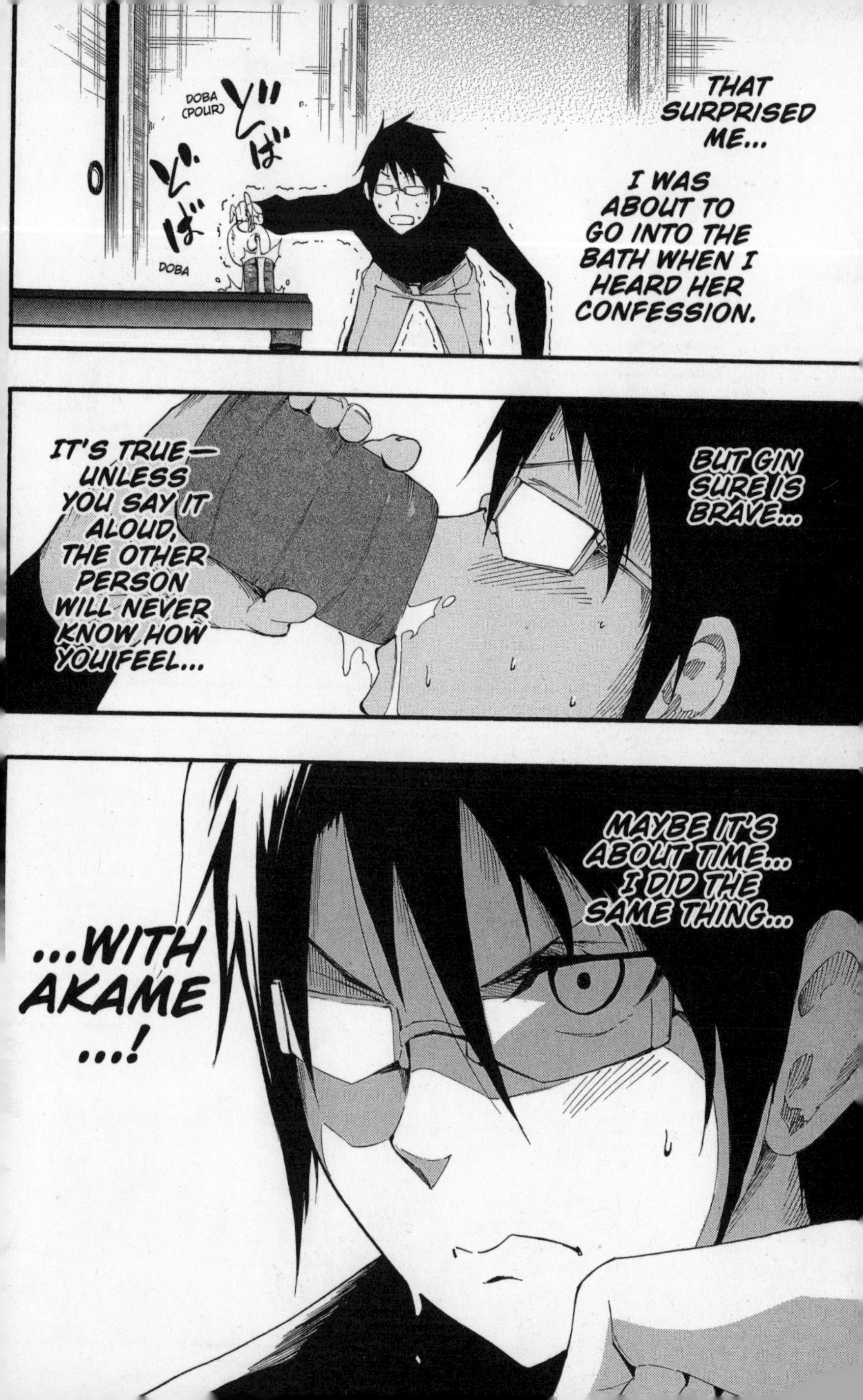
THAT SURPRISED ME...
I WAS ABOUT TO GO INTO THE BATH WHEN I HEARD HER CONFESSION.
どばどば
DOBA (POUR)
どばどば
DOBA
BUT GIN SURE IS BRAVE...
IT'S TRUE— UNLESS YOU SAY IT ALOUD, THE OTHER PERSON WILL NEVER KNOW HOW YOU FEEL...
MAYBE IT'S ABOUT TIME... I DID THE SAME THING...
...WITH AKAME ...!

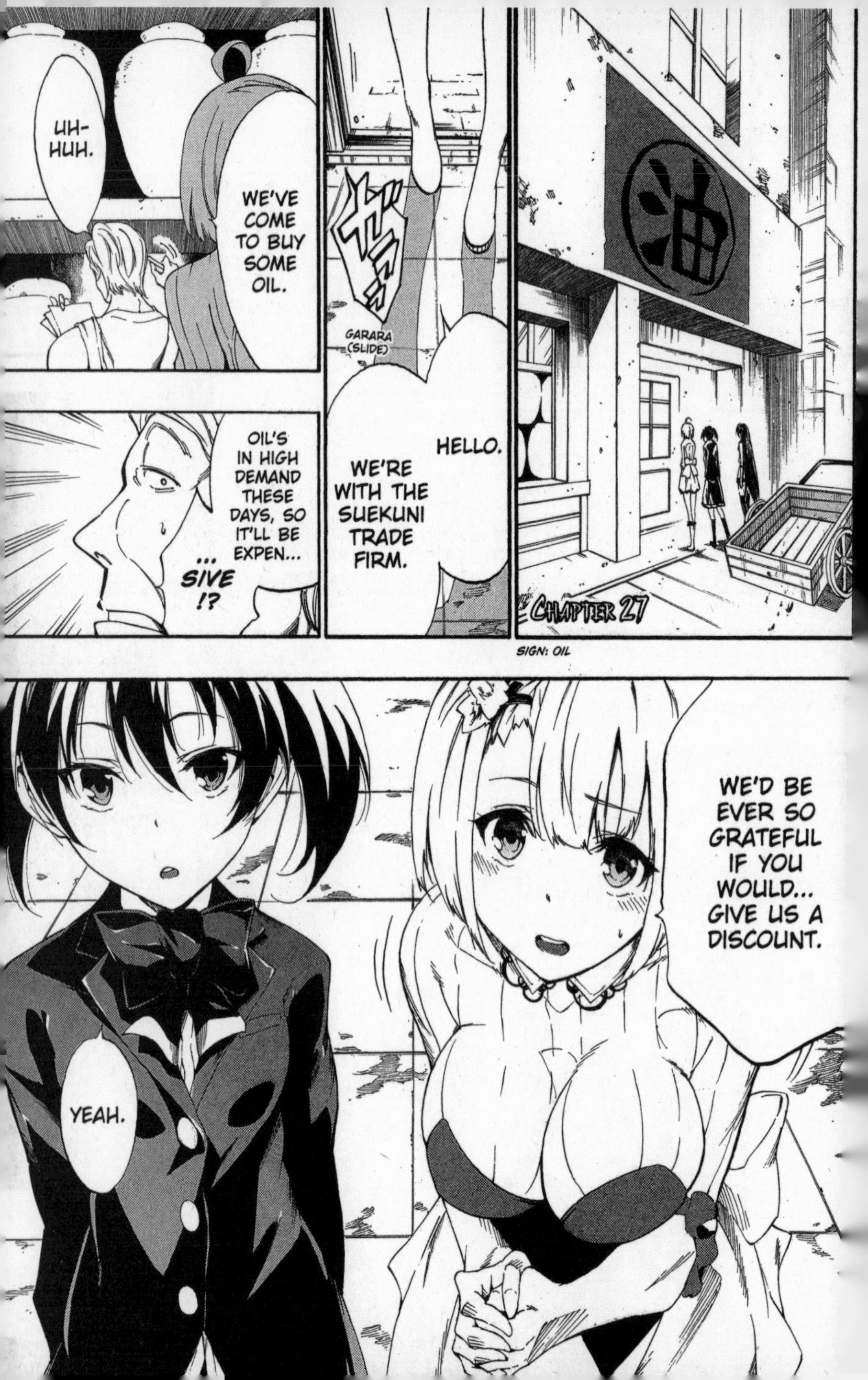
CHAPTER 27
SIGN: OIL
GARARA (SLIDE)
HELLO.
WE'RE WITH THE SUEKUNI TRADE FIRM.
WE'VE COME TO BUY SOME OIL.
UH-HUH.
OIL'S IN HIGH DEMAND THESE DAYS, SO IT'LL BE EXPEN...
...SIVE!?
WE'D BE EVER SO GRATEFUL IF YOU WOULD... GIVE US A DISCOUNT.
YEAH.

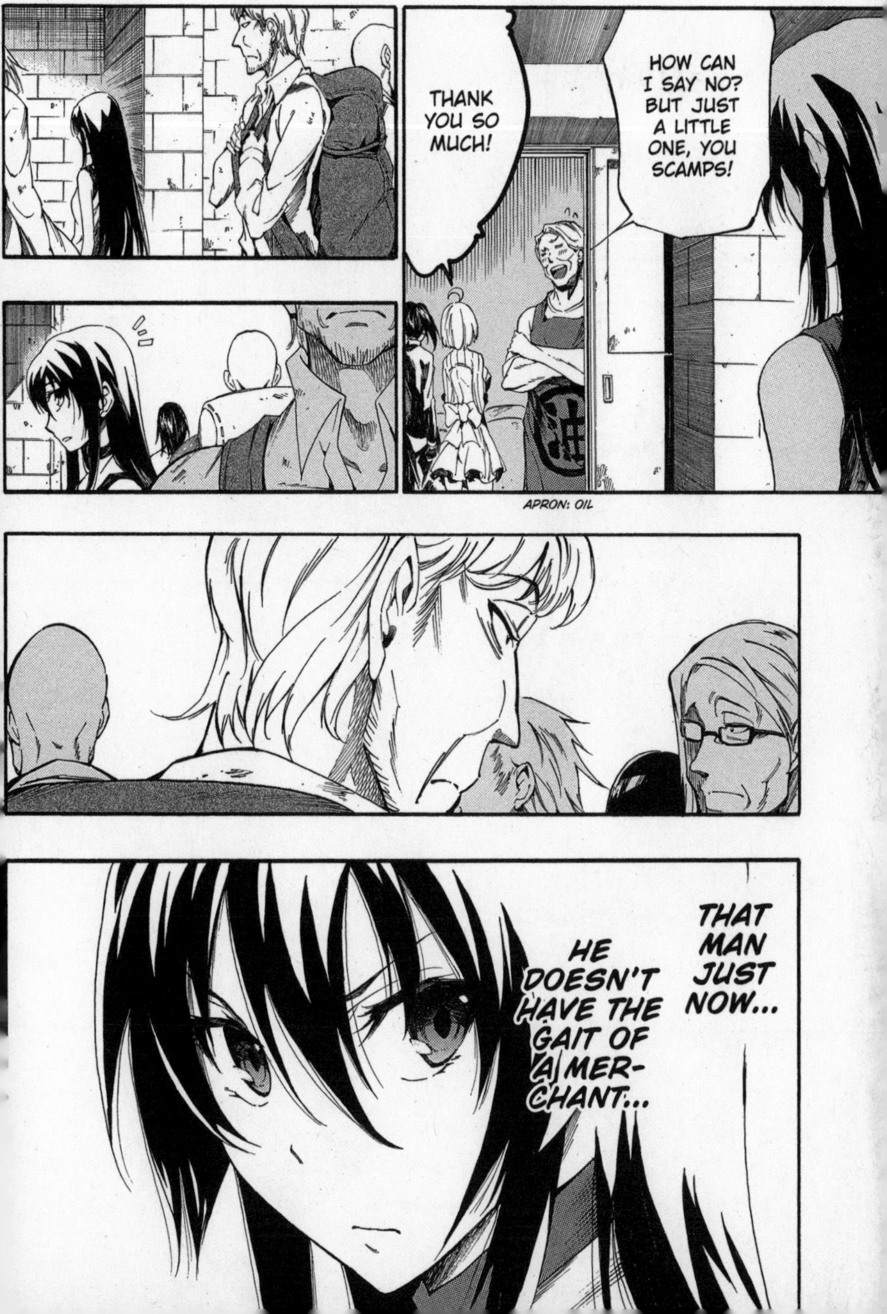
HOW CAN I SAY NO? BUT JUST A LITTLE ONE, YOU SCAMPS!
THANK YOU SO MUCH!
APRON: OIL
THAT MAN JUST NOW...
HE DOESN'T HAVE THE GAIT OF A MER-CHANT...

Chapter 27 - Confession

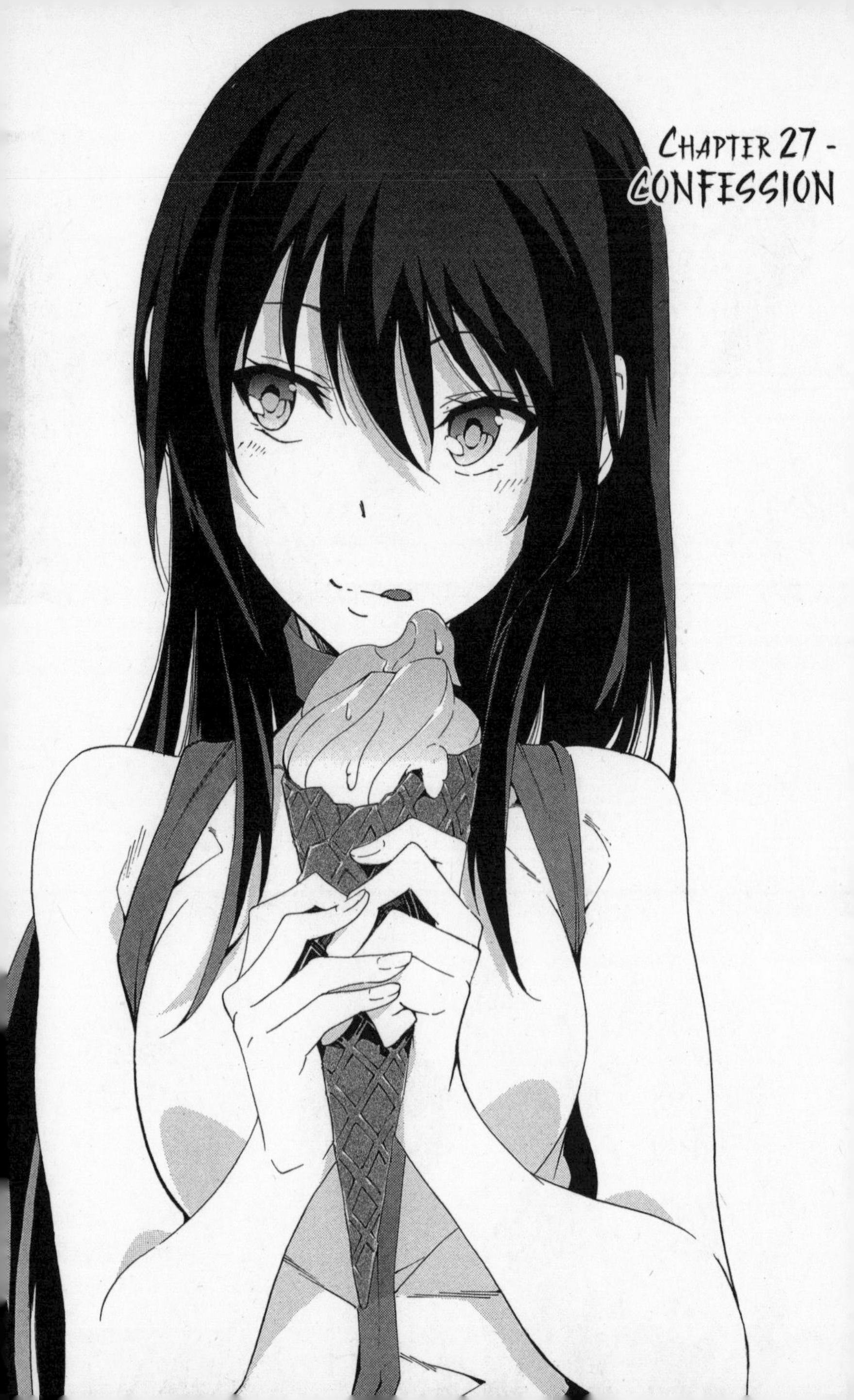

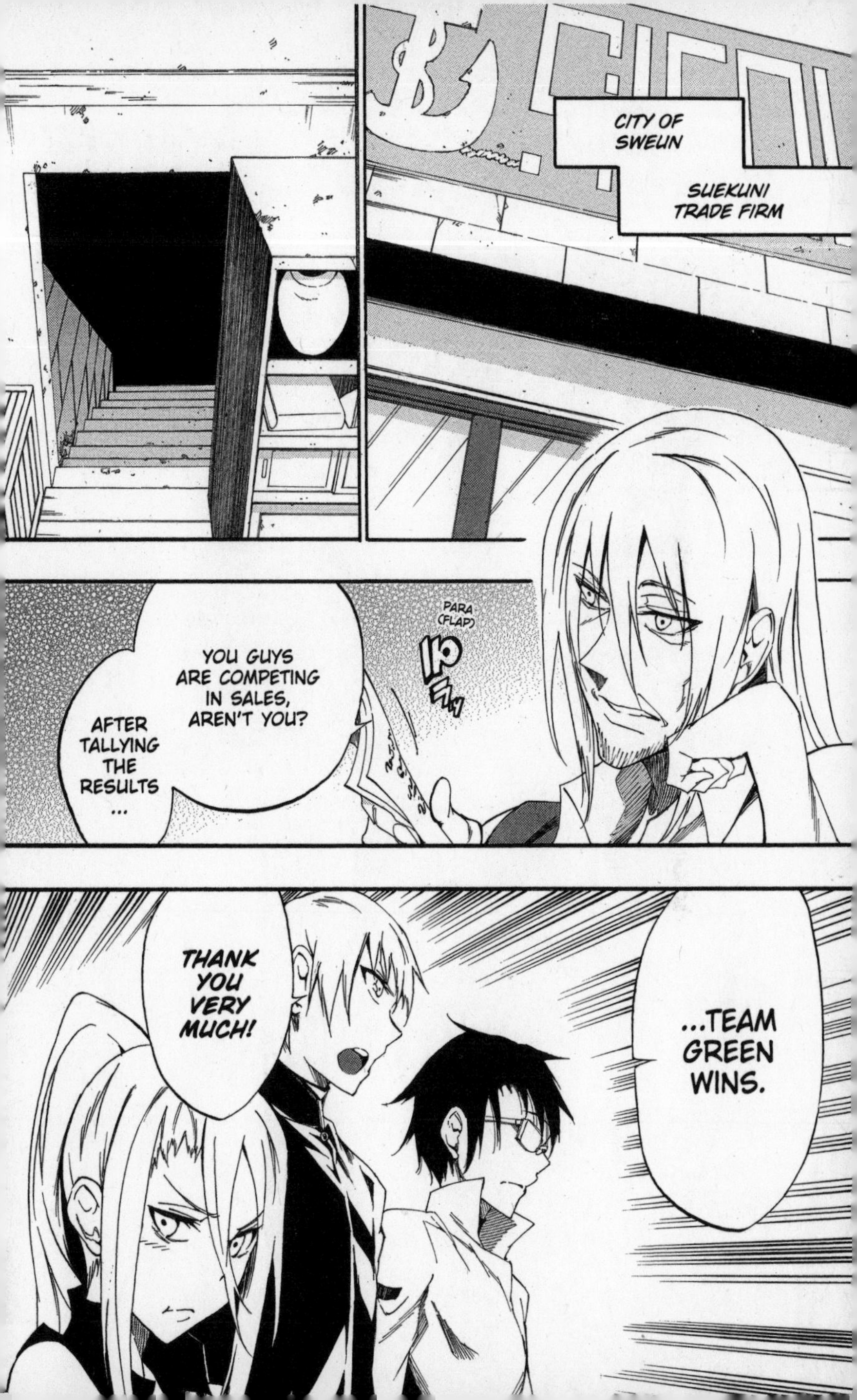
CITY OF SWEUN
SUEKUNI TRADE FIRM
PARA (FLAP)
YOU GUYS ARE COMPETING IN SALES, AREN'T YOU?
AFTER TALLYING THE RESULTS...
...TEAM GREEN WINS.
THANK YOU VERY MUCH!

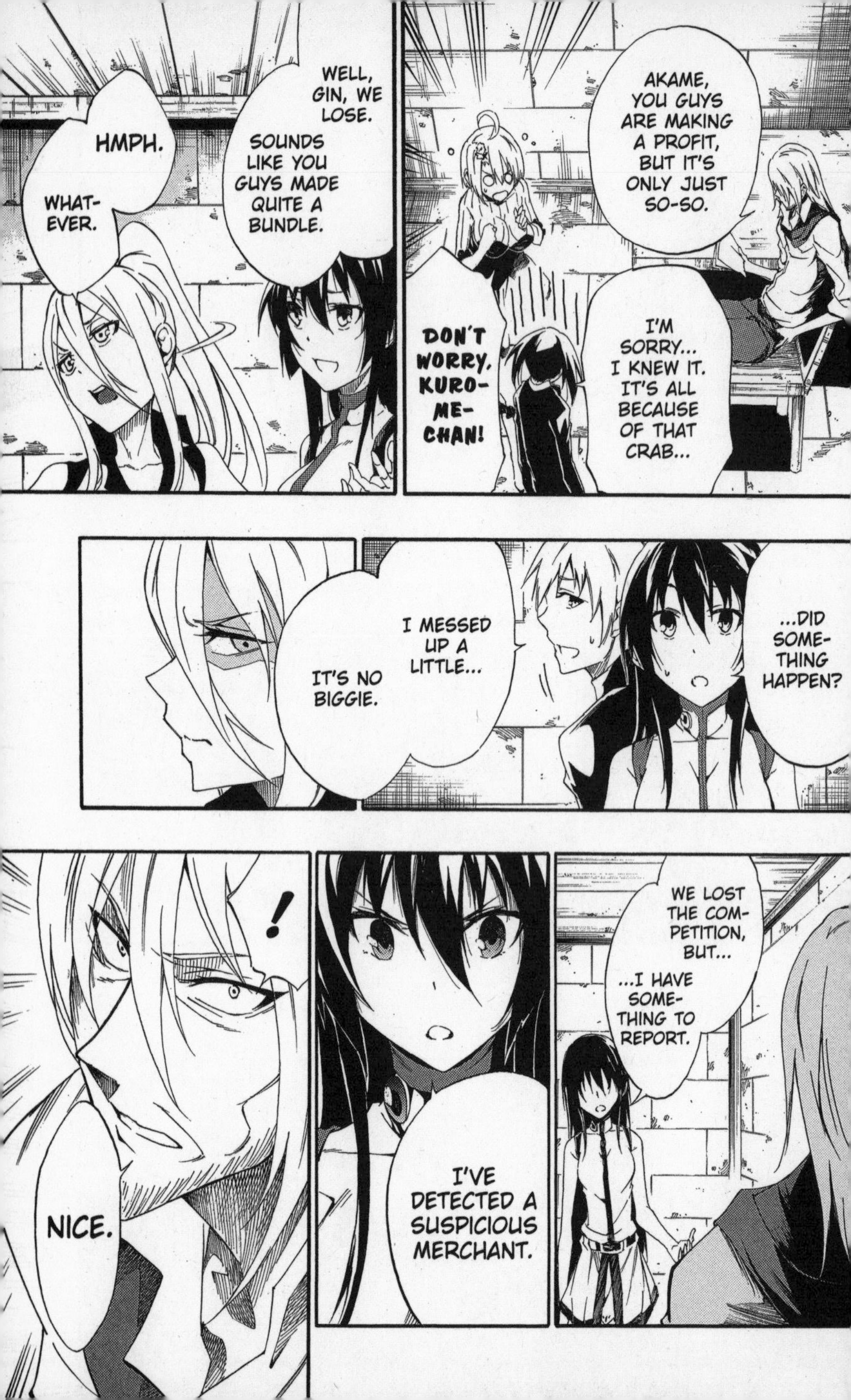
AKAME, YOU GUYS ARE MAKING A PROFIT, BUT IT'S ONLY JUST SO-SO.
I'M SORRY... I KNEW IT. IT'S ALL BECAUSE OF THAT CRAB...
DON'T WORRY, KURO-ME-CHAN!
WELL, GIN, WE LOSE.
SOUNDS LIKE YOU GUYS MADE QUITE A BUNDLE.
HMPH.
WHAT-EVER.
...DID SOME-THING HAPPEN?
I MESSED UP A LITTLE...
IT'S NO BIGGIE.
WE LOST THE COM-PETITION, BUT...
...I HAVE SOME-THING TO REPORT.
I'VE DETECTED A SUSPICIOUS MERCHANT.
!
NICE.

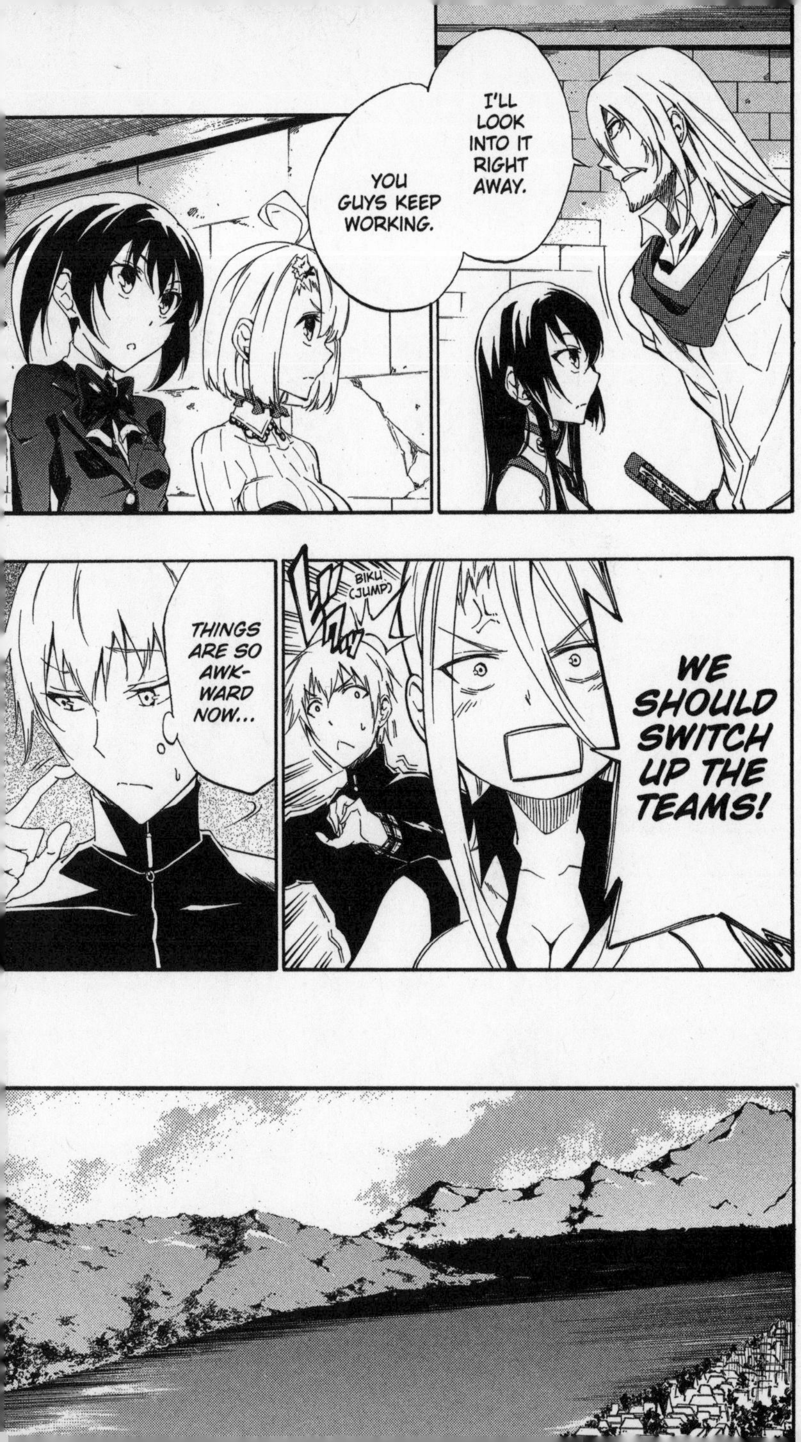
I'LL LOOK INTO IT RIGHT AWAY.
YOU GUYS KEEP WORKING.
WE SHOULD SWITCH UP THE TEAMS!
BIKU (JUMP)
THINGS ARE SO AWK-WARD NOW...

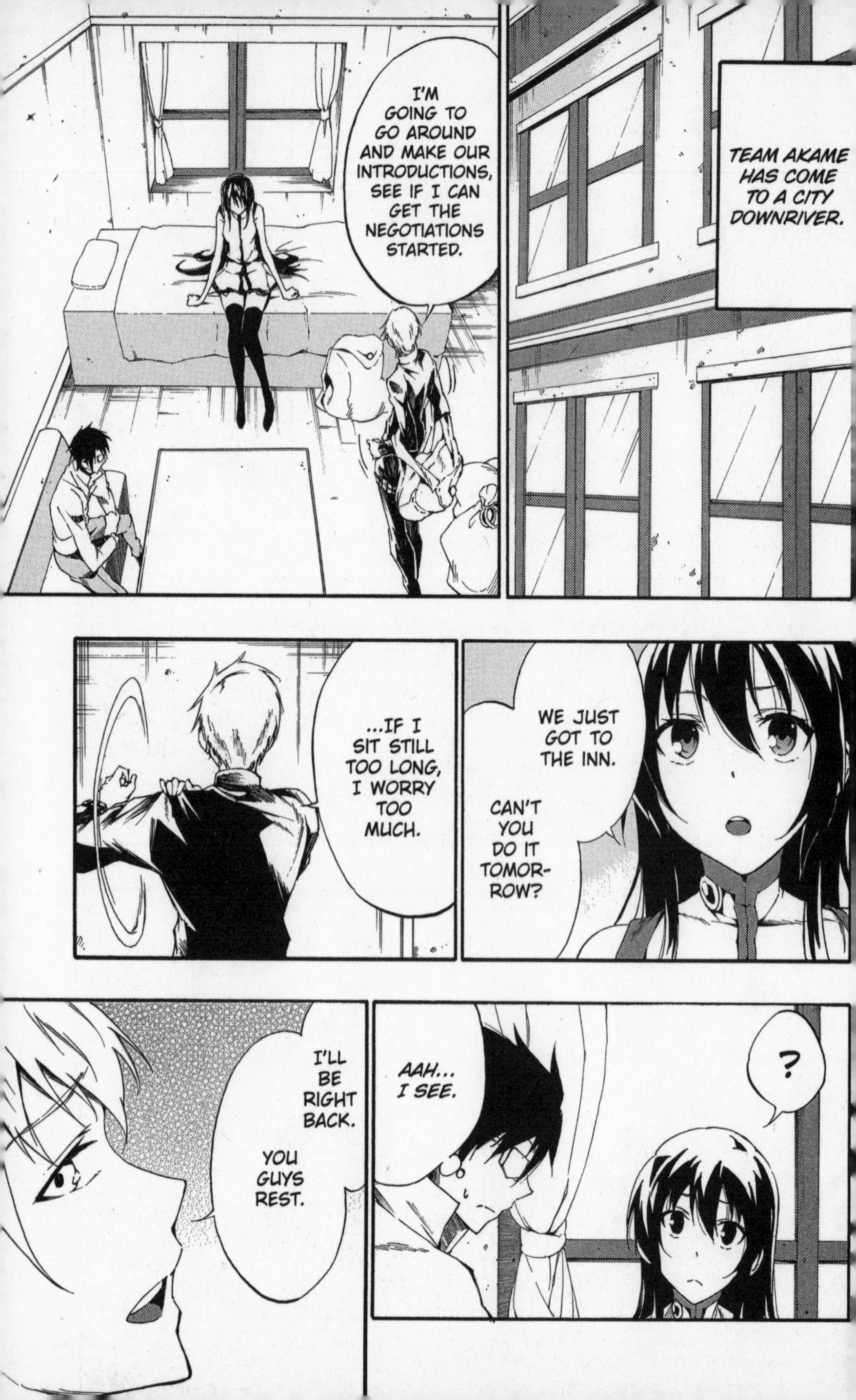
TEAM AKAME HAS COME TO A CITY DOWNRIVER.
I'M GOING TO GO AROUND AND MAKE OUR INTRODUCTIONS, SEE IF I CAN GET THE NEGOTIATIONS STARTED.
WE JUST GOT TO THE INN.
CAN'T YOU DO IT TOMOR-ROW?
...IF I SIT STILL TOO LONG, I WORRY TOO MUCH.
?
AAH... I SEE.
I'LL BE RIGHT BACK.
YOU GUYS REST.

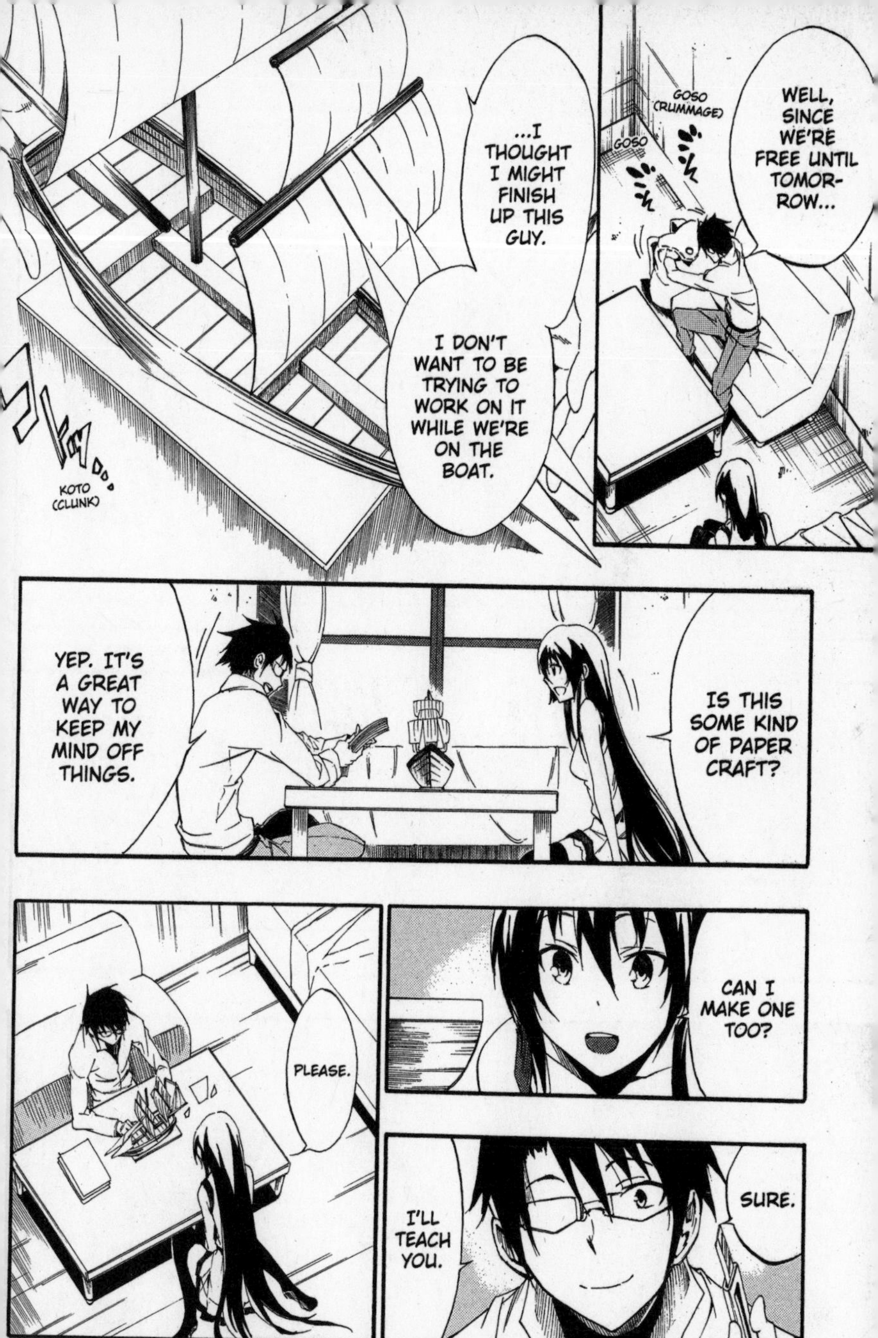
WELL, SINCE WE'RE FREE UNTIL TOMOR-ROW...
GOSO (RUMMAGE)
GOSO
...I THOUGHT I MIGHT FINISH UP THIS GUY.
I DON'T WANT TO BE TRYING TO WORK ON IT WHILE WE'RE ON THE BOAT.
KOTO (CLUNK)
IS THIS SOME KIND OF PAPER CRAFT?
YEP. IT'S A GREAT WAY TO KEEP MY MIND OFF THINGS.
CAN I MAKE ONE TOO?
SURE.
I'LL TEACH YOU.
PLEASE.

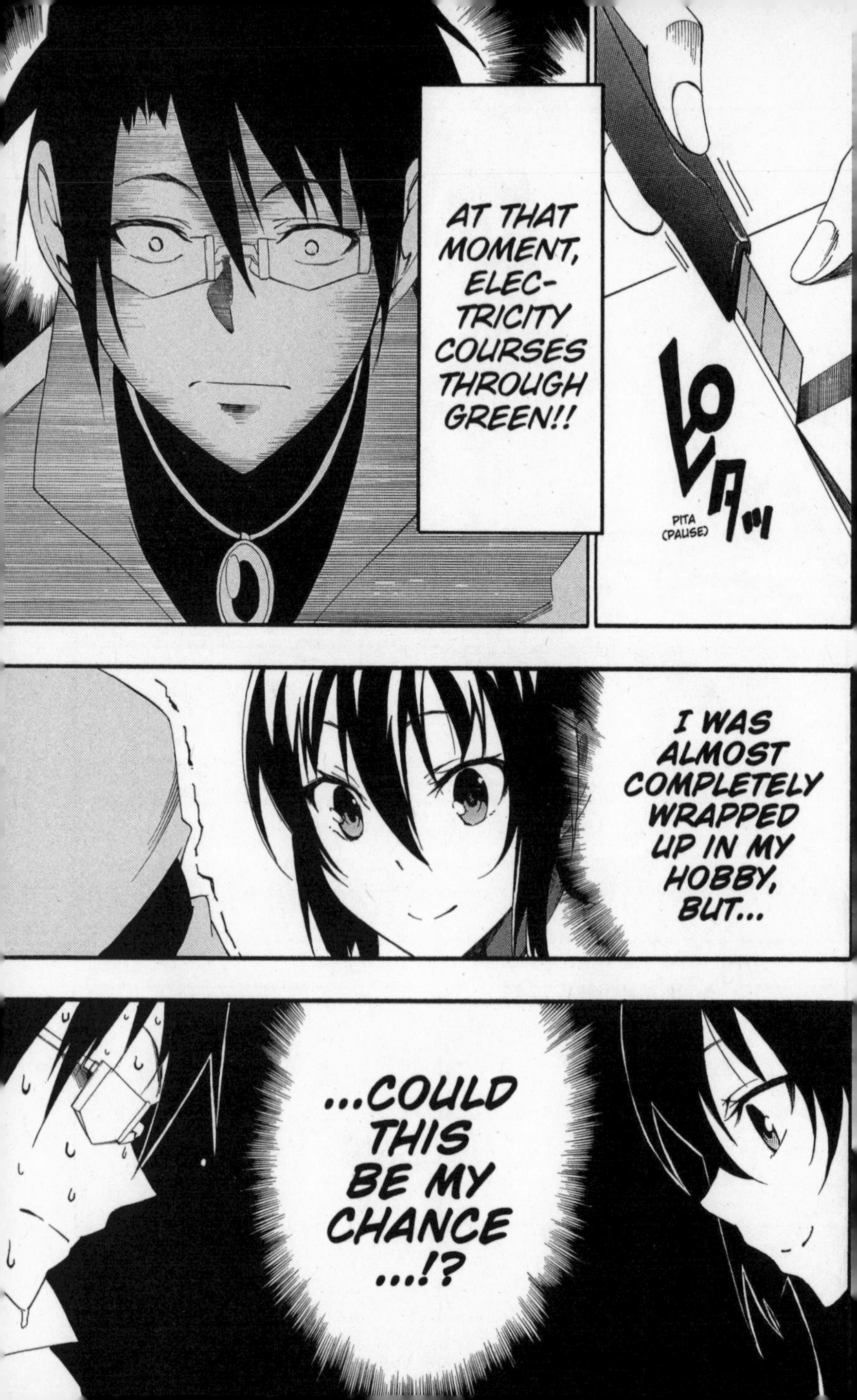
PITA (PAUSE)
AT THAT MOMENT, ELEC-TRICITY COURSES THROUGH GREEN!!
I WAS ALMOST COMPLETELY WRAPPED UP IN MY HOBBY, BUT...
...COULD THIS BE MY CHANCE ...!?

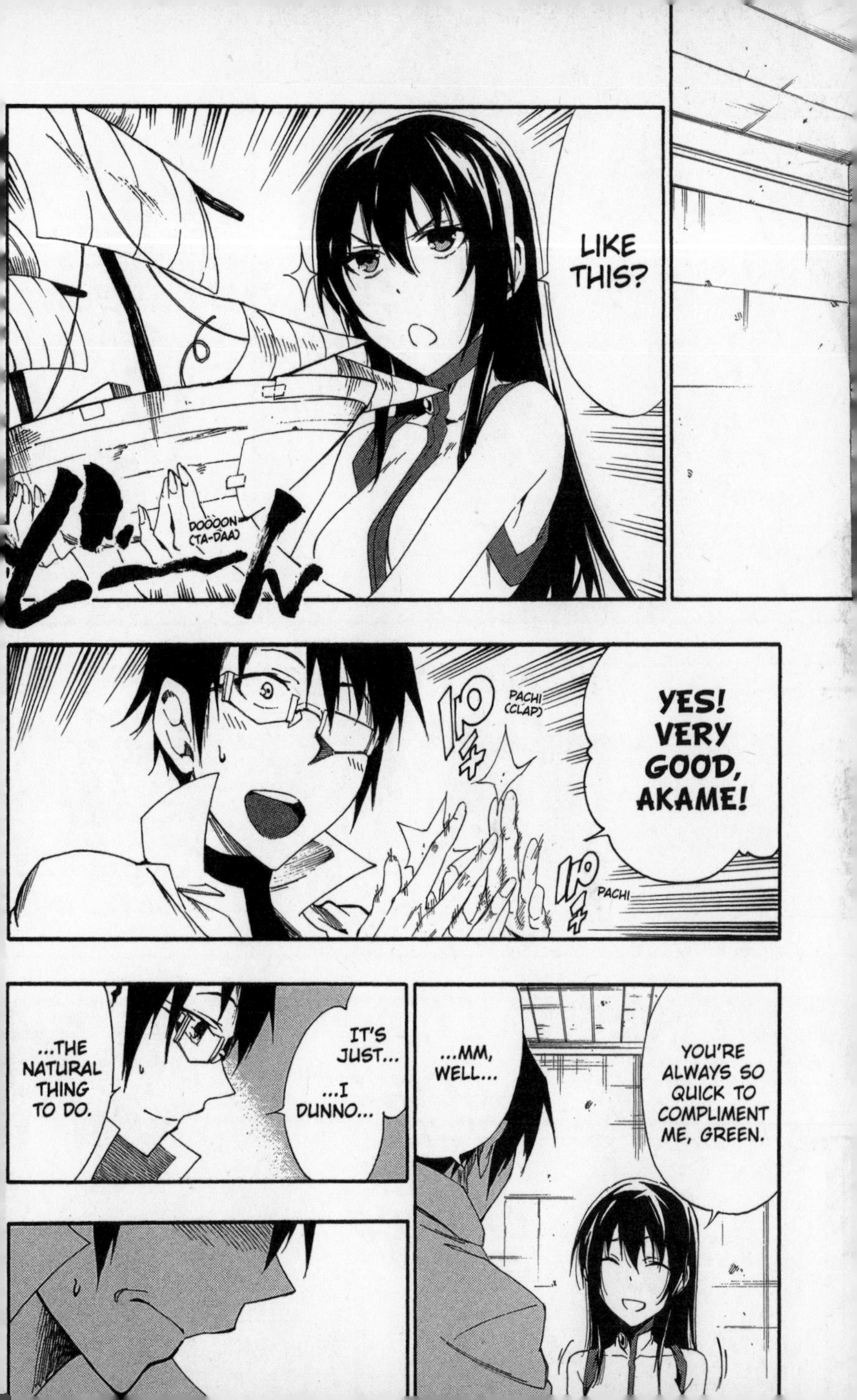
LIKE THIS?
DOOOON (TA-DAA)
YES! VERY GOOD, AKAME!
PACHI (CLAP)
PACHI
YOU'RE ALWAYS SO QUICK TO COMPLIMENT ME, GREEN.
...MM, WELL...
IT'S JUST...
...I DUNNO...
...THE NATURAL THING TO DO.

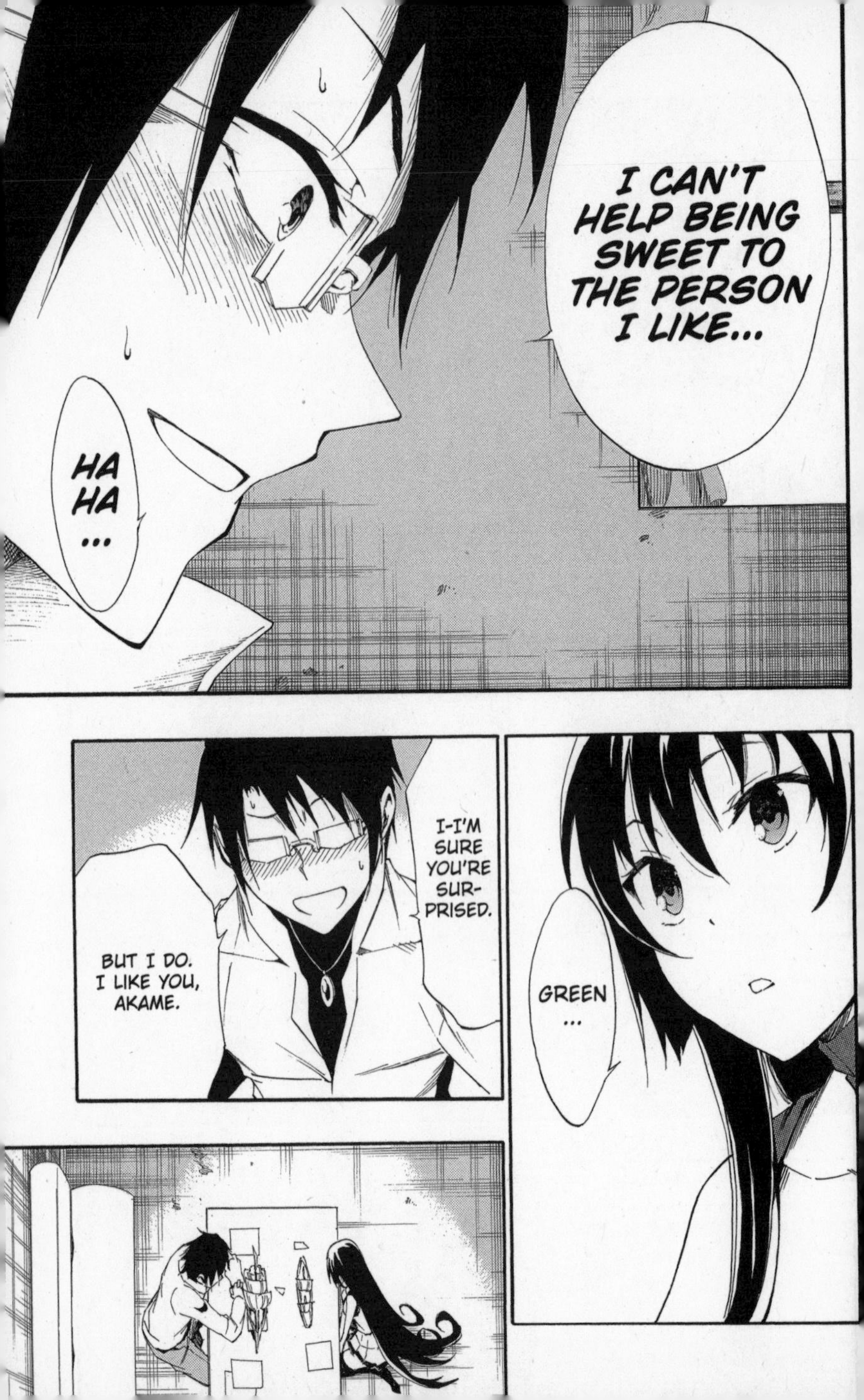
I CAN'T HELP BEING SWEET TO THE PERSON I LIKE...
HA HA ...
GREEN ...
I-I'M SURE YOU'RE SUR-PRISED.
BUT I DO. I LIKE YOU, AKAME.

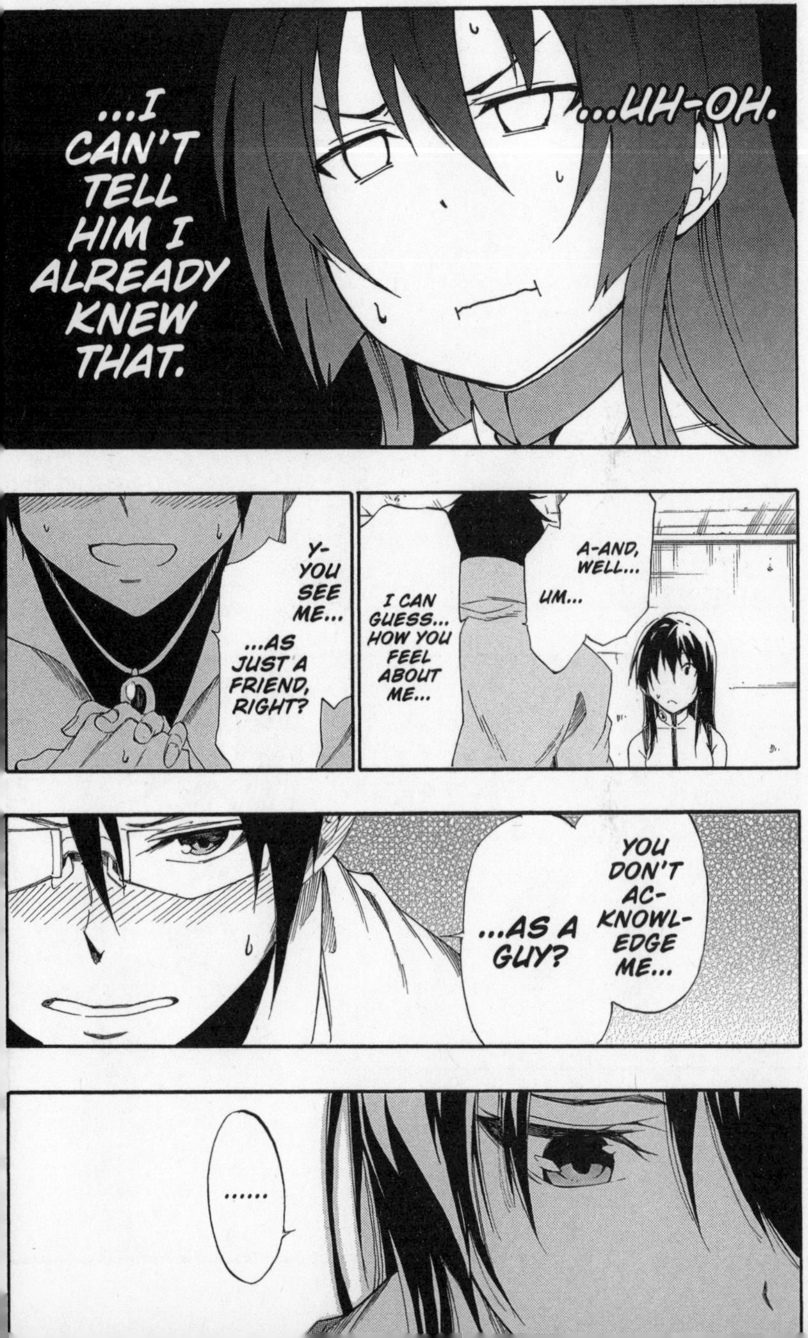
...UH-OH.
...I CAN'T TELL HIM I ALREADY KNEW THAT.
A-AND, WELL...
UM...
I CAN GUESS... HOW YOU FEEL ABOUT ME...
Y-YOU SEE ME...
...AS JUST A FRIEND, RIGHT?
YOU DON'T AC-KNOWL-EDGE ME...
...AS A GUY?
......

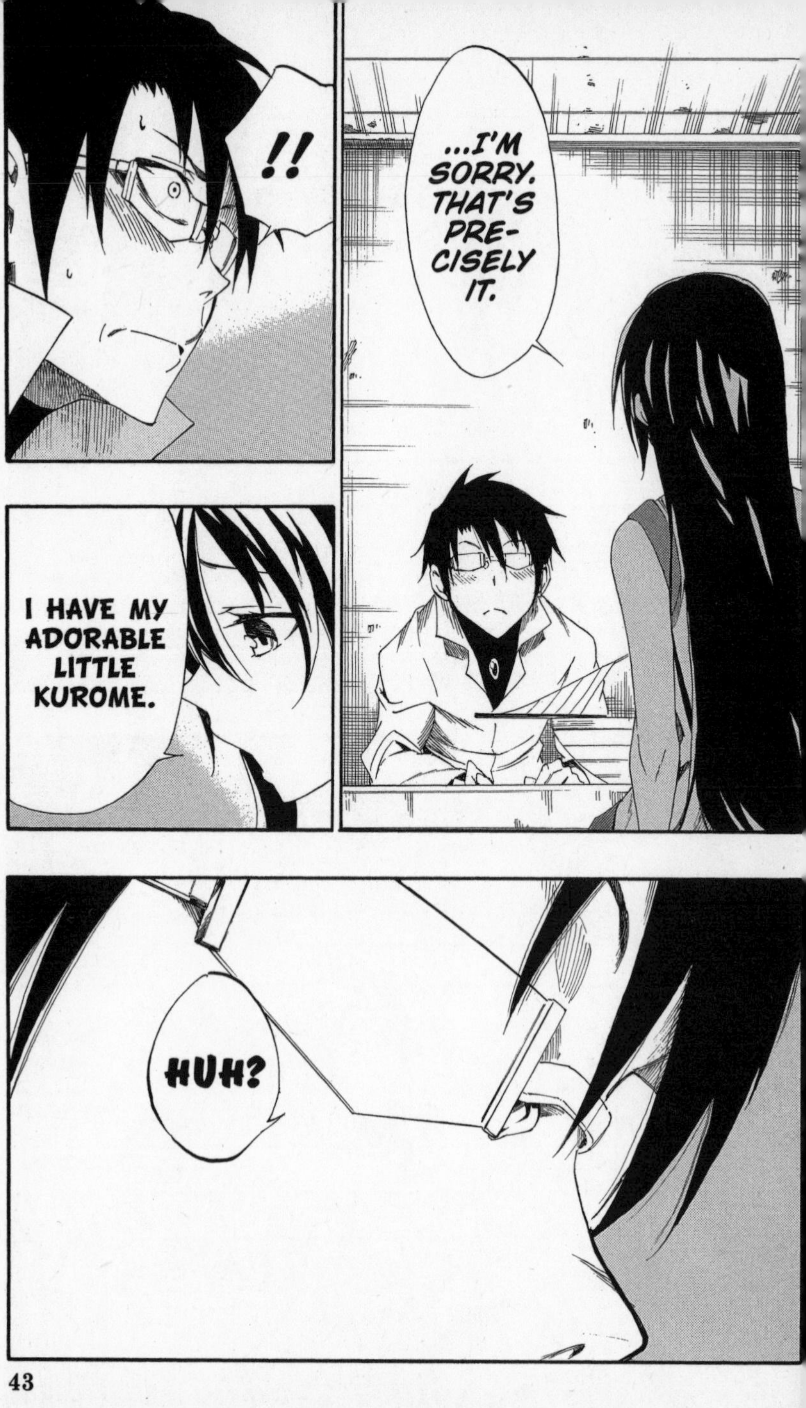
...I'M SORRY. THAT'S PRE- CISELY IT.
!!
I HAVE MY ADORABLE LITTLE KUROME.
HUH?

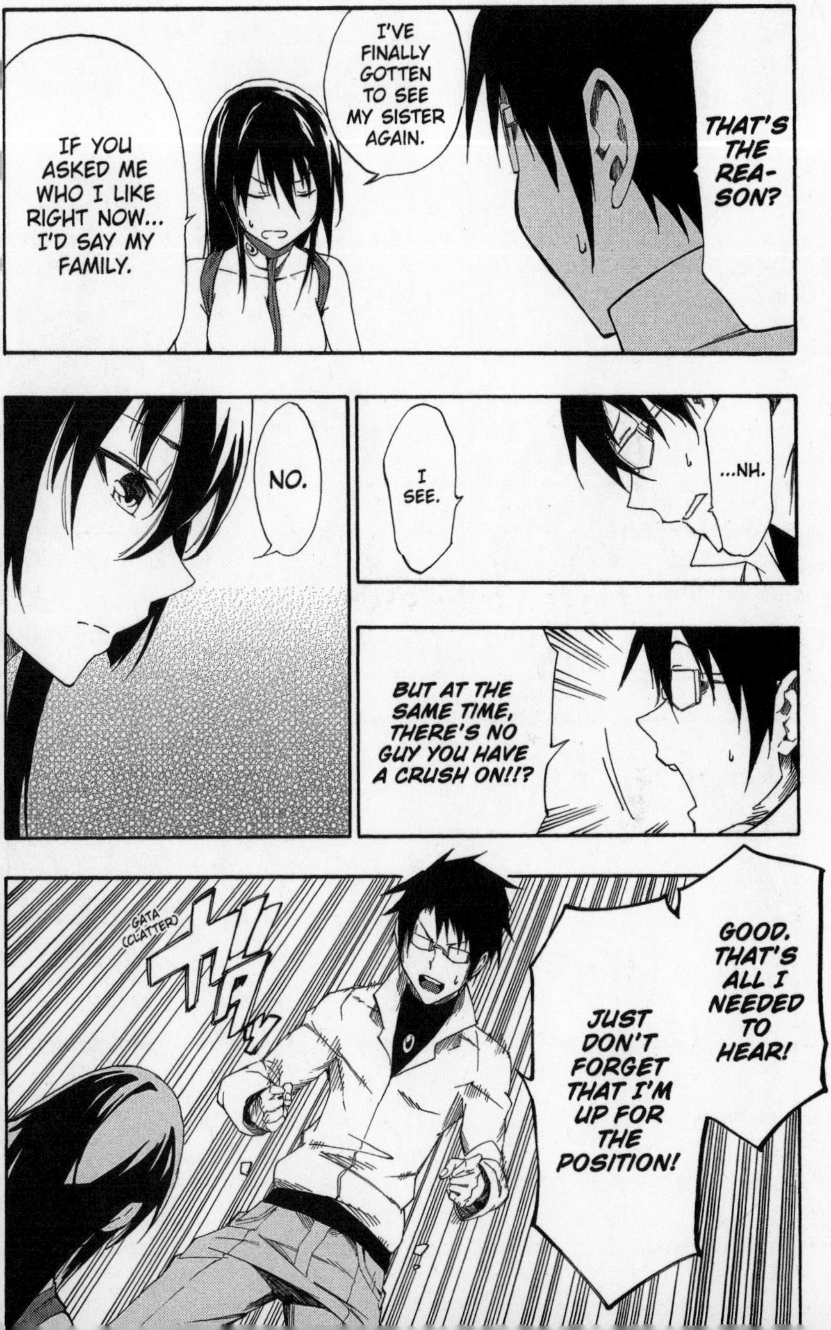
I'VE FINALLY GOTTEN TO SEE MY SISTER AGAIN.
IF YOU ASKED ME WHO I LIKE RIGHT NOW... I'D SAY MY FAMILY.
THAT'S THE REA-SON?
...NH.
I SEE.
BUT AT THE SAME TIME, THERE'S NO GUY YOU HAVE A CRUSH ON!!?
NO.
GOOD. THAT'S ALL I NEEDED TO HEAR!
JUST DON'T FORGET THAT I'M UP FOR THE POSITION!
GATA (CLATTER)

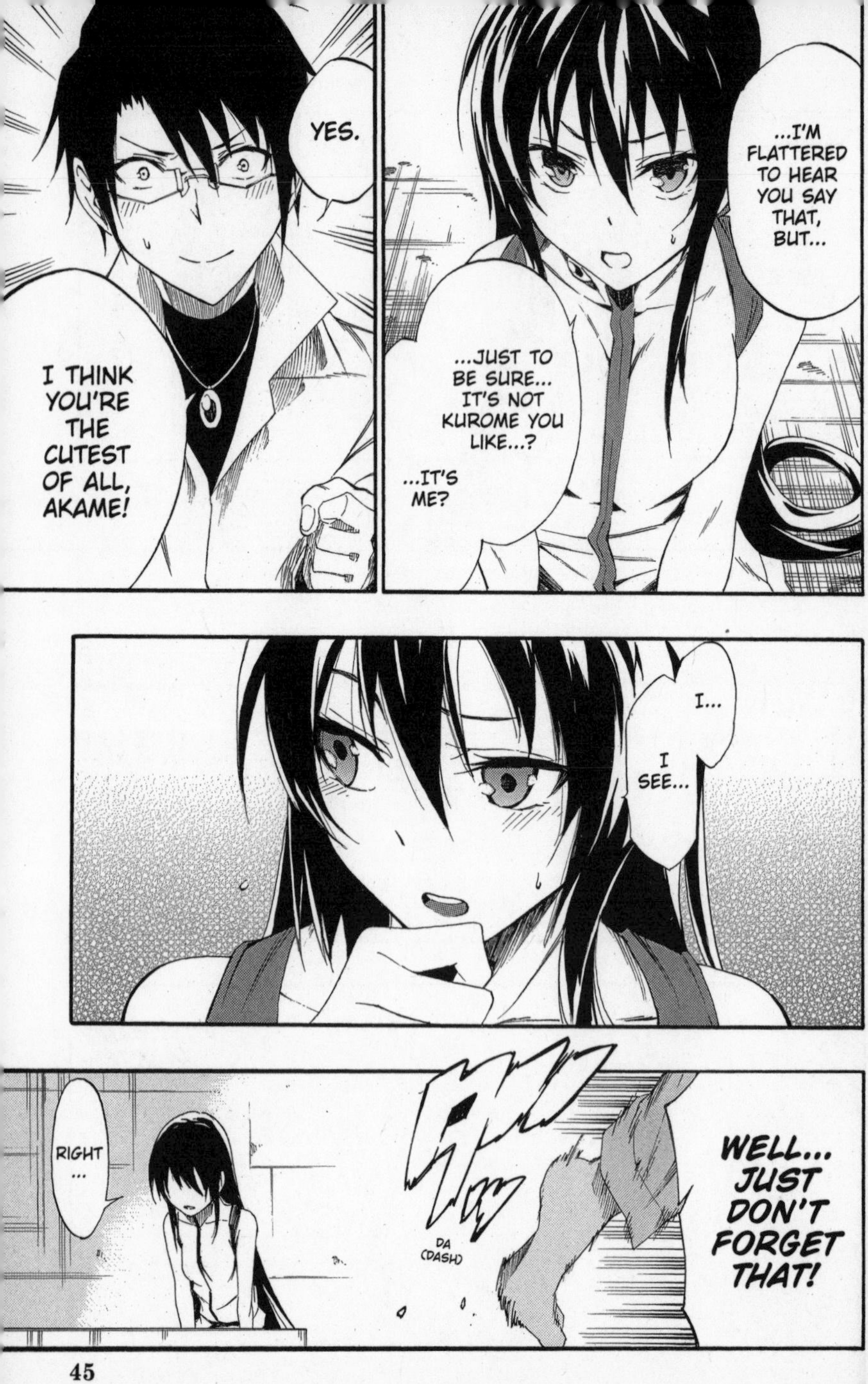
...I'M FLATTERED TO HEAR YOU SAY THAT, BUT...
...JUST TO BE SURE... IT'S NOT KUROME YOU LIKE...?
...IT'S ME?
YES.
I THINK YOU'RE THE CUTEST OF ALL, AKAME!
I...
I SEE...
WELL... JUST DON'T FORGET THAT!
DA (DASH)
RIGHT...

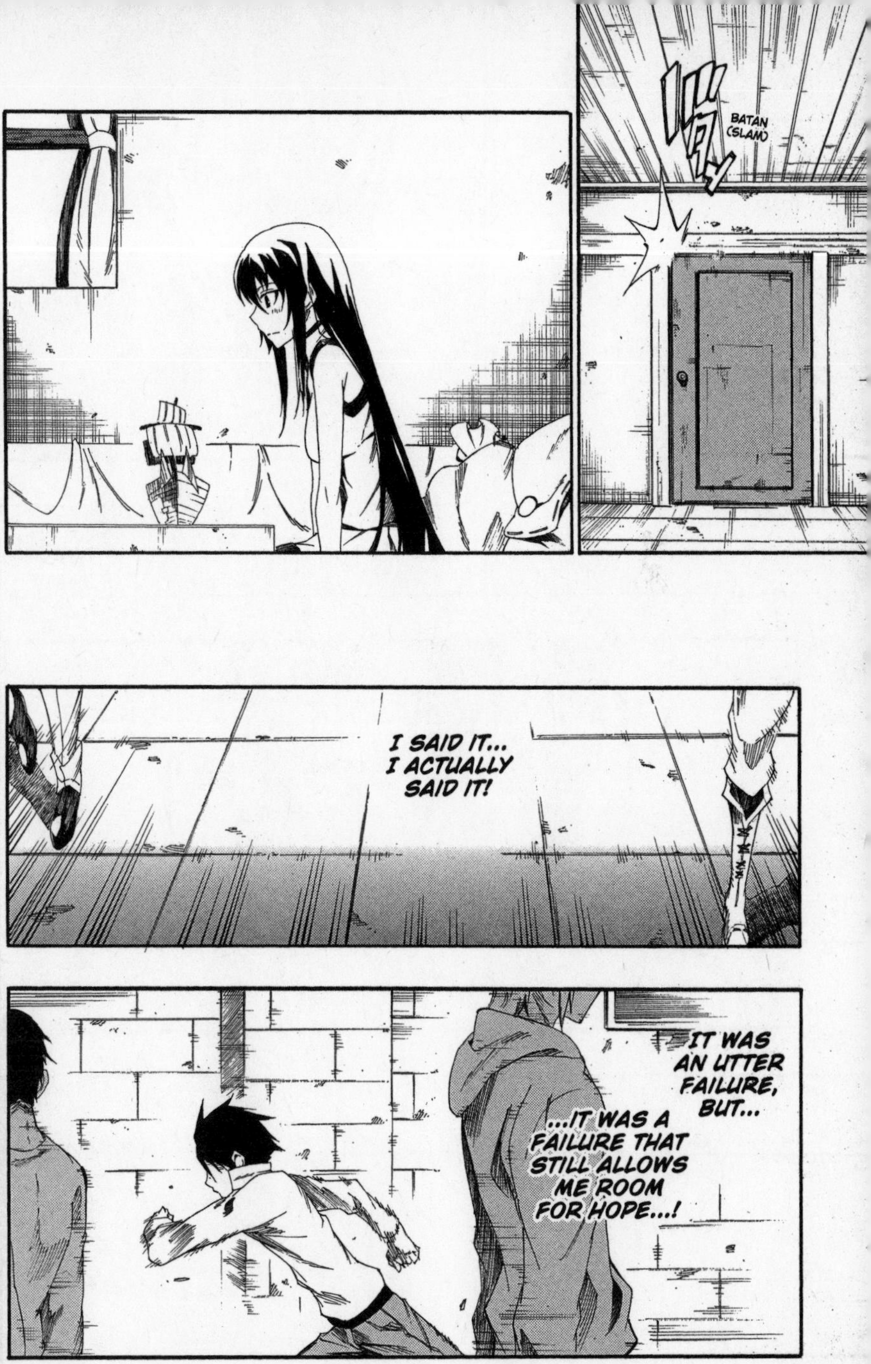
BATAN (SLAM)
I SAID IT... I ACTUALLY SAID IT!
IT WAS AN UTTER FAILURE, BUT...
...IT WAS A FAILURE THAT STILL ALLOWS ME ROOM FOR HOPE...!

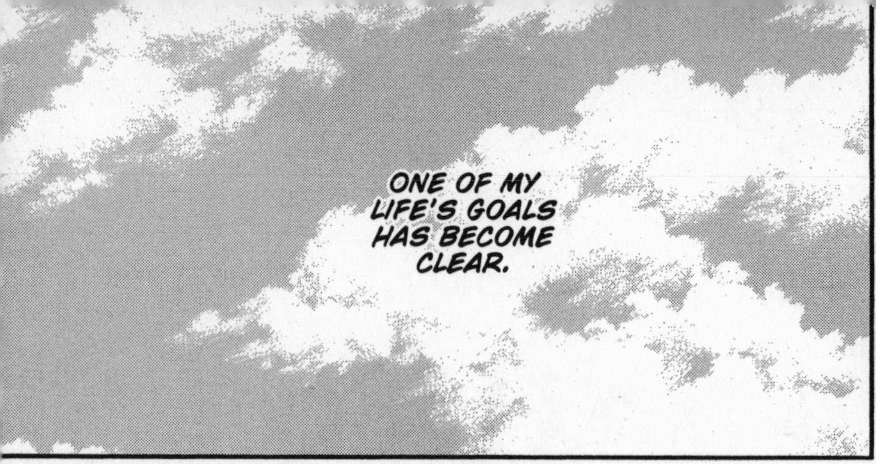
ONE OF MY LIFE'S GOALS HAS BECOME CLEAR.

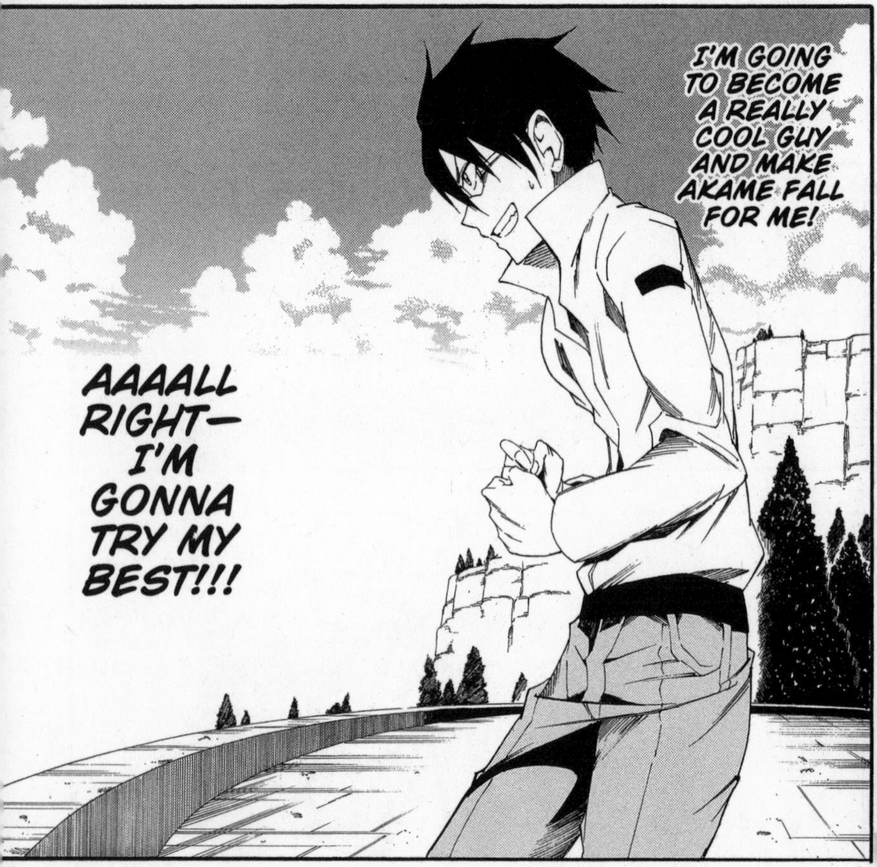
I'M GOING TO BECOME A REALLY COOL GUY AND MAKE AKAME FALL FOR ME!
AAAALL RIGHT— I'M GONNA TRY MY BEST!!!

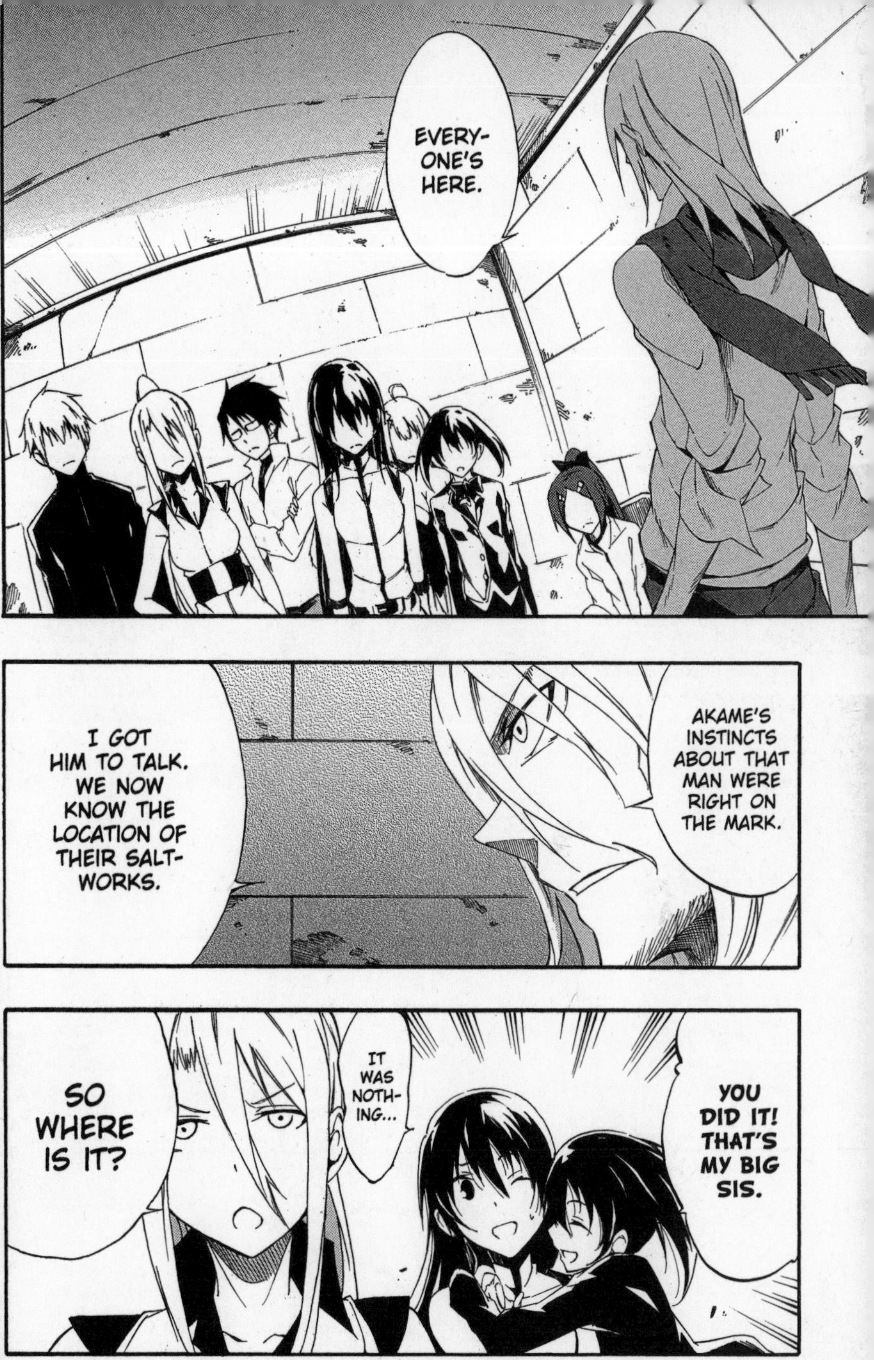
EVERYONE'S HERE.
AKAME'S INSTINCTS ABOUT THAT MAN WERE RIGHT ON THE MARK.
I GOT HIM TO TALK. WE NOW KNOW THE LOCATION OF THEIR SALTWORKS.
YOU DID IT! THAT'S MY BIG SIS.
IT WAS NOTHING...
SO WHERE IS IT?

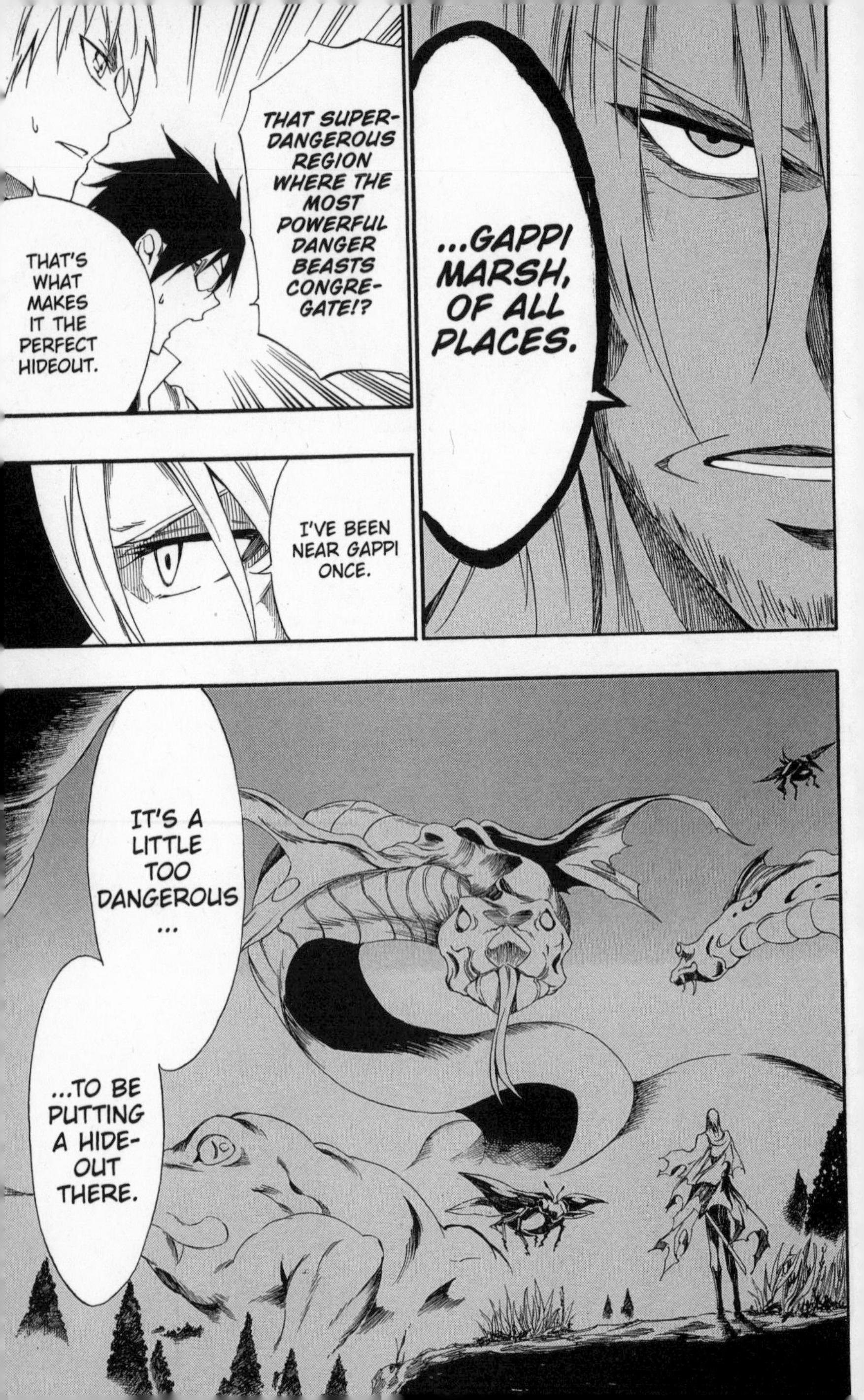
...GAPPI MARSH, OF ALL PLACES.
THAT SUPER-DANGEROUS REGION WHERE THE MOST POWERFUL DANGER BEASTS CONGREGATE!?
THAT'S WHAT MAKES IT THE PERFECT HIDEOUT.
I'VE BEEN NEAR GAPPI ONCE.
IT'S A LITTLE TOO DANGEROUS...
...TO BE PUTTING A HIDE-OUT THERE.

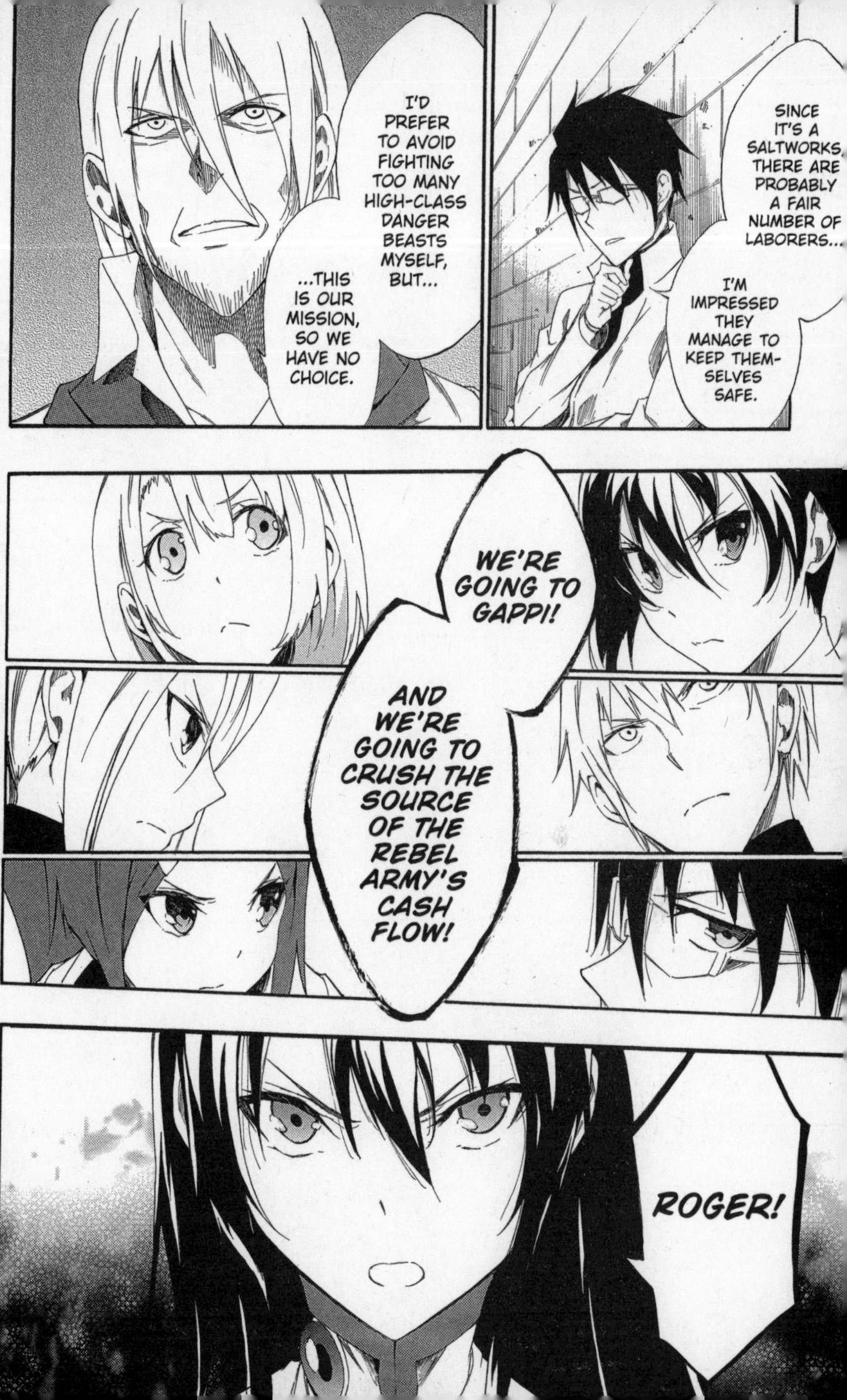
SINCE IT'S A SALTWORKS, THERE ARE PROBABLY A FAIR NUMBER OF LABORERS...
I'M IMPRESSED THEY MANAGE TO KEEP THEMSELVES SAFE.
I'D PREFER TO AVOID FIGHTING TOO MANY HIGH-CLASS DANGER BEASTS MYSELF, BUT...
...THIS IS OUR MISSION, SO WE HAVE NO CHOICE.
WE'RE GOING TO GAPPI!
AND WE'RE GOING TO CRUSH THE SOURCE OF THE REBEL ARMY'S CASH FLOW!
ROGER!

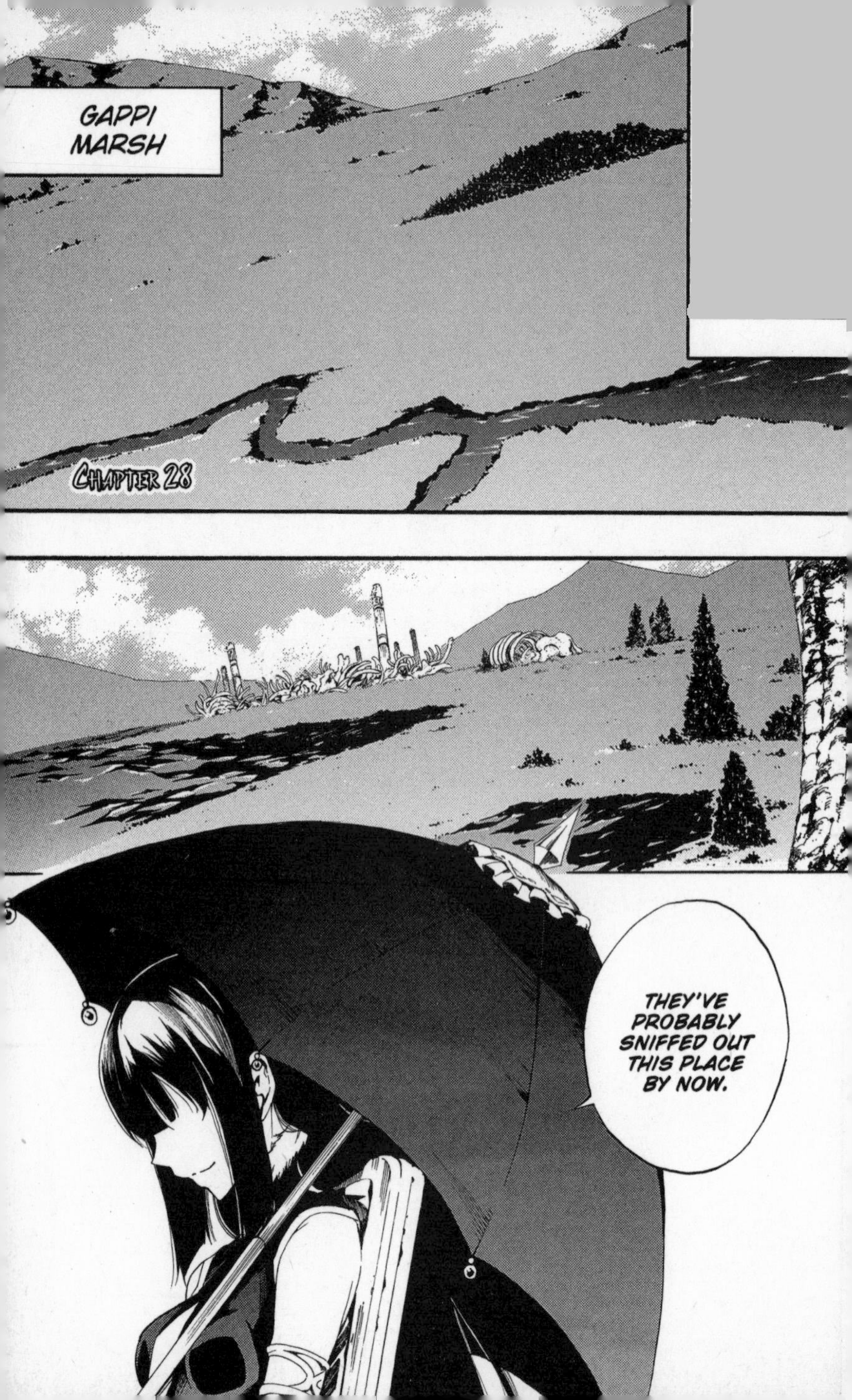
GAPPI MARSH
CHAPTER 28
THEY'VE PROBABLY SNIFFED OUT THIS PLACE BY NOW.

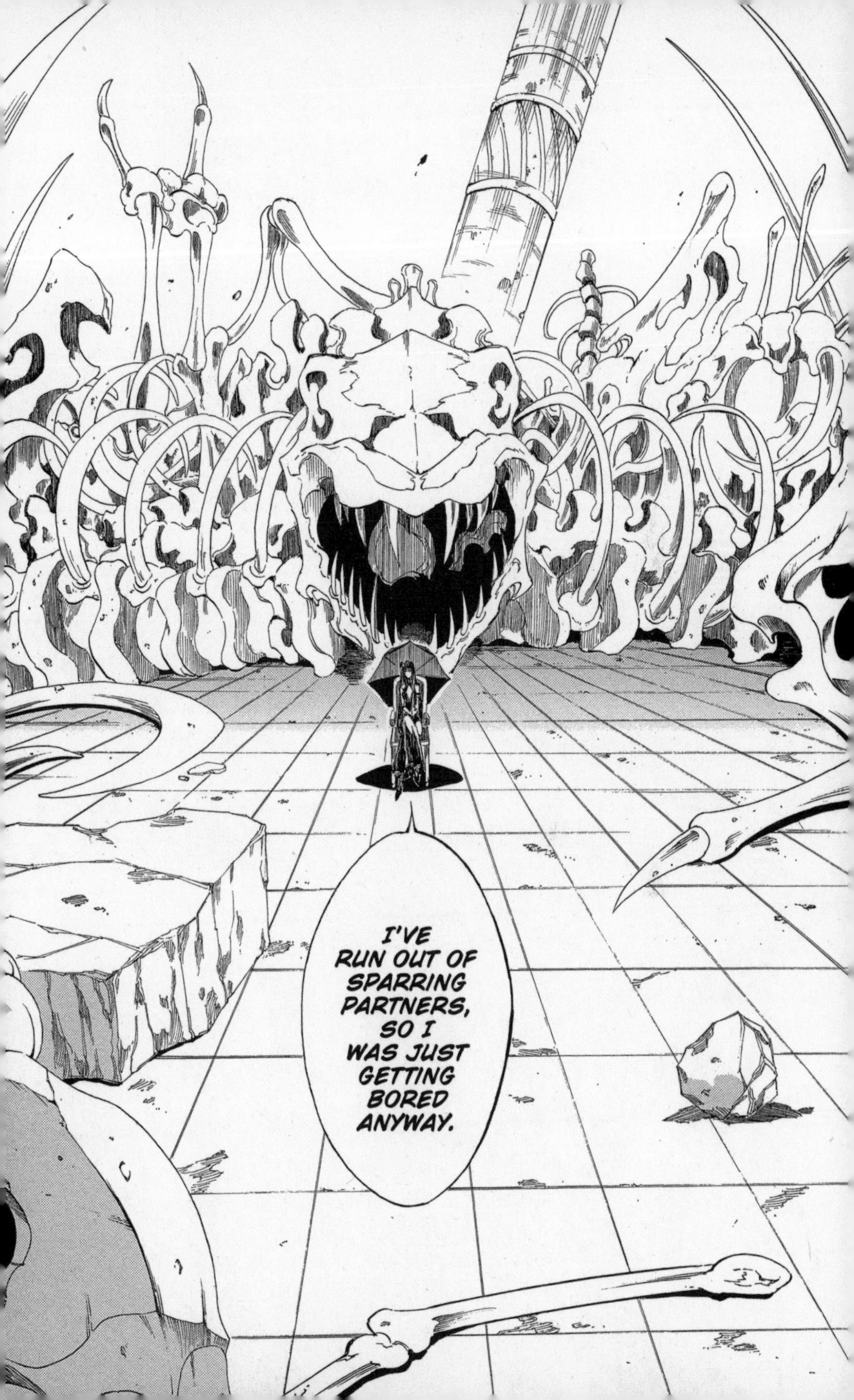
I'VE RUN OUT OF SPARRING PARTNERS, SO I WAS JUST GETTING BORED ANYWAY.

COM-
ING.

GATA
(CLATTER)

MADAM
MERA.

DINNER IS
READY.

KO
(CLIK)

KO

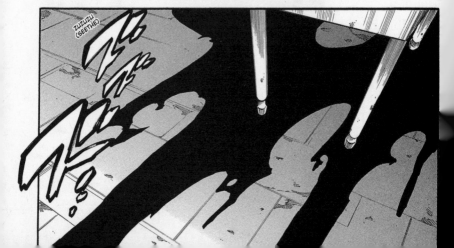

ZUZUZU
(SEETHE)

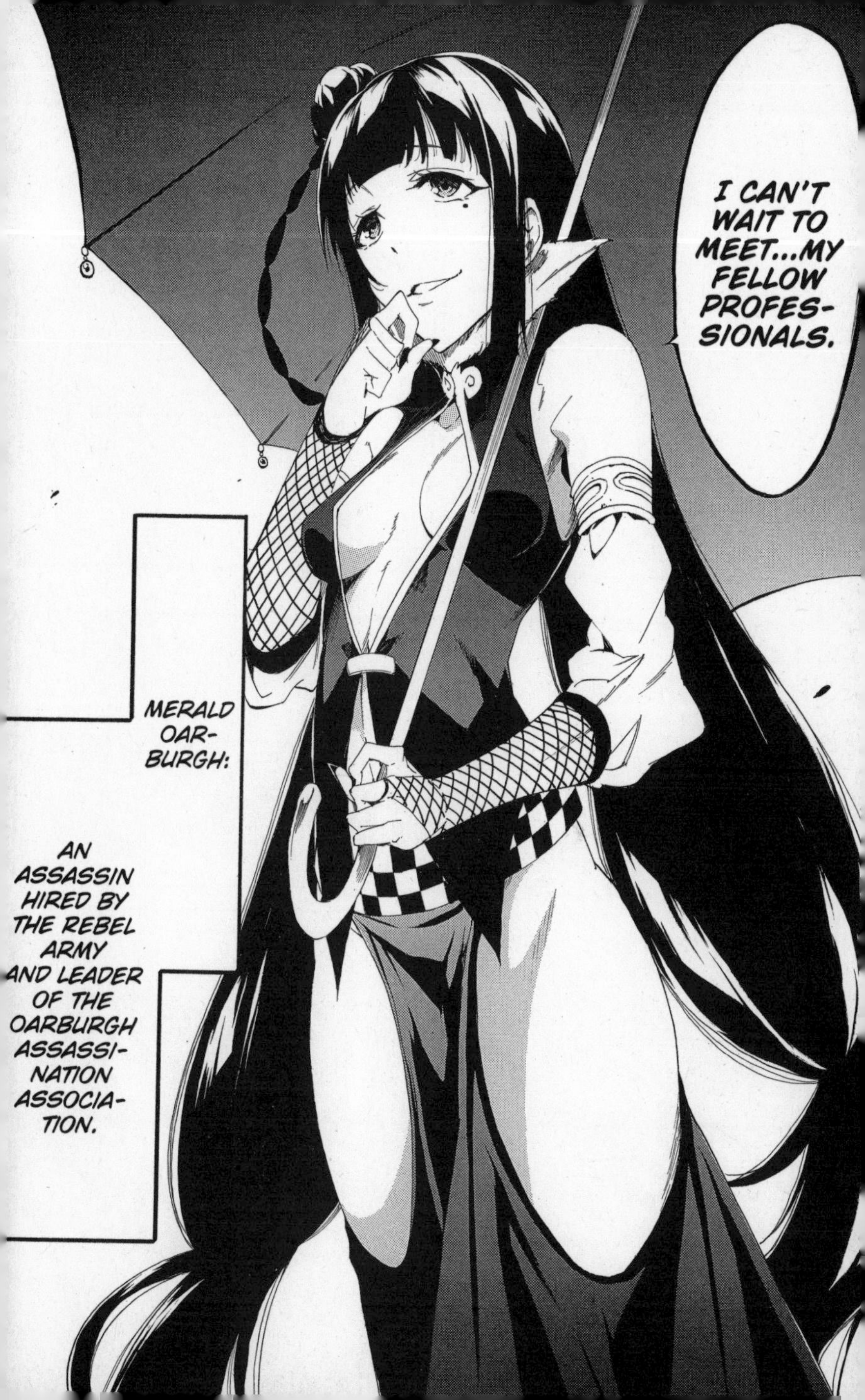
I CAN'T WAIT TO MEET...MY FELLOW PROFES-SIONALS.
MERALD OAR-BURGH:
AN ASSASSIN HIRED BY THE REBEL ARMY AND LEADER OF THE OARBURGH ASSASSI-NATION ASSOCIA-TION.

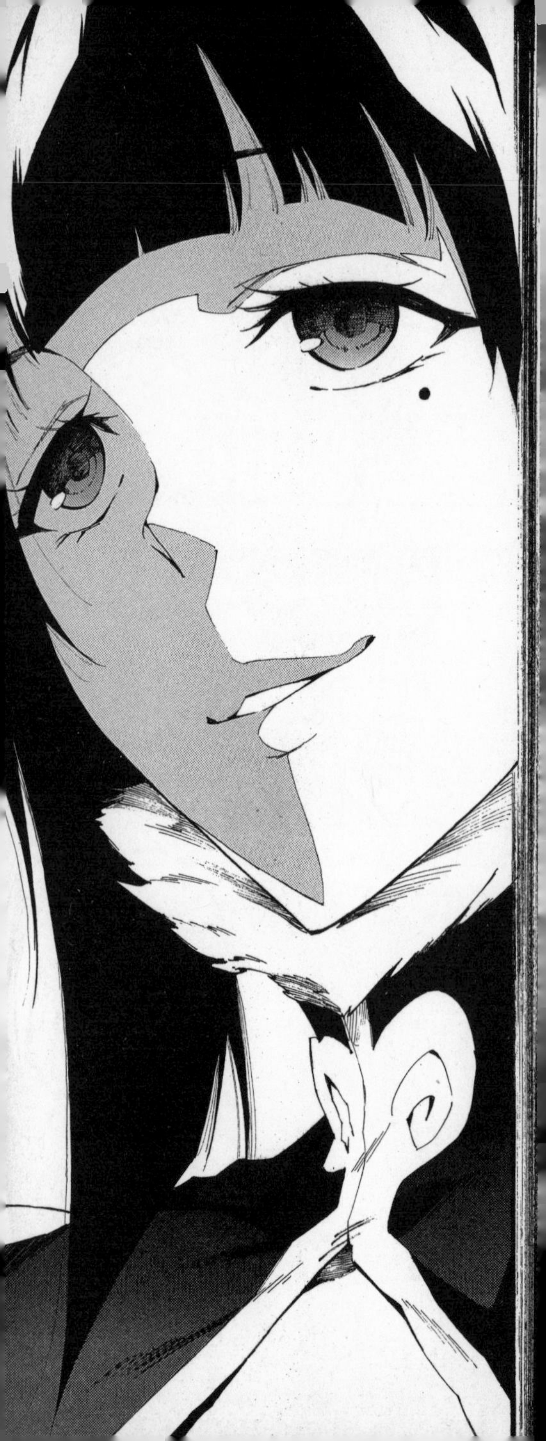

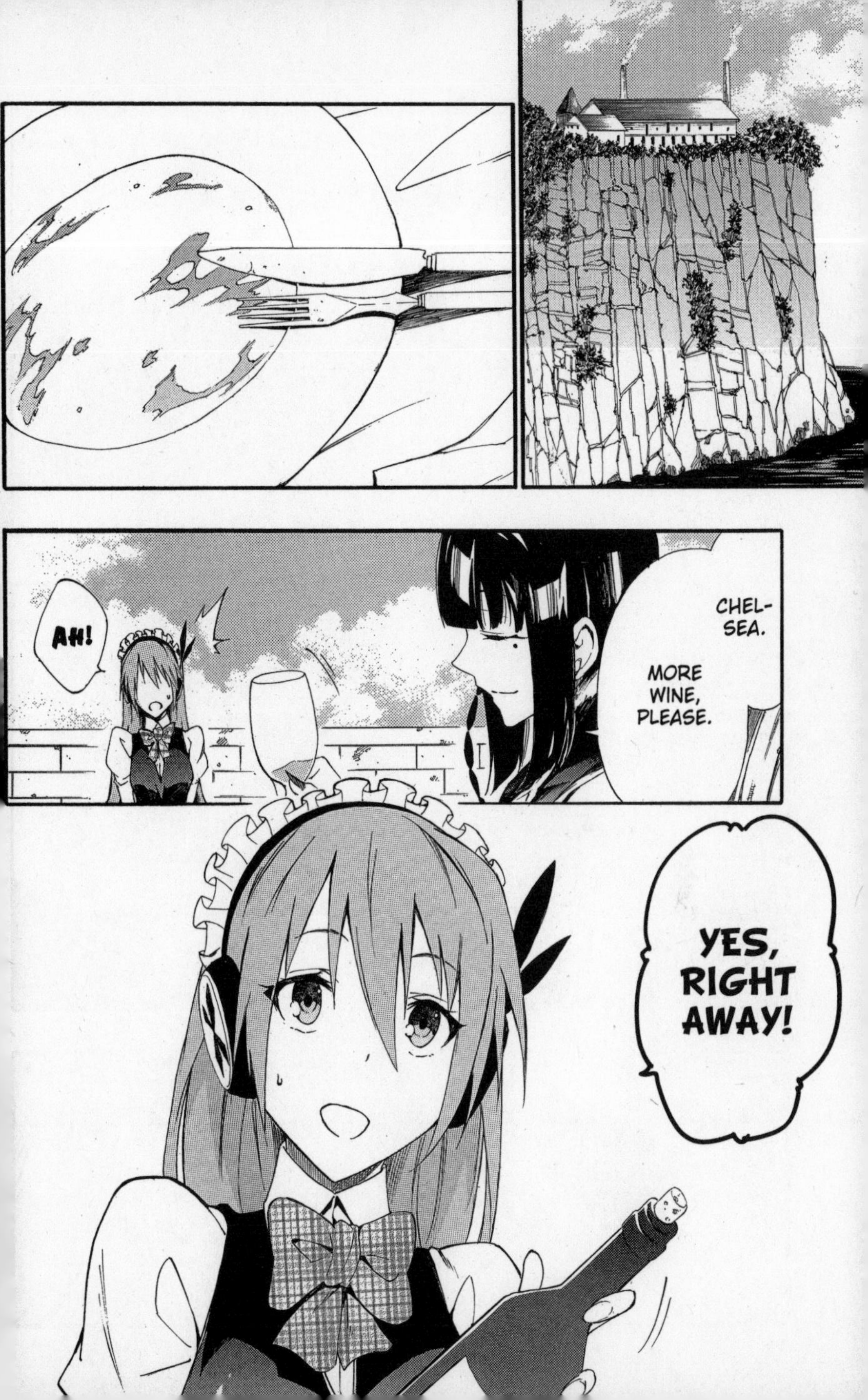
CHEL-SEA.
MORE WINE, PLEASE.
AH!
YES, RIGHT AWAY!

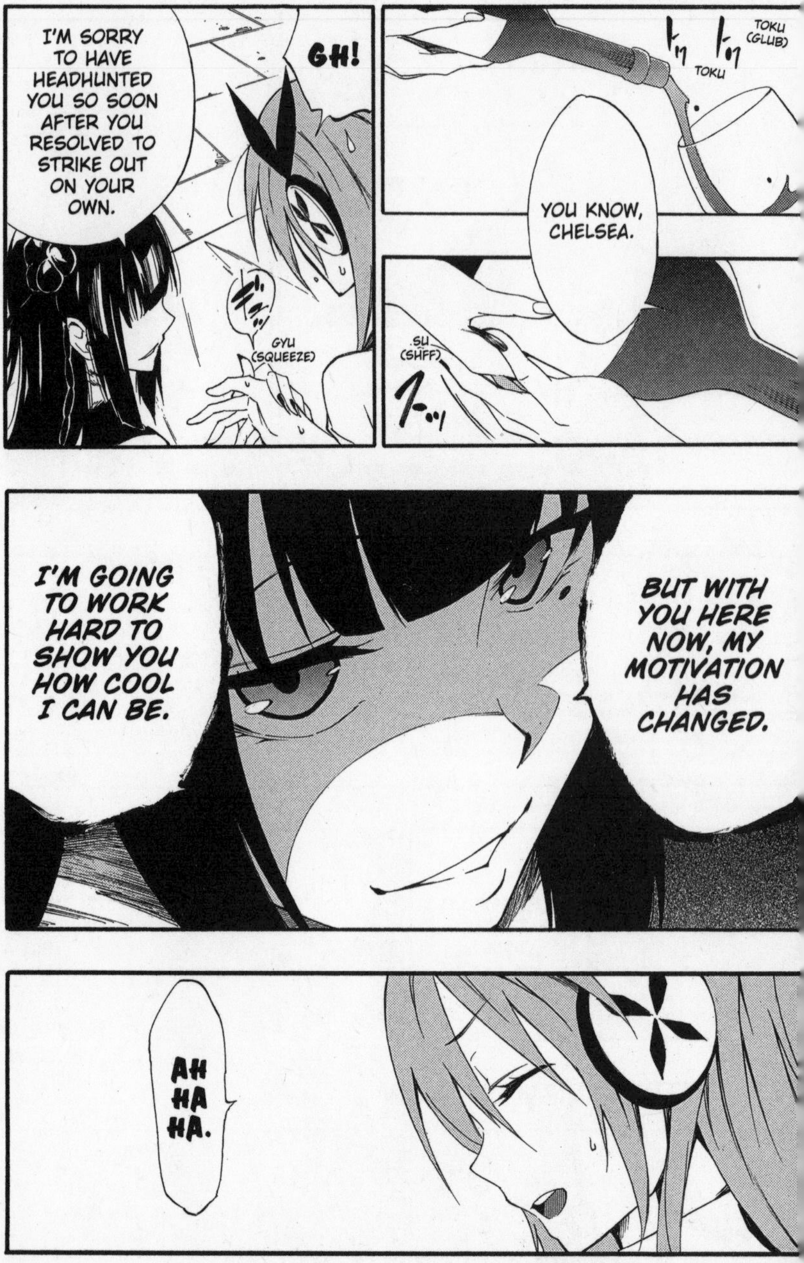

TOKU (GLUB)
TOKU
YOU KNOW, CHELSEA.
SU (SHFF)
I'M SORRY TO HAVE HEADHUNTED YOU SO SOON AFTER YOU RESOLVED TO STRIKE OUT ON YOUR OWN.
GH!
GYU (SQUEEZE)
BUT WITH YOU HERE NOW, MY MOTIVATION HAS CHANGED.
I'M GOING TO WORK HARD TO SHOW YOU HOW COOL I CAN BE.
AH HA HA.

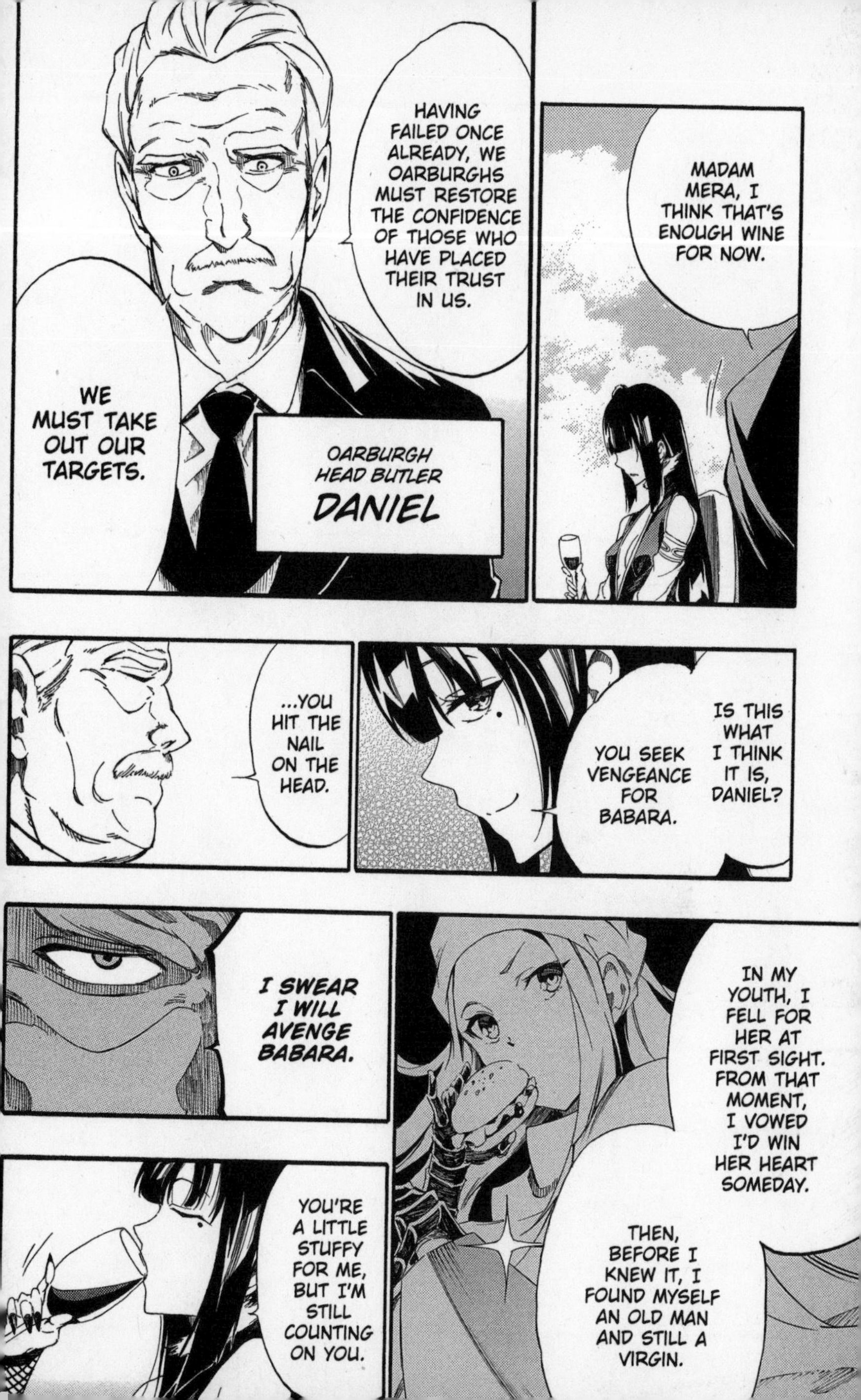
MADAM MERA, I THINK THAT'S ENOUGH WINE FOR NOW.
HAVING FAILED ONCE ALREADY, WE OARBURGHS MUST RESTORE THE CONFIDENCE OF THOSE WHO HAVE PLACED THEIR TRUST IN US.
WE MUST TAKE OUT OUR TARGETS.
OARBURGH HEAD BUTLER DANIEL
IS THIS WHAT I THINK IT IS, DANIEL?
YOU SEEK VENGEANCE FOR BABARA.
...YOU HIT THE NAIL ON THE HEAD.
IN MY YOUTH, I FELL FOR HER AT FIRST SIGHT. FROM THAT MOMENT, I VOWED I'D WIN HER HEART SOMEDAY.
THEN, BEFORE I KNEW IT, I FOUND MYSELF AN OLD MAN AND STILL A VIRGIN.
I SWEAR I WILL AVENGE BABARA.
YOU'RE A LITTLE STUFFY FOR ME, BUT I'M STILL COUNTING ON YOU.

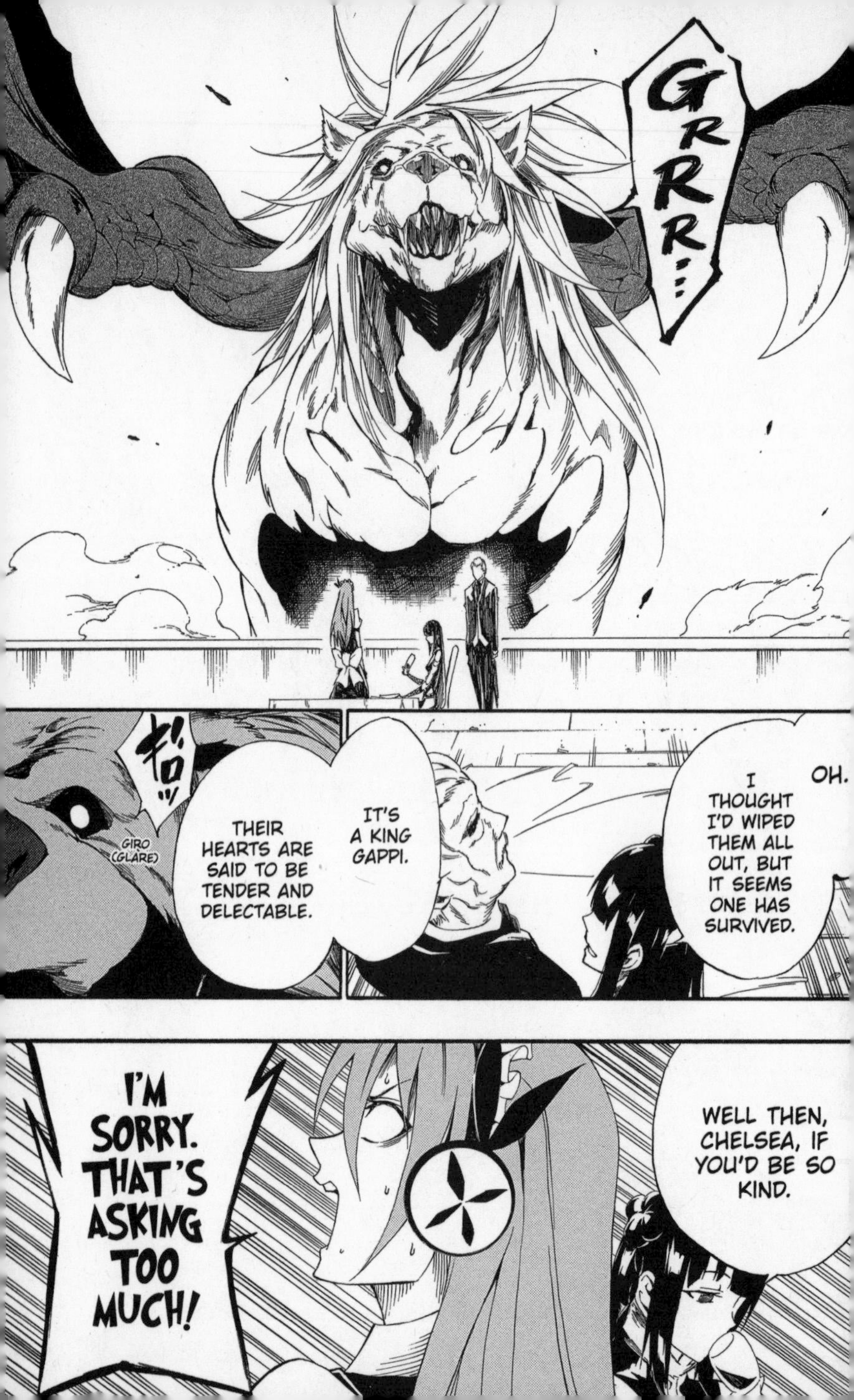
GRRR…
OH.
I THOUGHT I'D WIPED THEM ALL OUT, BUT IT SEEMS ONE HAS SURVIVED.
IT'S A KING GAPPI.
THEIR HEARTS ARE SAID TO BE TENDER AND DELECTABLE.
ギロッ
GIRO (GLARE)
WELL THEN, CHELSEA, IF YOU'D BE SO KIND.
I'M SORRY. THAT'S ASKING TOO MUCH!

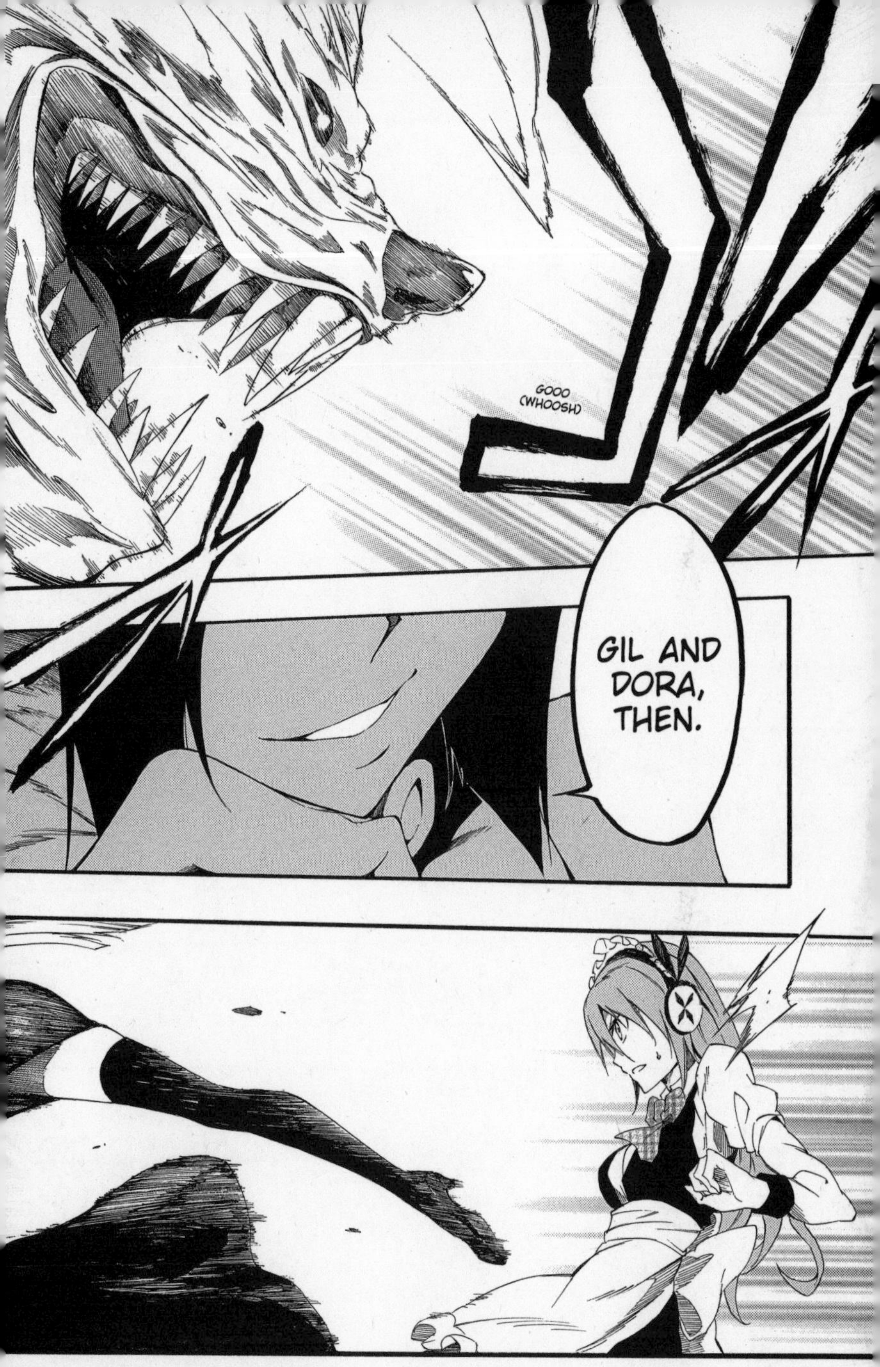
GOOO
(WHOOSH)
GIL AND DORA, THEN.

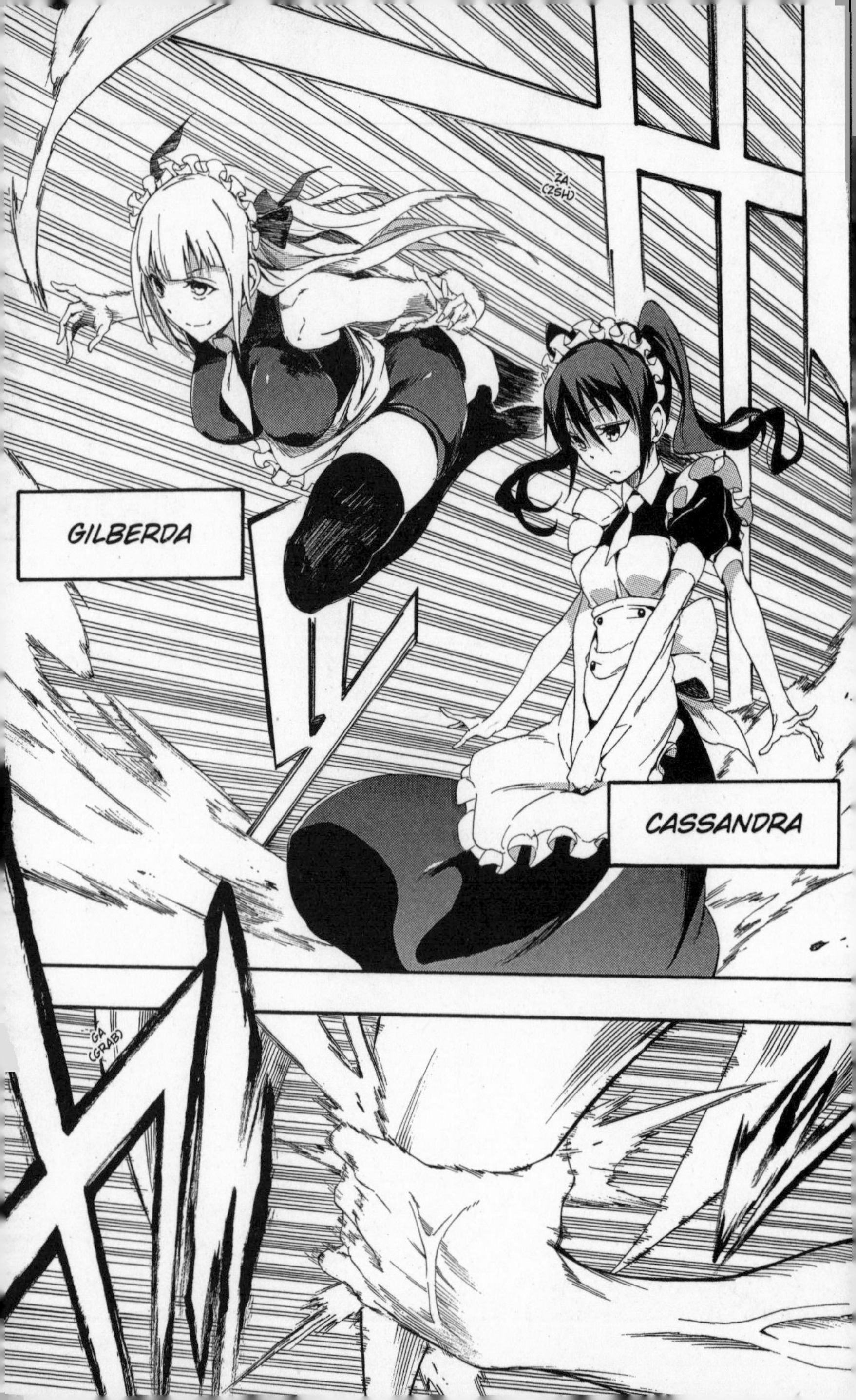
ZA (ZSH)
GILBERDA
CASSANDRA
GA (GRAB)

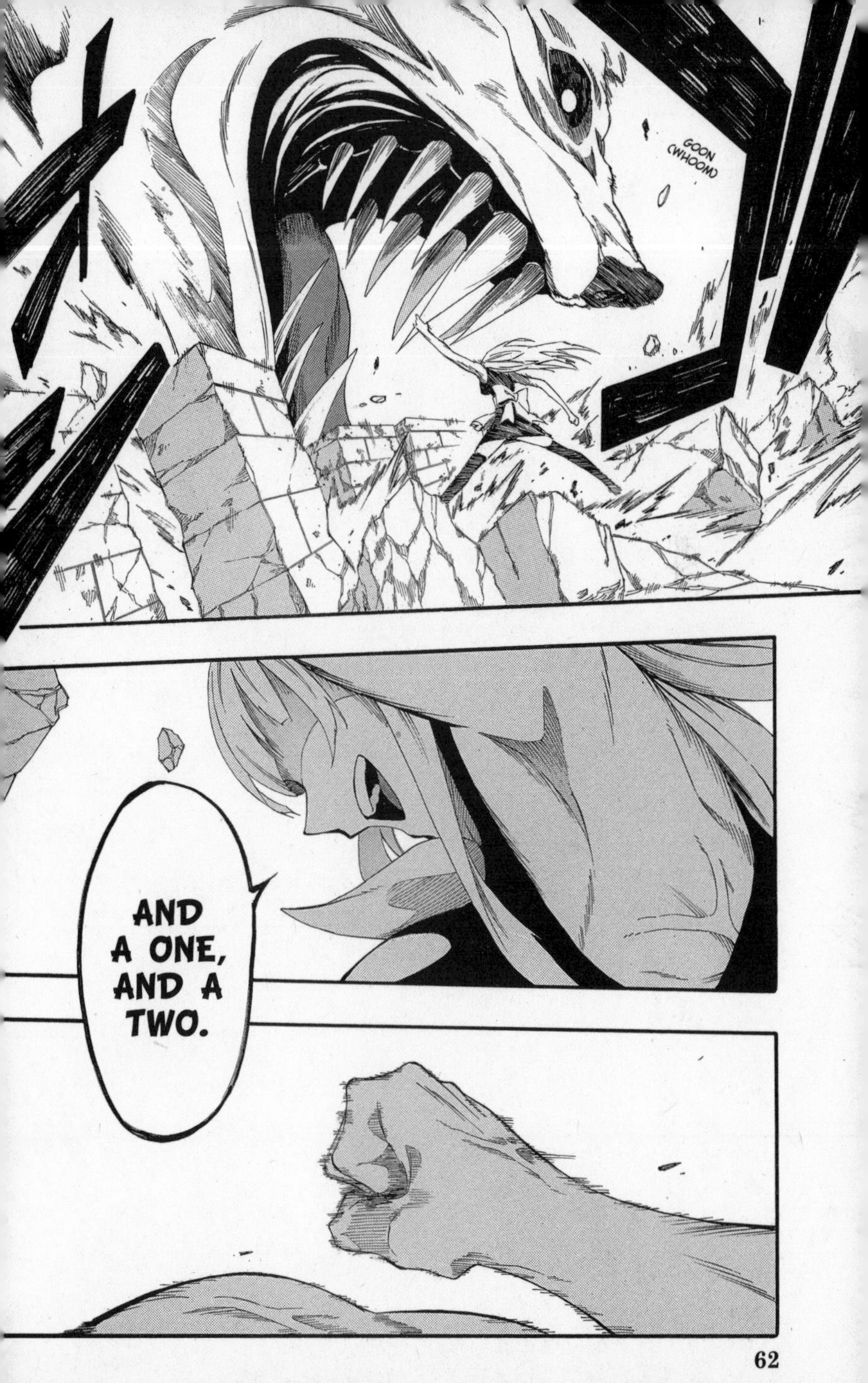
GOON (WHOOM)
AND A ONE, AND A TWO.

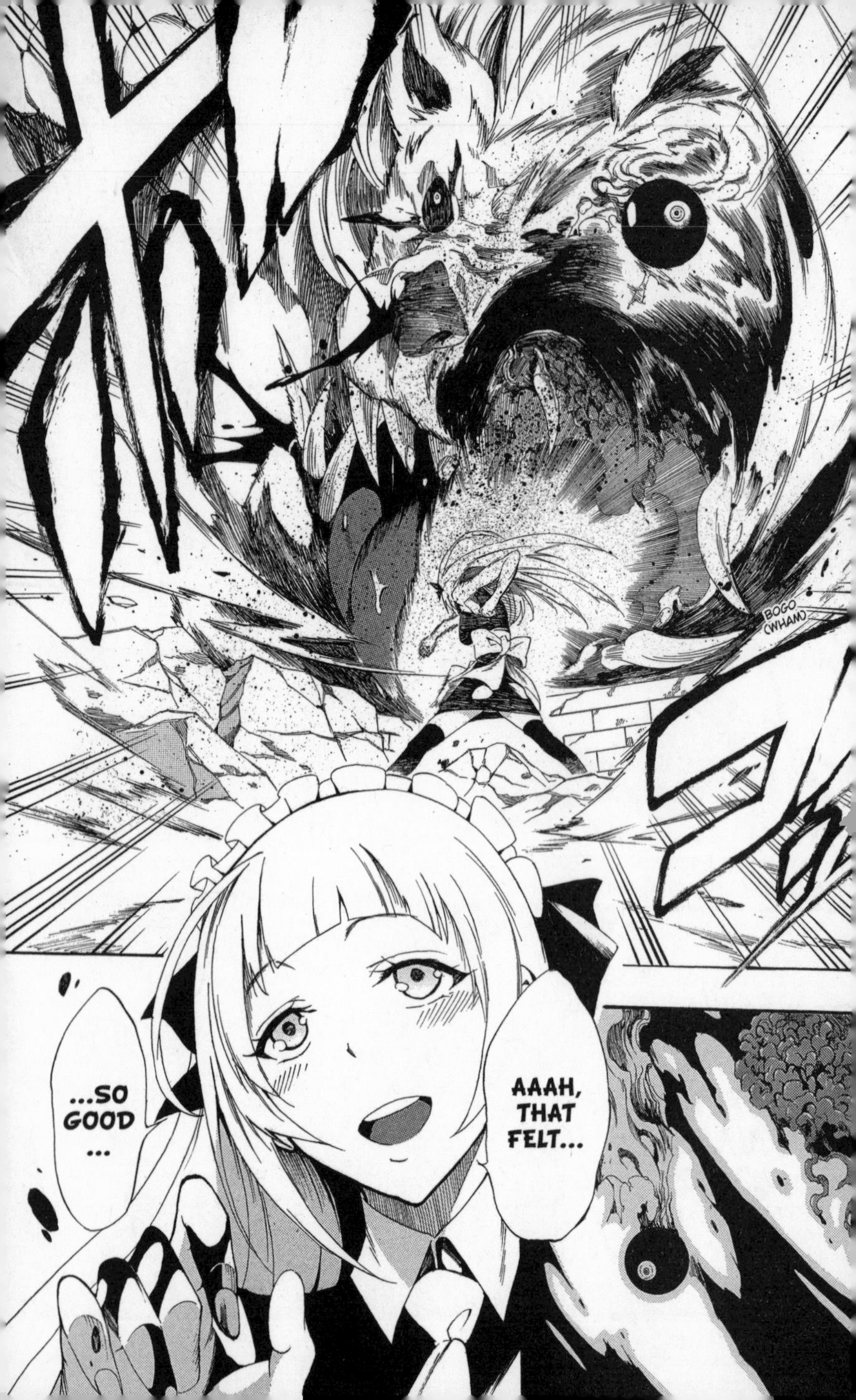
BOGO (WHAM)
AAAH, THAT FELT...
...SO GOOD ...

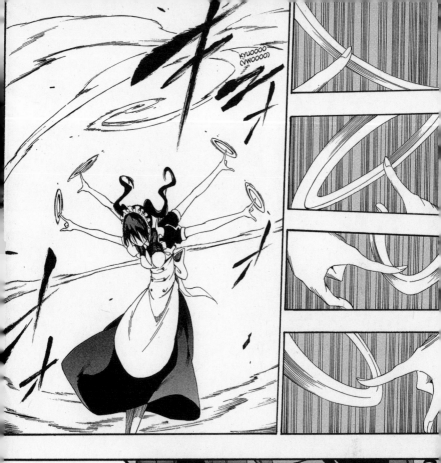

KYUOOOO
(VWOOOO)

NOW DOING THE FINAL DINNER PREP.

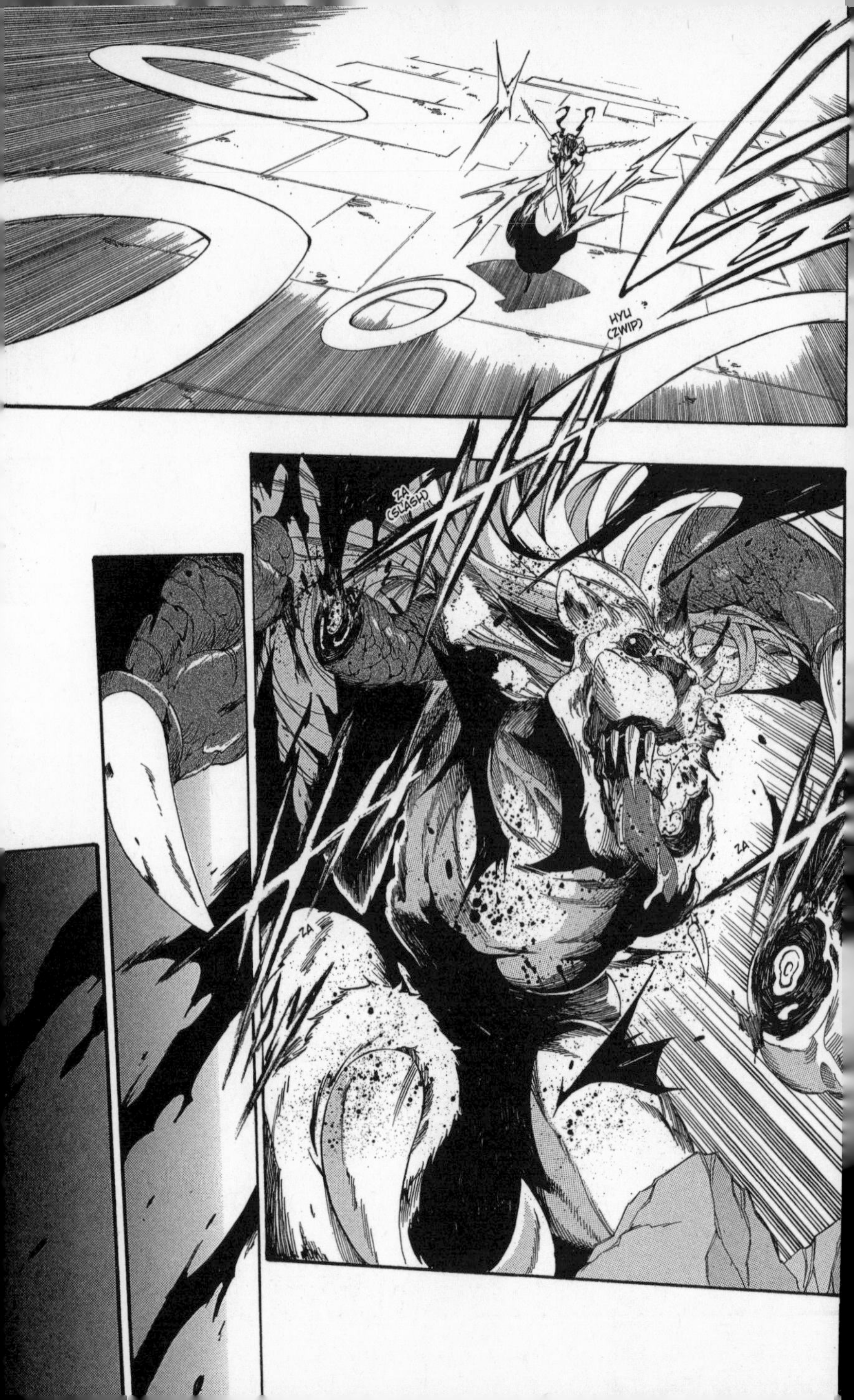
HYU
(ZWIP)
ZA
(SLASH)
ZA
ZA

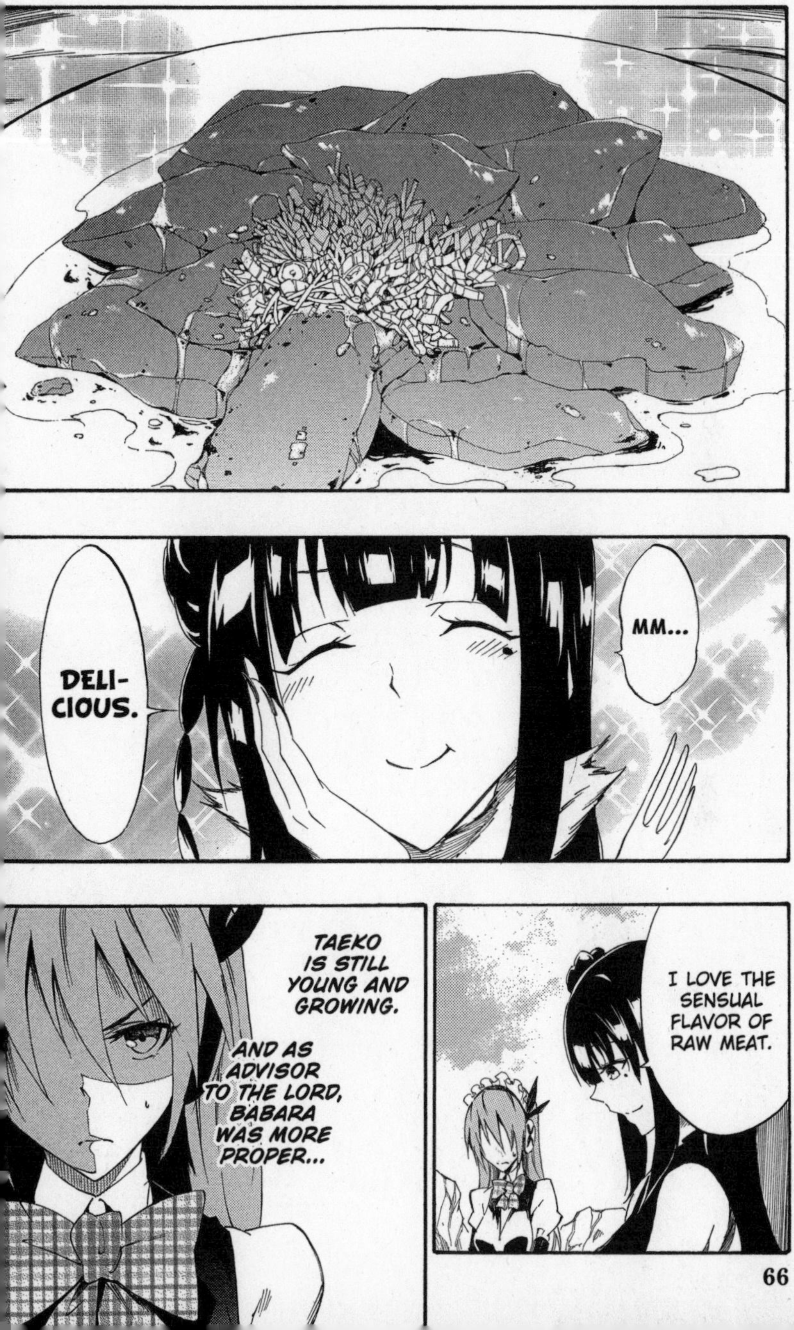
MM...
DELI-
CIOUS.
I LOVE THE SENSUAL FLAVOR OF RAW MEAT.
TAEKO IS STILL YOUNG AND GROWING.
AND AS ADVISOR TO THE LORD, BABARA WAS MORE PROPER...

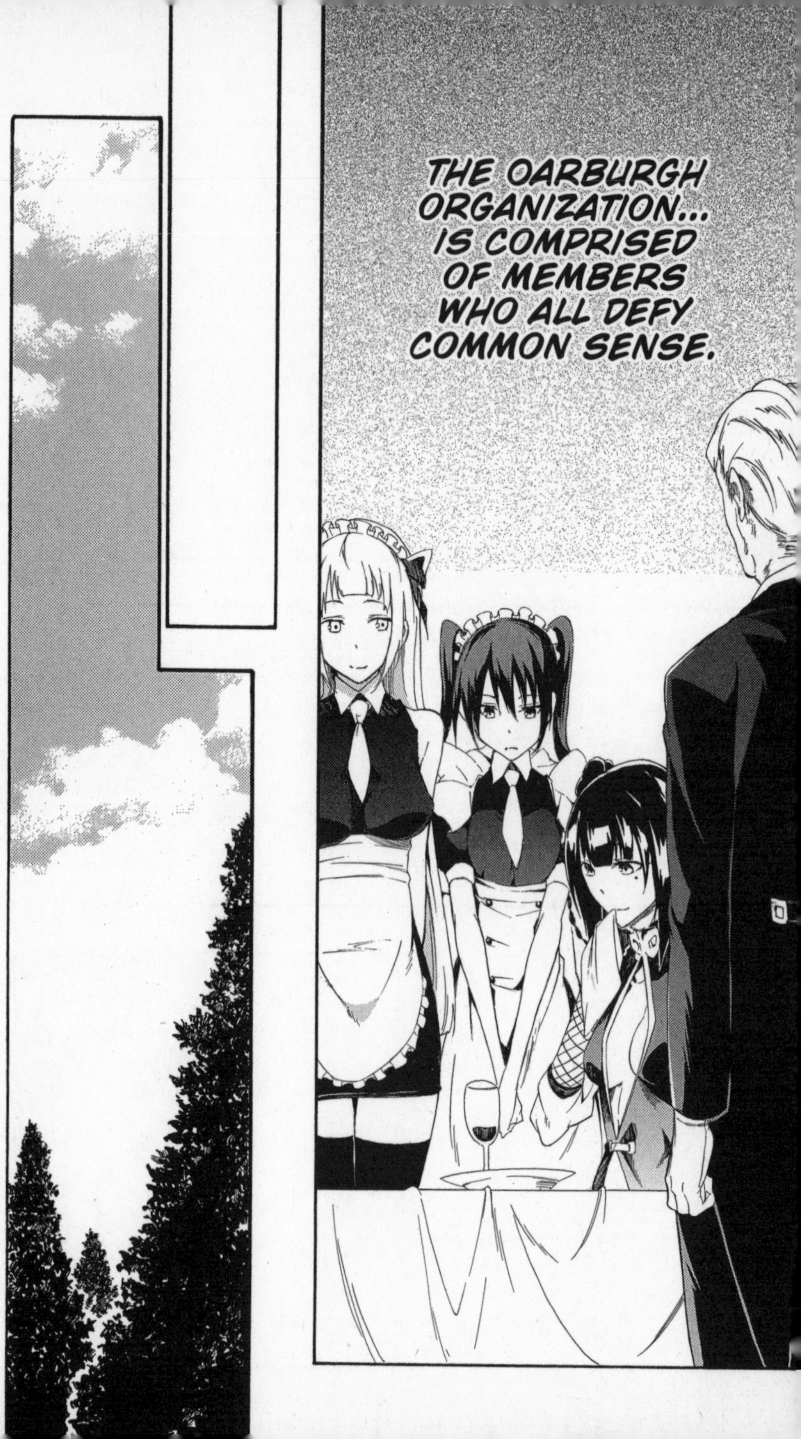
THE OARBURGH ORGANIZATION... IS COMPRISED OF MEMBERS WHO ALL DEFY COMMON SENSE.

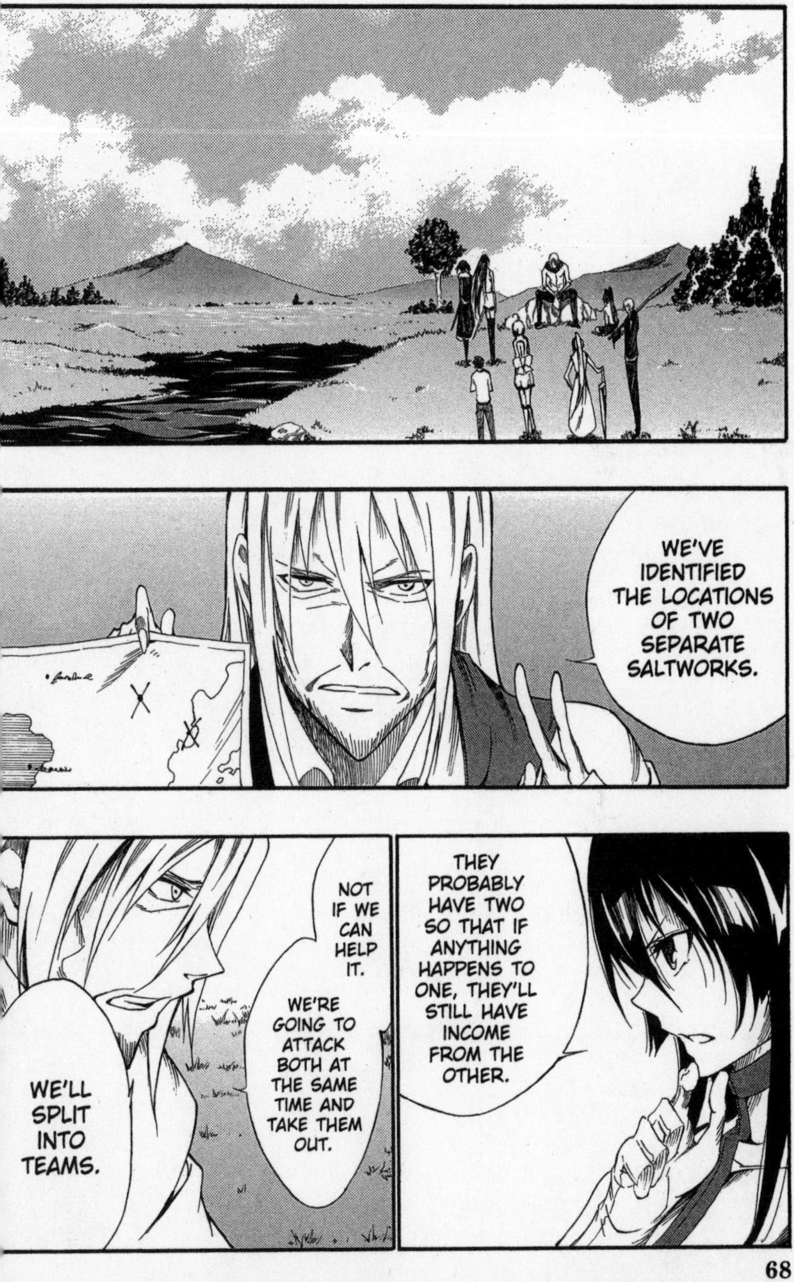
WE'VE IDENTIFIED THE LOCATIONS OF TWO SEPARATE SALTWORKS.
THEY PROBABLY HAVE TWO SO THAT IF ANYTHING HAPPENS TO ONE, THEY'LL STILL HAVE INCOME FROM THE OTHER.
NOT IF WE CAN HELP IT.
WE'RE GOING TO ATTACK BOTH AT THE SAME TIME AND TAKE THEM OUT.
WE'LL SPLIT INTO TEAMS.

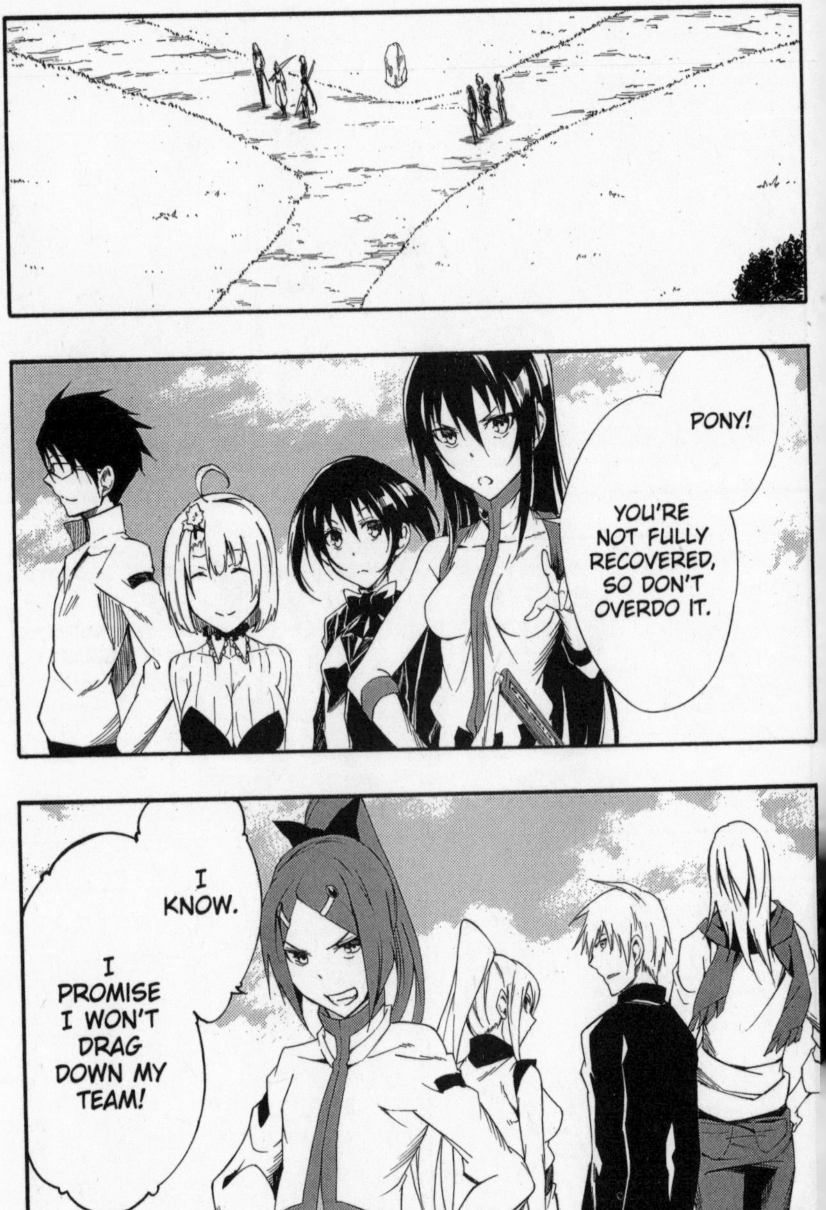
PONY!
YOU'RE NOT FULLY RECOVERED, SO DON'T OVERDO IT.
I KNOW.
I PROMISE I WON'T DRAG DOWN MY TEAM!

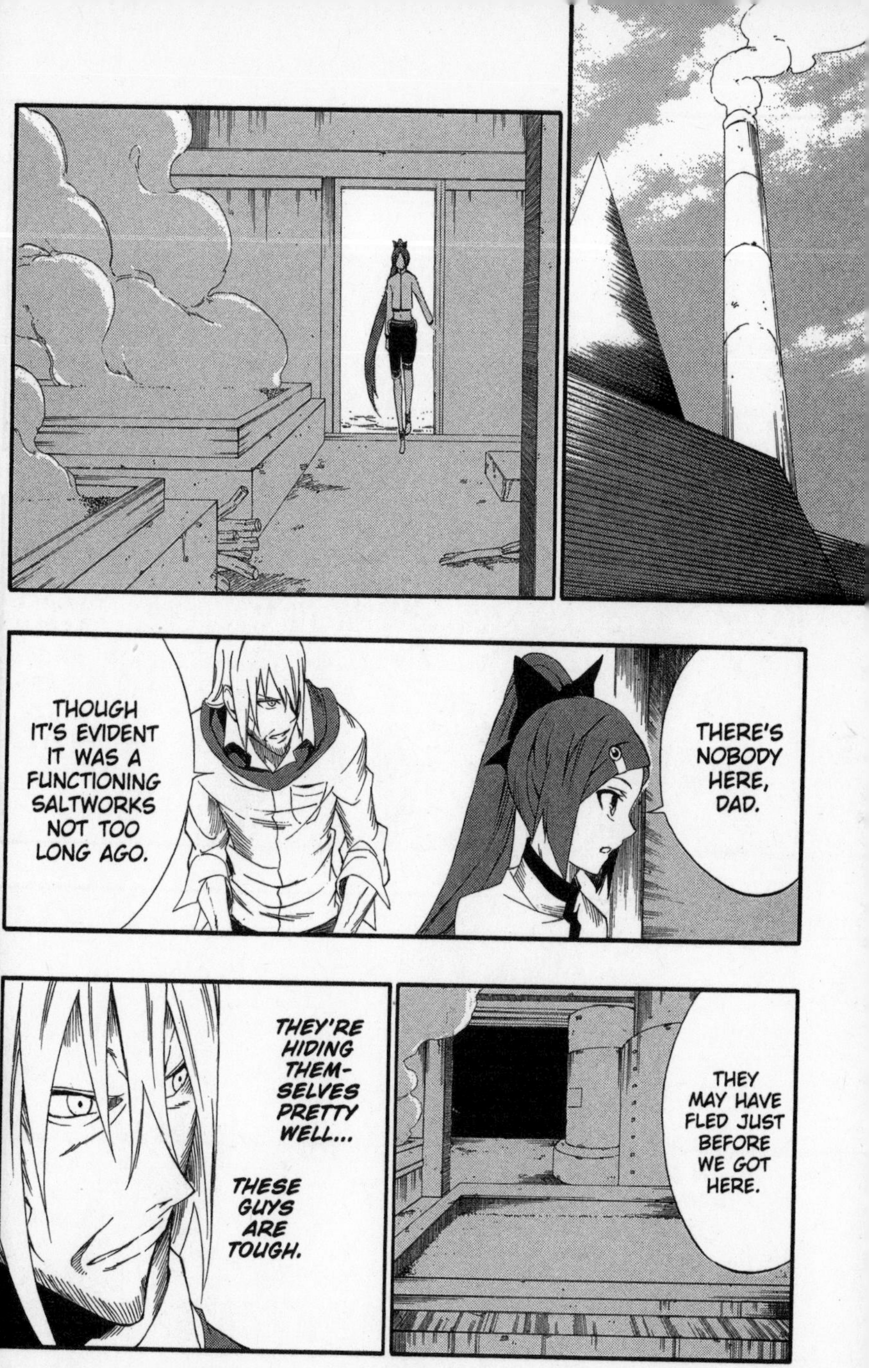
THERE'S NOBODY HERE, DAD.
THOUGH IT'S EVIDENT IT WAS A FUNCTIONING SALTWORKS NOT TOO LONG AGO.
THEY MAY HAVE FLED JUST BEFORE WE GOT HERE.
THEY'RE HIDING THEM-SELVES PRETTY WELL...
THESE GUYS ARE TOUGH.

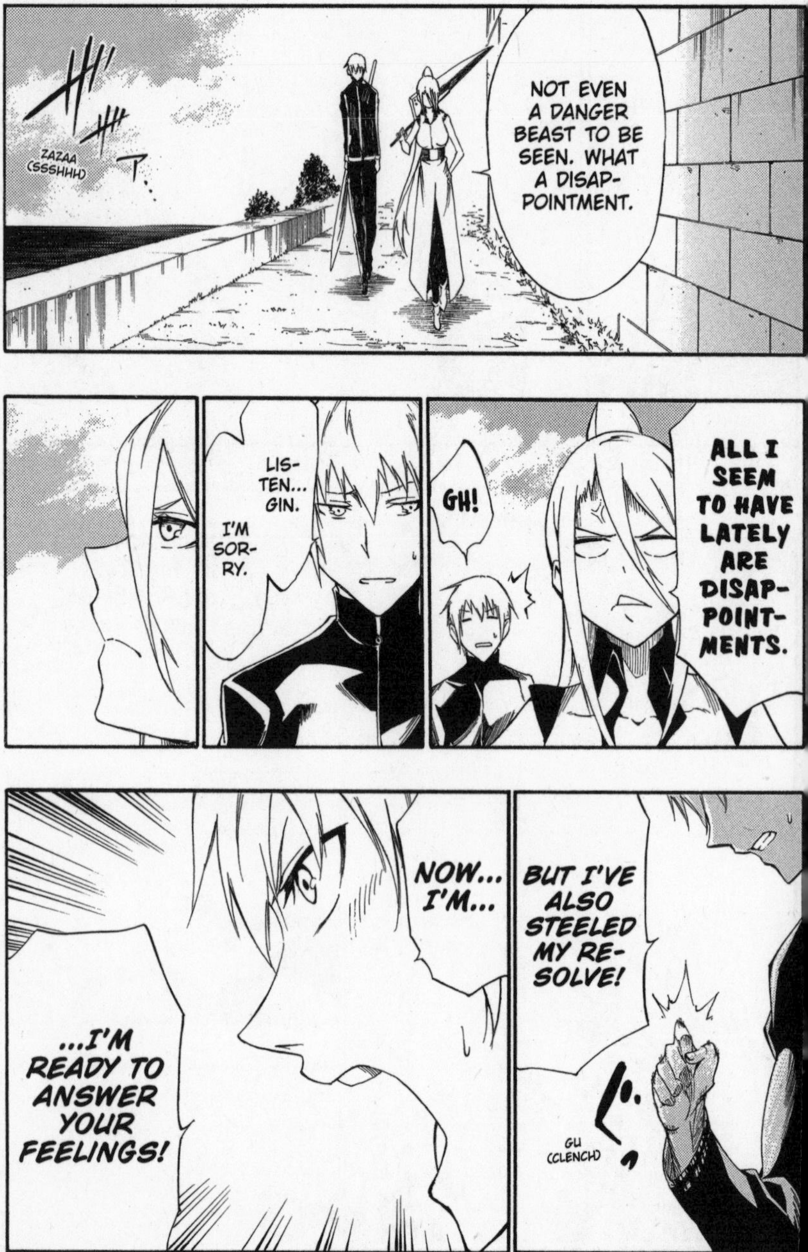
NOT EVEN A DANGER BEAST TO BE SEEN. WHAT A DISAPPOINTMENT.
ZAZAA (SSSHHH)
ALL I SEEM TO HAVE LATELY ARE DISAPPOINTMENTS.
GH!
LISTEN... GIN.
I'M SORRY.
BUT I'VE ALSO STEELED MY RESOLVE!
GU (CLENCH)
NOW... I'M...
...I'M READY TO ANSWER YOUR FEELINGS!

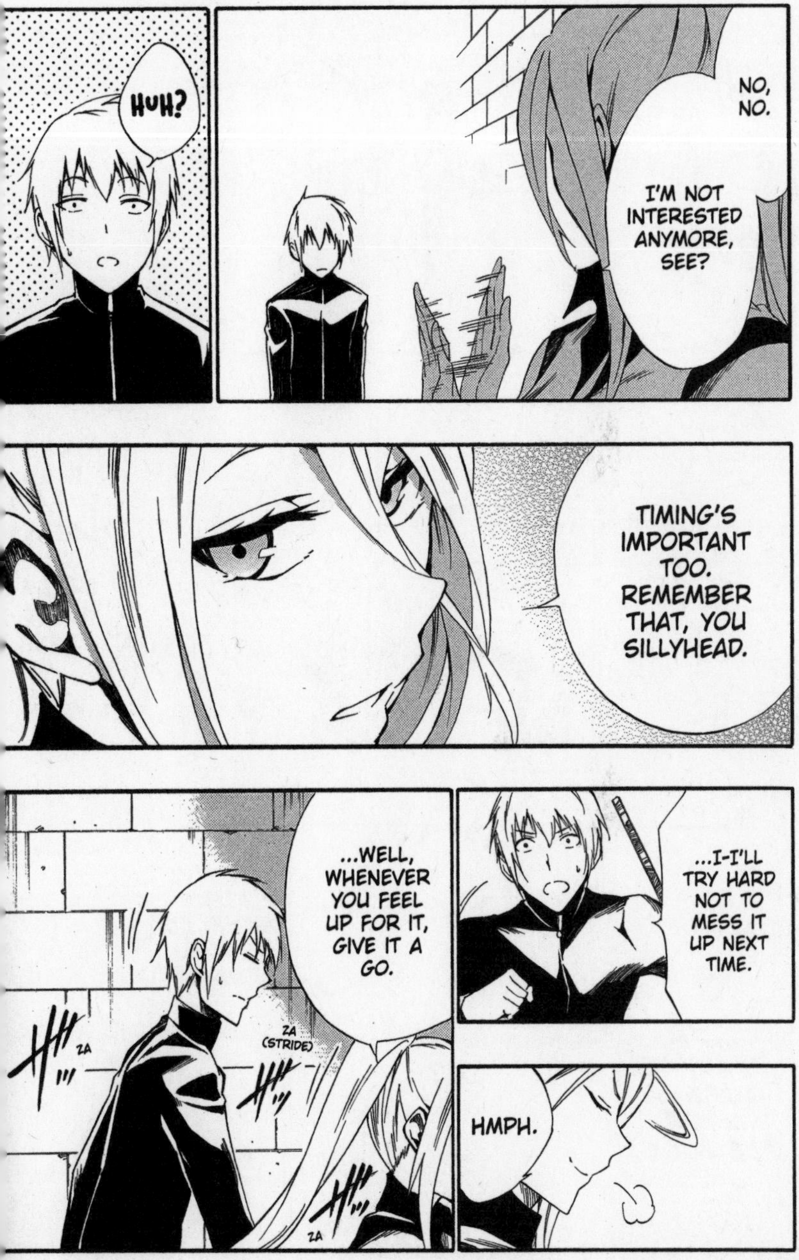
NO, NO.
I'M NOT INTERESTED ANYMORE, SEE?
HUH?
TIMING'S IMPORTANT TOO. REMEMBER THAT, YOU SILLYHEAD.
...I-I'LL TRY HARD NOT TO MESS IT UP NEXT TIME.
HMPH.
...WELL, WHENEVER YOU FEEL UP FOR IT, GIVE IT A GO.
ZA (STRIDE)
ZA
ZA

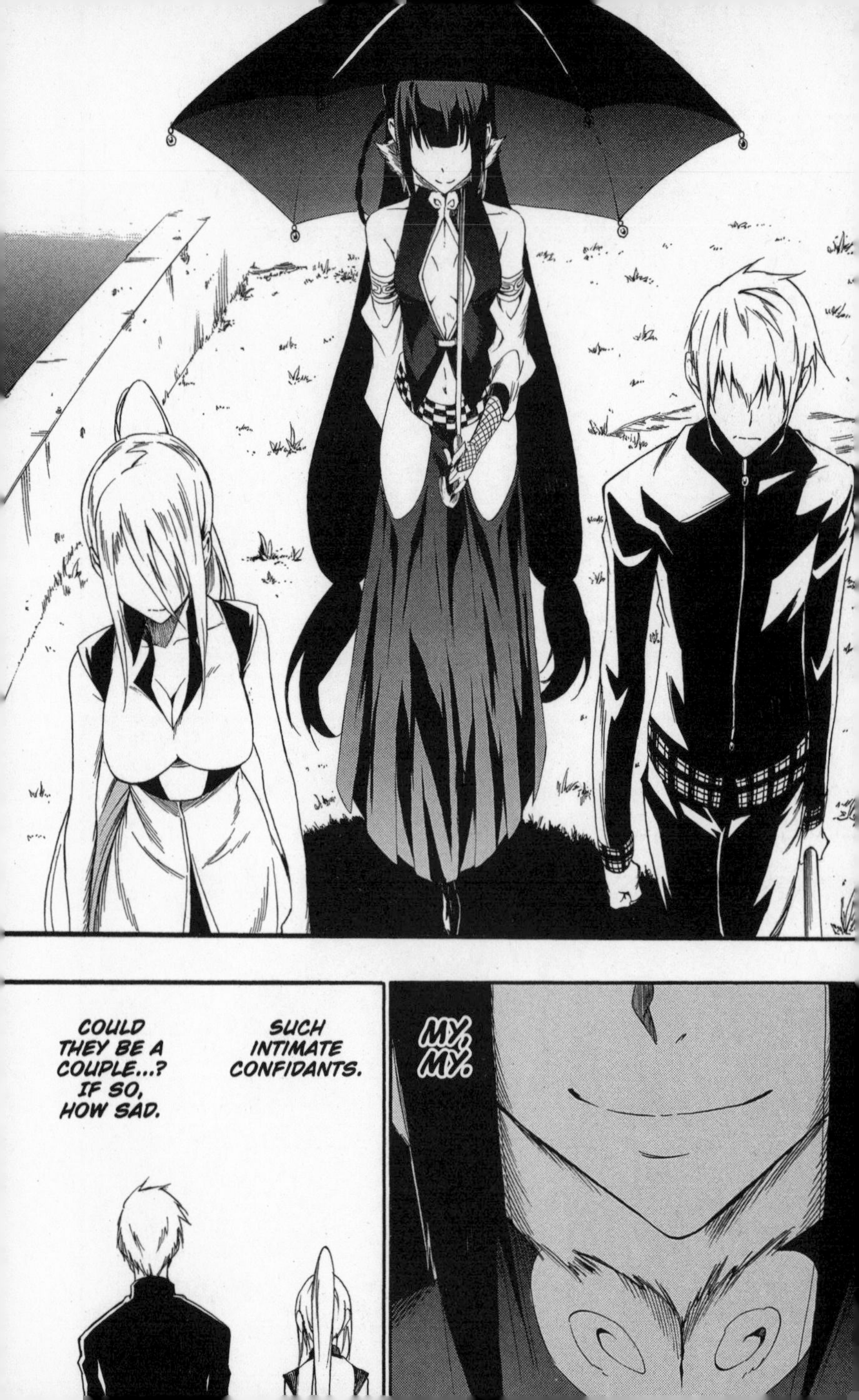
MY, MY.
SUCH INTIMATE CONFIDANTS.
COULD THEY BE A COUPLE...? IF SO, HOW SAD.

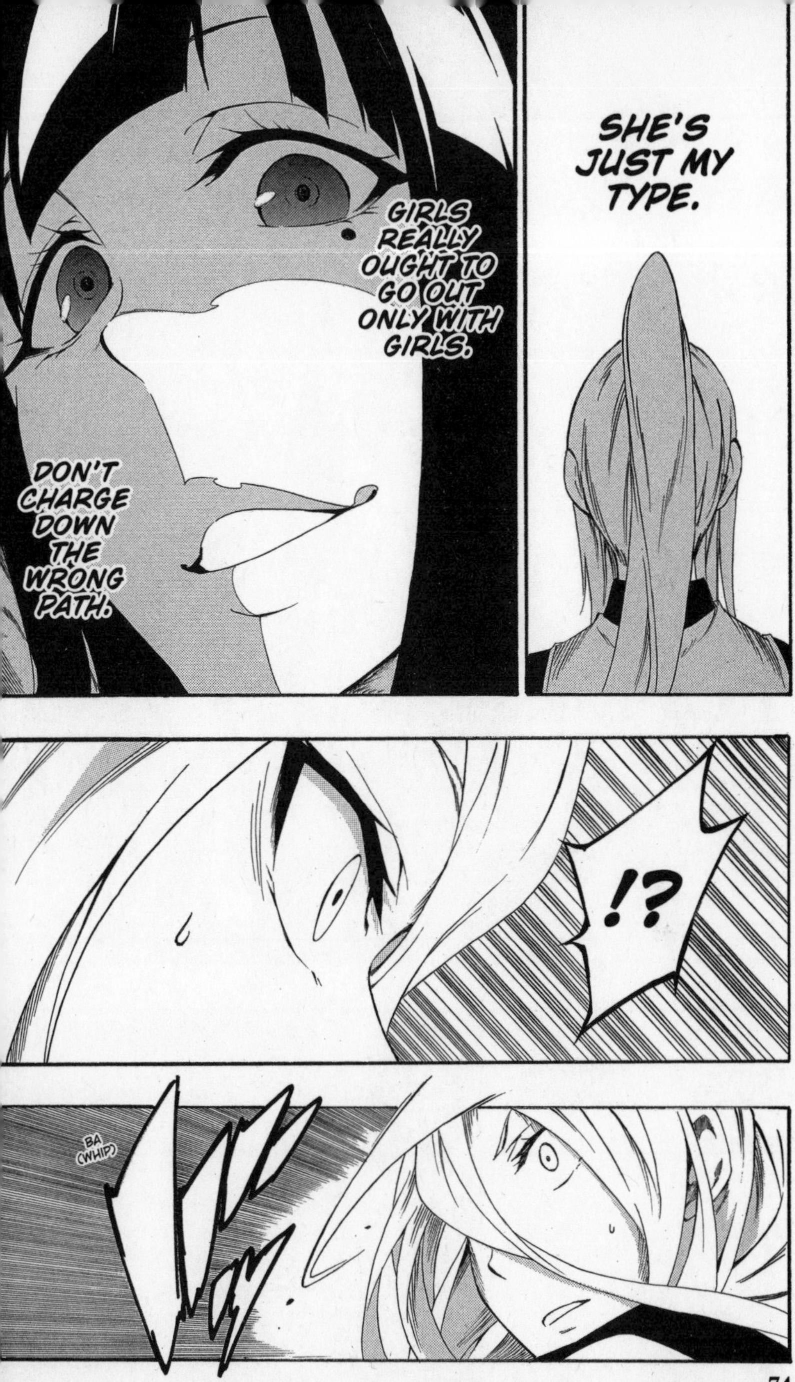
SHE'S JUST MY TYPE.
GIRLS REALLY OUGHT TO GO OUT ONLY WITH GIRLS.
DON'T CHARGE DOWN THE WRONG PATH.
!?
BA (WHIP)

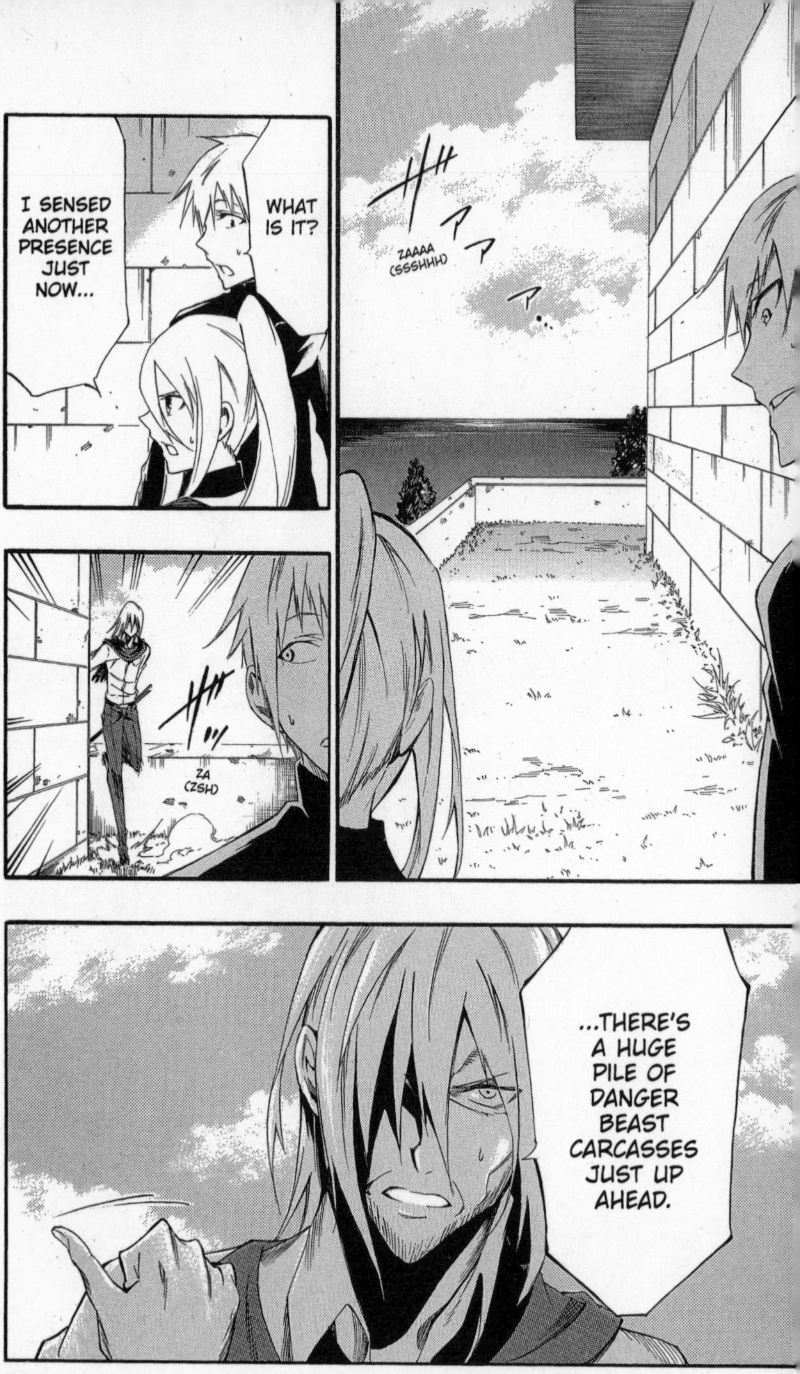
ZAAAA (SSSHHH)
WHAT IS IT?
I SENSED ANOTHER PRESENCE JUST NOW...
ZA (ZSH)
...THERE'S A HUGE PILE OF DANGER BEAST CARCASSES JUST UP AHEAD.

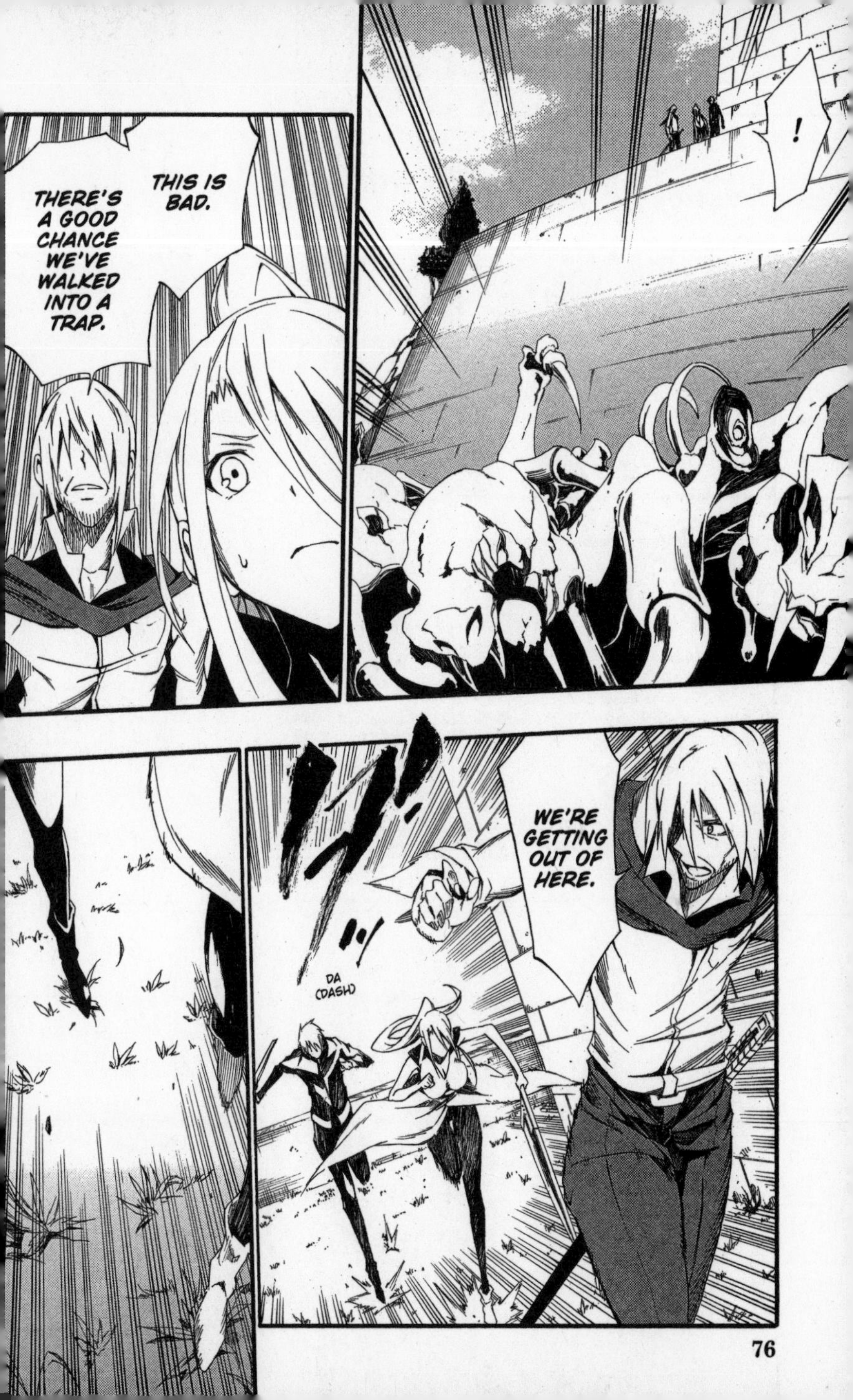
!
THIS IS BAD.
THERE'S A GOOD CHANCE WE'VE WALKED INTO A TRAP.
WE'RE GETTING OUT OF HERE.
DA (DASH)

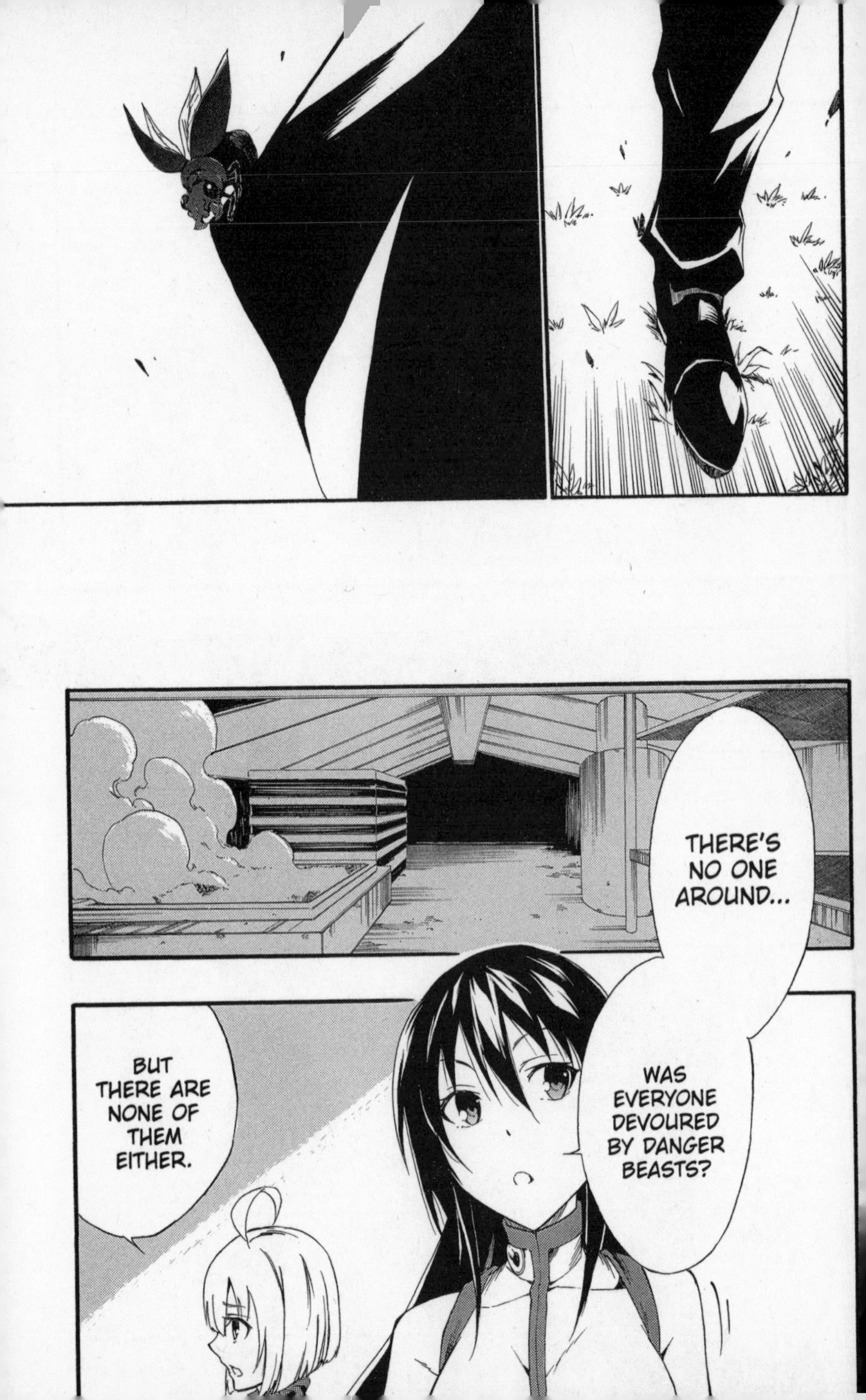
THERE'S NO ONE AROUND...
WAS EVERYONE DEVOURED BY DANGER BEASTS?
BUT THERE ARE NONE OF THEM EITHER.

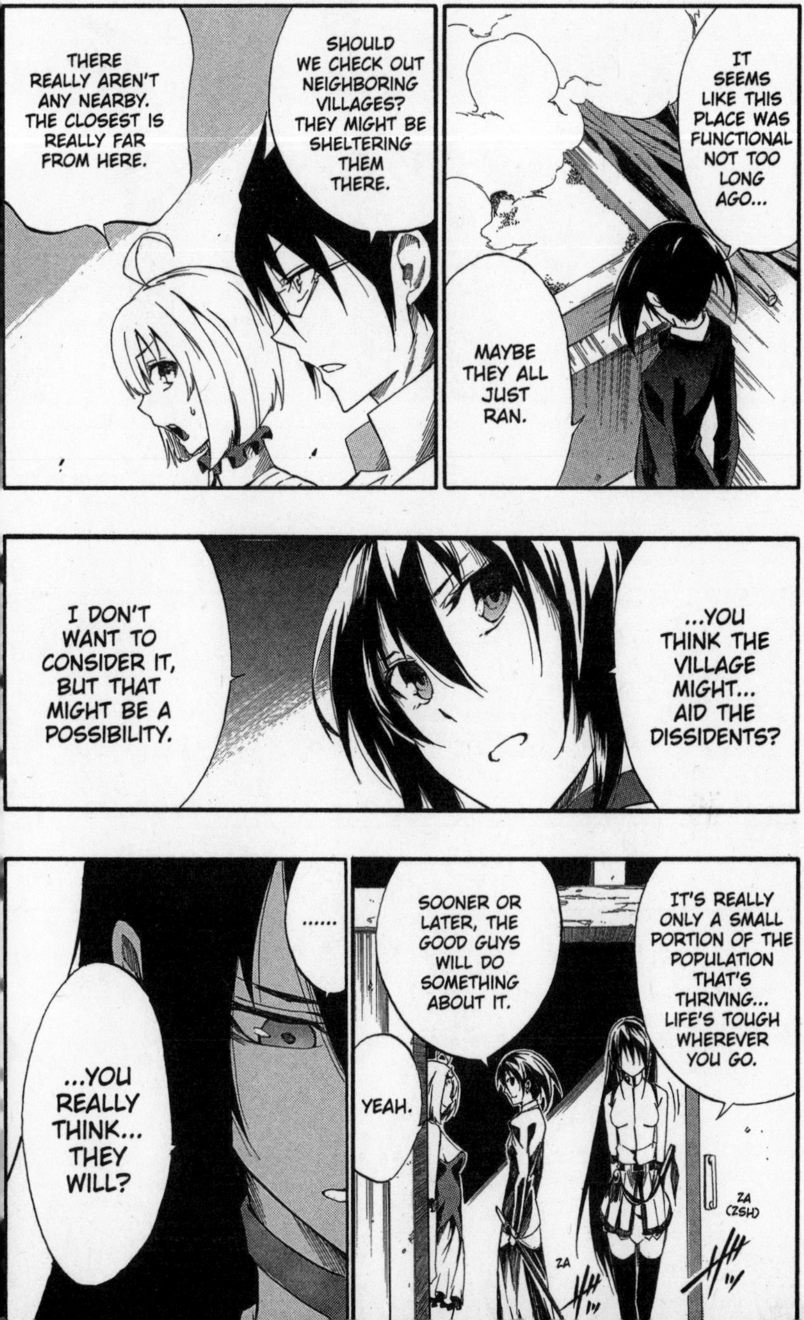
IT SEEMS LIKE THIS PLACE WAS FUNCTIONAL NOT TOO LONG AGO...
MAYBE THEY ALL JUST RAN.
SHOULD WE CHECK OUT NEIGHBORING VILLAGES? THEY MIGHT BE SHELTERING THEM THERE.
THERE REALLY AREN'T ANY NEARBY. THE CLOSEST IS REALLY FAR FROM HERE.
...YOU THINK THE VILLAGE MIGHT... AID THE DISSIDENTS?
I DON'T WANT TO CONSIDER IT, BUT THAT MIGHT BE A POSSIBILITY.
IT'S REALLY ONLY A SMALL PORTION OF THE POPULATION THAT'S THRIVING... LIFE'S TOUGH WHEREVER YOU GO.
SOONER OR LATER, THE GOOD GUYS WILL DO SOMETHING ABOUT IT.
YEAH.
ZA (ZSH)
ZA
......
...YOU REALLY THINK... THEY WILL?

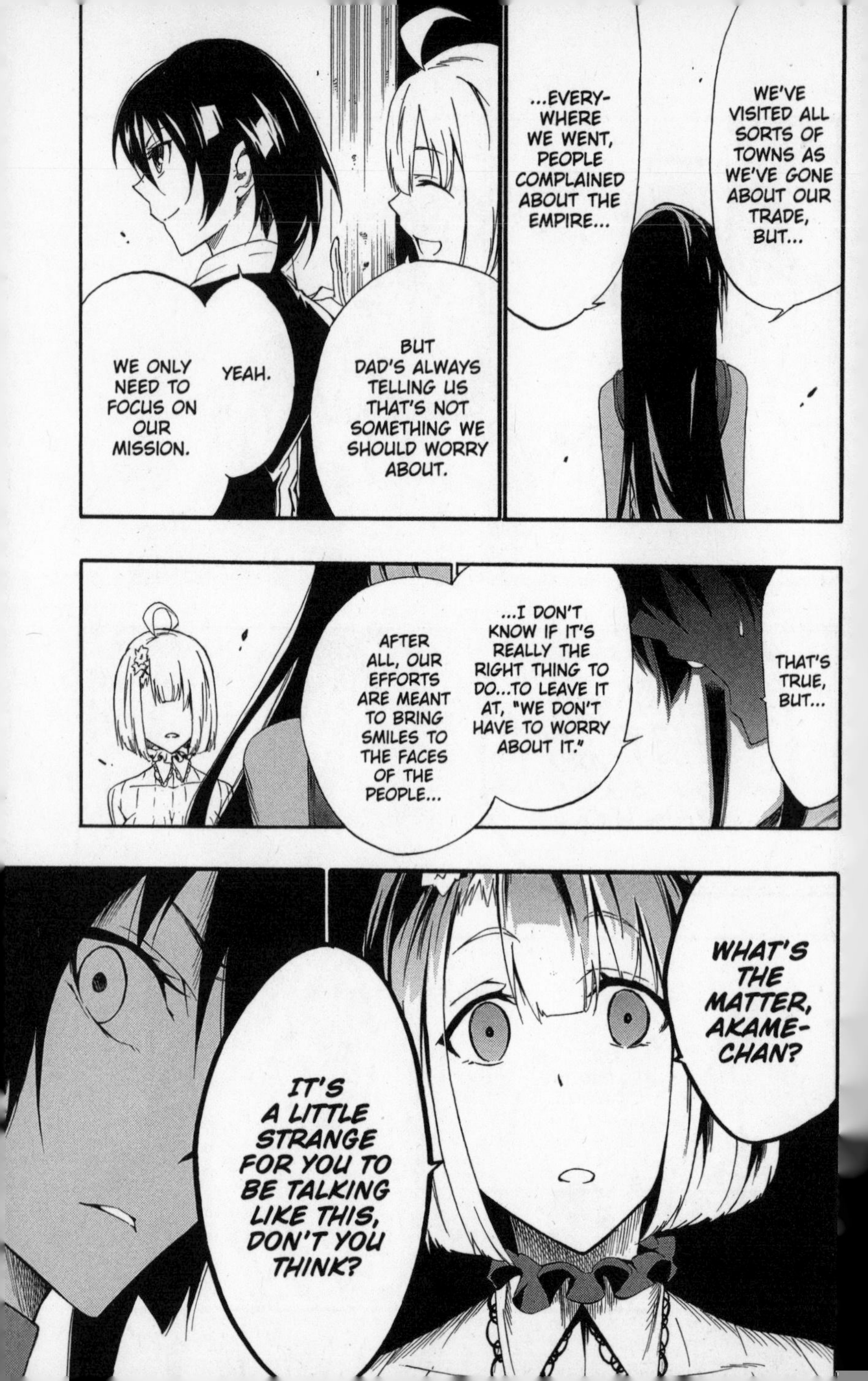
WE'VE VISITED ALL SORTS OF TOWNS AS WE'VE GONE ABOUT OUR TRADE, BUT...
...EVERY-WHERE WE WENT, PEOPLE COMPLAINED ABOUT THE EMPIRE...
BUT DAD'S ALWAYS TELLING US THAT'S NOT SOMETHING WE SHOULD WORRY ABOUT.
YEAH.
WE ONLY NEED TO FOCUS ON OUR MISSION.
THAT'S TRUE, BUT...
...I DON'T KNOW IF IT'S REALLY THE RIGHT THING TO DO...TO LEAVE IT AT, "WE DON'T HAVE TO WORRY ABOUT IT."
AFTER ALL, OUR EFFORTS ARE MEANT TO BRING SMILES TO THE FACES OF THE PEOPLE...
WHAT'S THE MATTER, AKAME-CHAN?
IT'S A LITTLE STRANGE FOR YOU TO BE TALKING LIKE THIS, DON'T YOU THINK?

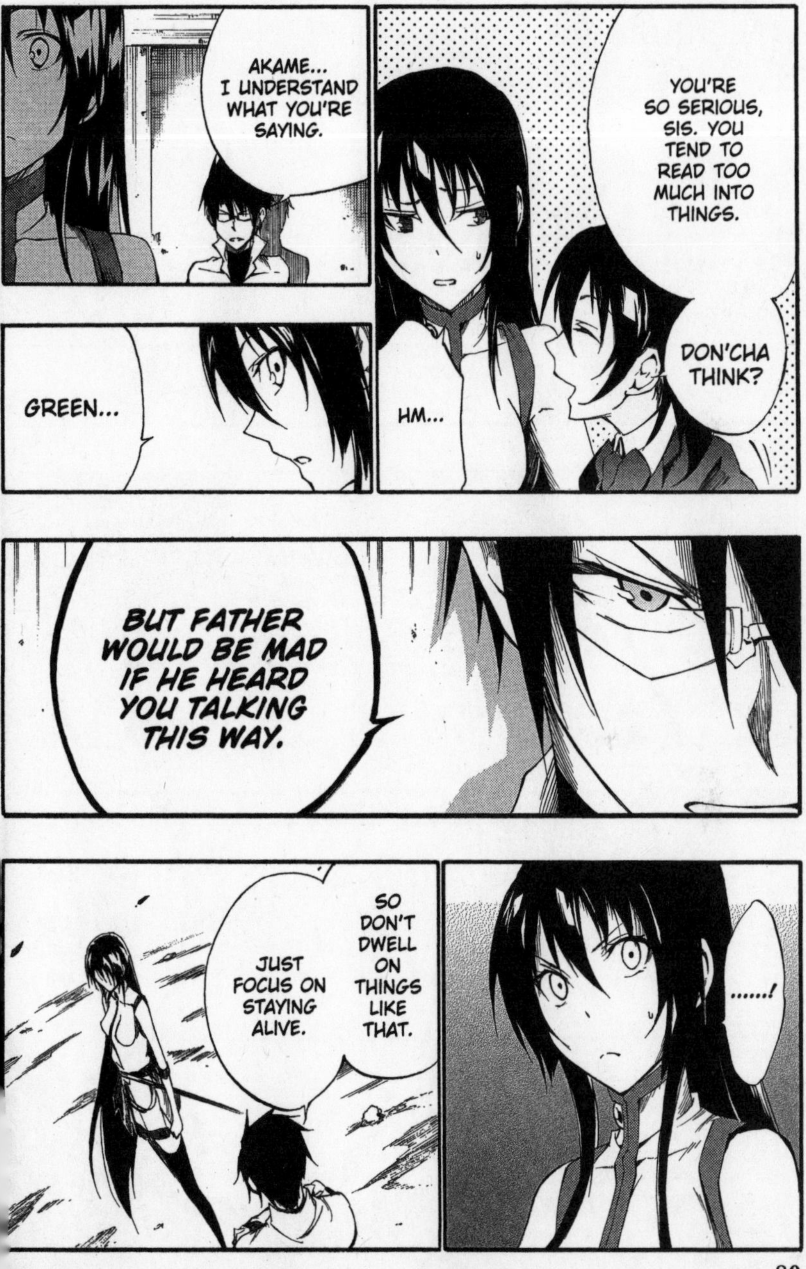

YOU'RE SO SERIOUS, SIS. YOU TEND TO READ TOO MUCH INTO THINGS.
DON'CHA THINK?
HM...
AKAME... I UNDERSTAND WHAT YOU'RE SAYING.
GREEN...
BUT FATHER WOULD BE MAD IF HE HEARD YOU TALKING THIS WAY.
......!
SO DON'T DWELL ON THINGS LIKE THAT.
JUST FOCUS ON STAYING ALIVE.

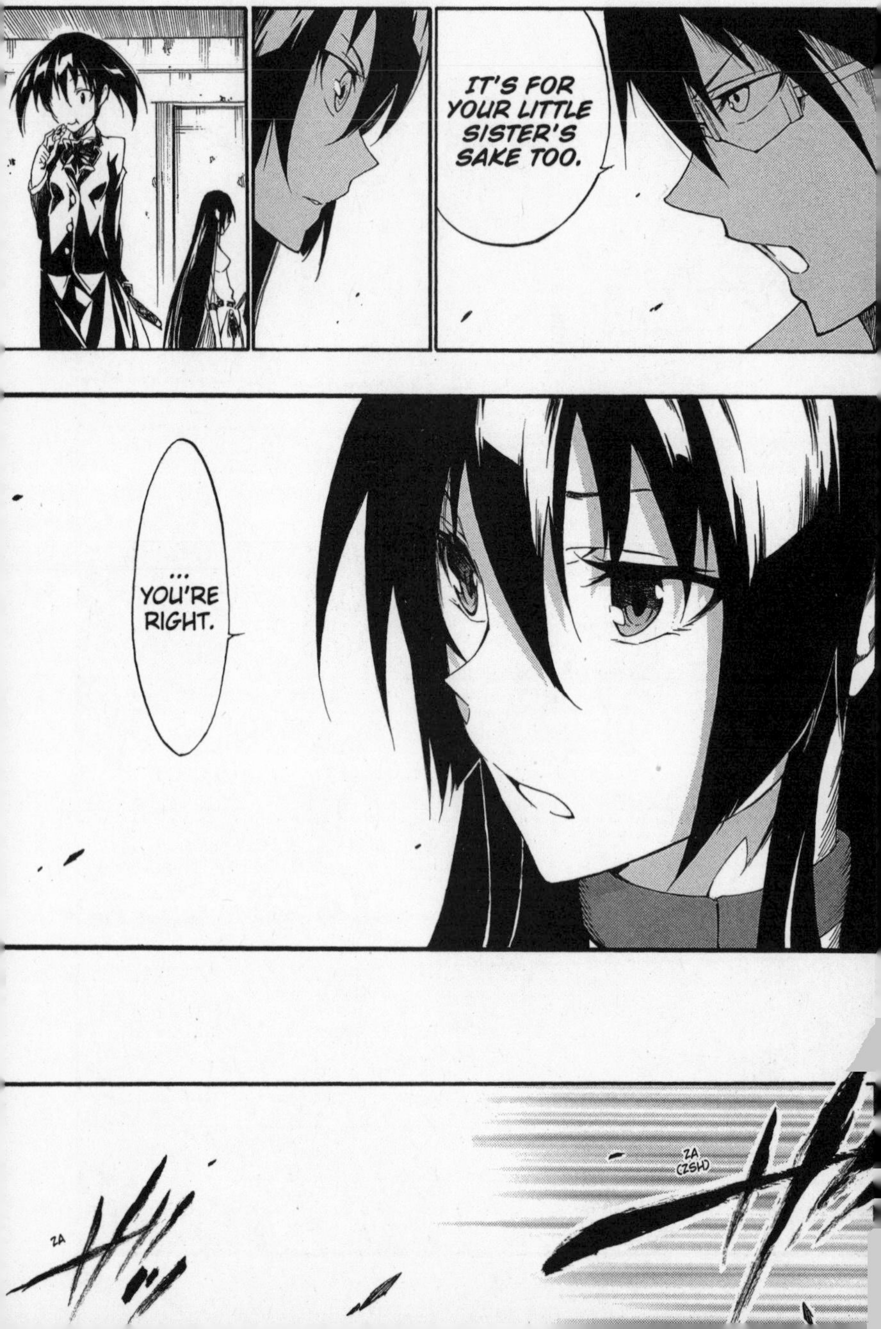
IT'S FOR YOUR LITTLE SISTER'S SAKE TOO.
...YOU'RE RIGHT.
ZA (ZSH)
ZA

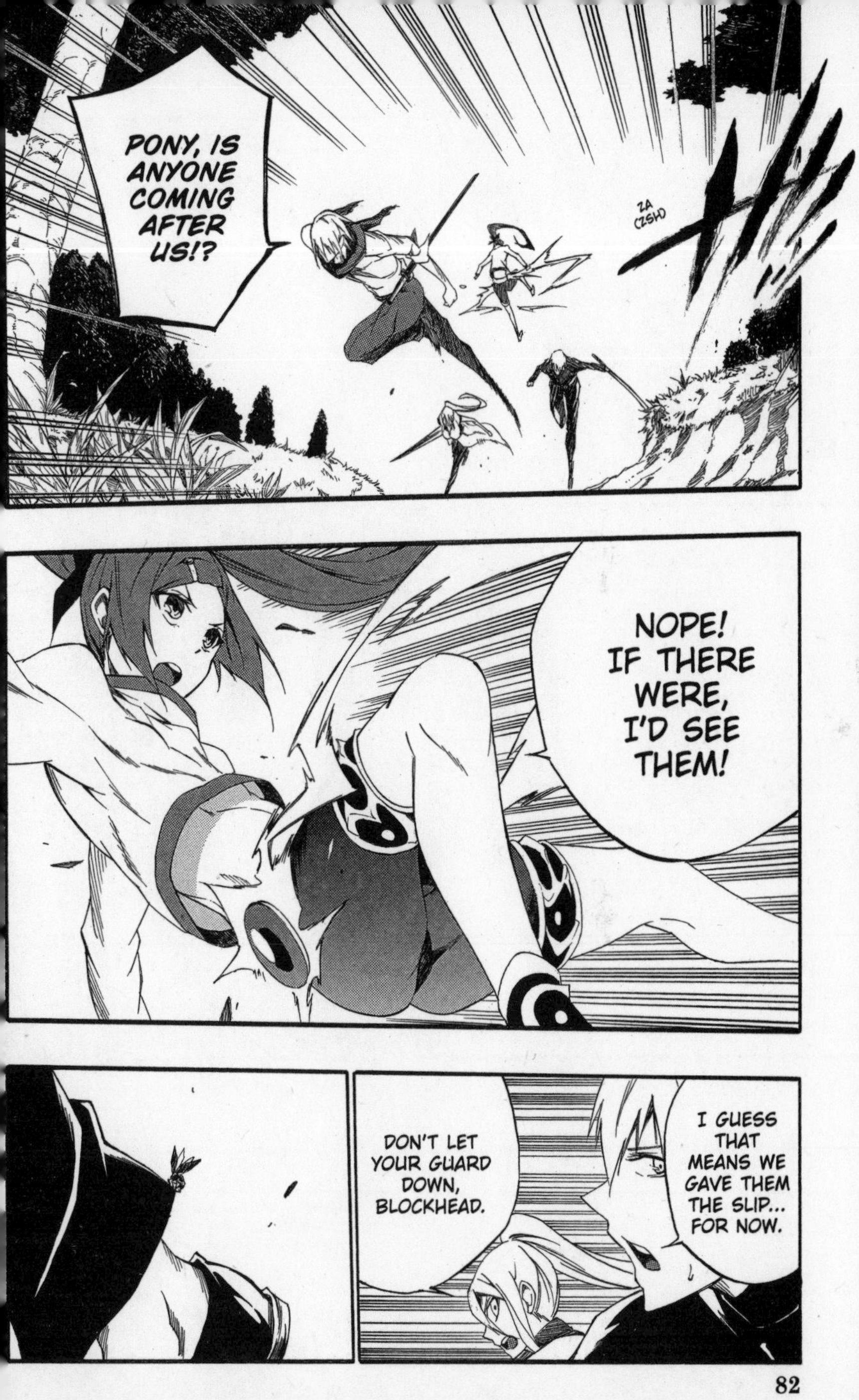
PONY, IS ANYONE COMING AFTER US!?
ZA (ZSH)
NOPE! IF THERE WERE, I'D SEE THEM!
I GUESS THAT MEANS WE GAVE THEM THE SLIP... FOR NOW.
DON'T LET YOUR GUARD DOWN, BLOCKHEAD.

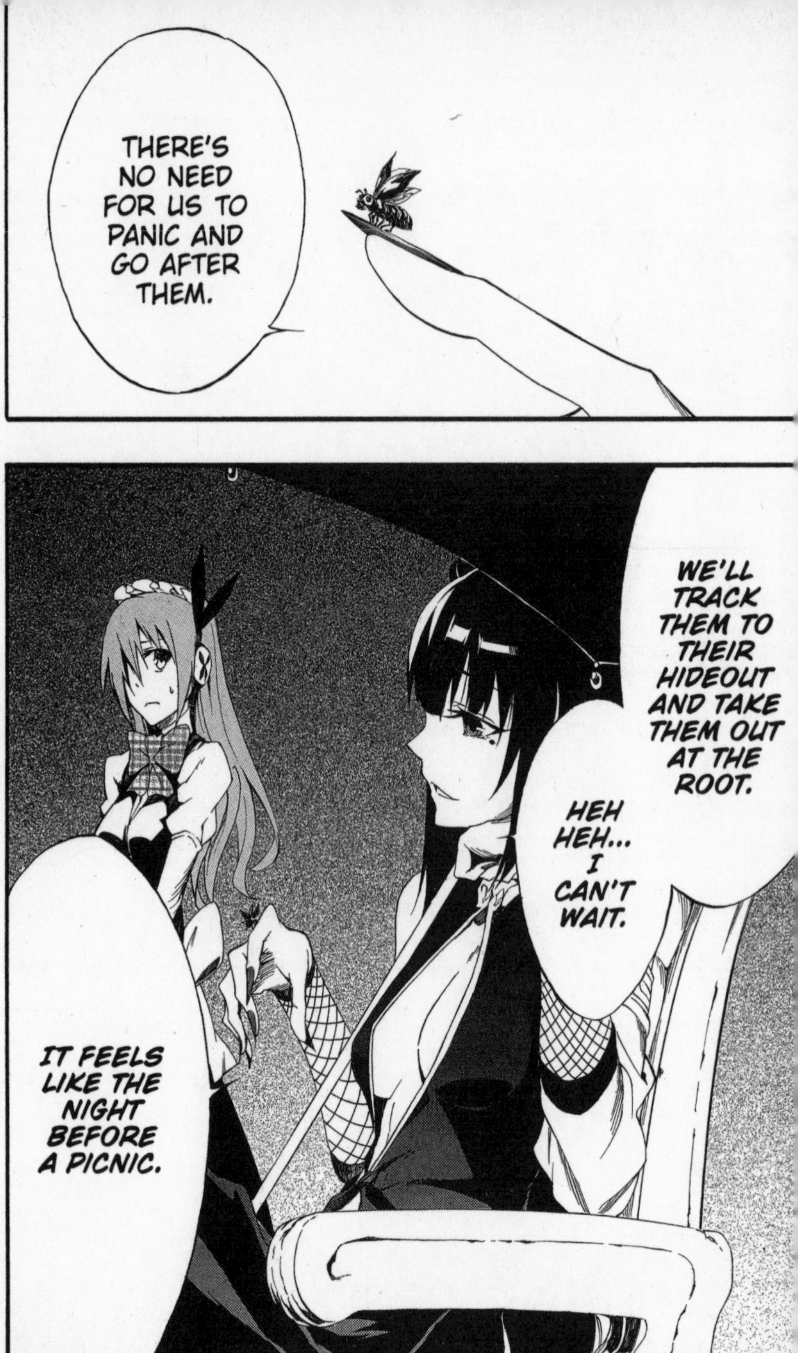
THERE'S NO NEED FOR US TO PANIC AND GO AFTER THEM.
WE'LL TRACK THEM TO THEIR HIDEOUT AND TAKE THEM OUT AT THE ROOT.
HEH HEH... I CAN'T WAIT.
IT FEELS LIKE THE NIGHT BEFORE A PICNIC.

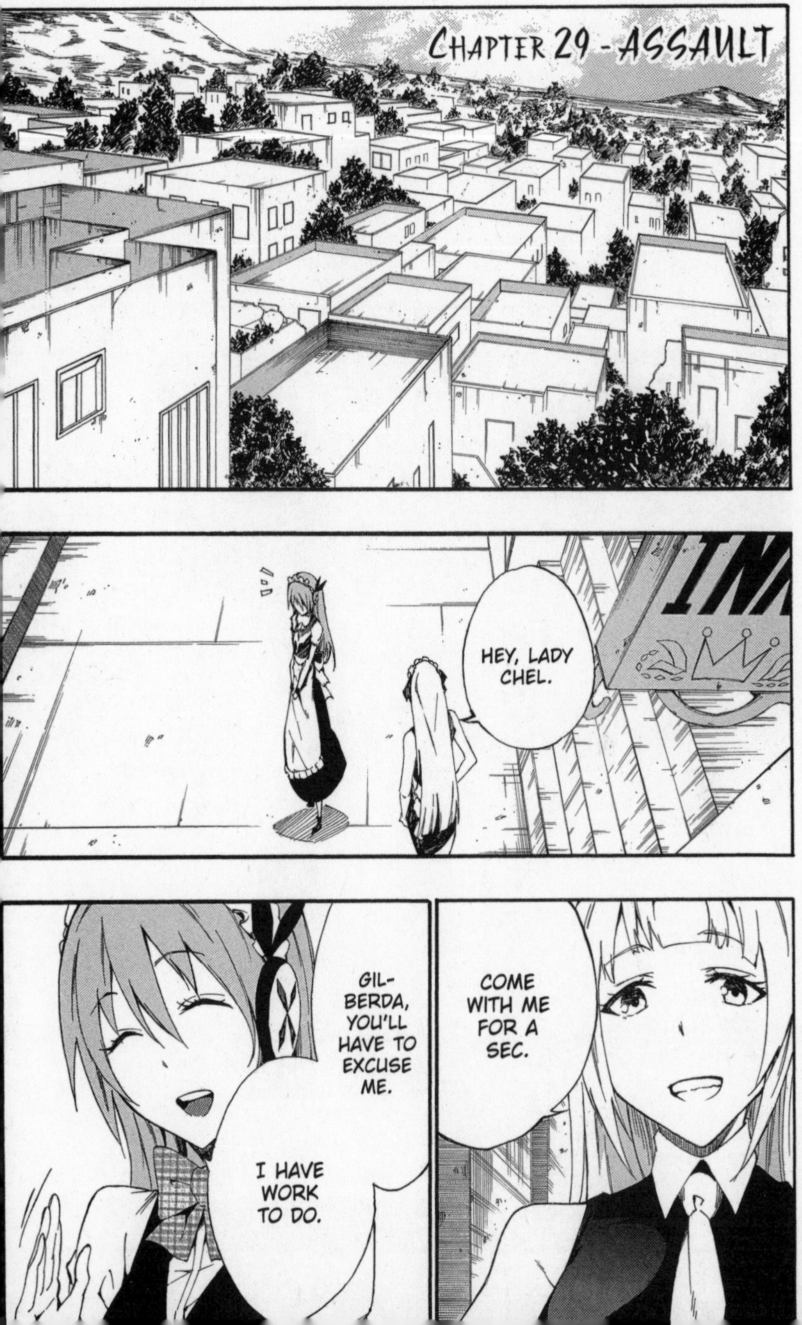
Chapter 29 - Assault
HEY, LADY CHEL.
COME WITH ME FOR A SEC.
GIL-BERDA, YOU'LL HAVE TO EXCUSE ME.
I HAVE WORK TO DO.

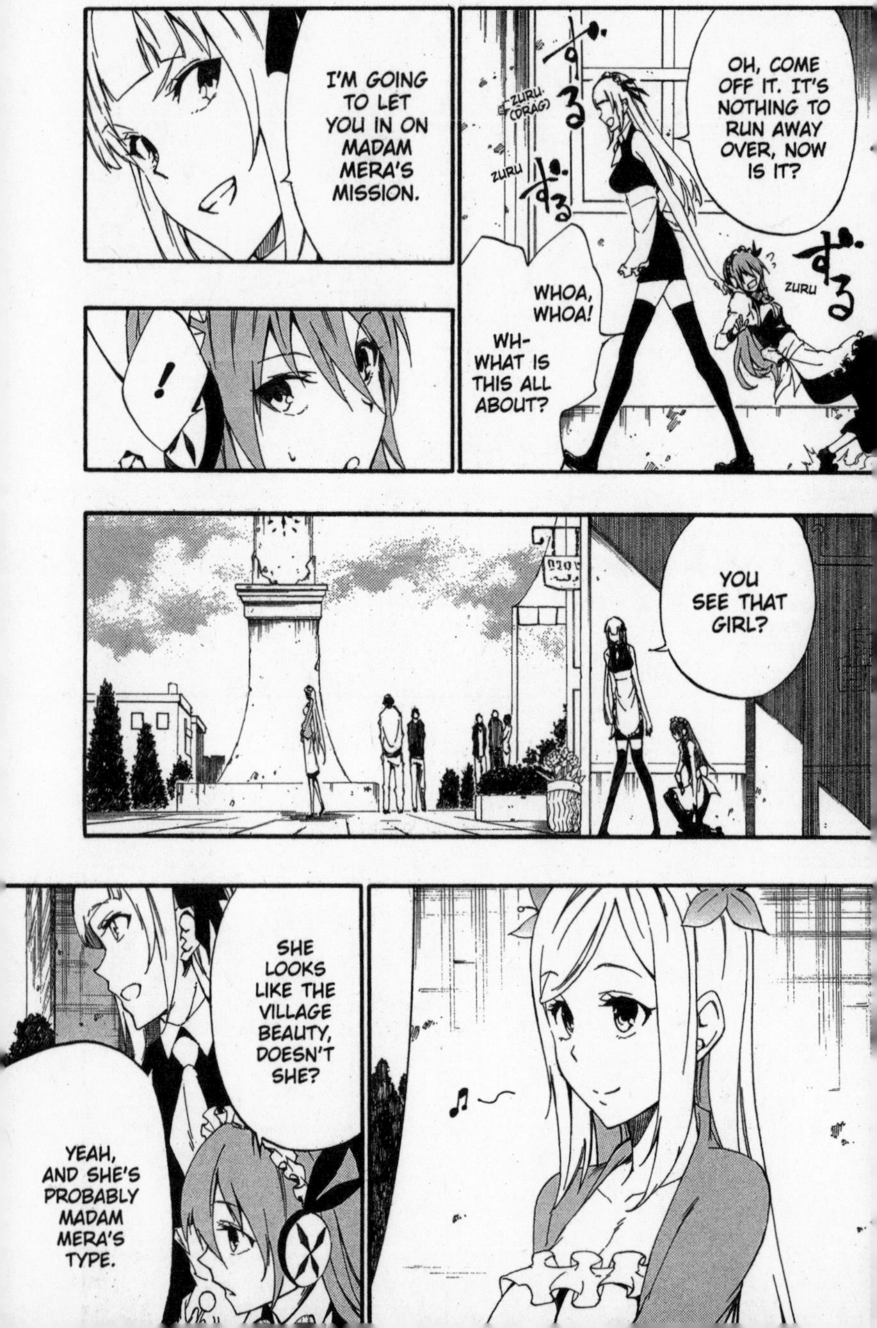
OH, COME OFF IT. IT'S NOTHING TO RUN AWAY OVER, NOW IS IT?
ずる
ZURU (DRAG)
ずる
ZURU
ずる
ZURU
WHOA, WHOA!
WH- WHAT IS THIS ALL ABOUT?
I'M GOING TO LET YOU IN ON MADAM MERA'S MISSION.
!
YOU SEE THAT GIRL?
♪~
SHE LOOKS LIKE THE VILLAGE BEAUTY, DOESN'T SHE?
YEAH, AND SHE'S PROBABLY MADAM MERA'S TYPE.

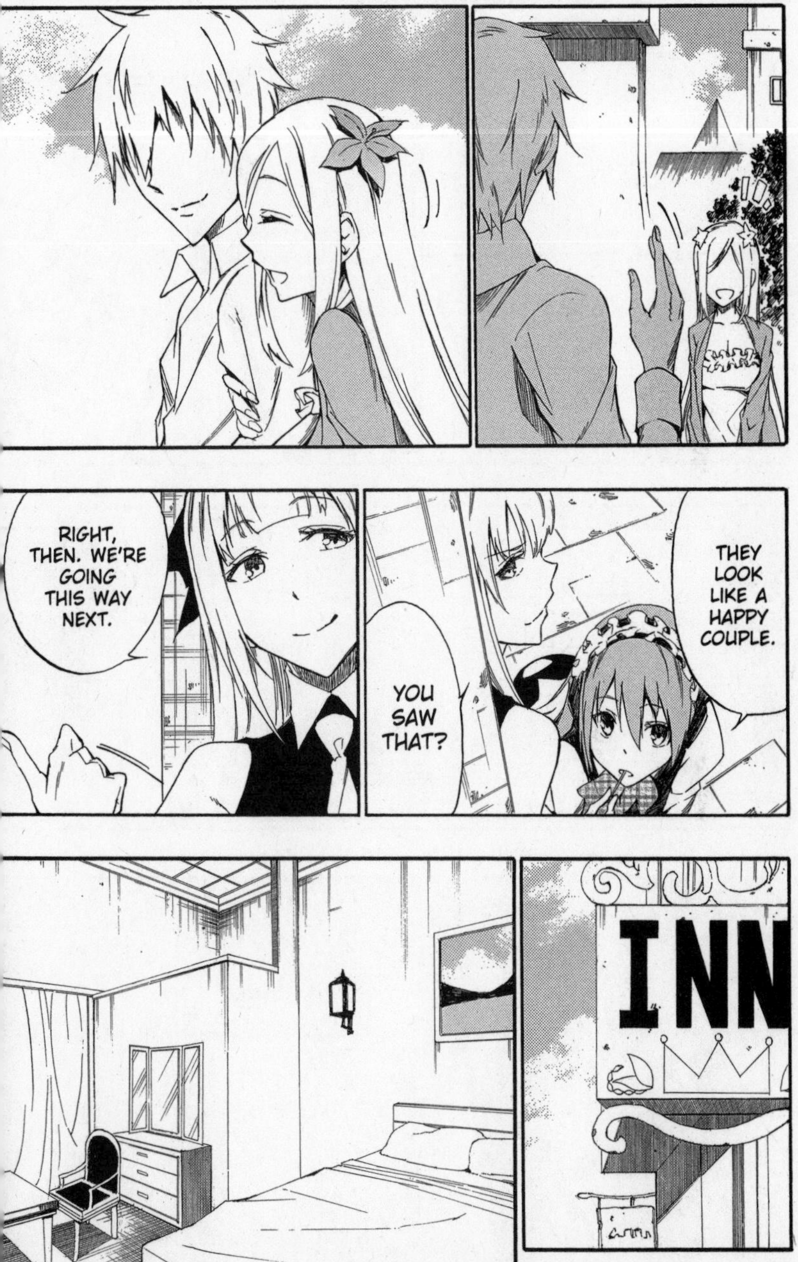
!!
THEY LOOK LIKE A HAPPY COUPLE.
YOU SAW THAT?
RIGHT, THEN. WE'RE GOING THIS WAY NEXT.
INN

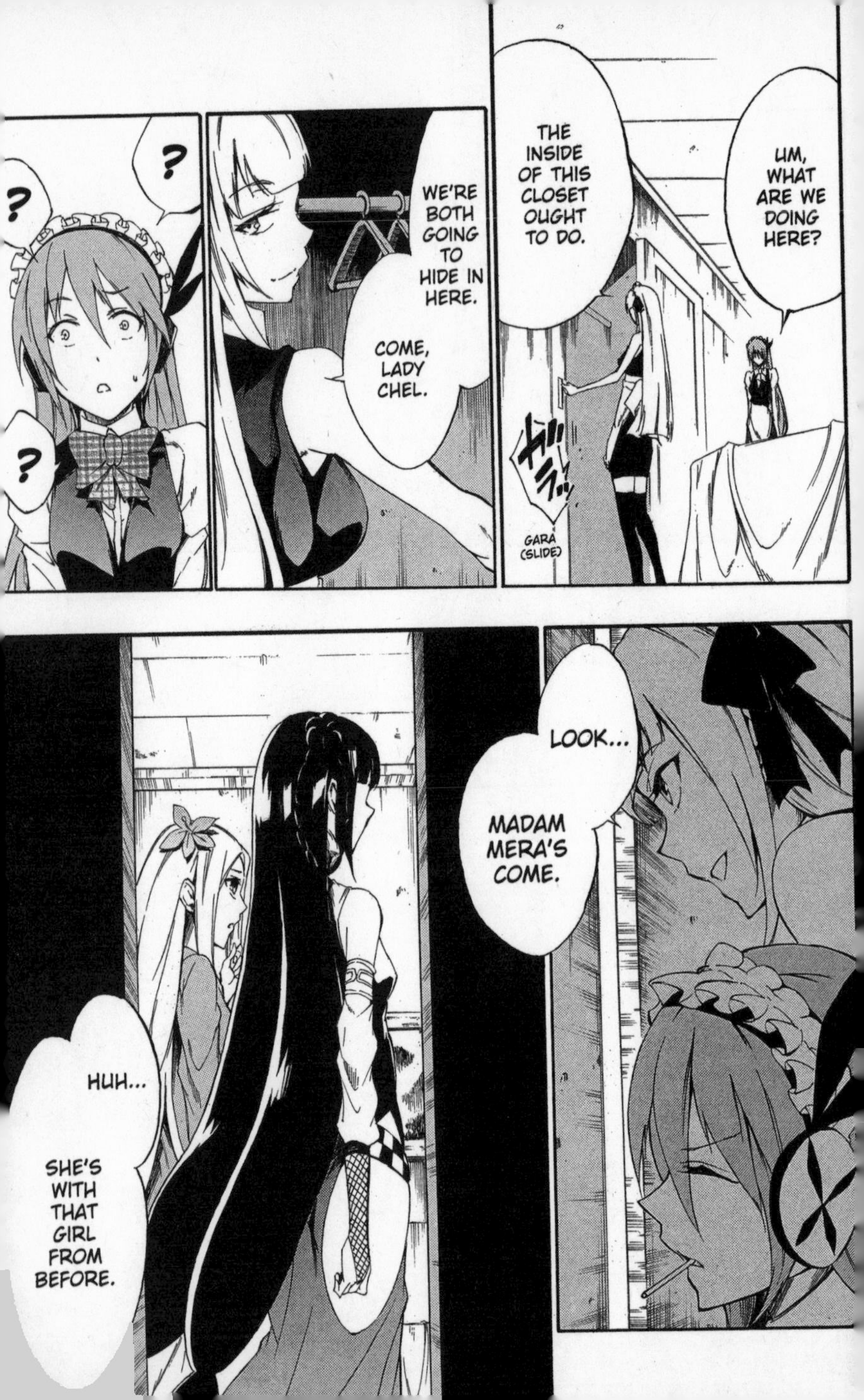
UM, WHAT ARE WE DOING HERE?
THE INSIDE OF THIS CLOSET OUGHT TO DO.
GARA (SLIDE)
WE'RE BOTH GOING TO HIDE IN HERE.
COME, LADY CHEL.
?
?
?
LOOK...
MADAM MERA'S COME.
HUH...
SHE'S WITH THAT GIRL FROM BEFORE.

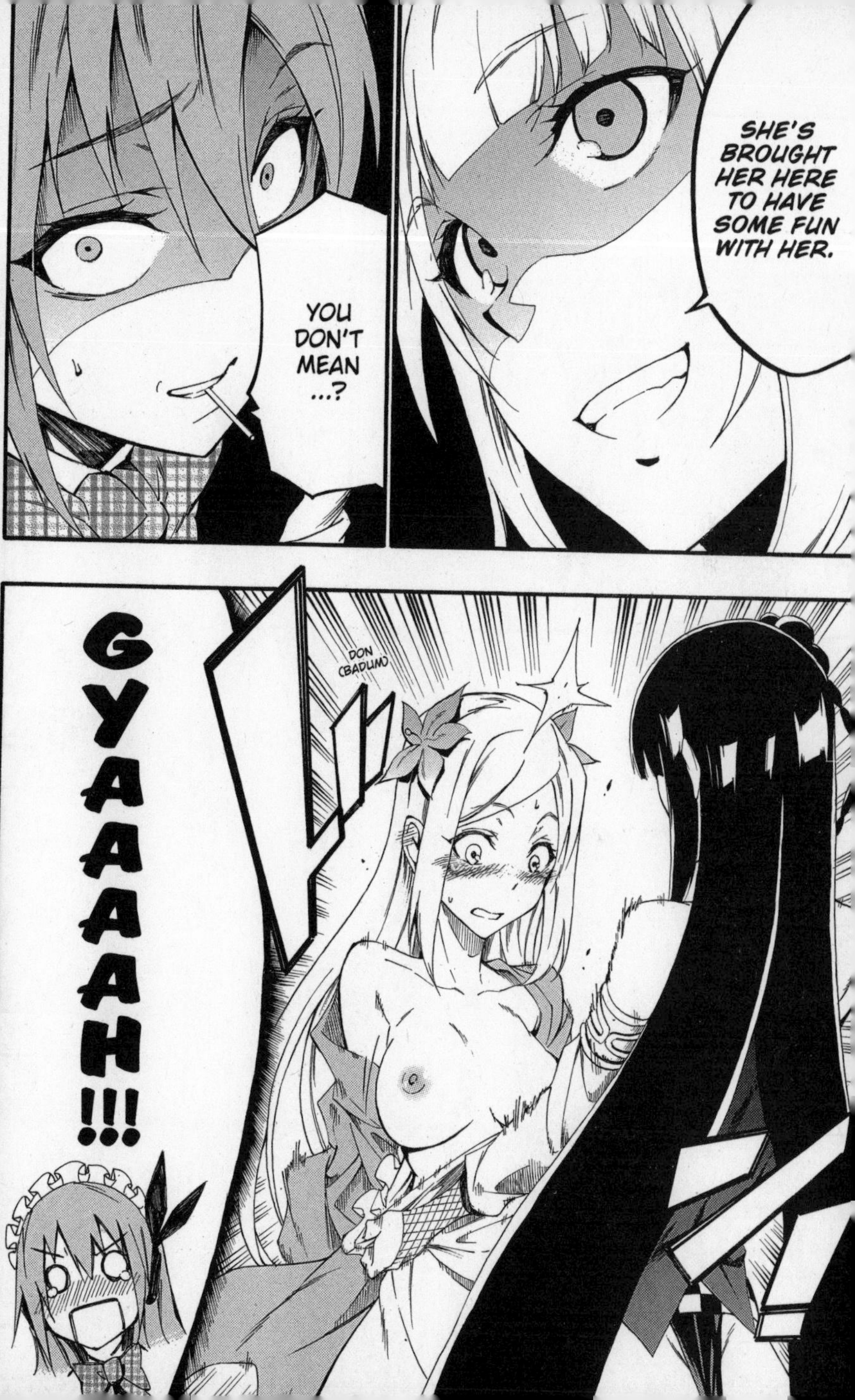
SHE'S BROUGHT HER HERE TO HAVE SOME FUN WITH HER.
YOU DON'T MEAN ...?
DON (BADUM)
GYAAAAAH!!!

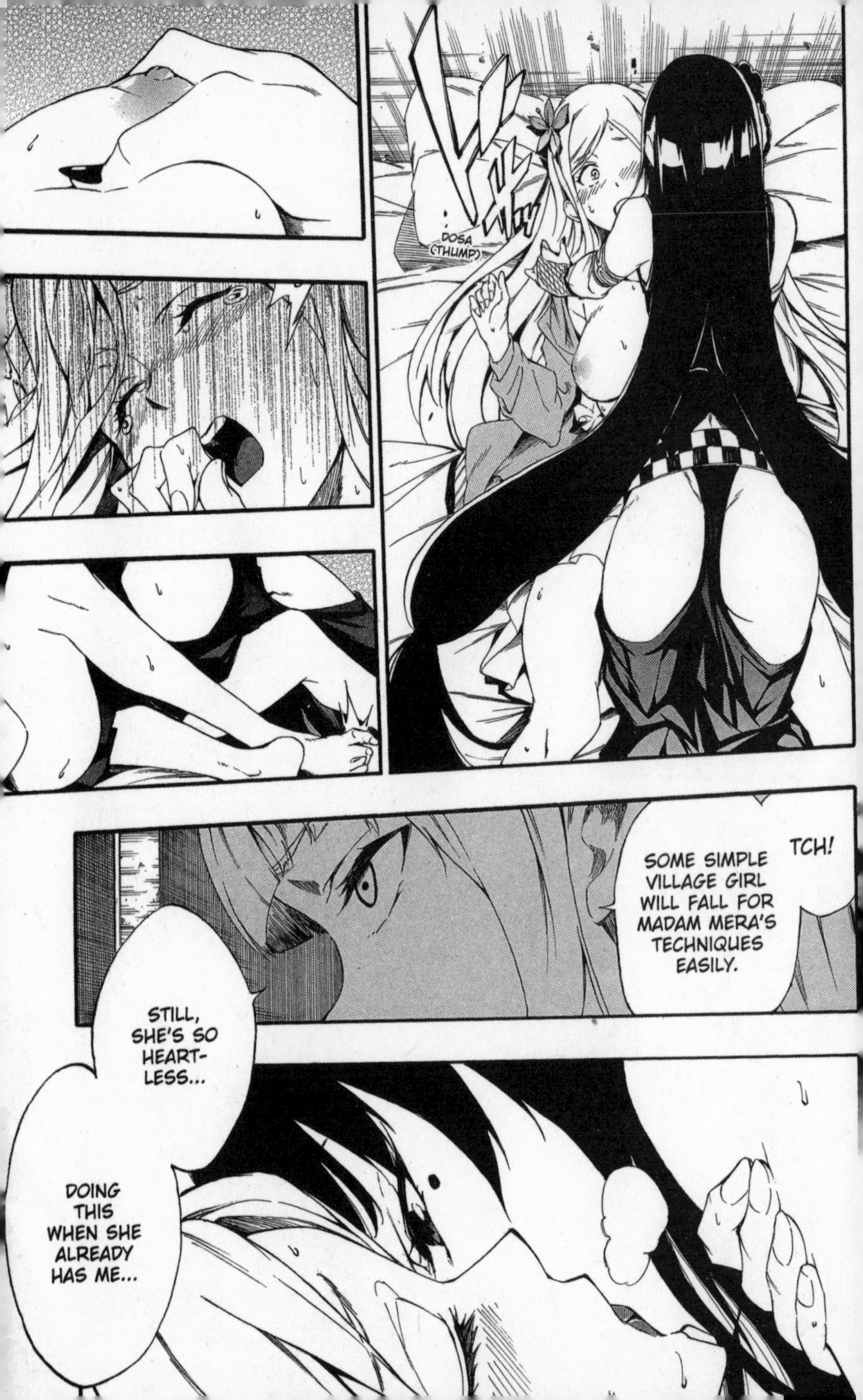
DOSA (THUMP)
TCH!
SOME SIMPLE VILLAGE GIRL WILL FALL FOR MADAM MERA'S TECHNIQUES EASILY.
STILL, SHE'S SO HEART-LESS...
DOING THIS WHEN SHE ALREADY HAS ME...

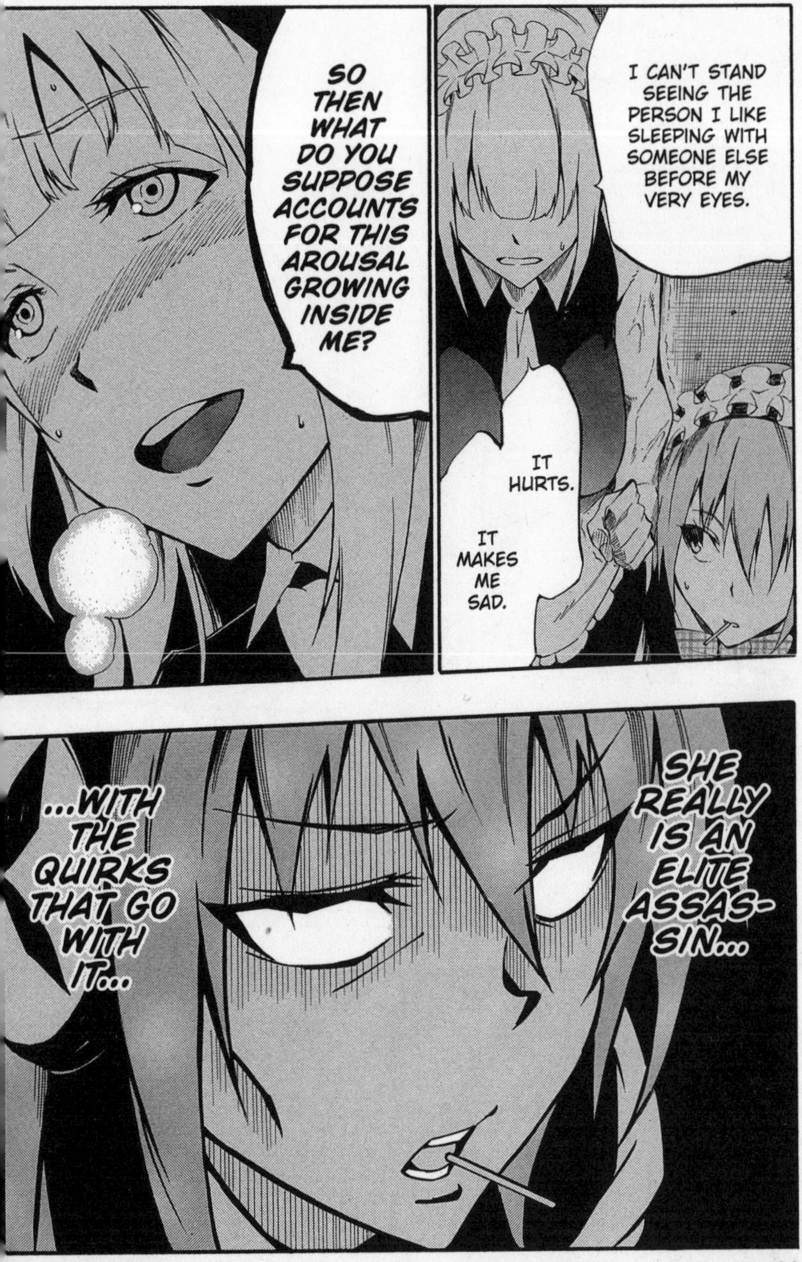
I CAN'T STAND SEEING THE PERSON I LIKE SLEEPING WITH SOMEONE ELSE BEFORE MY VERY EYES.
IT HURTS.
IT MAKES ME SAD.
SO THEN WHAT DO YOU SUPPOSE ACCOUNTS FOR THIS AROUSAL GROWING INSIDE ME?
SHE REALLY IS AN ELITE ASSAS-SIN...
...WITH THE QUIRKS THAT GO WITH IT...

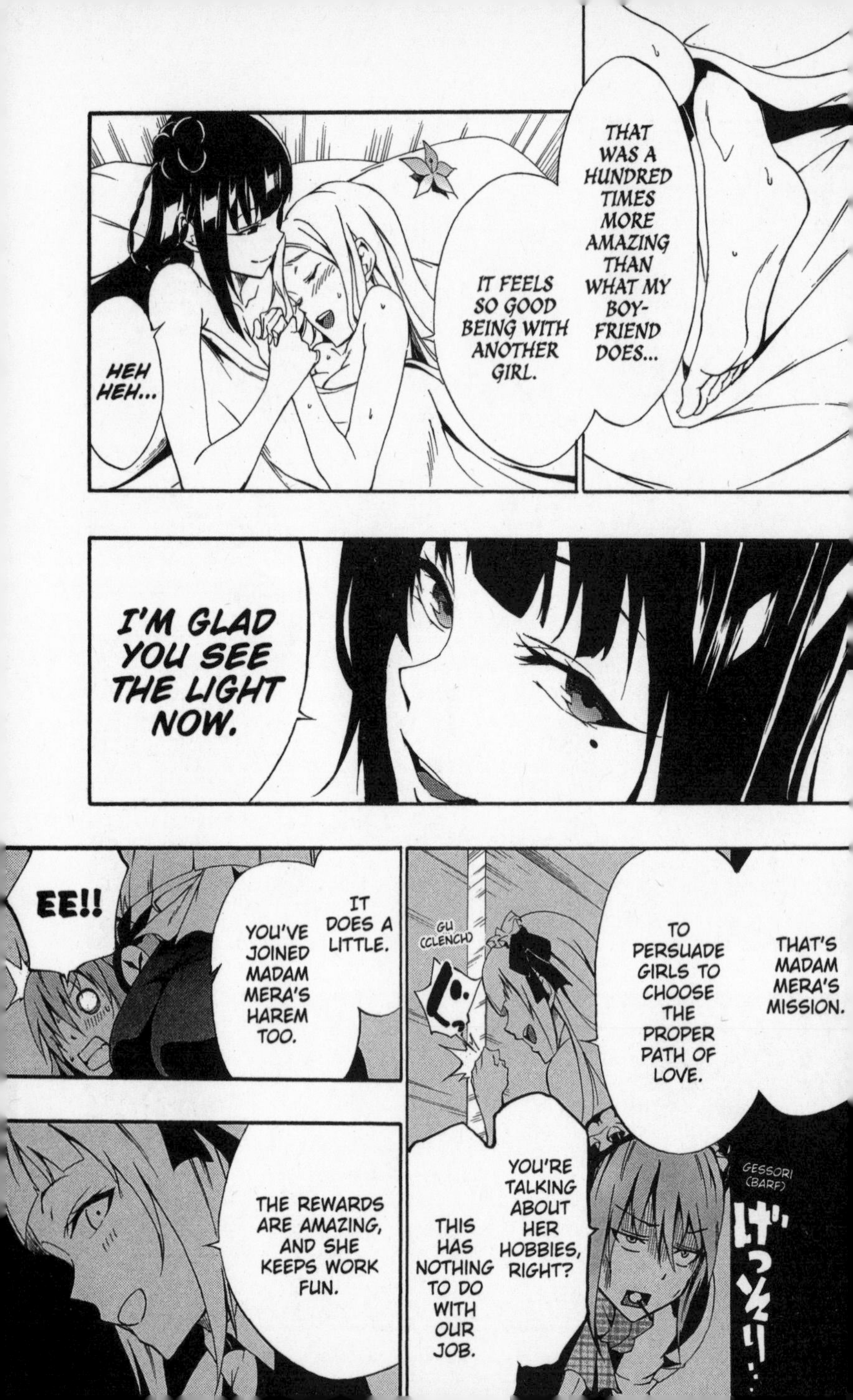
THAT WAS A HUNDRED TIMES MORE AMAZING THAN WHAT MY BOY-FRIEND DOES...
IT FEELS SO GOOD BEING WITH ANOTHER GIRL.
HEH HEH...
I'M GLAD YOU SEE THE LIGHT NOW.
THAT'S MADAM MERA'S MISSION.
TO PERSUADE GIRLS TO CHOOSE THE PROPER PATH OF LOVE.
GU (CLENCH)
YOU'RE TALKING ABOUT HER HOBBIES, RIGHT?
THIS HAS NOTHING TO DO WITH OUR JOB.
GESSORI (BARF)
げっそり…
IT DOES A LITTLE.
YOU'VE JOINED MADAM MERA'S HAREM TOO.
EE!!
THE REWARDS ARE AMAZING, AND SHE KEEPS WORK FUN.

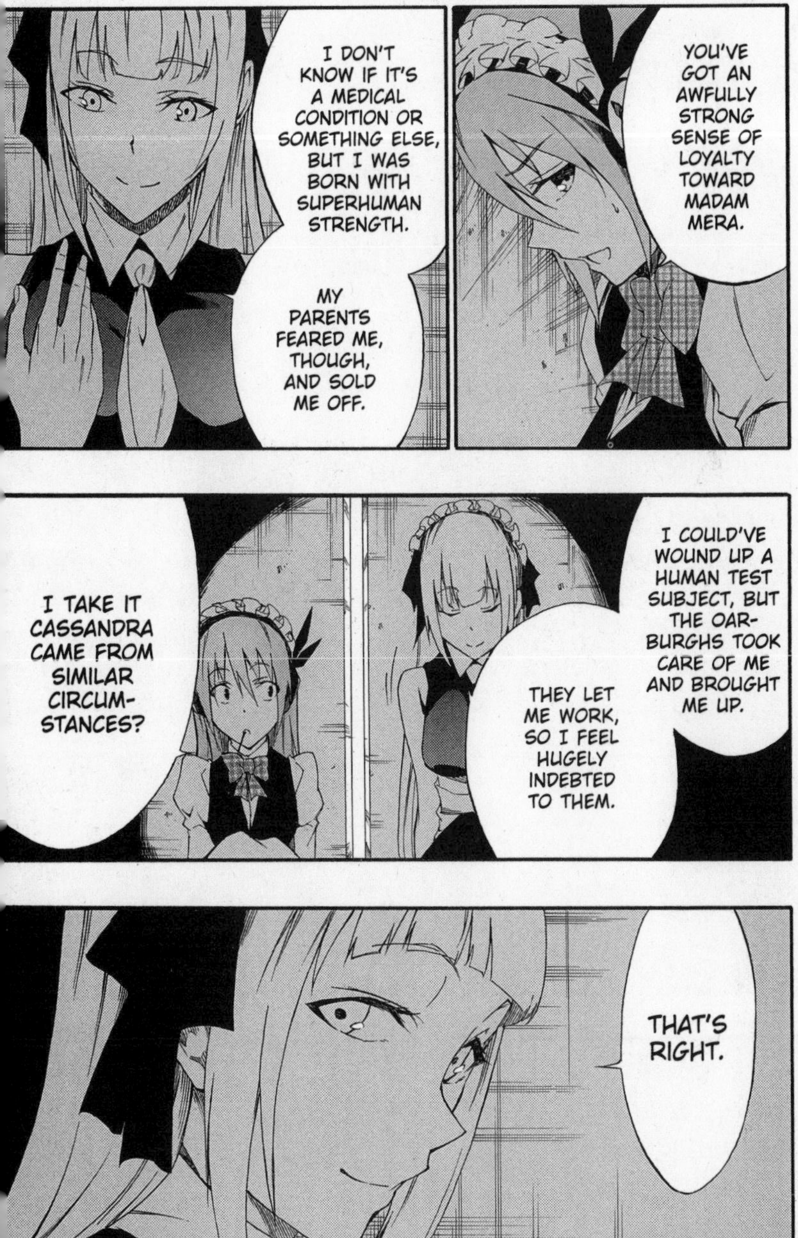
YOU'VE GOT AN AWFULLY STRONG SENSE OF LOYALTY TOWARD MADAM MERA.
I DON'T KNOW IF IT'S A MEDICAL CONDITION OR SOMETHING ELSE, BUT I WAS BORN WITH SUPERHUMAN STRENGTH.
MY PARENTS FEARED ME, THOUGH, AND SOLD ME OFF.
I COULD'VE WOUND UP A HUMAN TEST SUBJECT, BUT THE OAR-BURGHS TOOK CARE OF ME AND BROUGHT ME UP.
THEY LET ME WORK, SO I FEEL HUGELY INDEBTED TO THEM.
I TAKE IT CASSANDRA CAME FROM SIMILAR CIRCUM-STANCES?
THAT'S RIGHT.

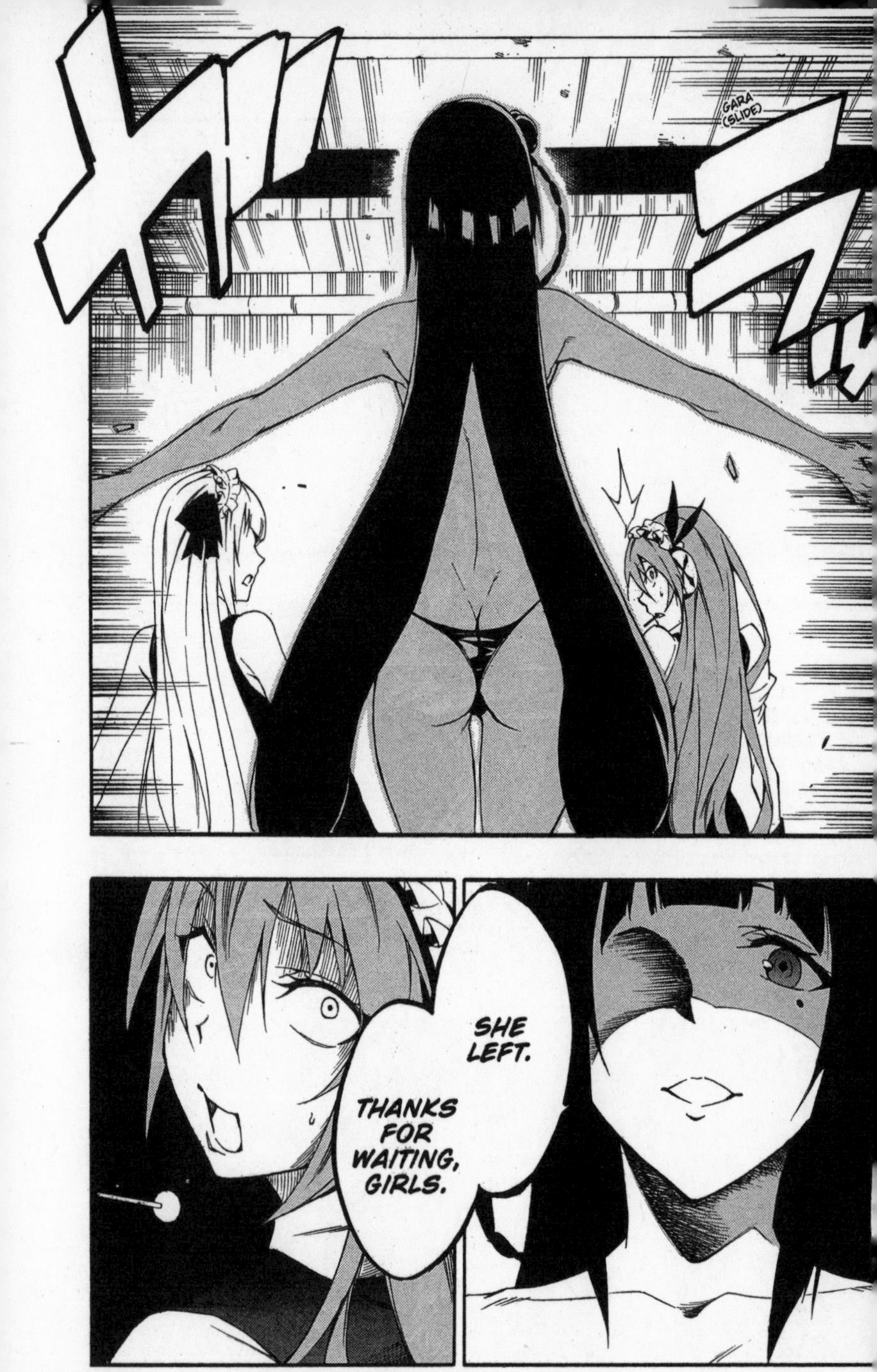
GARA (SLIDE)
SHE LEFT.
THANKS FOR WAITING, GIRLS.

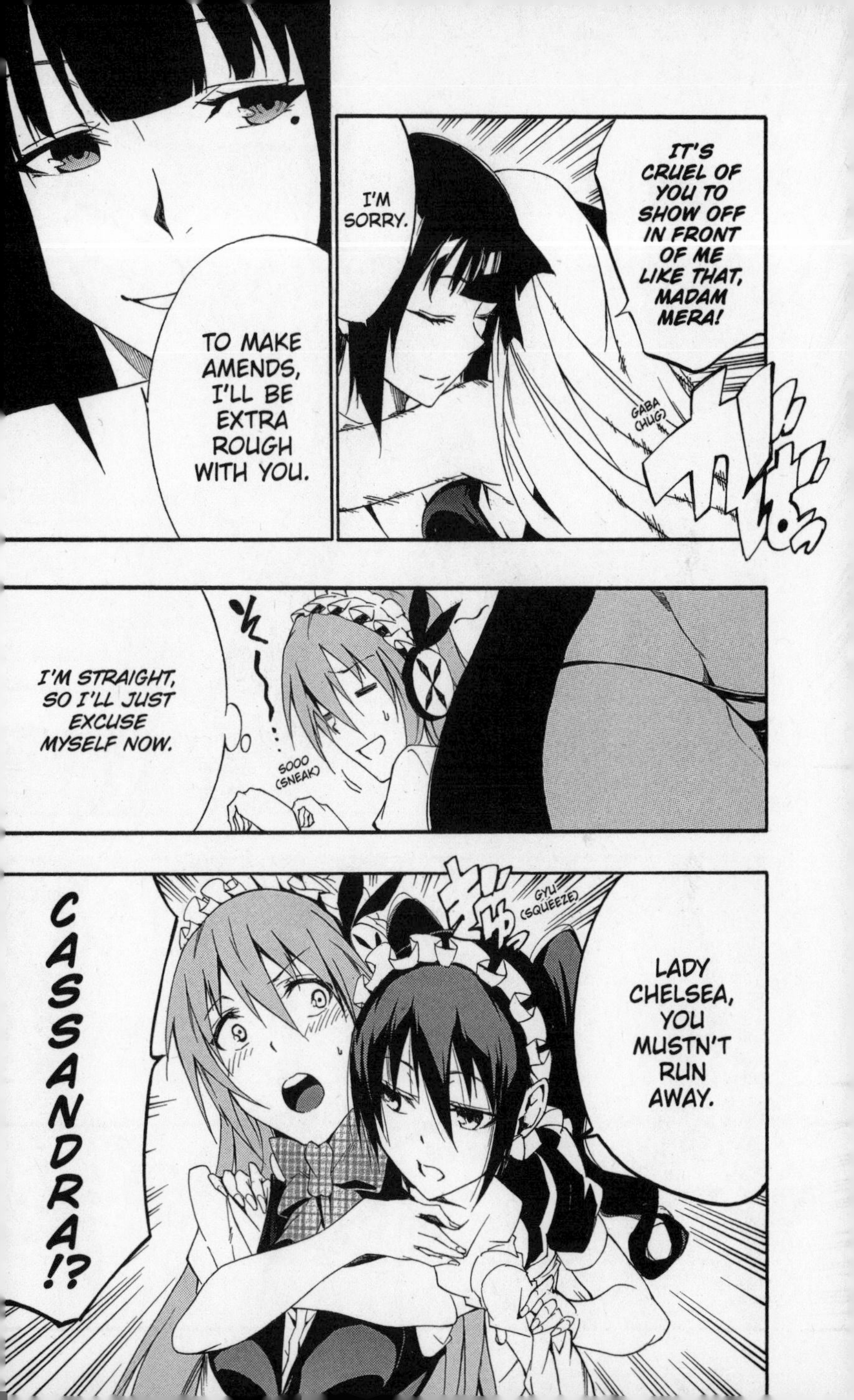
IT'S CRUEL OF YOU TO SHOW OFF IN FRONT OF ME LIKE THAT, MADAM MERA!
I'M SORRY.
GABA (HUG)
TO MAKE AMENDS, I'LL BE EXTRA ROUGH WITH YOU.
I'M STRAIGHT, SO I'LL JUST EXCUSE MYSELF NOW.
SOOO (SNEAK)
GYU (SQUEEZE)
LADY CHELSEA, YOU MUSTN'T RUN AWAY.
CASSANDRA!?

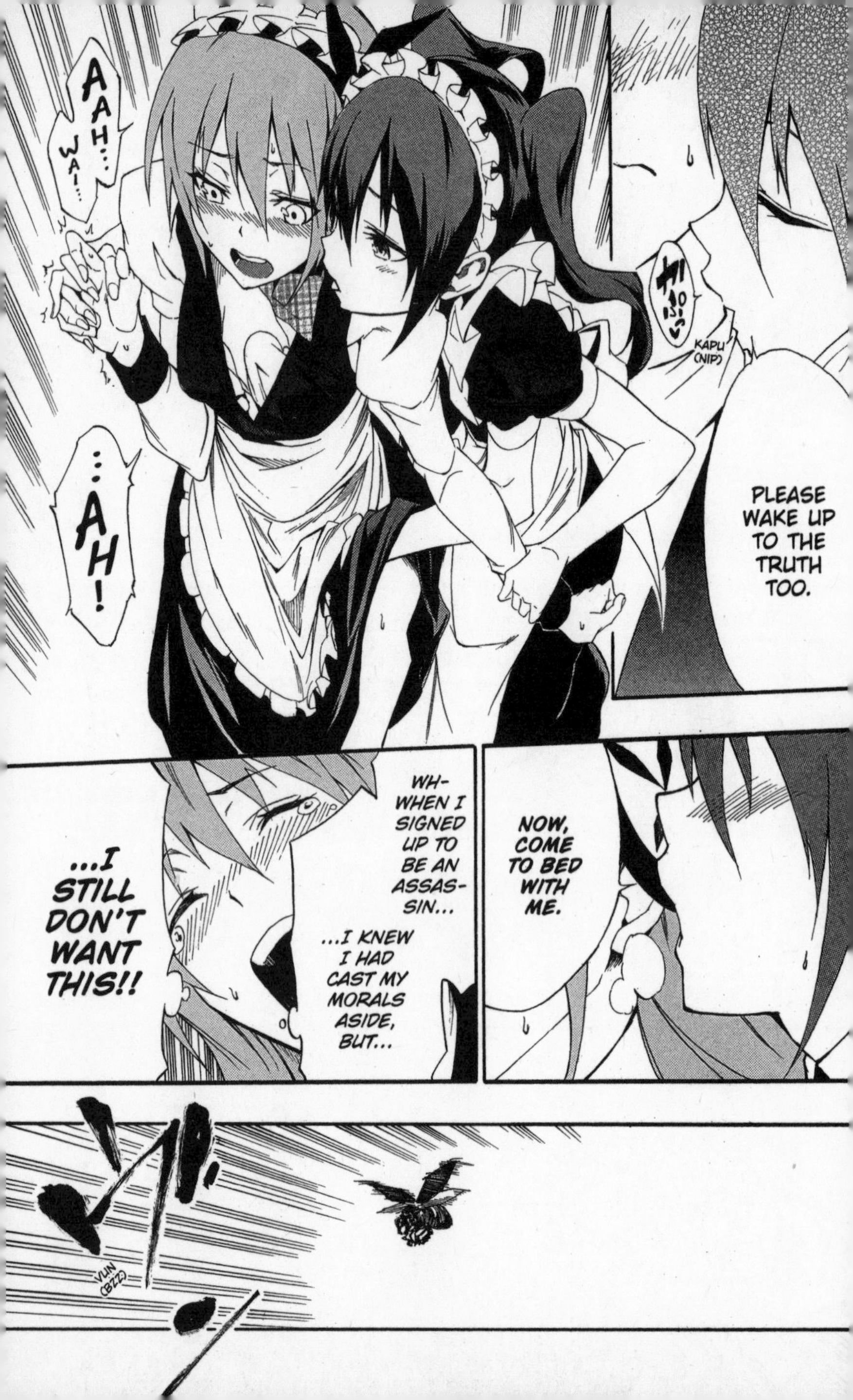
KAPU (NIP)
PLEASE WAKE UP TO THE TRUTH TOO.
AAH... WAI...
...AH!
NOW, COME TO BED WITH ME.
WH- WHEN I SIGNED UP TO BE AN ASSAS-SIN...
...I KNEW I HAD CAST MY MORALS ASIDE, BUT...
...I STILL DON'T WANT THIS!!
VUN (BZZ)

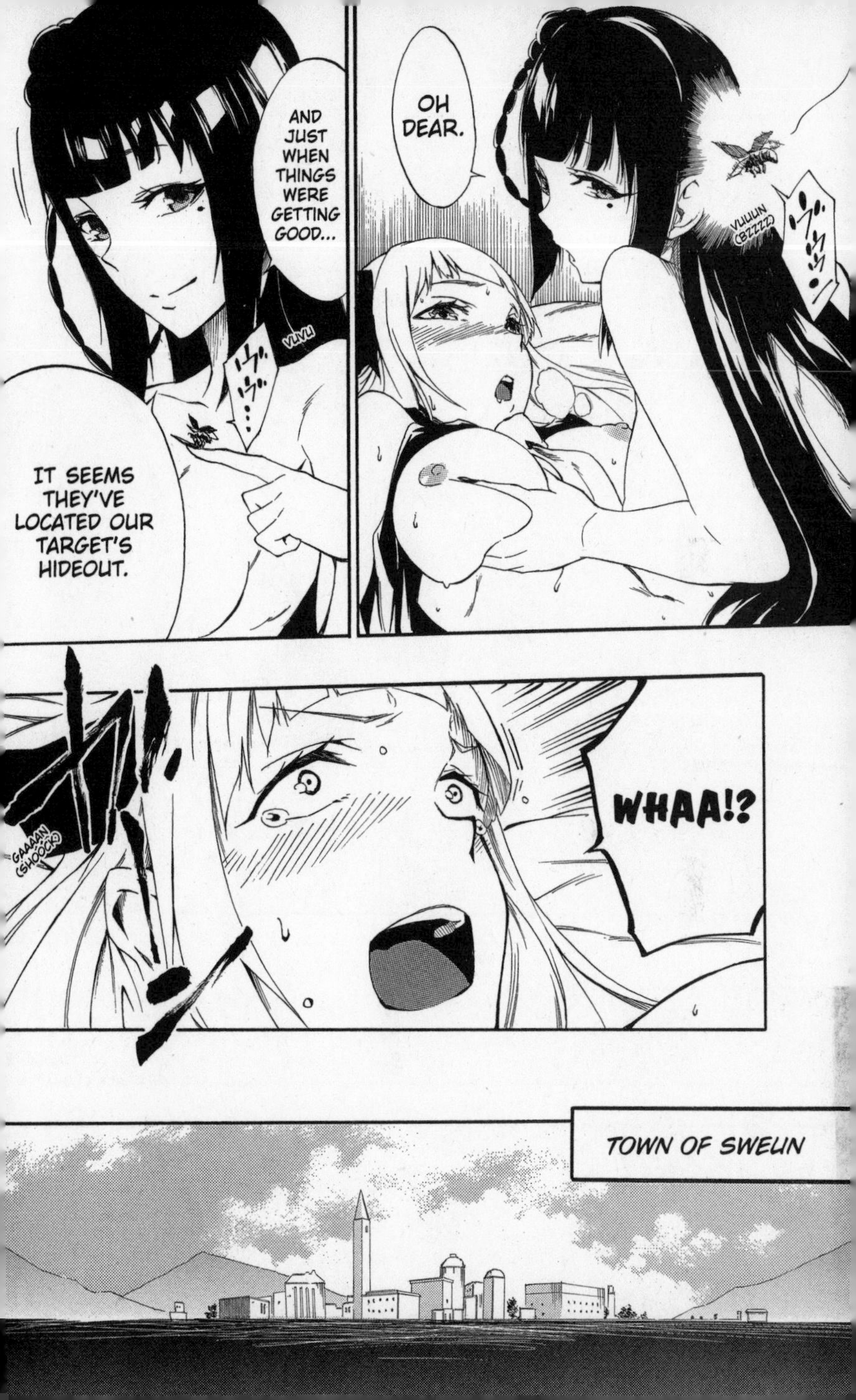
VUUUN (BZZZZ)
OH DEAR.
AND JUST WHEN THINGS WERE GETTING GOOD...
VUVU
IT SEEMS THEY'VE LOCATED OUR TARGET'S HIDEOUT.
WHAA!?
GAAAAN (SHOCK)
TOWN OF SWELIN

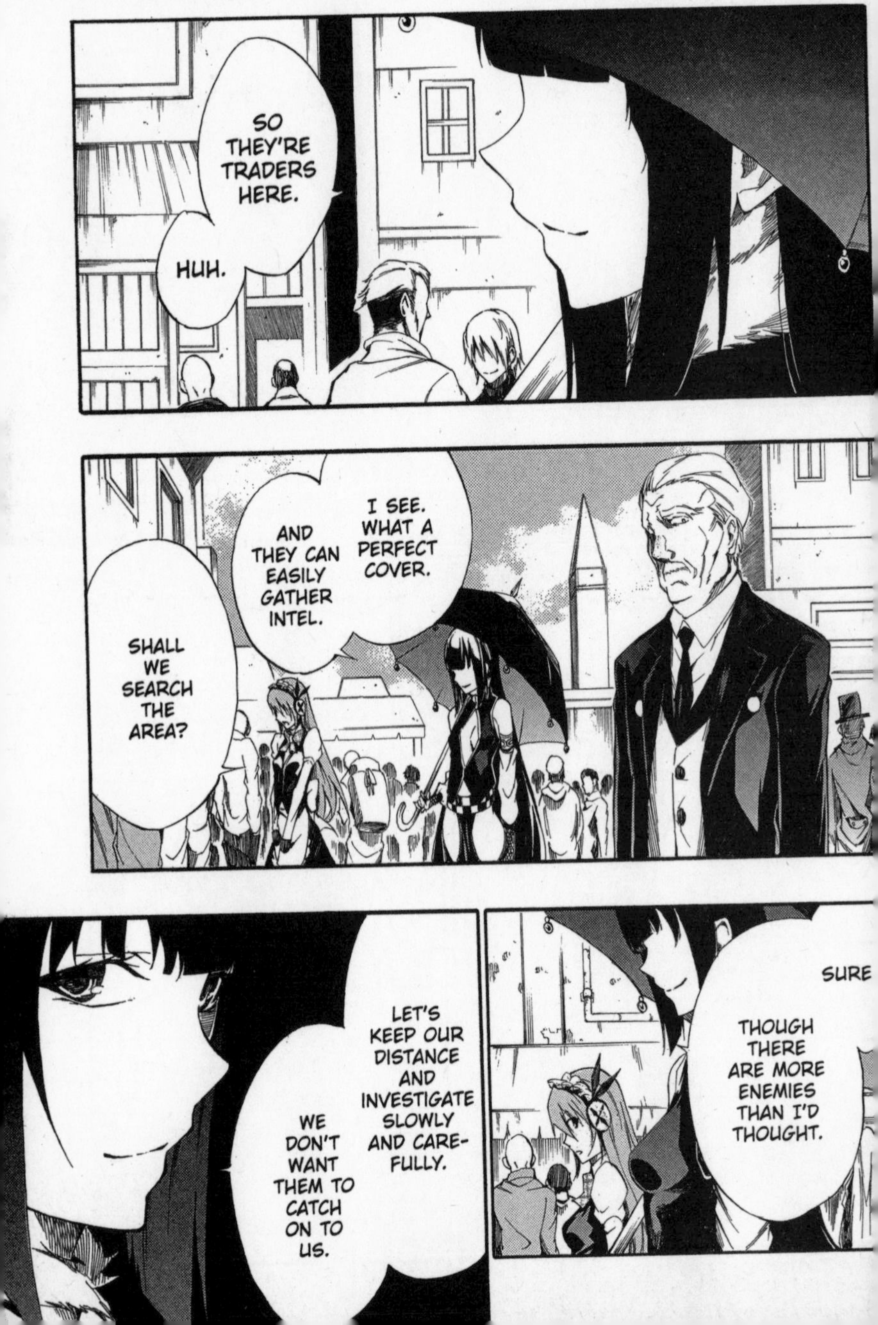
SO THEY'RE TRADERS HERE.
HUH.
I SEE. WHAT A PERFECT COVER.
AND THEY CAN EASILY GATHER INTEL.
SHALL WE SEARCH THE AREA?
SURE
THOUGH THERE ARE MORE ENEMIES THAN I'D THOUGHT.
LET'S KEEP OUR DISTANCE AND INVESTIGATE SLOWLY AND CARE-FULLY.
WE DON'T WANT THEM TO CATCH ON TO US.

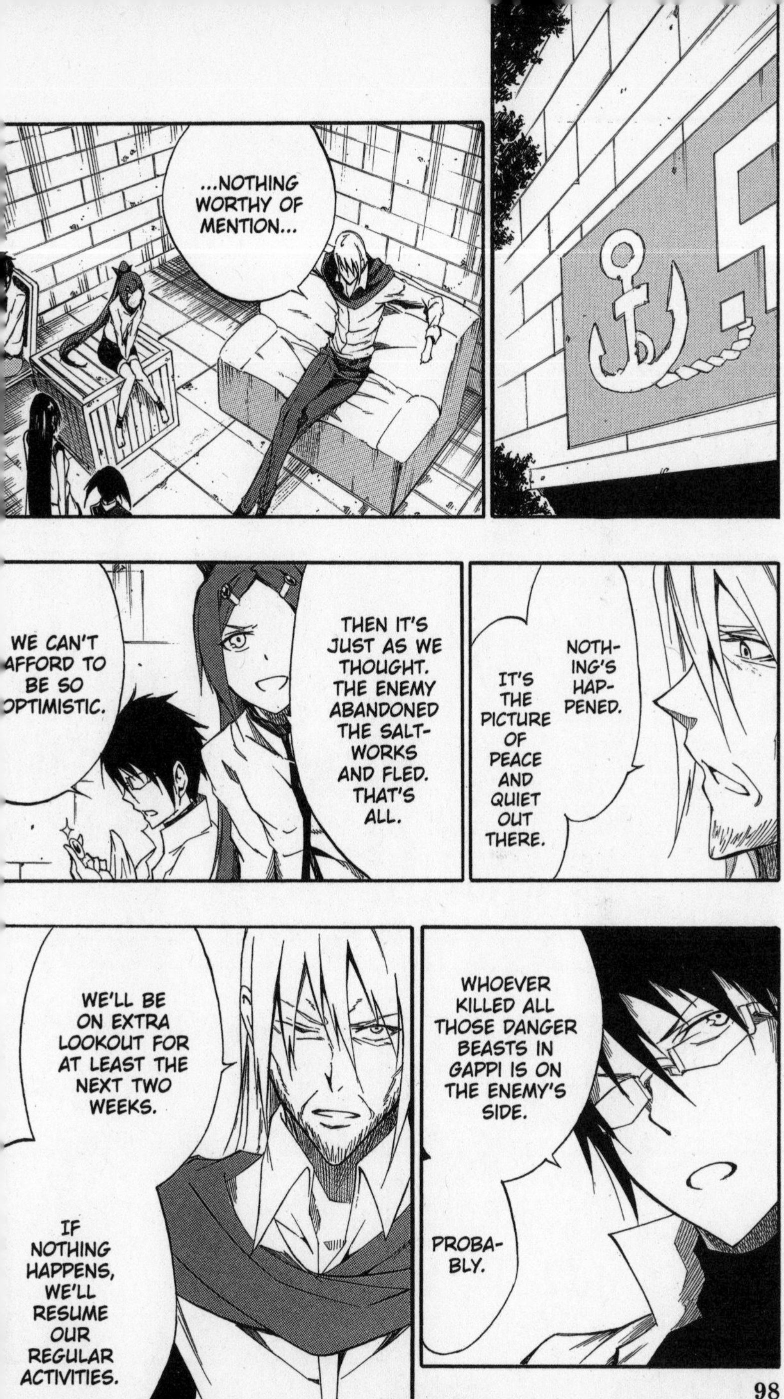
...NOTHING WORTHY OF MENTION...
NOTHING'S HAPPENED.
IT'S THE PICTURE OF PEACE AND QUIET OUT THERE.
THEN IT'S JUST AS WE THOUGHT. THE ENEMY ABANDONED THE SALTWORKS AND FLED. THAT'S ALL.
WE CAN'T AFFORD TO BE SO OPTIMISTIC.
WHOEVER KILLED ALL THOSE DANGER BEASTS IN GAPPI IS ON THE ENEMY'S SIDE.
PROBABLY.
WE'LL BE ON EXTRA LOOKOUT FOR AT LEAST THE NEXT TWO WEEKS.
IF NOTHING HAPPENS, WE'LL RESUME OUR REGULAR ACTIVITIES.

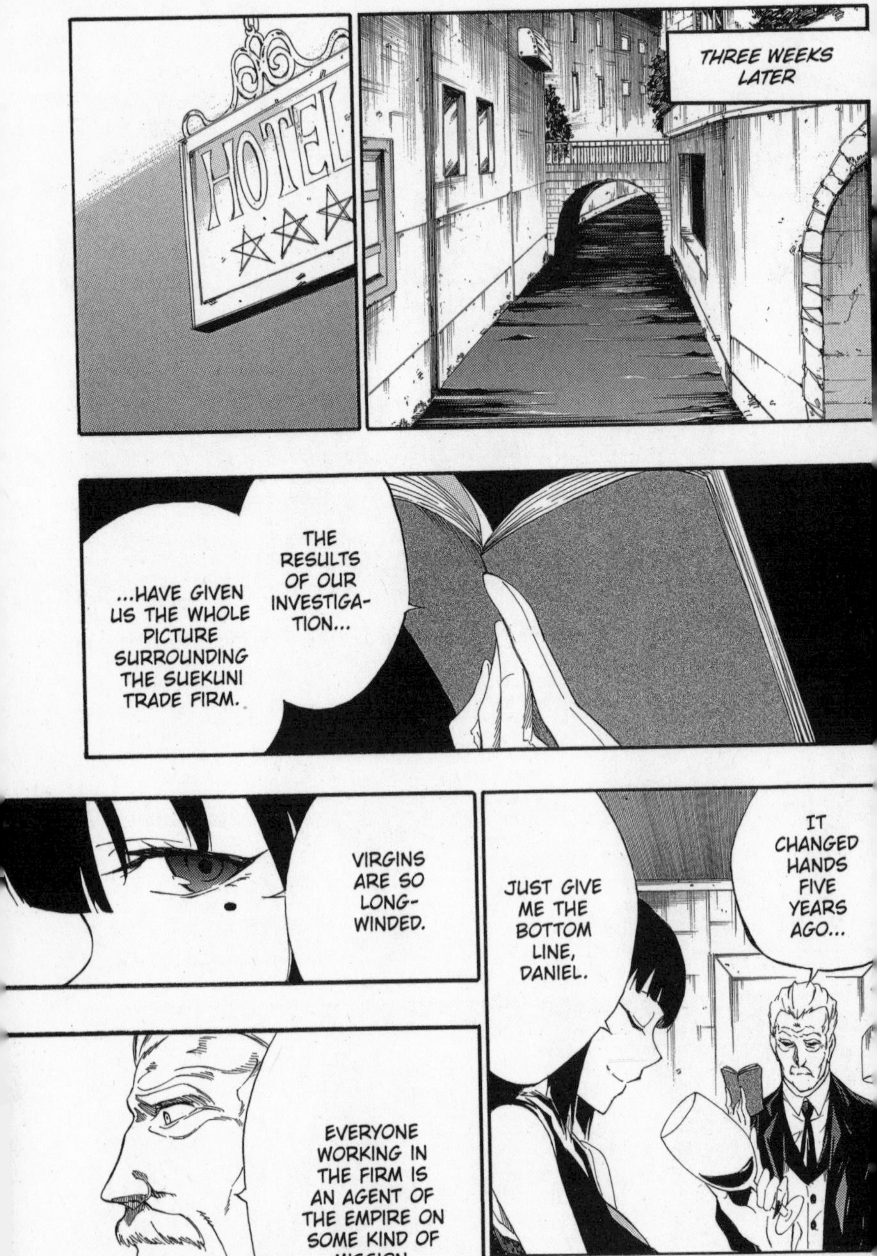
THREE WEEKS LATER
HOTEL
THE RESULTS OF OUR INVESTIGATION...
...HAVE GIVEN US THE WHOLE PICTURE SURROUNDING THE SUEKUNI TRADE FIRM.
IT CHANGED HANDS FIVE YEARS AGO...
JUST GIVE ME THE BOTTOM LINE, DANIEL.
VIRGINS ARE SO LONG-WINDED.
EVERYONE WORKING IN THE FIRM IS AN AGENT OF THE EMPIRE ON SOME KIND OF MISSION.

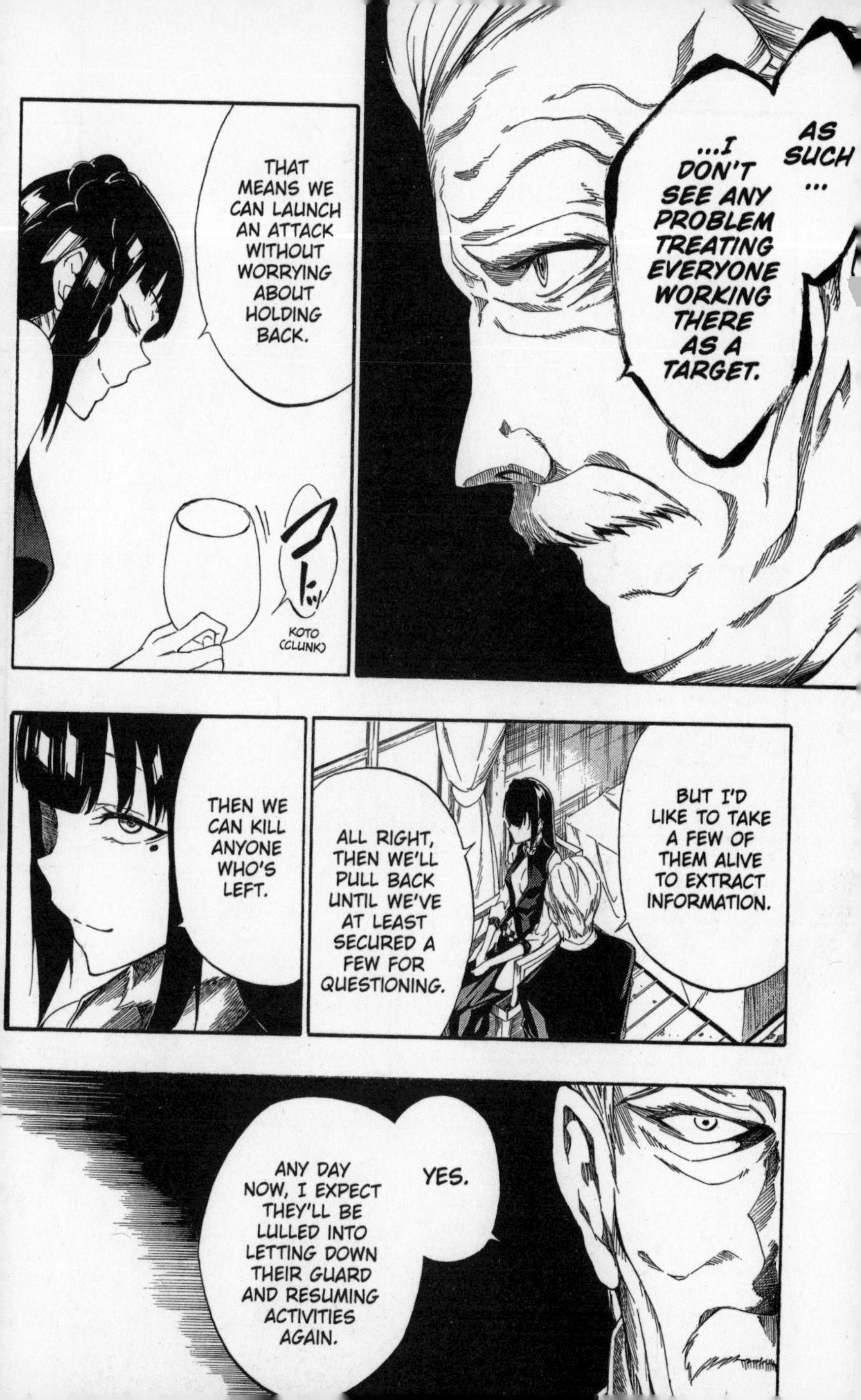
AS SUCH...
...I DON'T SEE ANY PROBLEM TREATING EVERYONE WORKING THERE AS A TARGET.
THAT MEANS WE CAN LAUNCH AN ATTACK WITHOUT WORRYING ABOUT HOLDING BACK.
KOTO (CLUNK)
BUT I'D LIKE TO TAKE A FEW OF THEM ALIVE TO EXTRACT INFORMATION.
ALL RIGHT, THEN WE'LL PULL BACK UNTIL WE'VE AT LEAST SECURED A FEW FOR QUESTIONING.
THEN WE CAN KILL ANYONE WHO'S LEFT.
YES.
ANY DAY NOW, I EXPECT THEY'LL BE LULLED INTO LETTING DOWN THEIR GUARD AND RESUMING ACTIVITIES AGAIN.

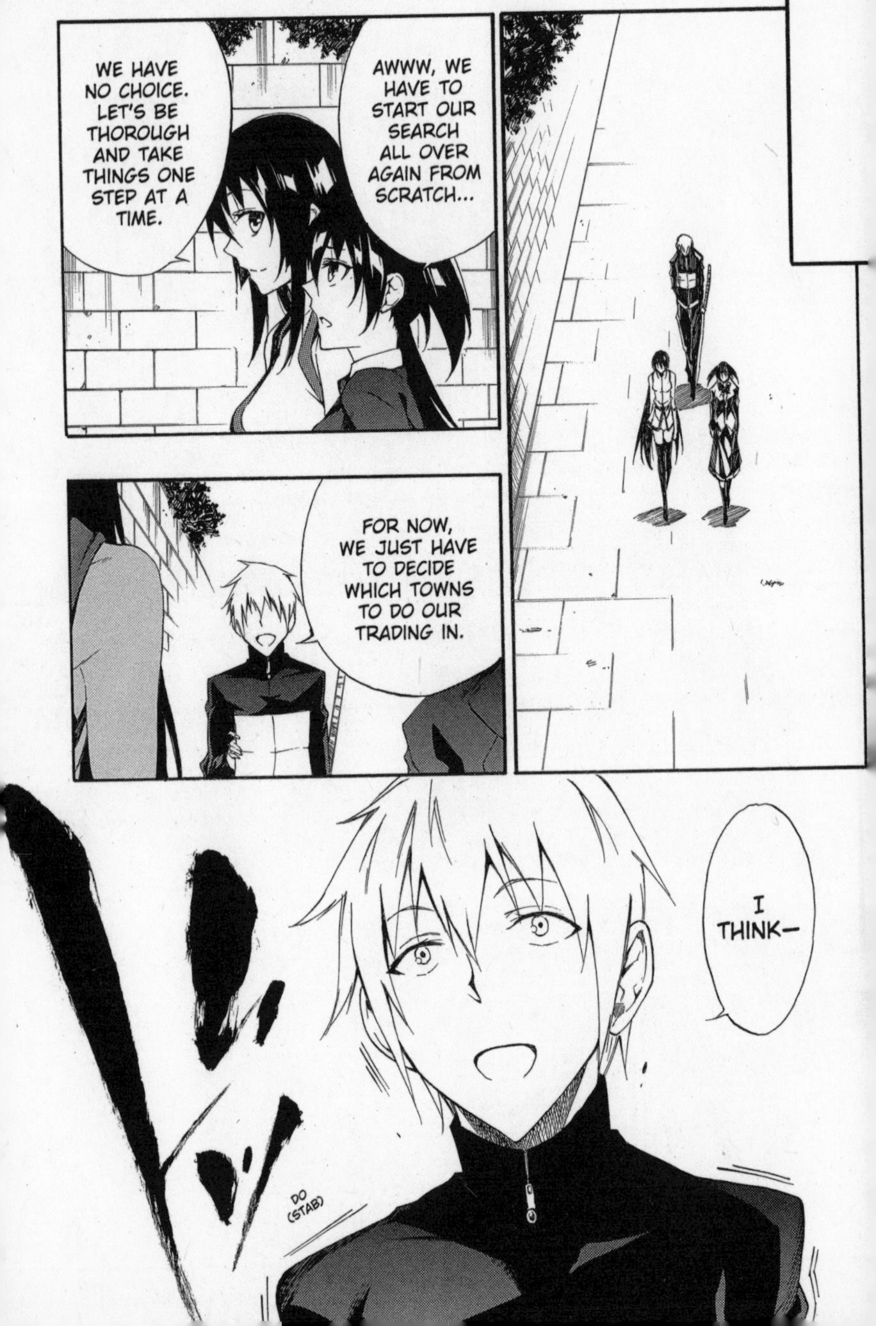
AWWW, WE HAVE TO START OUR SEARCH ALL OVER AGAIN FROM SCRATCH...
WE HAVE NO CHOICE. LET'S BE THOROUGH AND TAKE THINGS ONE STEP AT A TIME.
FOR NOW, WE JUST HAVE TO DECIDE WHICH TOWNS TO DO OUR TRADING IN.
I THINK—
DO (STAB)

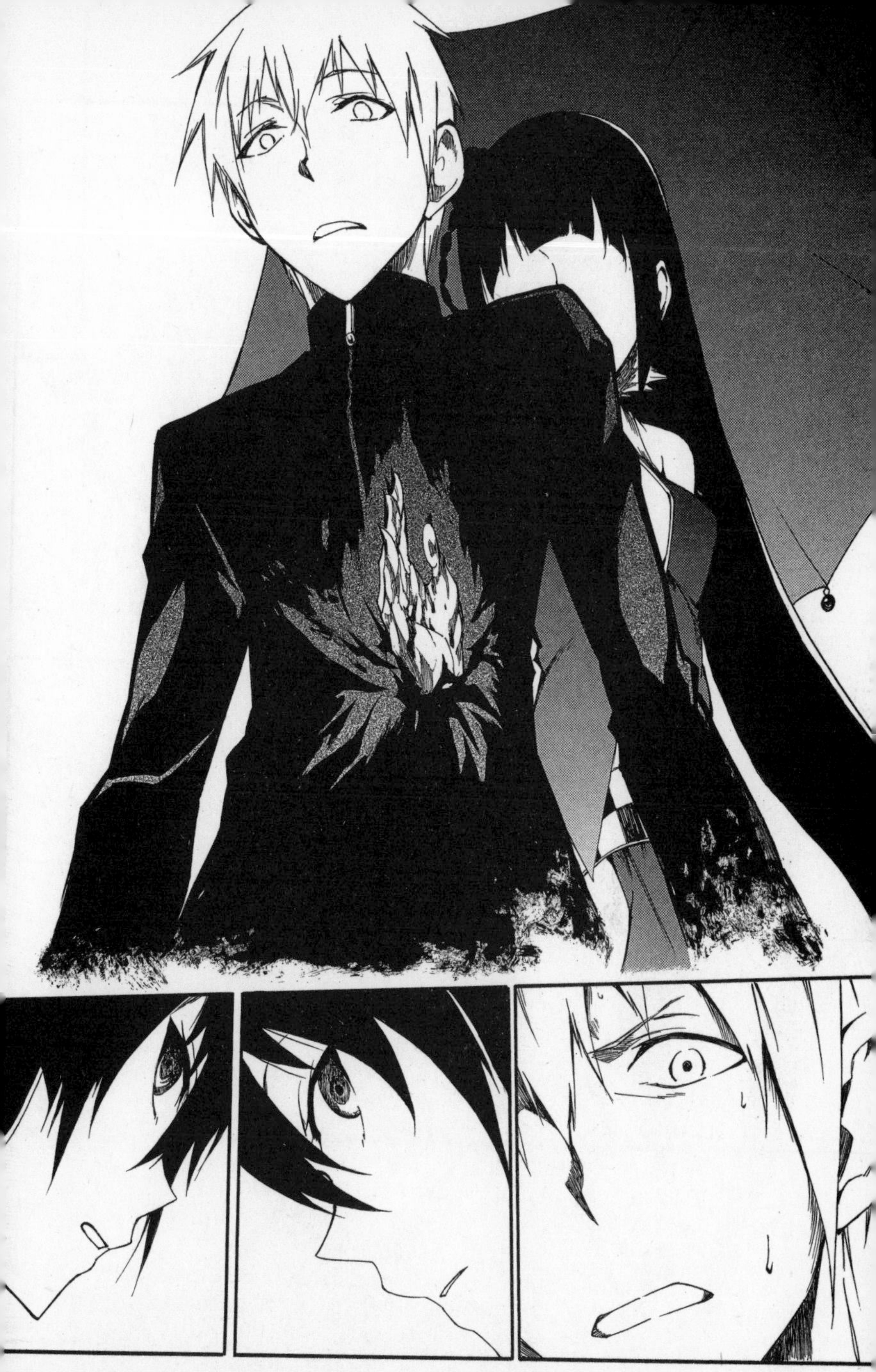

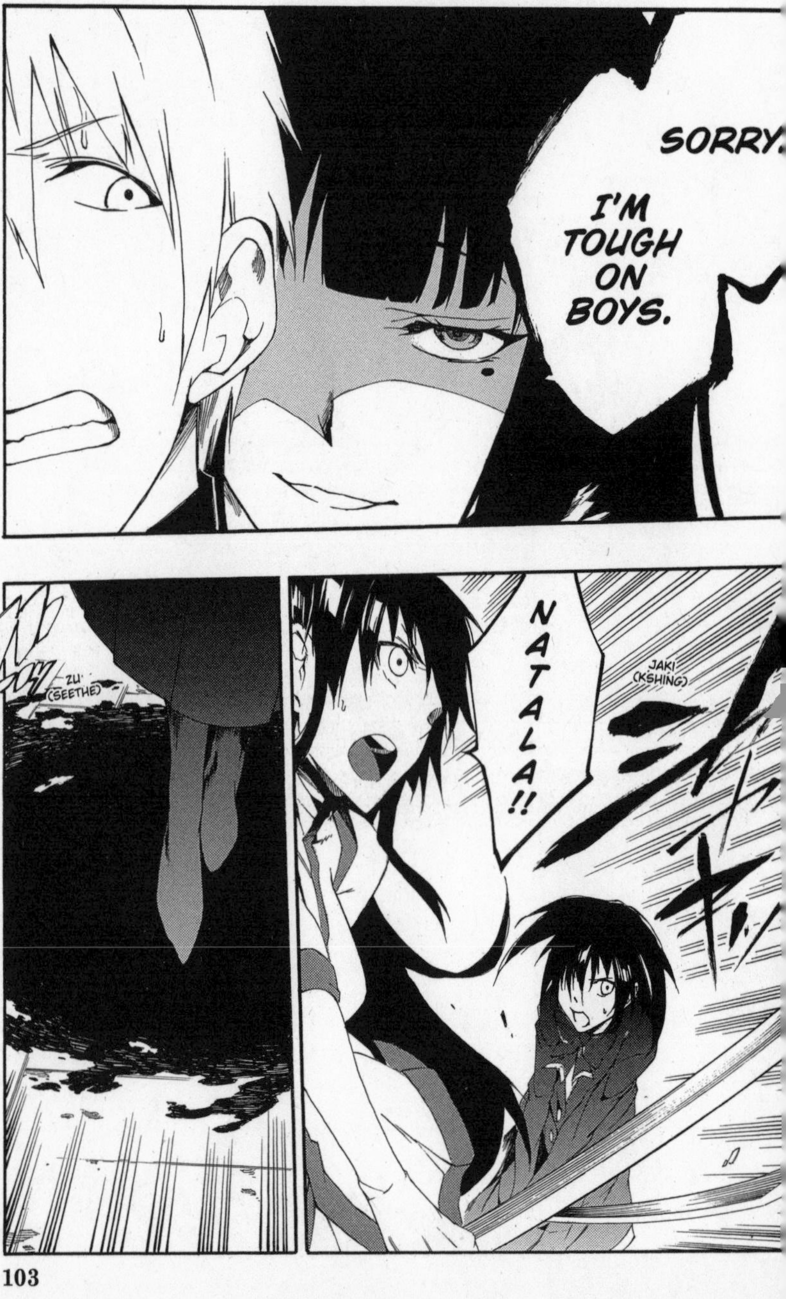
SORRY.
I'M TOUGH ON BOYS.
NATALA!!
JAKI (KSHING)
ZU (SEETHE)

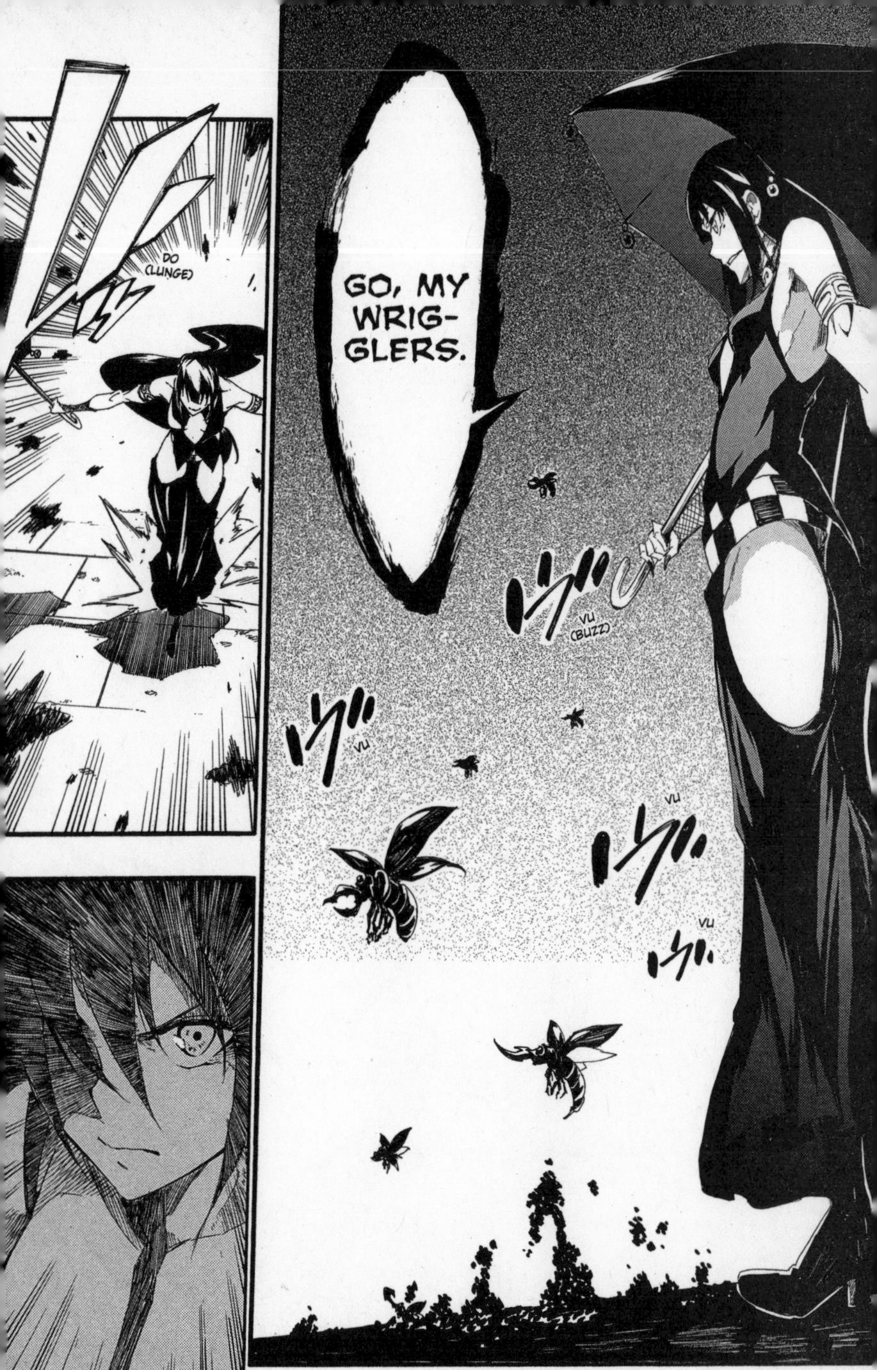
GO, MY WRIG-GLERS.
VU (BUZZ)
VU
VU
VU
DO (LUNGE)

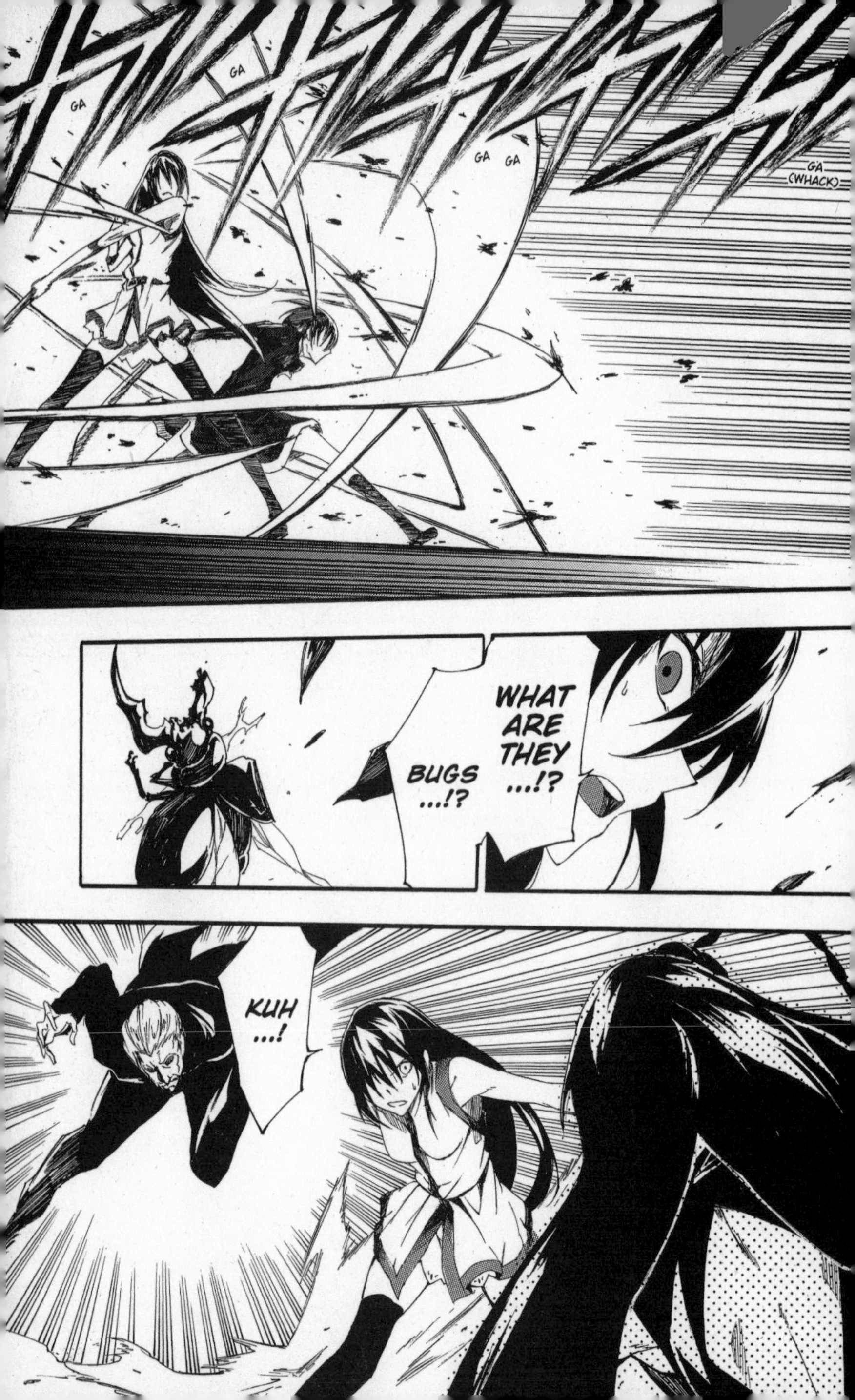
GA
(WHACK)
GA
GA
GA
GA
WHAT ARE THEY ...!?
BUGS ...!?
KUH ...!

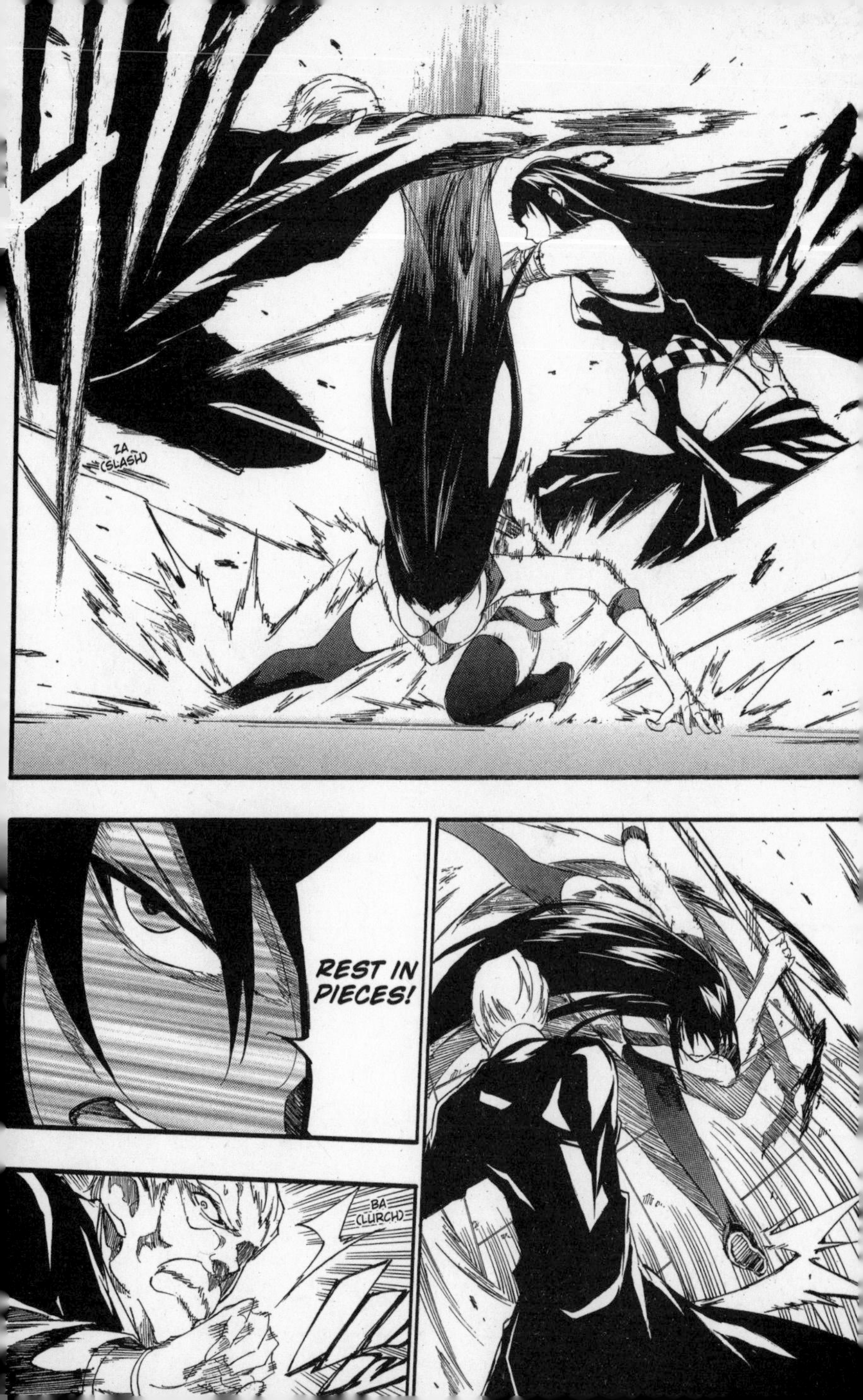
ZA (SLASH)
BA (CLURCH)
REST IN PIECES!

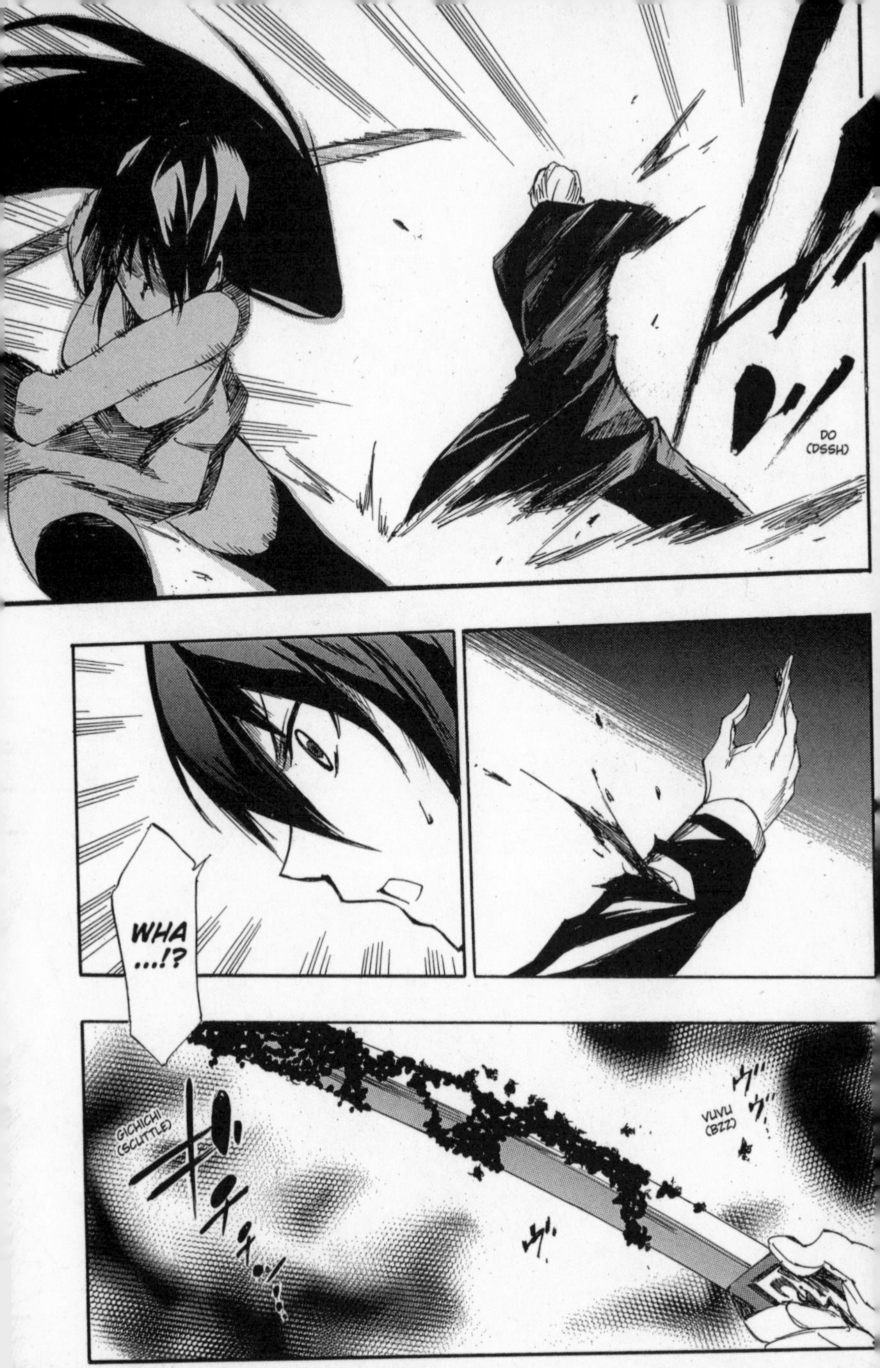
DO (DSSH)
WHA ...!?
VUVU (BZZ)
GICHICHI (SCUTTLE)

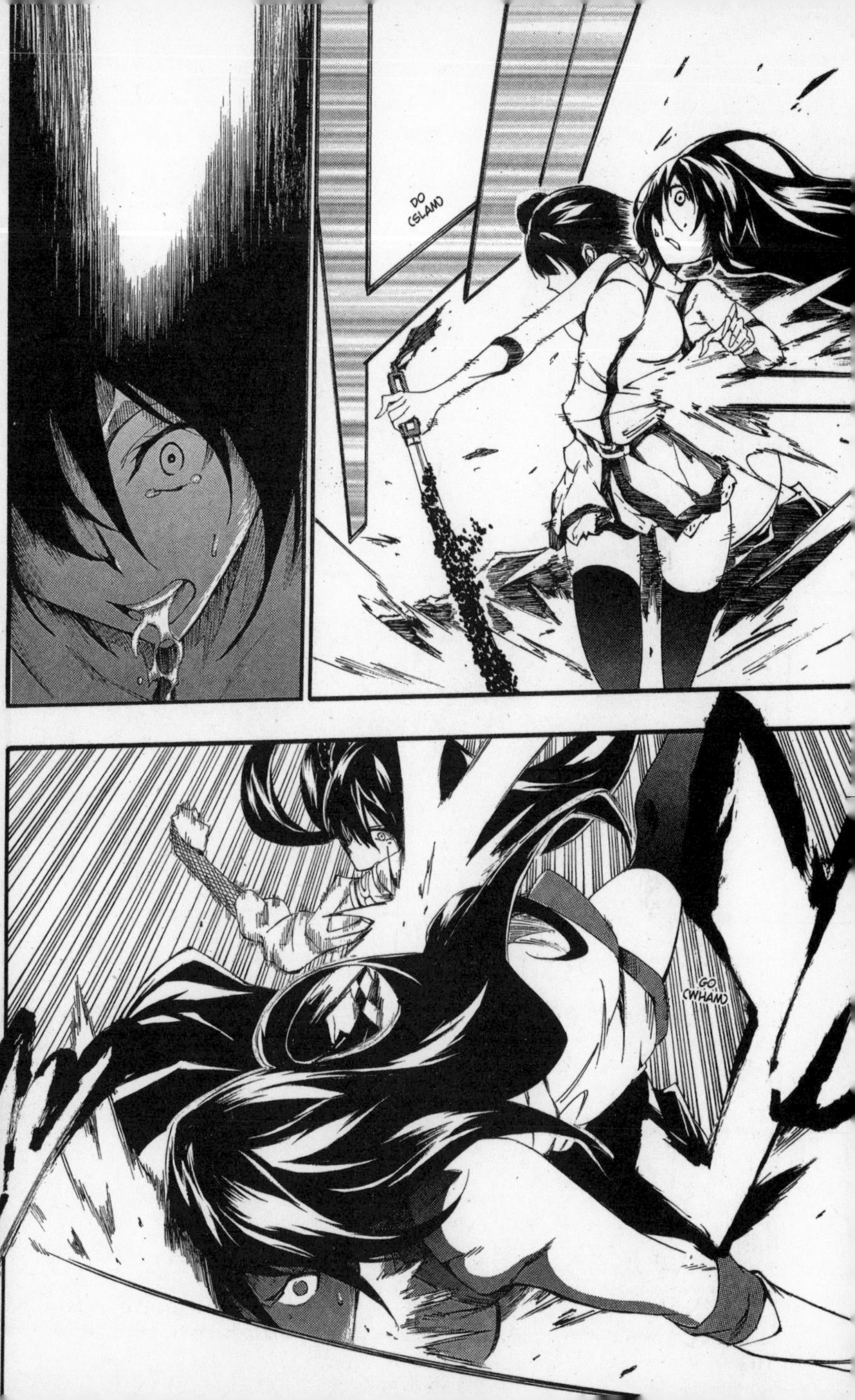
DO
(SLAM)
GO
(WHAM)

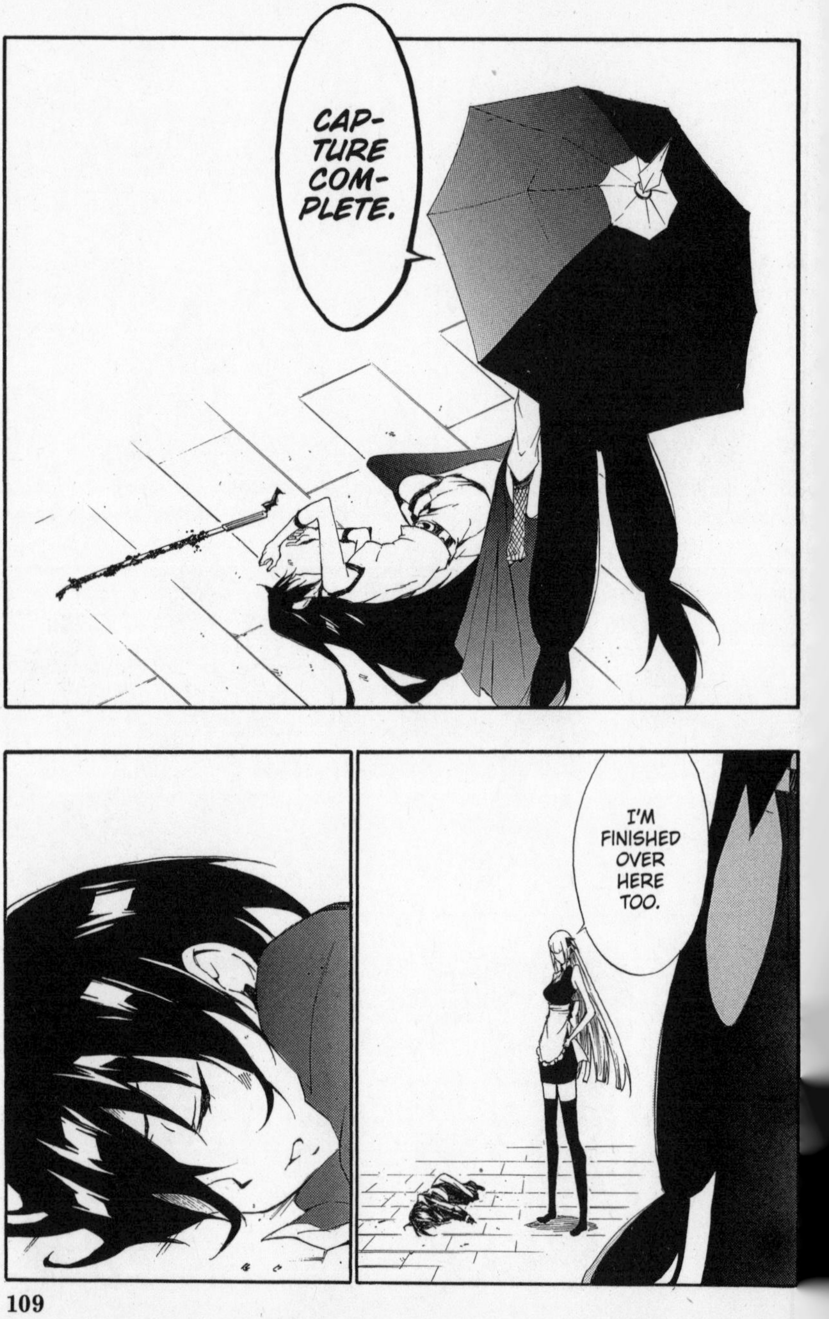
CAP-
TURE
COM-
PLETE.
I'M
FINISHED
OVER
HERE
TOO.

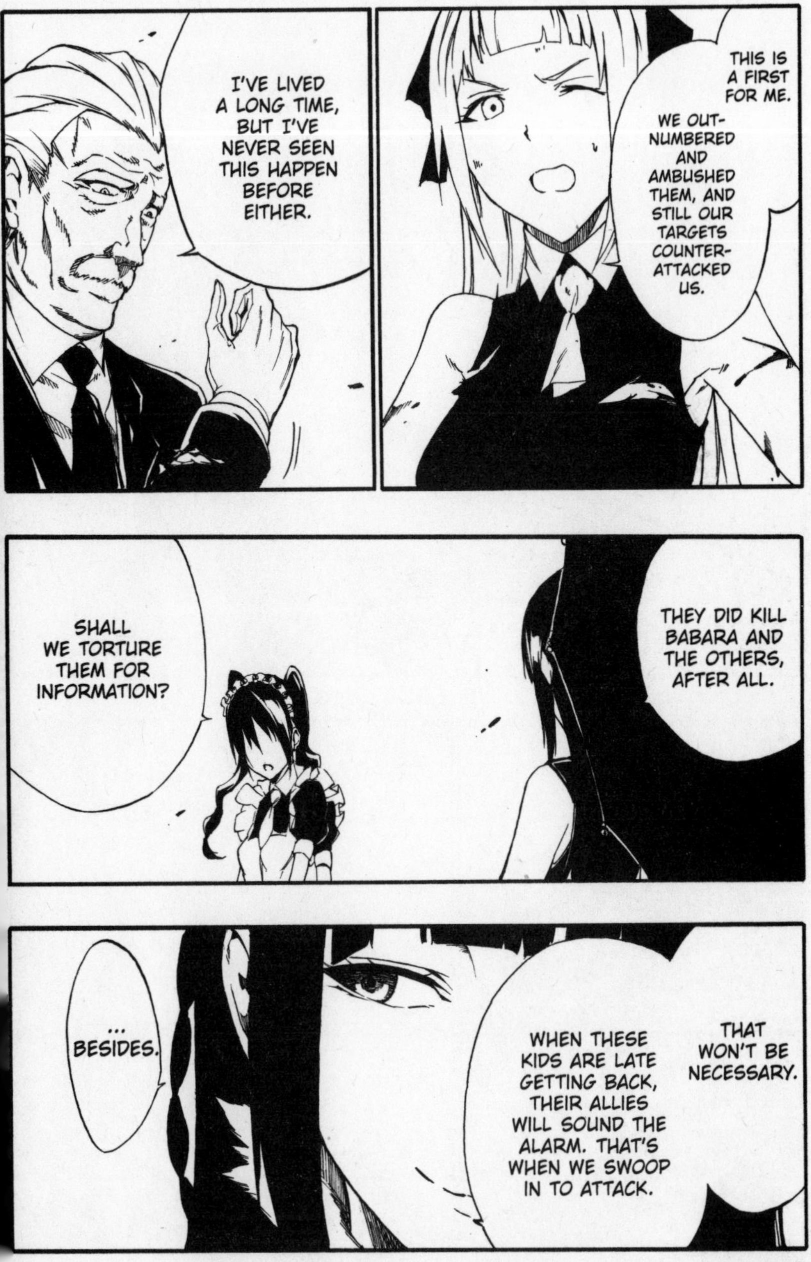
THIS IS A FIRST FOR ME.
WE OUT-NUMBERED AND AMBUSHED THEM, AND STILL OUR TARGETS COUNTER-ATTACKED US.
I'VE LIVED A LONG TIME, BUT I'VE NEVER SEEN THIS HAPPEN BEFORE EITHER.
THEY DID KILL BABARA AND THE OTHERS, AFTER ALL.
SHALL WE TORTURE THEM FOR INFORMATION?
THAT WON'T BE NECESSARY.
WHEN THESE KIDS ARE LATE GETTING BACK, THEIR ALLIES WILL SOUND THE ALARM. THAT'S WHEN WE SWOOP IN TO ATTACK.
...BESIDES.

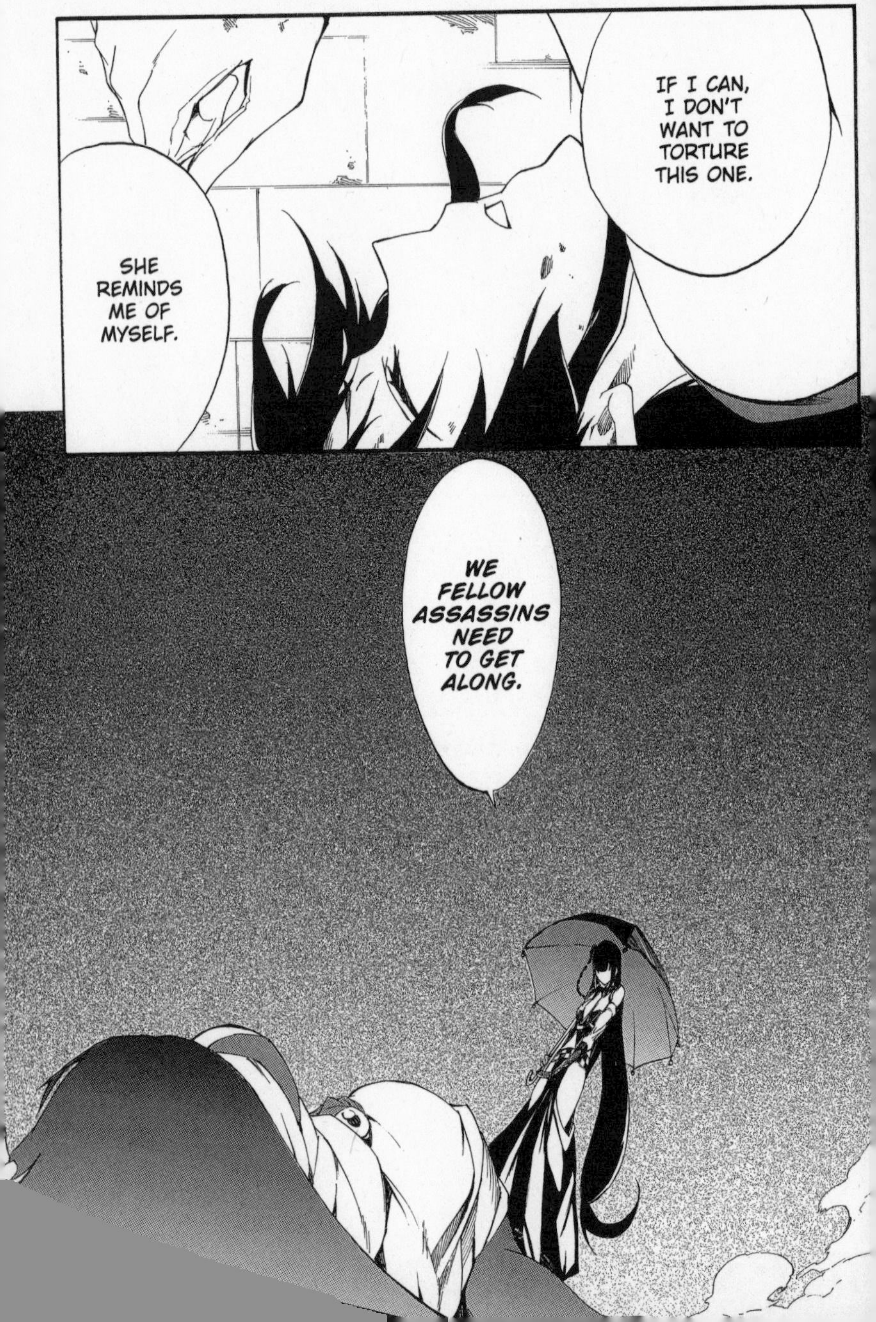
IF I CAN, I DON'T WANT TO TORTURE THIS ONE.
SHE REMINDS ME OF MYSELF.
WE FELLOW ASSASSINS NEED TO GET ALONG.

Akame ga KILL! ZERO

Rough Sketches

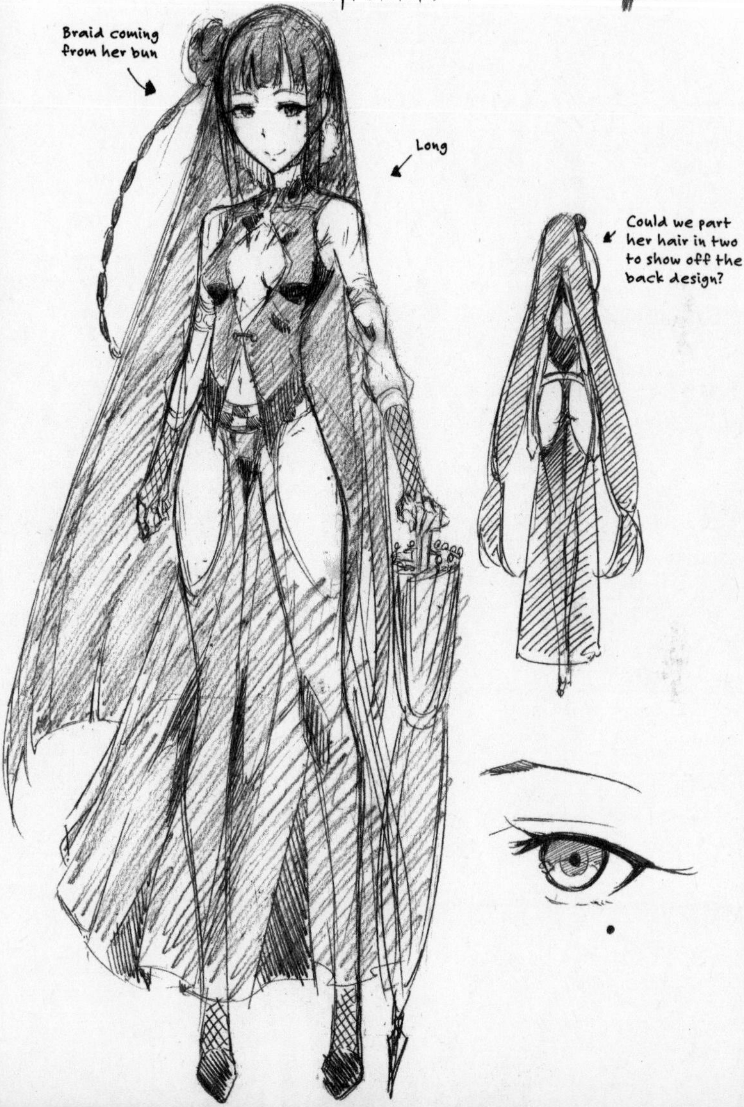

Braid coming from her bun
Long
Could we part her hair in two to show off the back design?

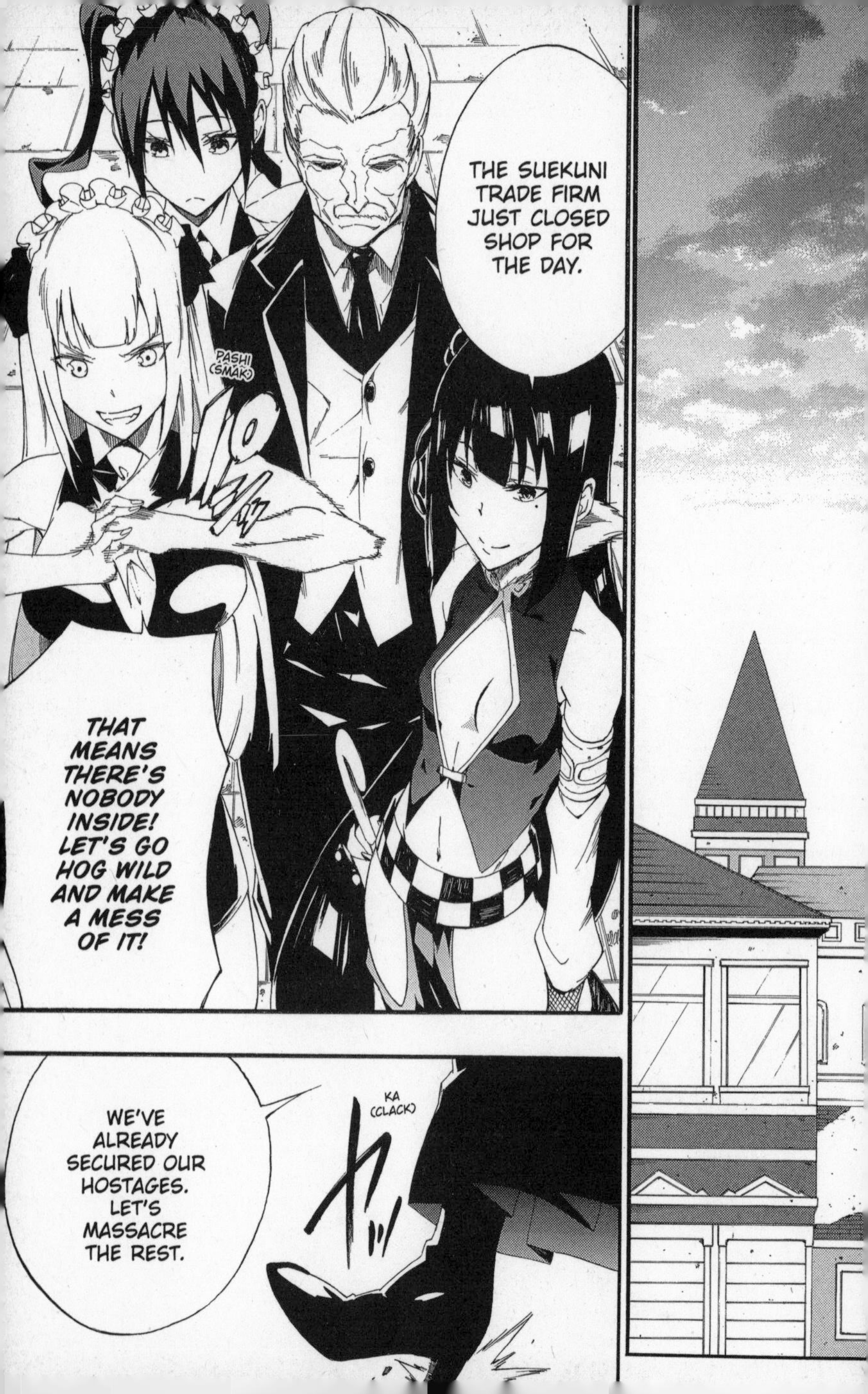
THE SUEKUNI TRADE FIRM JUST CLOSED SHOP FOR THE DAY.
PASHI (SMAK)
THAT MEANS THERE'S NOBODY INSIDE! LET'S GO HOG WILD AND MAKE A MESS OF IT!
KA (CLACK)
WE'VE ALREADY SECURED OUR HOSTAGES. LET'S MASSACRE THE REST.

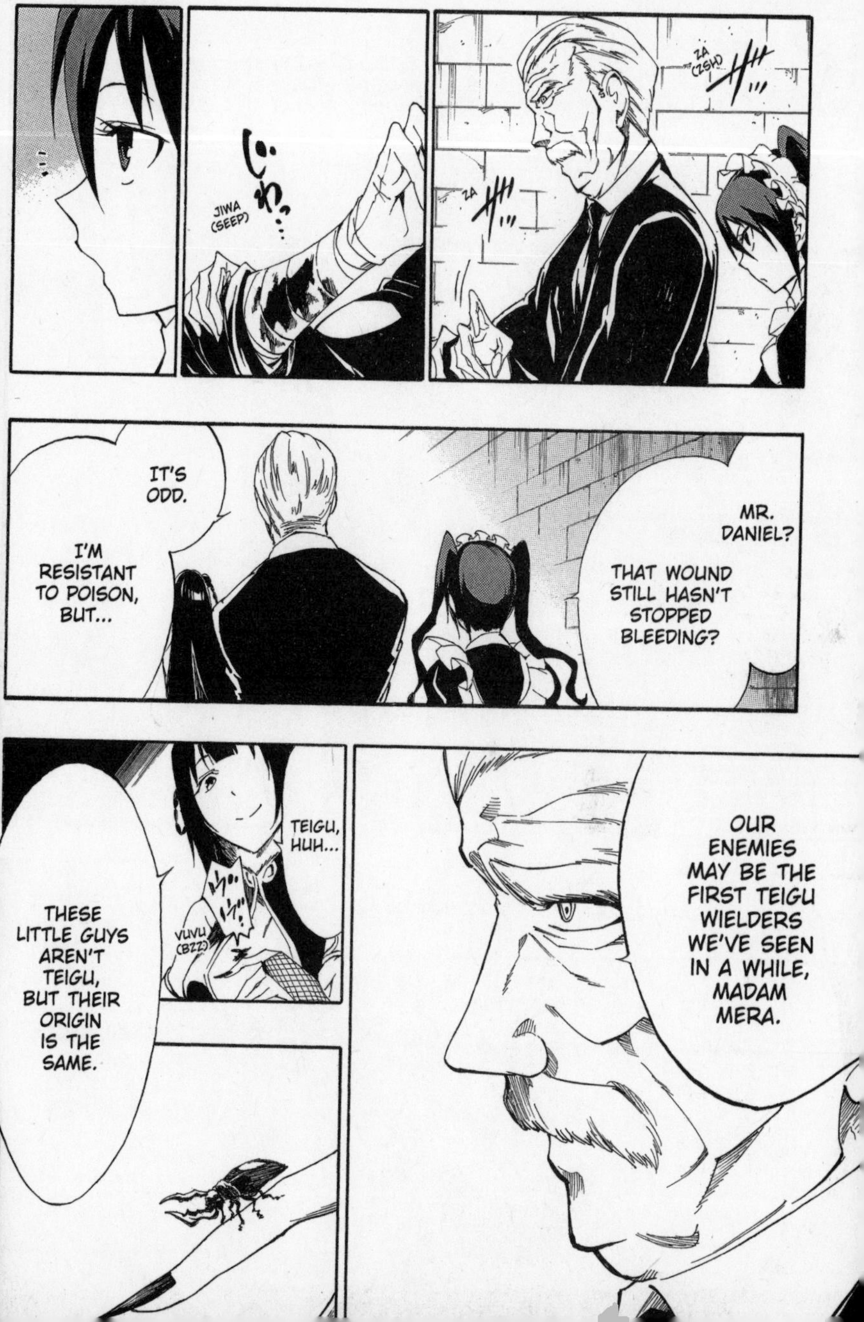
ZA (ZSH)
ZA
JIWA (SEEP)
MR. DANIEL? THAT WOUND STILL HASN'T STOPPED BLEEDING?
IT'S ODD.
I'M RESISTANT TO POISON, BUT...
OUR ENEMIES MAY BE THE FIRST TEIGU WIELDERS WE'VE SEEN IN A WHILE, MADAM MERA.
TEIGU, HUH...
VUVU (BZZ)
THESE LITTLE GUYS AREN'T TEIGU, BUT THEIR ORIGIN IS THE SAME.

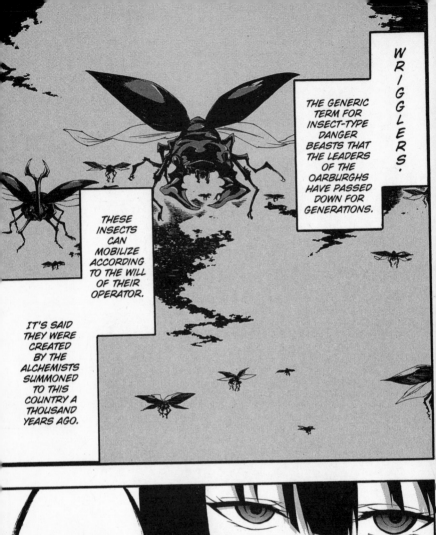

WRIGGLERS.

THE GENERIC TERM FOR INSECT-TYPE DANGER BEASTS THAT THE LEADERS OF THE OARBURGHS HAVE PASSED DOWN FOR GENERATIONS.

THESE INSECTS CAN MOBILIZE ACCORDING TO THE WILL OF THEIR OPERATOR.

IT'S SAID THEY WERE CREATED BY THE ALCHEMISTS SUMMONED TO THIS COUNTRY A THOUSAND YEARS AGO.

THEY'RE JUST THE THING FOR OUR OPPONENTS.

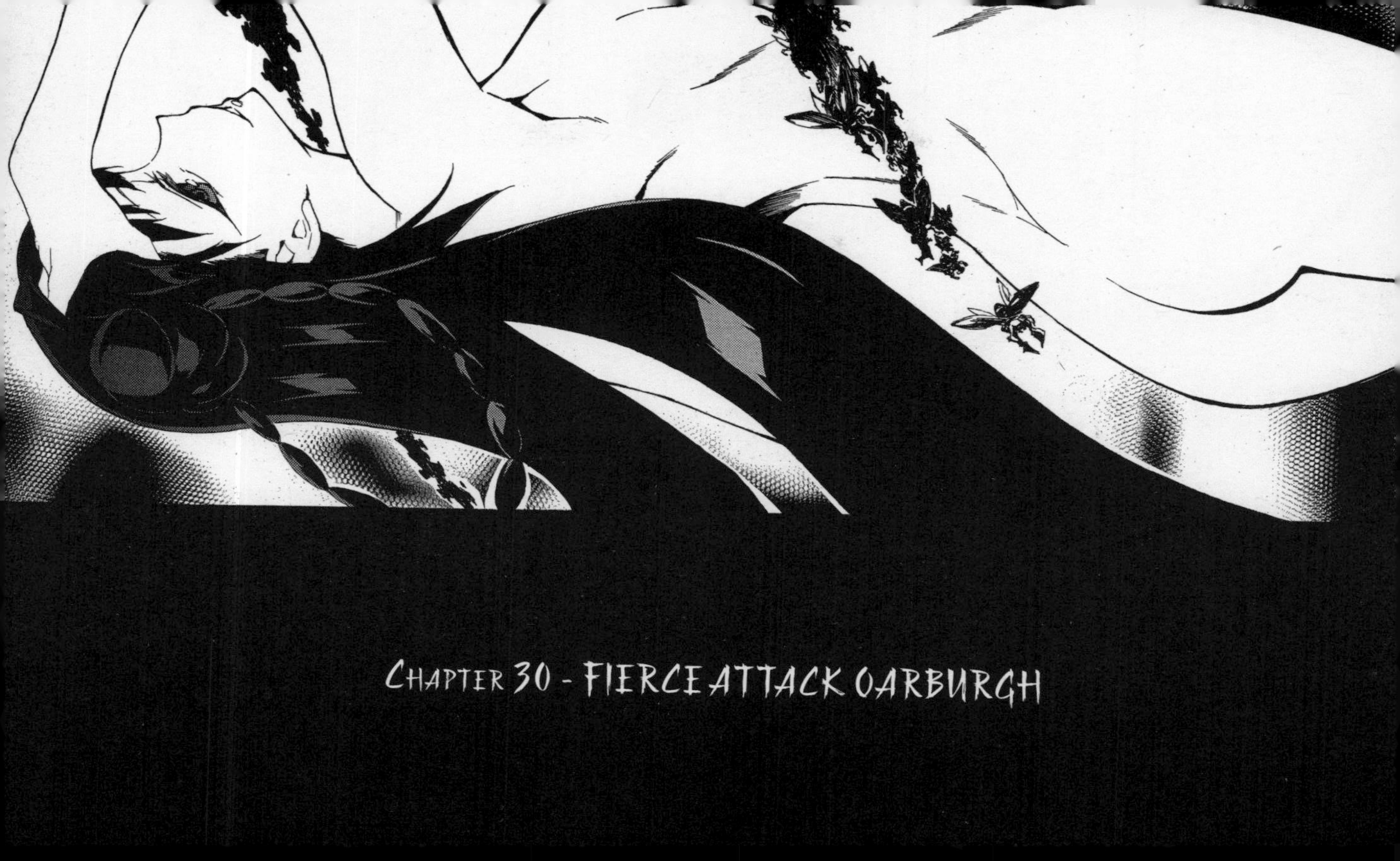
CHAPTER 30 - FIERCE ATTACK OARBURGH

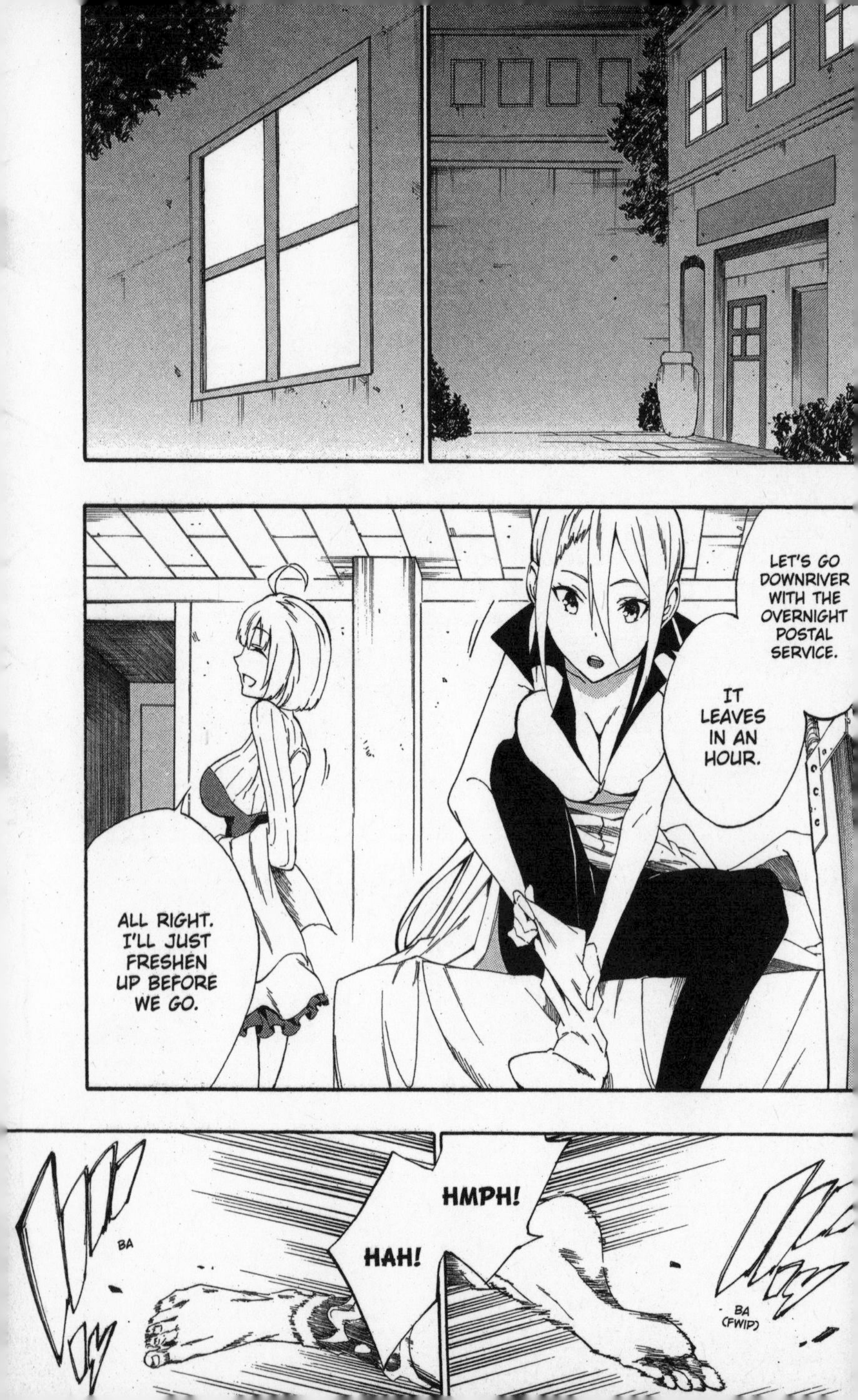
LET'S GO DOWNRIVER WITH THE OVERNIGHT POSTAL SERVICE.
IT LEAVES IN AN HOUR.
ALL RIGHT. I'LL JUST FRESHEN UP BEFORE WE GO.
BA (FWIP)
HMPH!
HAH!
BA

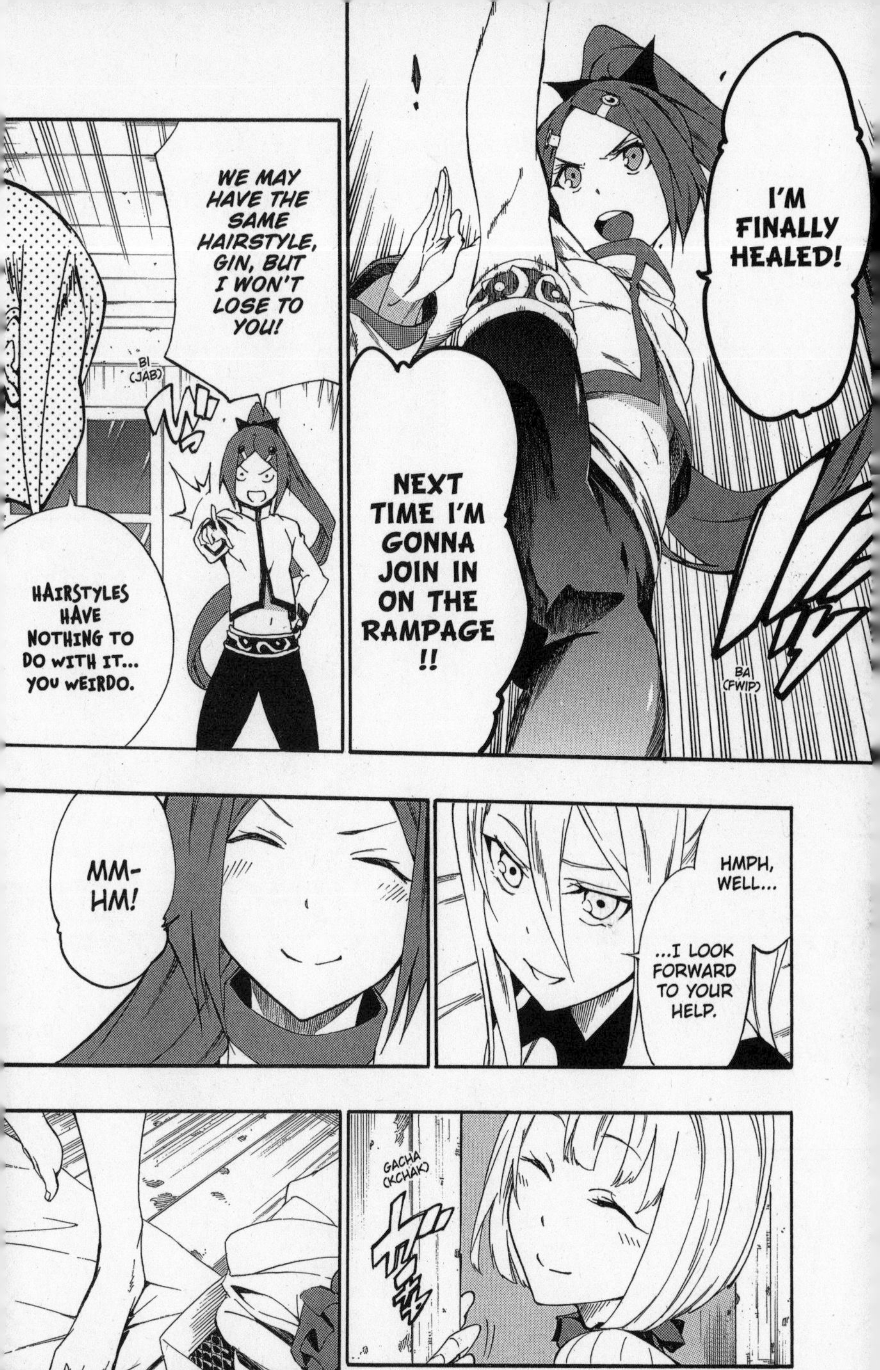
!
I'M FINALLY HEALED!
NEXT TIME I'M GONNA JOIN IN ON THE RAMPAGE!!
BA (FWIP)
WE MAY HAVE THE SAME HAIRSTYLE, GIN, BUT I WON'T LOSE TO YOU!
BI (JAB)
HAIRSTYLES HAVE NOTHING TO DO WITH IT... YOU WEIRDO.
HMPH, WELL...
...I LOOK FORWARD TO YOUR HELP.
MM-HM!
GACHA (KCHAK)

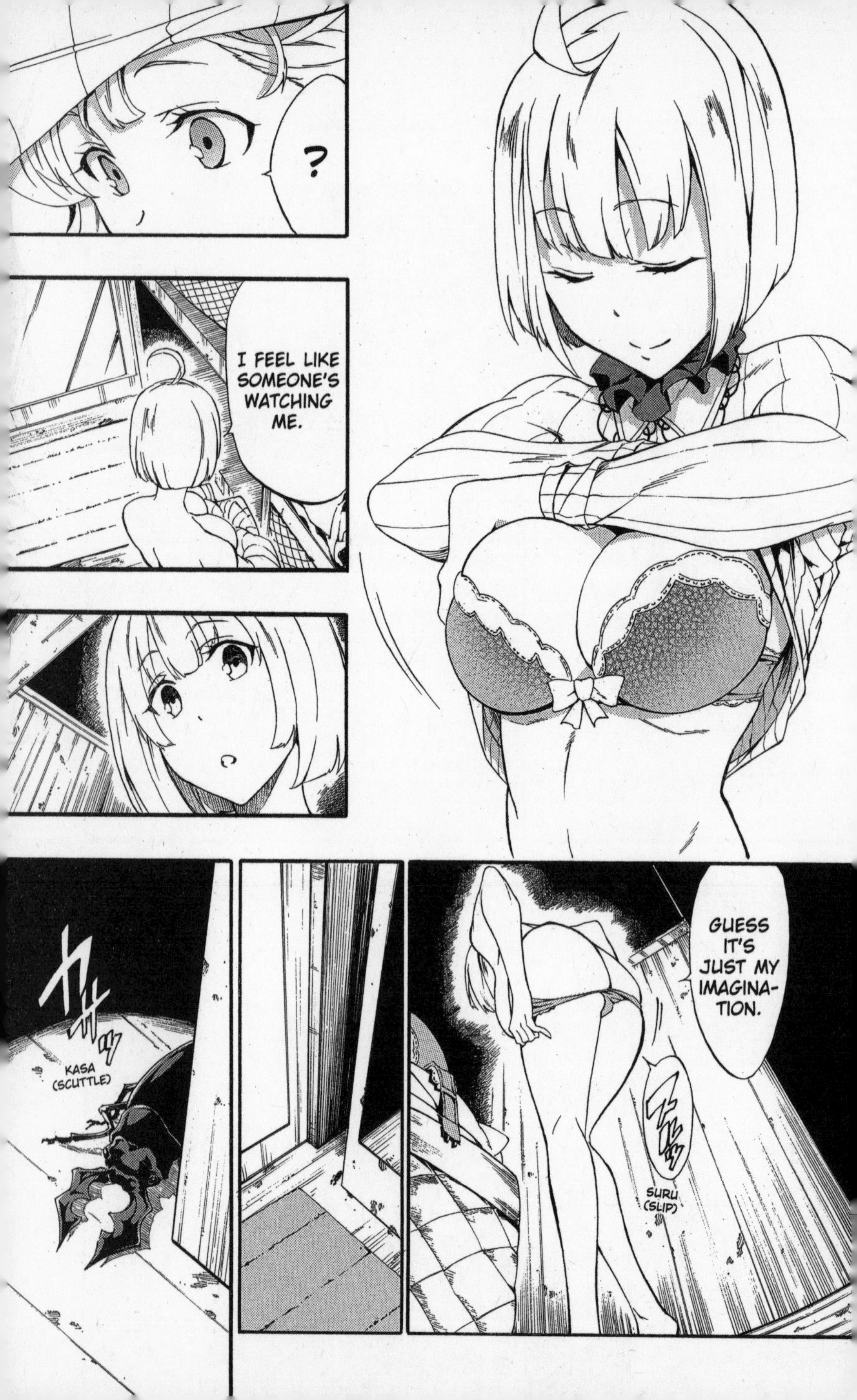
?
I FEEL LIKE SOMEONE'S WATCHING ME.
GUESS IT'S JUST MY IMAGINA-TION.
SURU (SLIP)
KASA (SCUTTLE)

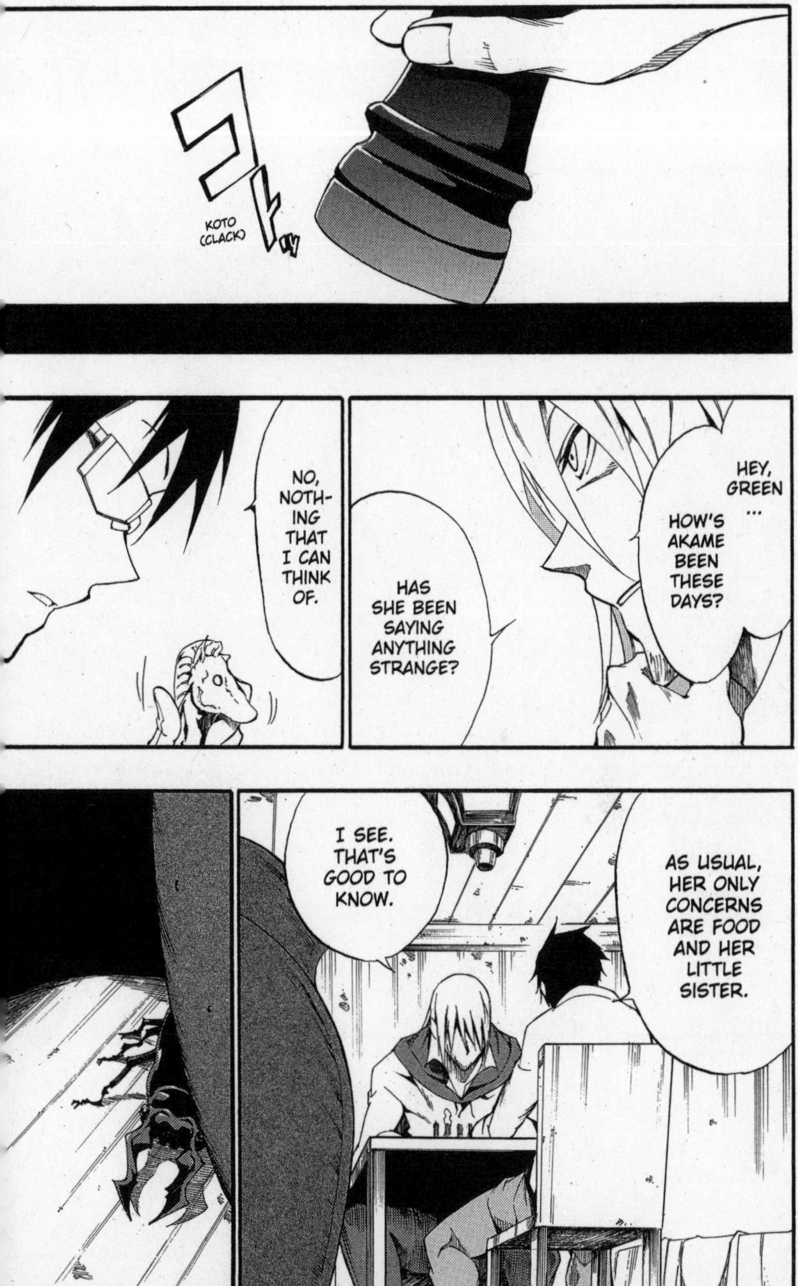
KOTO (CLACK)
HEY, GREEN ... HOW'S AKAME BEEN THESE DAYS?
HAS SHE BEEN SAYING ANYTHING STRANGE?
NO, NOTHING THAT I CAN THINK OF.
AS USUAL, HER ONLY CONCERNS ARE FOOD AND HER LITTLE SISTER.
I SEE. THAT'S GOOD TO KNOW.

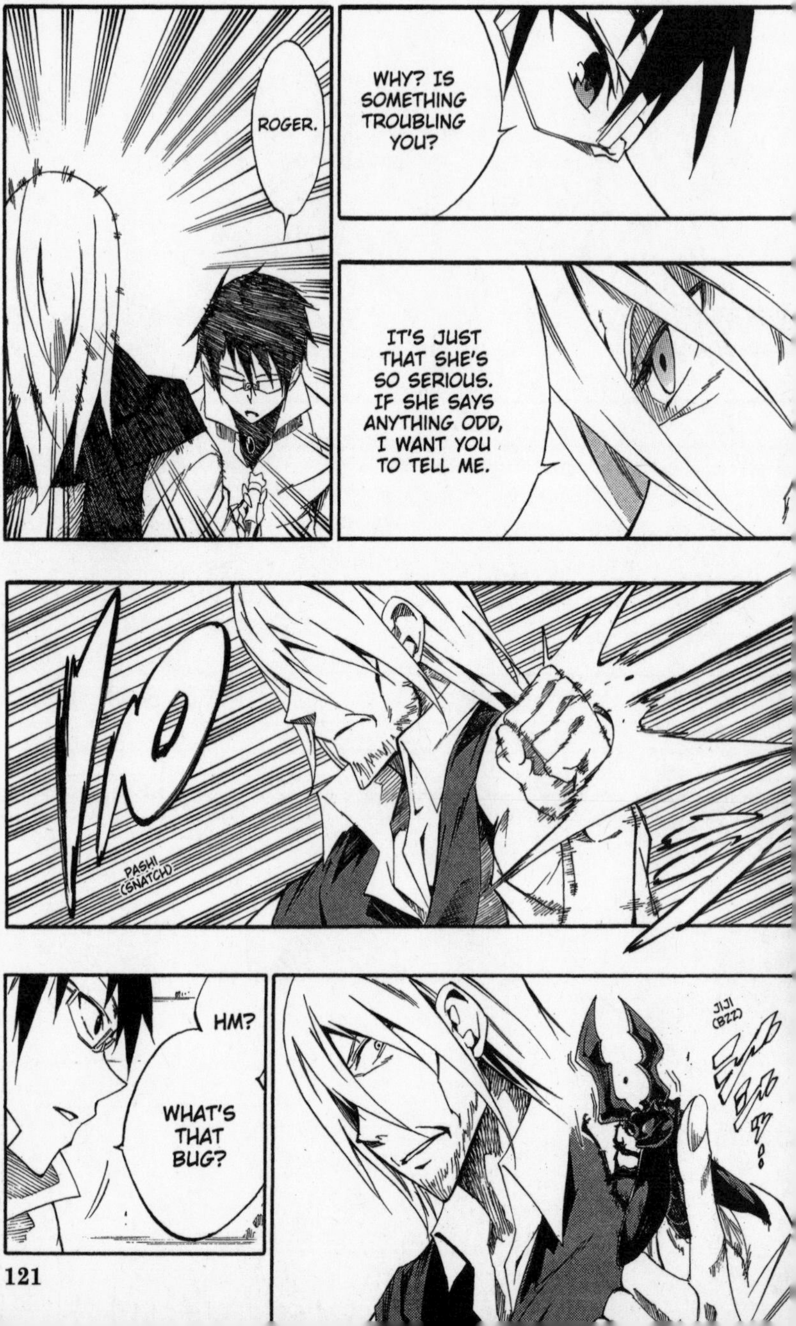
WHY? IS SOMETHING TROUBLING YOU?
IT'S JUST THAT SHE'S SO SERIOUS. IF SHE SAYS ANYTHING ODD, I WANT YOU TO TELL ME.
ROGER.
PASHI (SNATCH)
JIJI (BZZ)
HM?
WHAT'S THAT BUG?

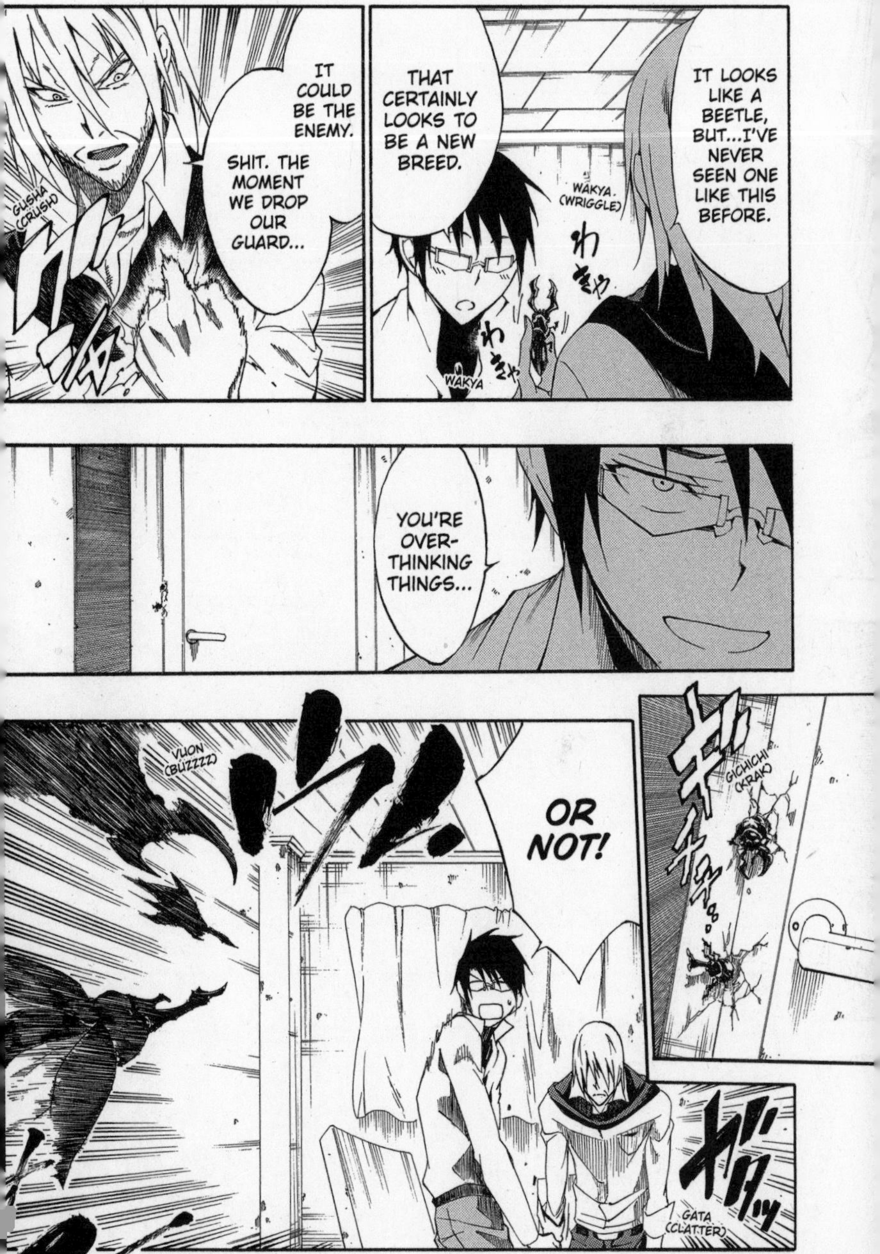
IT LOOKS LIKE A BEETLE, BUT...I'VE NEVER SEEN ONE LIKE THIS BEFORE.
WAKYA. (WRIGGLE)
WAKYA
THAT CERTAINLY LOOKS TO BE A NEW BREED.
IT COULD BE THE ENEMY.
SHIT. THE MOMENT WE DROP OUR GUARD...
GUSHA (CRUSH)
YOU'RE OVER-THINKING THINGS...
GICHICHI (KRAK)
OR NOT!
VUON (BUZZZZ)
GATA (CLATTER)

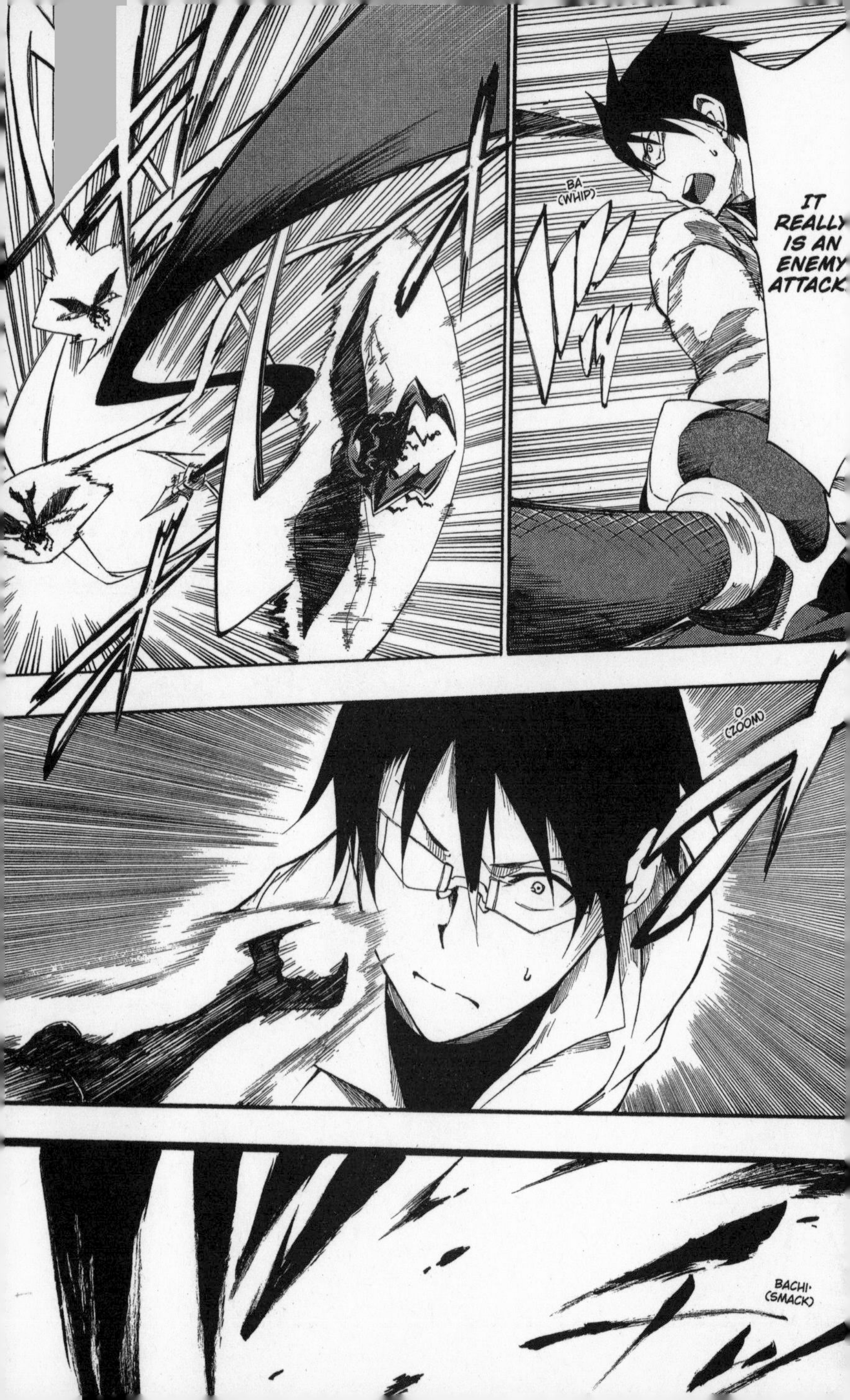
IT REALLY IS AN ENEMY ATTACK
BA (WHIP)
O (ZOOM)
BACHI· (SMACK)

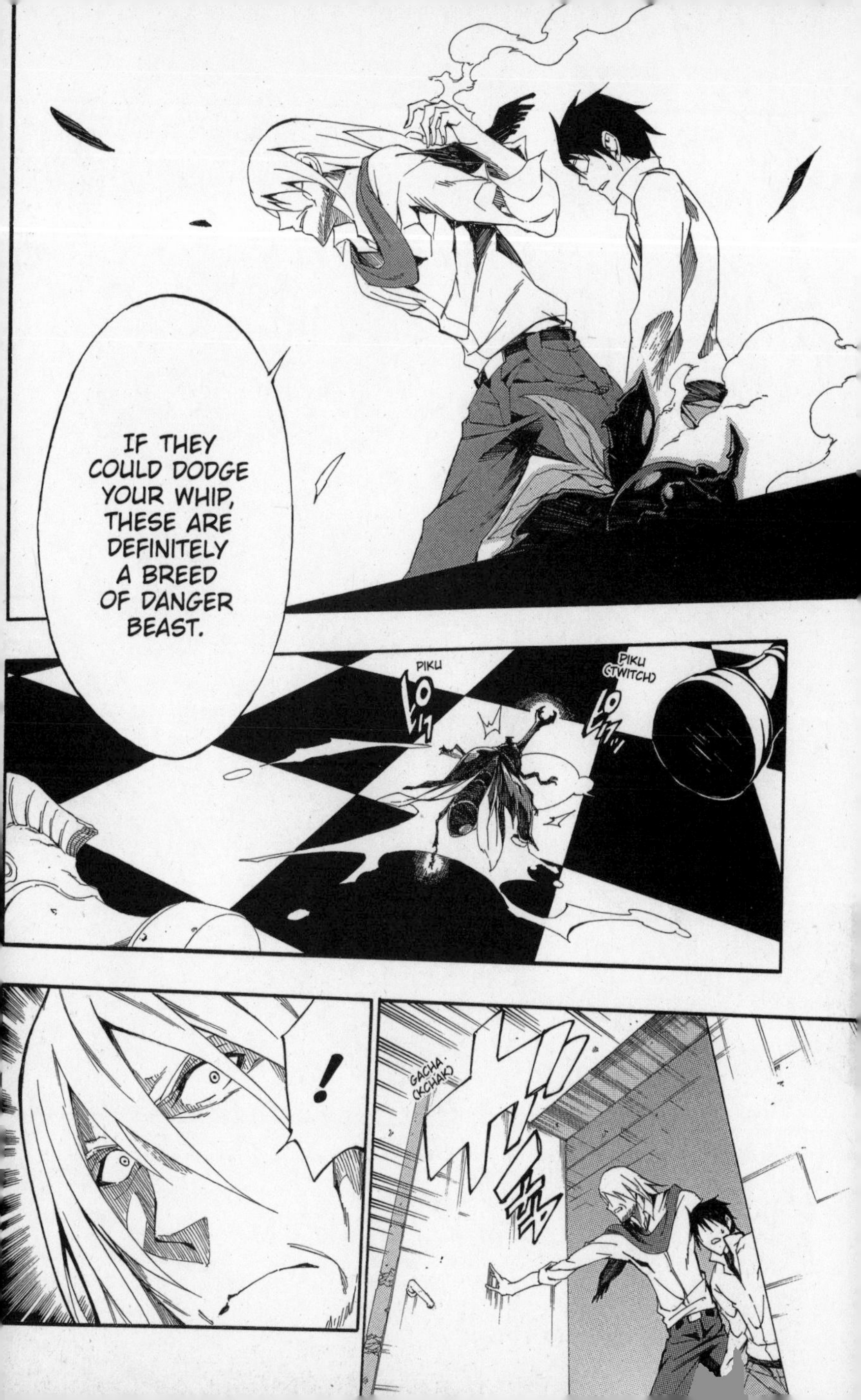
IF THEY COULD DODGE YOUR WHIP, THESE ARE DEFINITELY A BREED OF DANGER BEAST.
PIKU (TWITCH)
PIKU
!
GACHA (KCHAK)

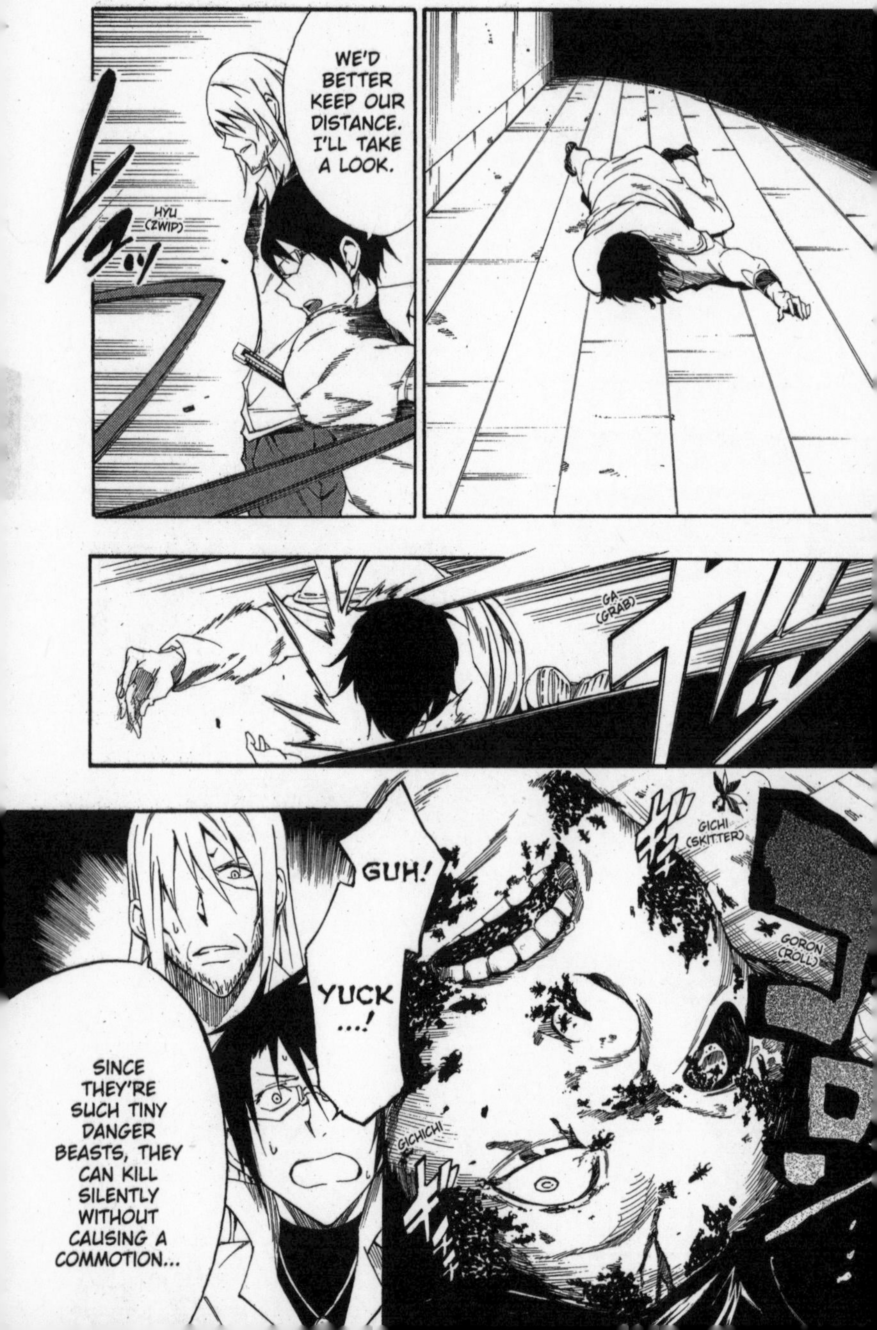
WE'D BETTER KEEP OUR DISTANCE. I'LL TAKE A LOOK.
HYU (ZWIP)
GA (GRAB)
GICHI (SKITTER)
GORON (ROLL)
GUH!
YUCK ...!
GICHICHI
SINCE THEY'RE SUCH TINY DANGER BEASTS, THEY CAN KILL SILENTLY WITHOUT CAUSING A COMMOTION...

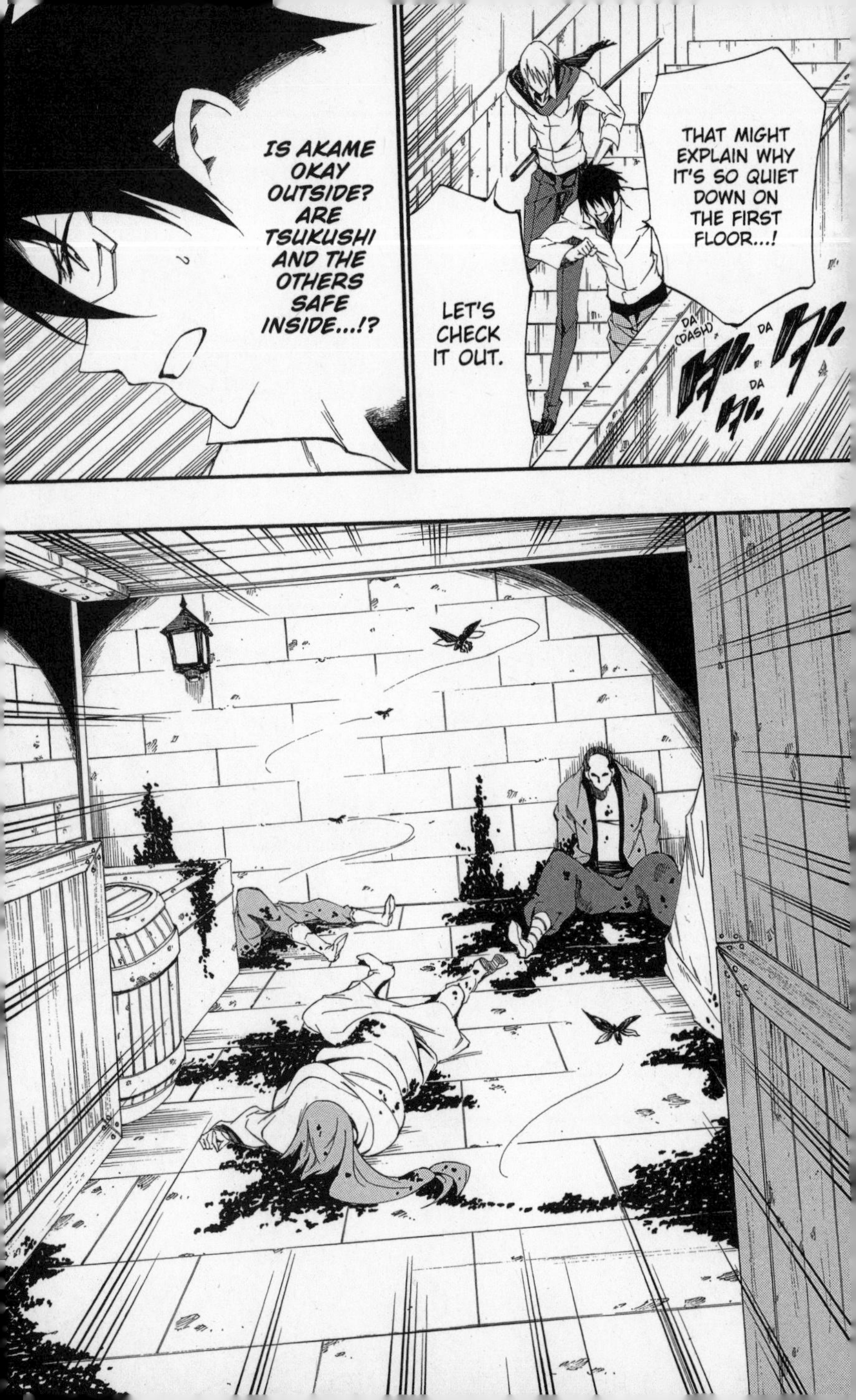
THAT MIGHT EXPLAIN WHY IT'S SO QUIET DOWN ON THE FIRST FLOOR...!
DA (DASH) DA DA
LET'S CHECK IT OUT.
IS AKAME OKAY OUTSIDE? ARE TSUKUSHI AND THE OTHERS SAFE INSIDE...!?

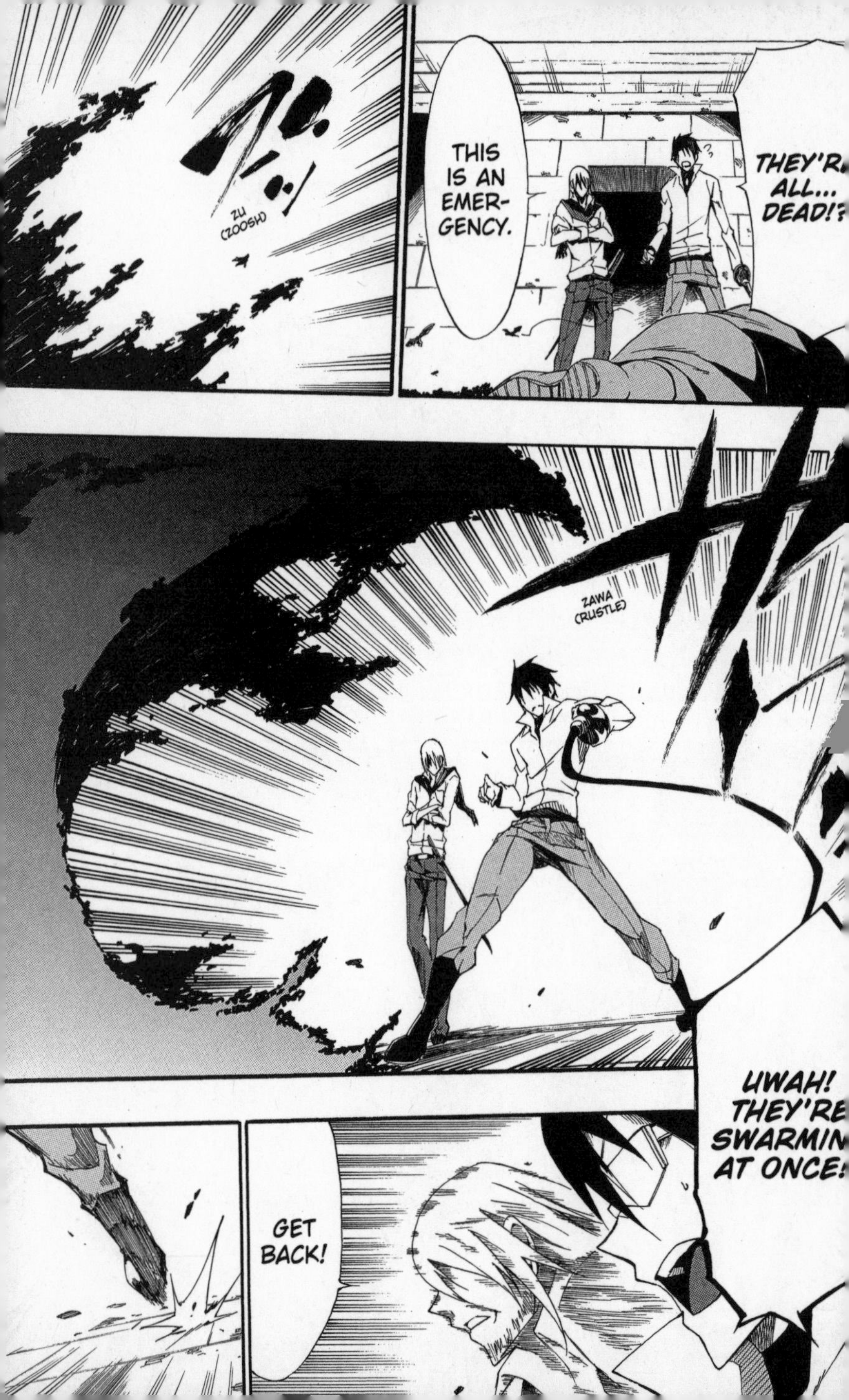
THEY'R... ALL... DEAD!?
THIS IS AN EMER-GENCY.
ZU (ZOOSH)
ZAWA (RUSTLE)
UWAH! THEY'RE SWARMIN AT ONCE!
GET BACK!

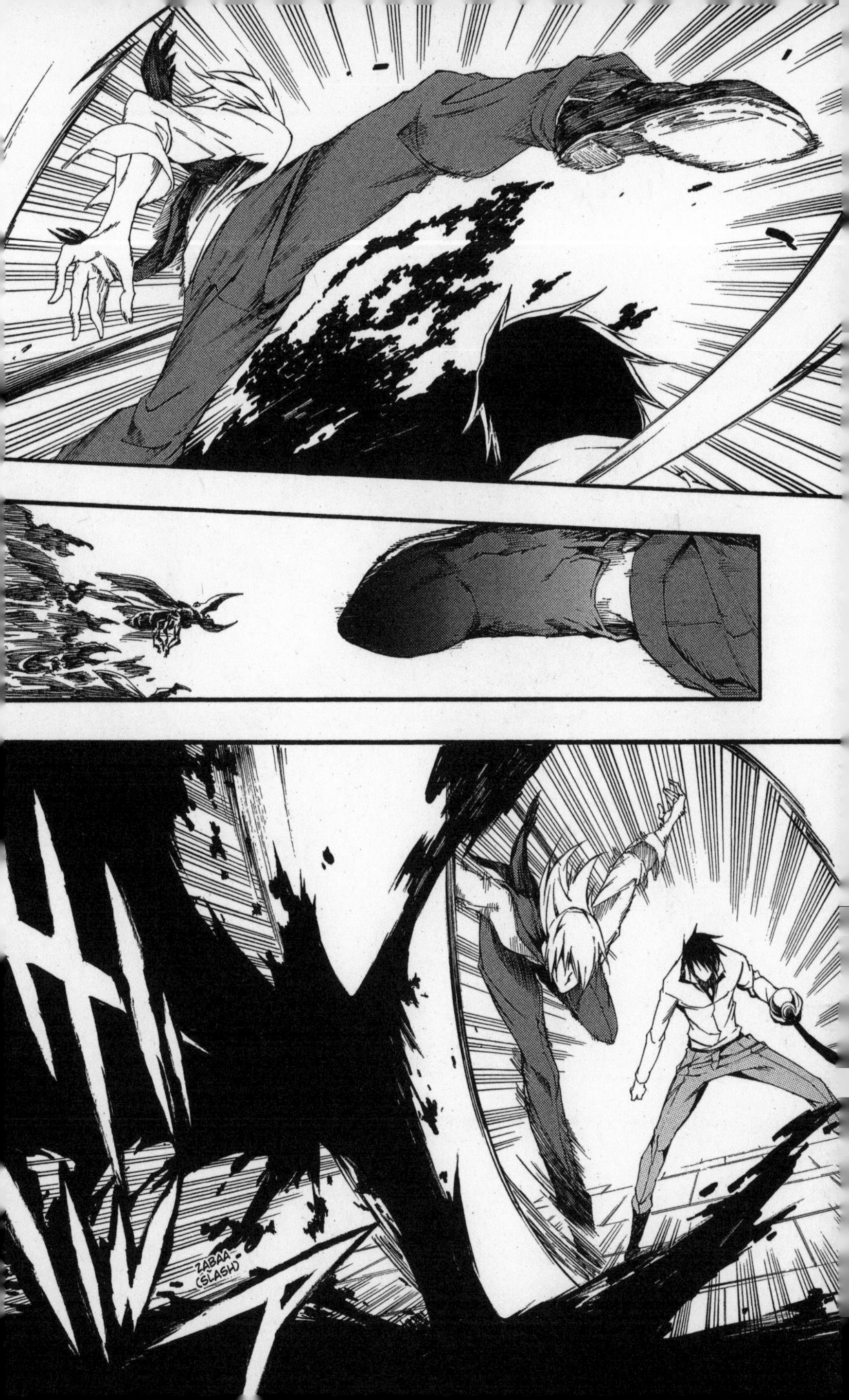
ZABAA
(SLASH)

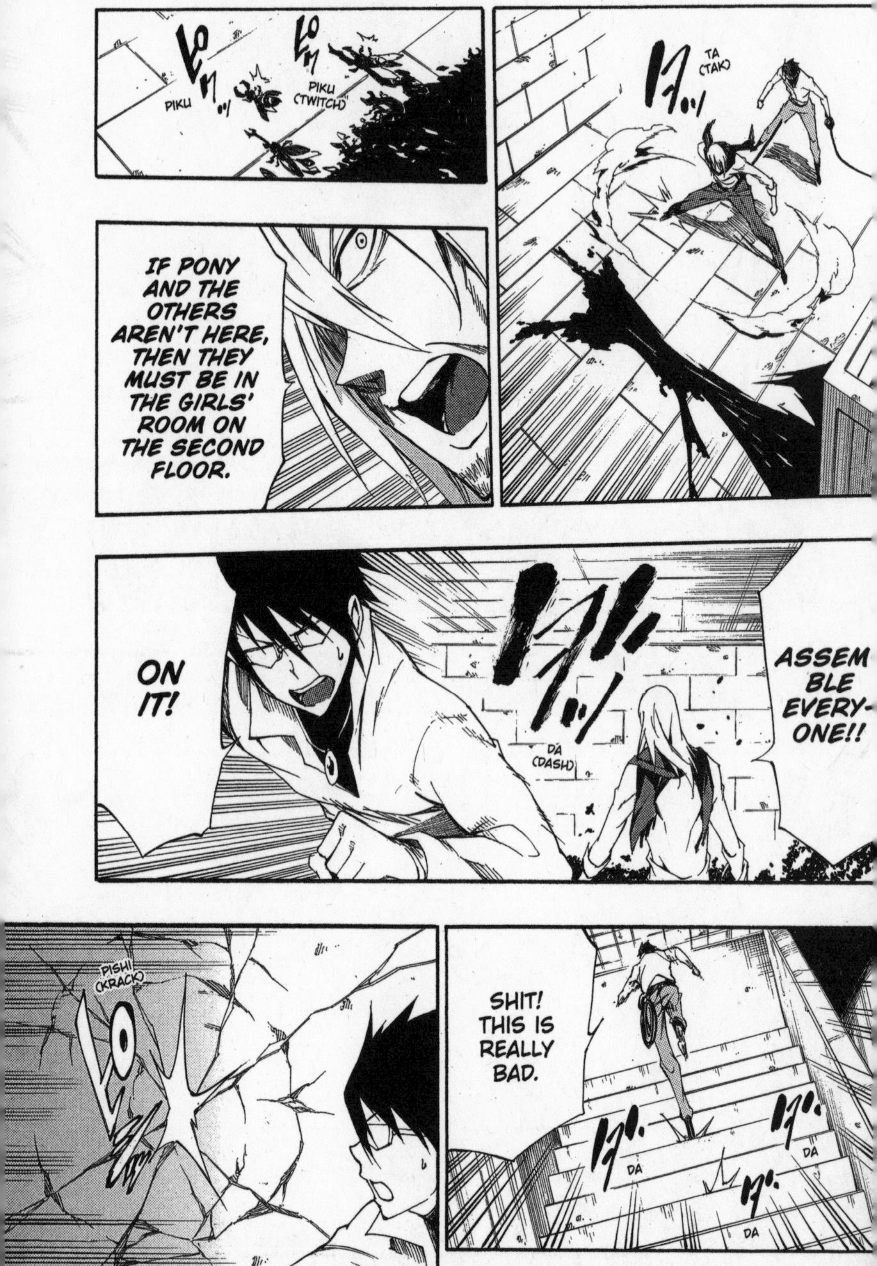
TA
(TAK)
PIKU
PIKU
(TWITCH)
IF PONY AND THE OTHERS AREN'T HERE, THEN THEY MUST BE IN THE GIRLS' ROOM ON THE SECOND FLOOR.
ASSEMBLE EVERYONE!!
DA
(DASH)
ON IT!
SHIT! THIS IS REALLY BAD.
DA
DA
DA
PISHI
(KRACK)

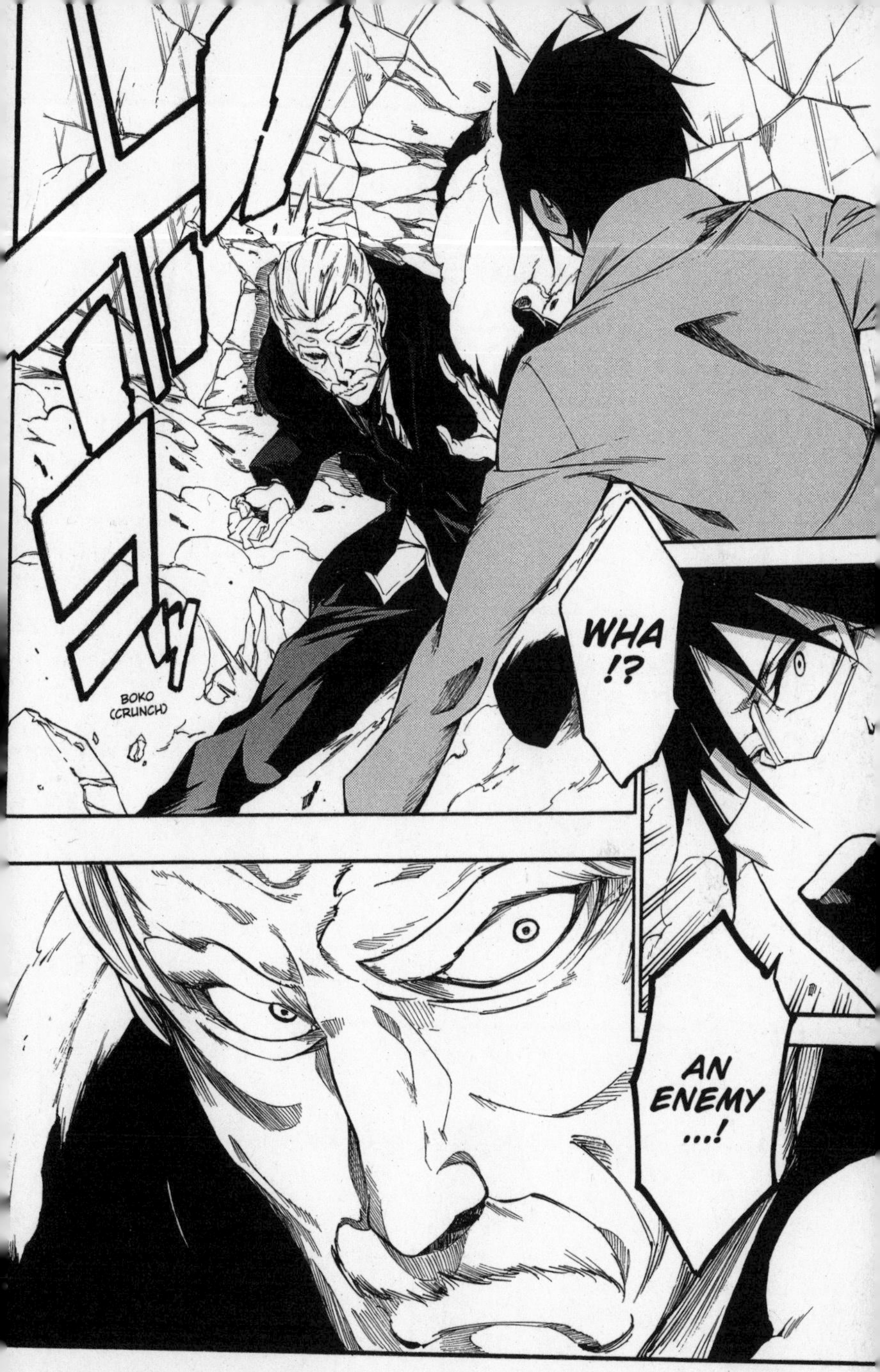
WHA !?
BOKO (CRUNCH)
AN ENEMY ...!

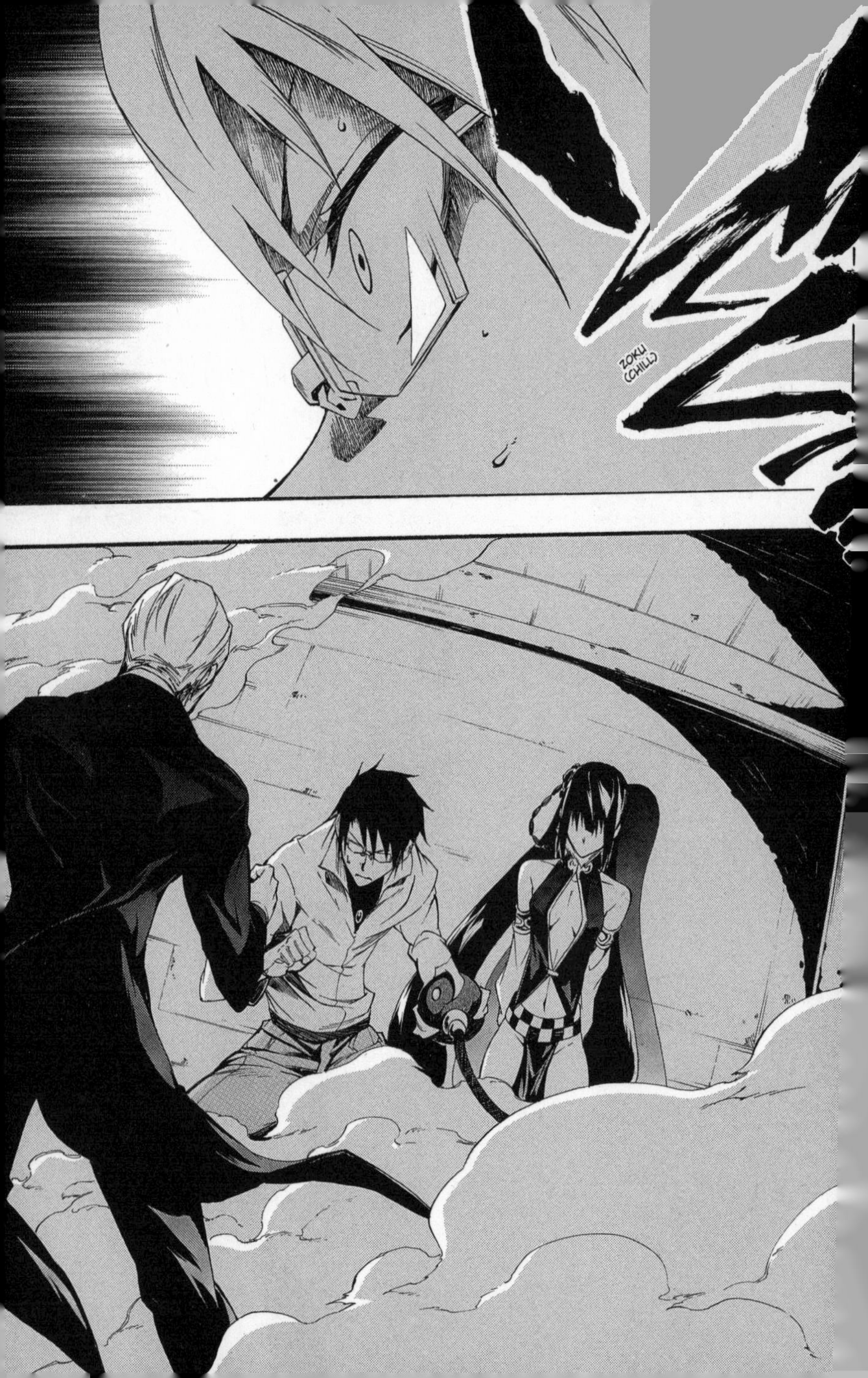
ZOKU
(CHILL)

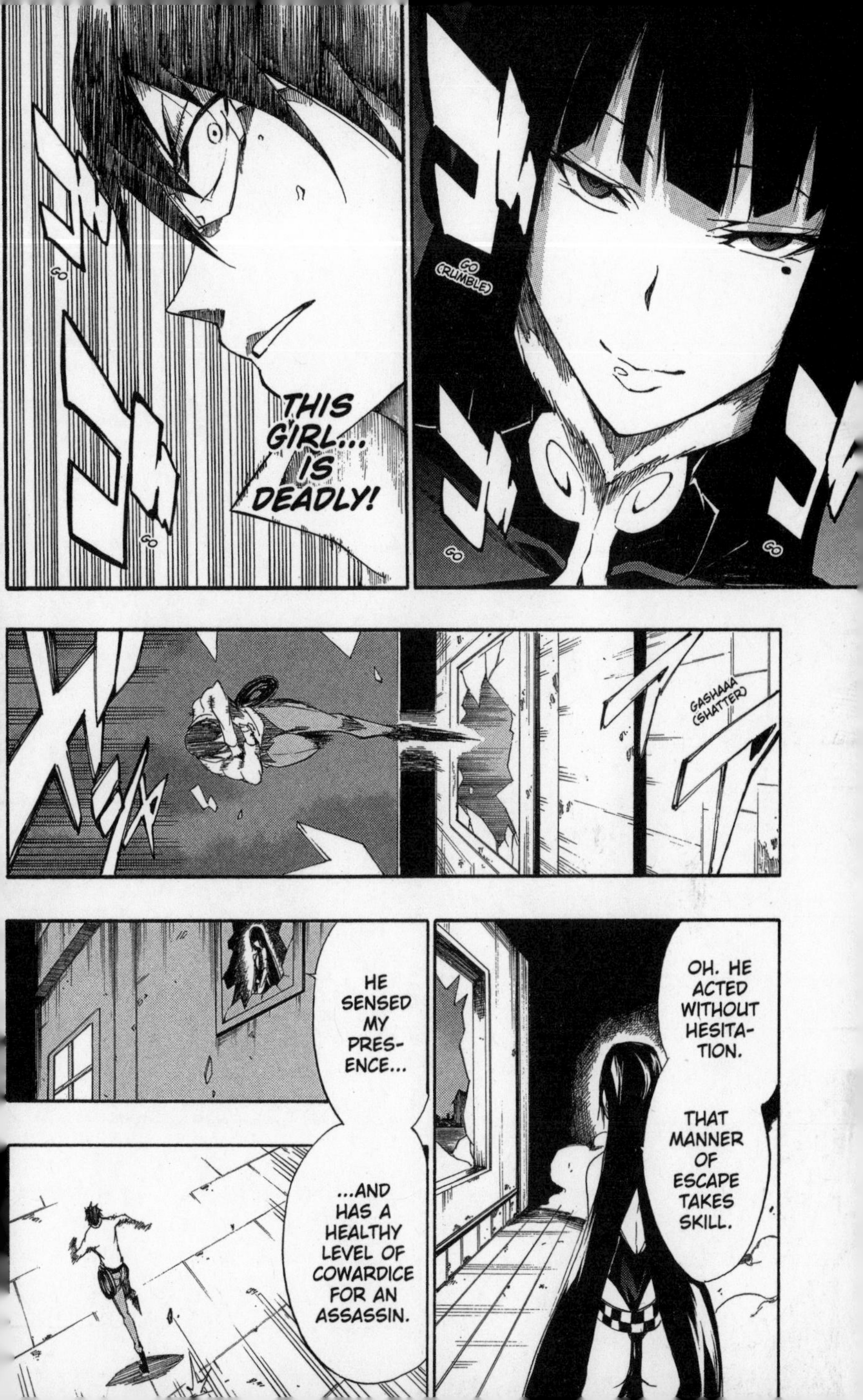
GO (RUMBLE)
GO
GO
GO
GO
THIS GIRL... IS DEADLY!
GASHAAA (SHATTER)
OH. HE ACTED WITHOUT HESITA-TION.
THAT MANNER OF ESCAPE TAKES SKILL.
HE SENSED MY PRES-ENCE...
...AND HAS A HEALTHY LEVEL OF COWARDICE FOR AN ASSASSIN.

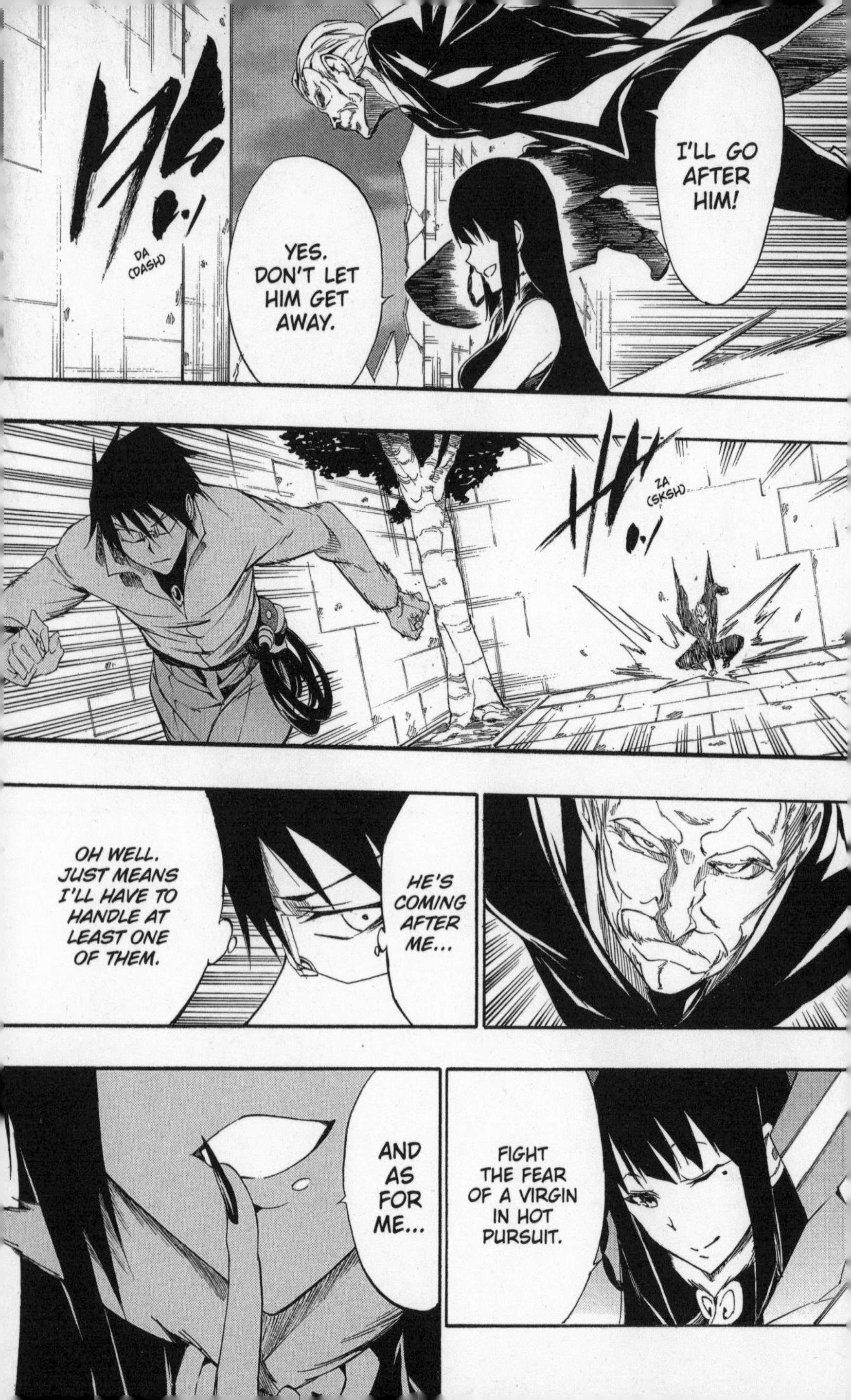
I'LL GO AFTER HIM!
YES. DON'T LET HIM GET AWAY.
DA (DASH)
ZA (SKSH)
HE'S COMING AFTER ME...
OH WELL. JUST MEANS I'LL HAVE TO HANDLE AT LEAST ONE OF THEM.
FIGHT THE FEAR OF A VIRGIN IN HOT PURSUIT.
AND AS FOR ME...

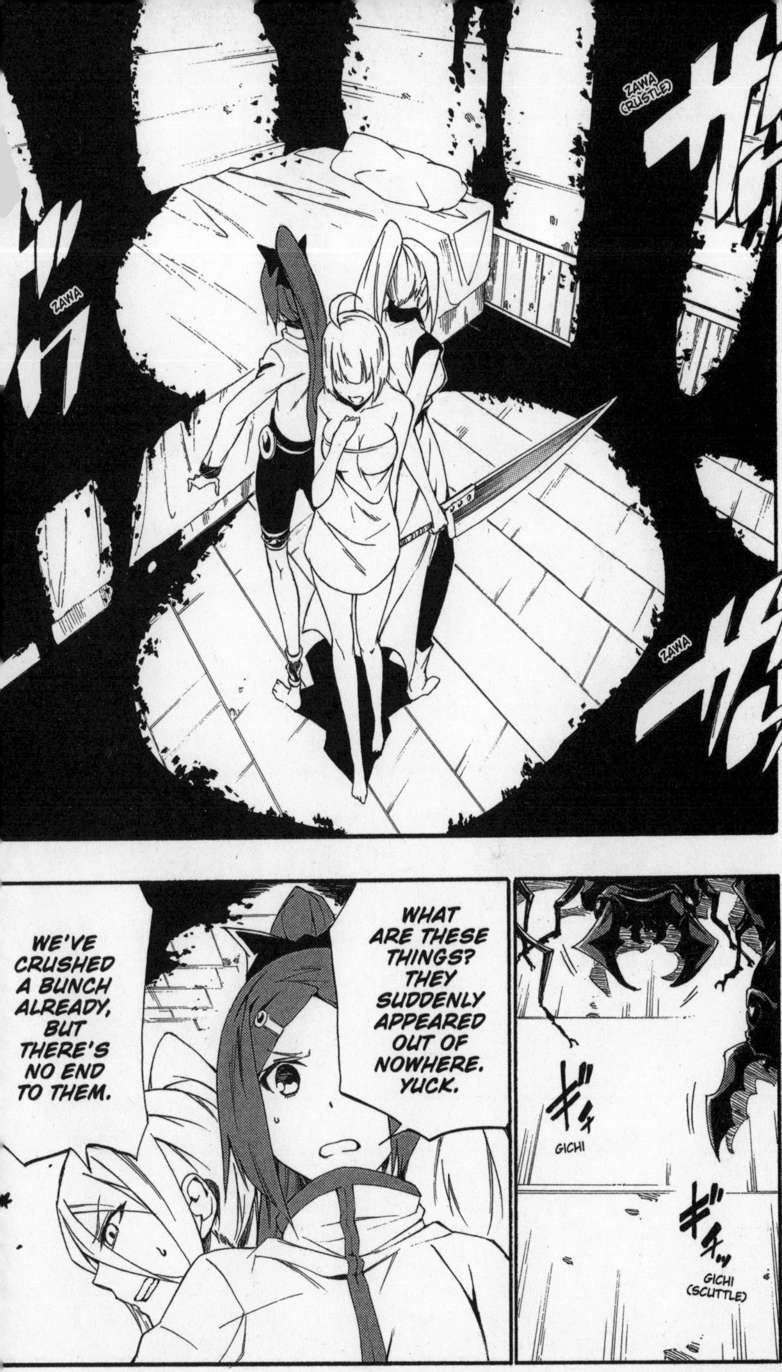
ZAWA (RUSTLE)
ZAWA
ZAWA
GICHI
GICHI (SCUTTLE)
WHAT ARE THESE THINGS? THEY SUDDENLY APPEARED OUT OF NOWHERE. YUCK.
WE'VE CRUSHED A BUNCH ALREADY, BUT THERE'S NO END TO THEM.

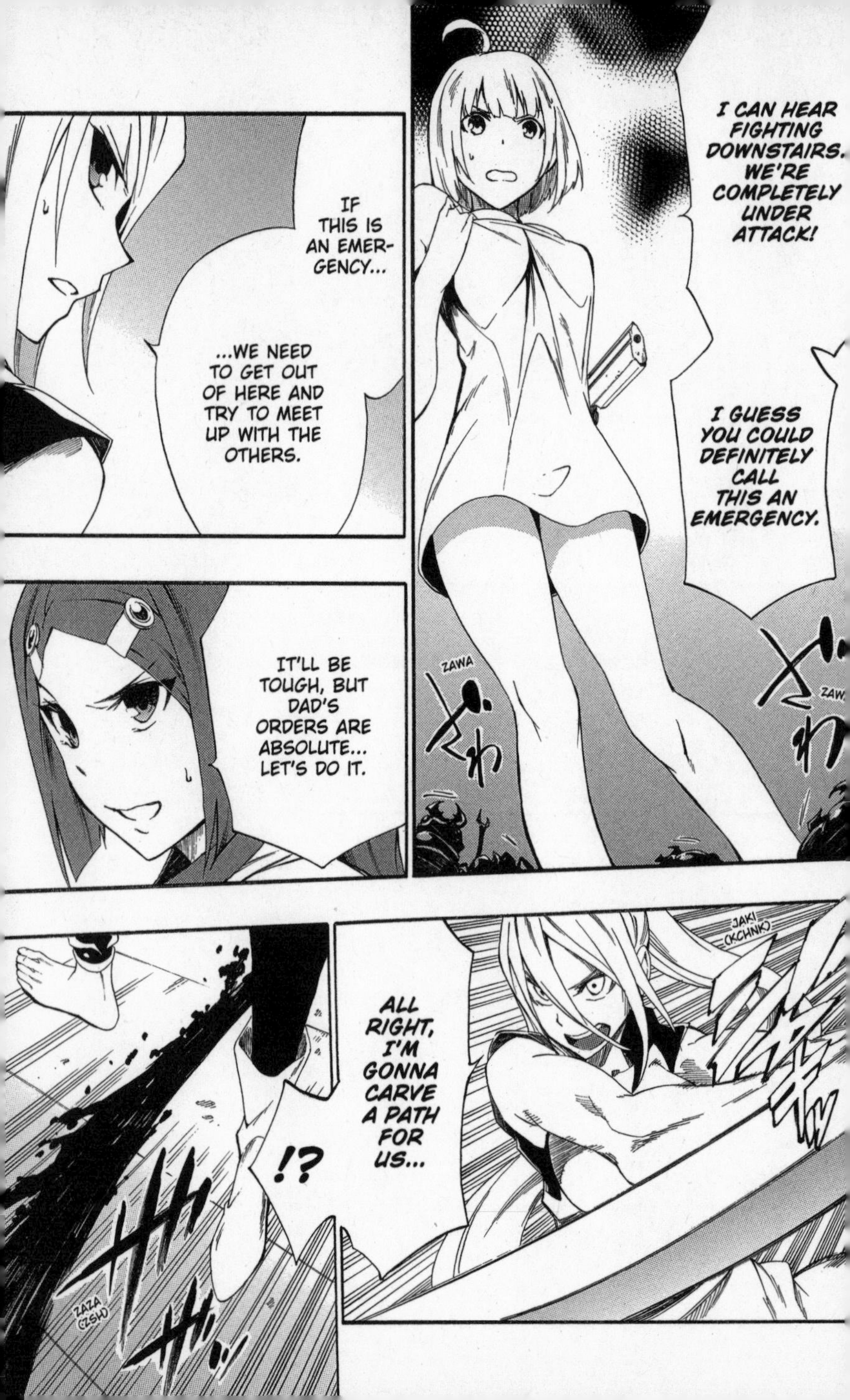
I CAN HEAR FIGHTING DOWNSTAIRS. WE'RE COMPLETELY UNDER ATTACK!
I GUESS YOU COULD DEFINITELY CALL THIS AN EMERGENCY.
ZAWA
IF THIS IS AN EMER-GENCY...
...WE NEED TO GET OUT OF HERE AND TRY TO MEET UP WITH THE OTHERS.
IT'LL BE TOUGH, BUT DAD'S ORDERS ARE ABSOLUTE... LET'S DO IT.
JAKI (KCHNK)
ALL RIGHT, I'M GONNA CARVE A PATH FOR US...
!?
ZAZA (ZSH)

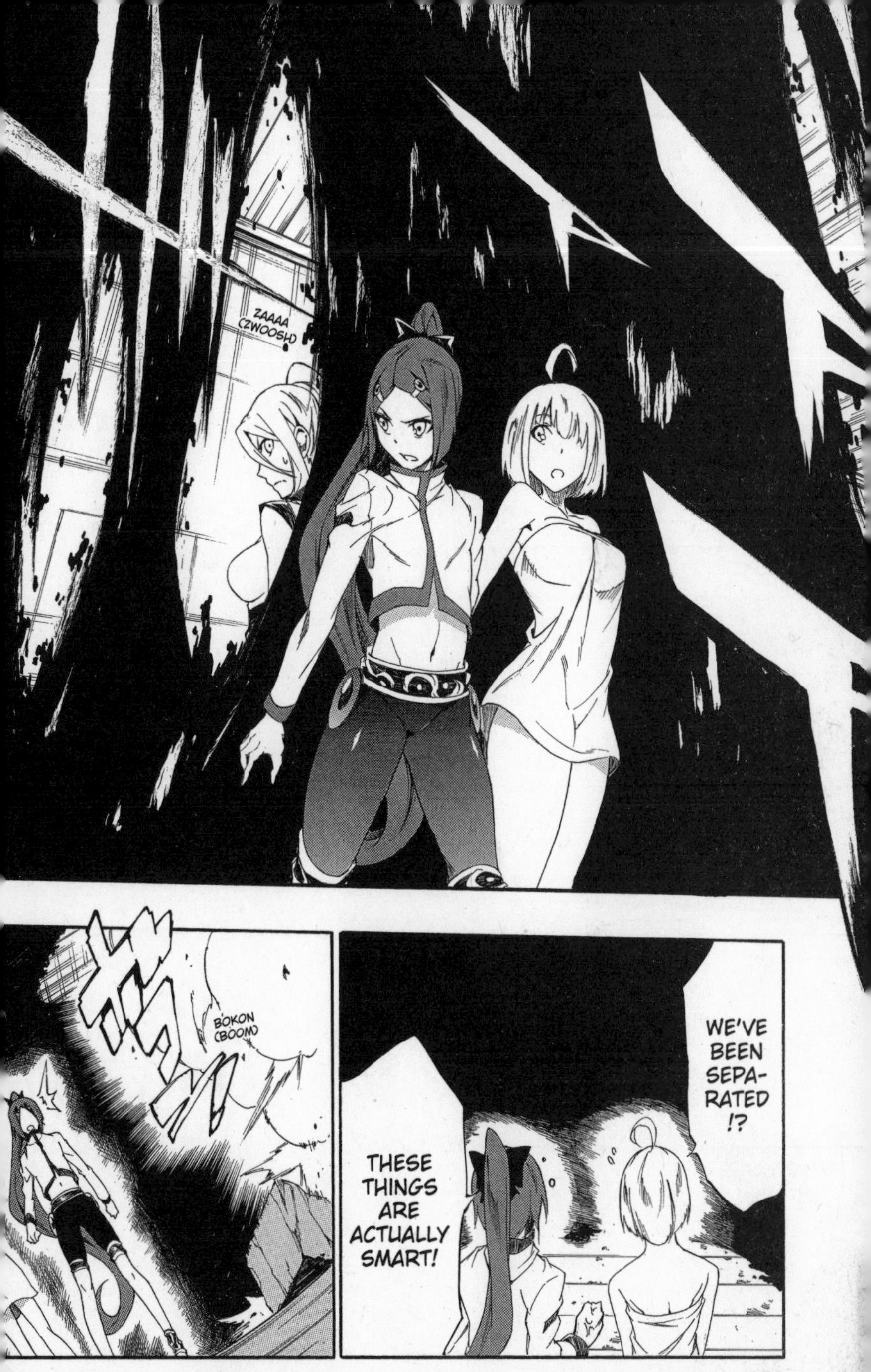
ZAAAA (ZWOOSH)
WE'VE BEEN SEPA-RATED!?
THESE THINGS ARE ACTUALLY SMART!
BOKON (BOOM)

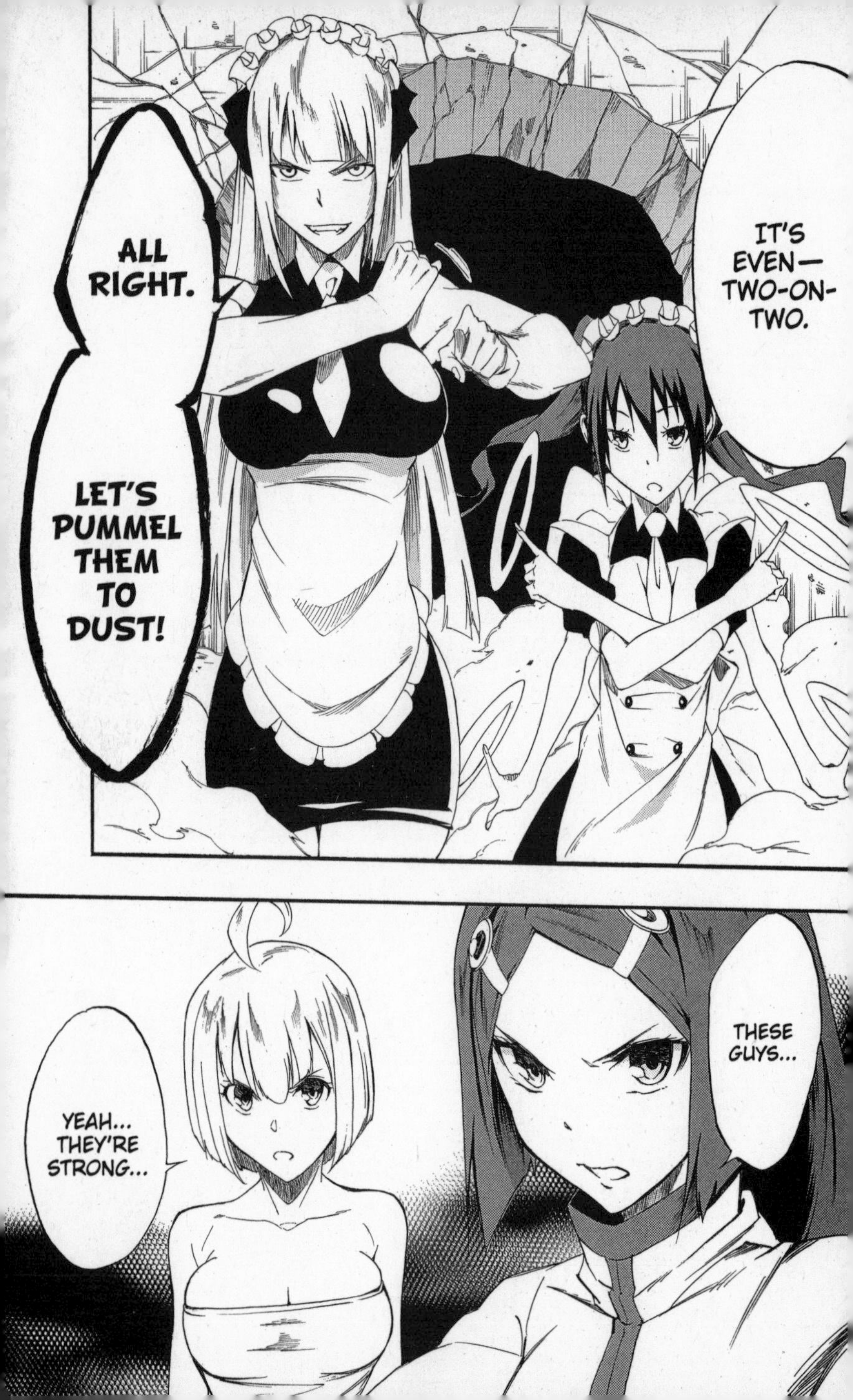
IT'S EVEN—TWO-ON-TWO.
ALL RIGHT.
LET'S PUMMEL THEM TO DUST!
THESE GUYS...
YEAH... THEY'RE STRONG...

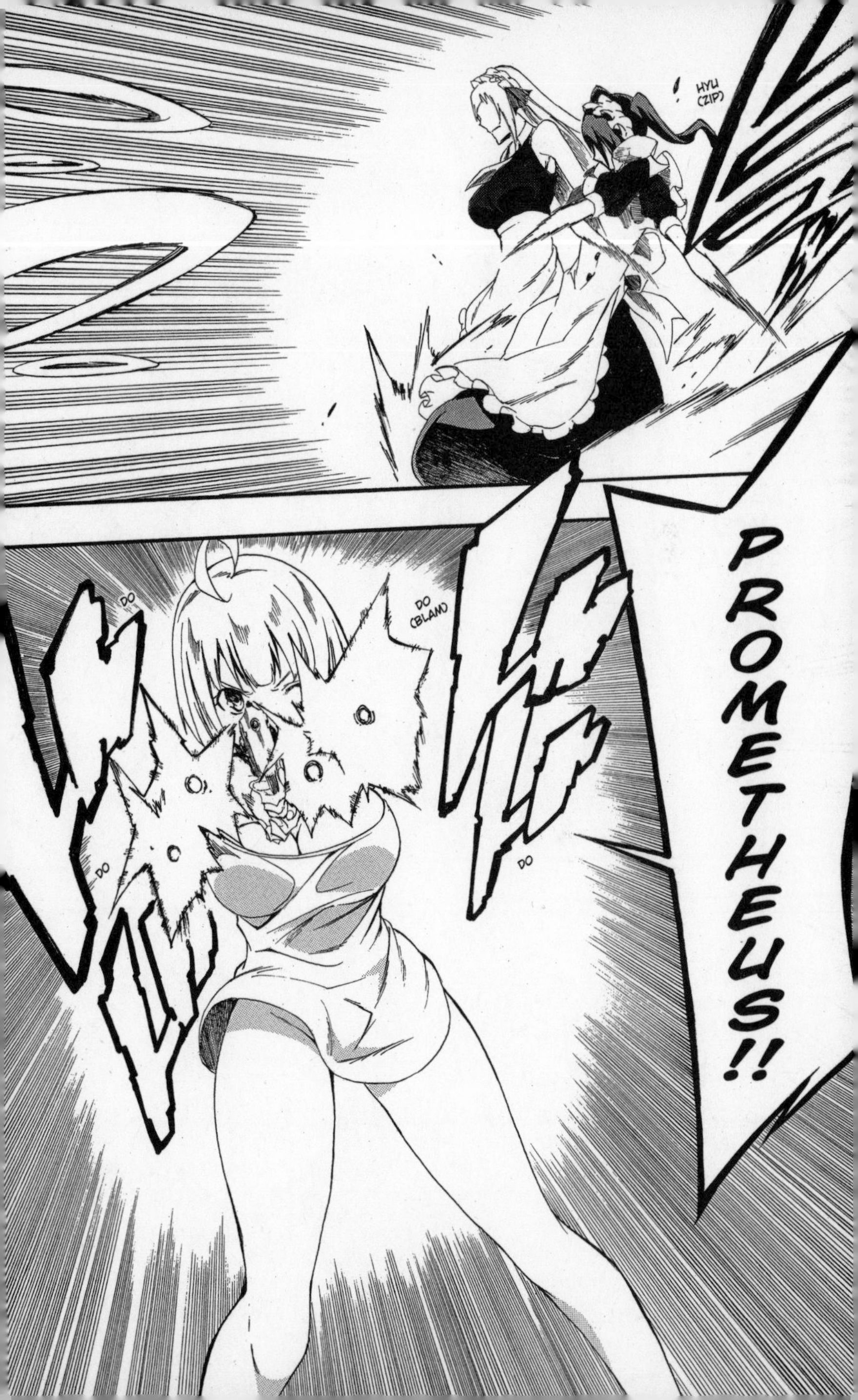
HYU (ZIP)
PROMETHEUS!!
DO (BLAM)
DO
DO
DO

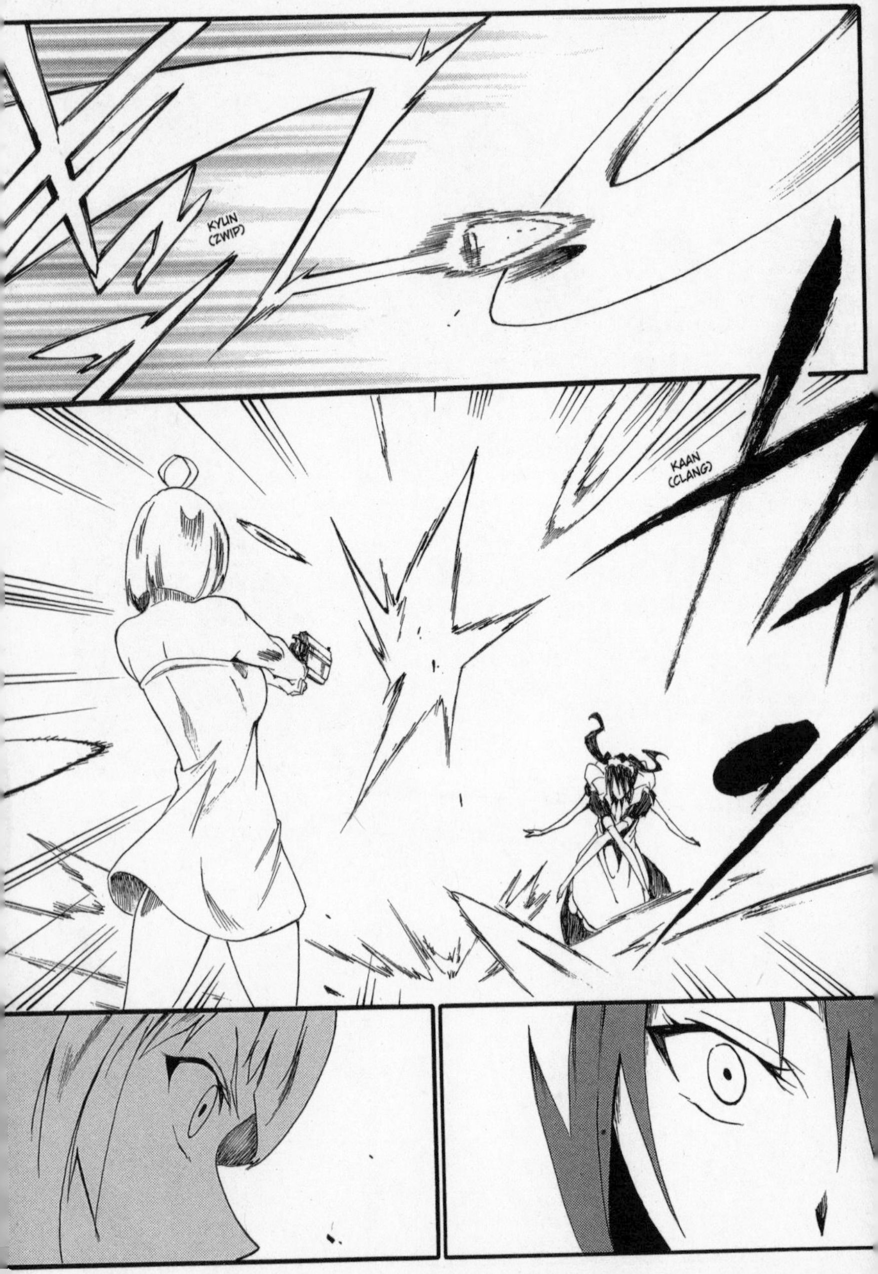
KYUN
(ZWIP)
KAAN
(CLANG)

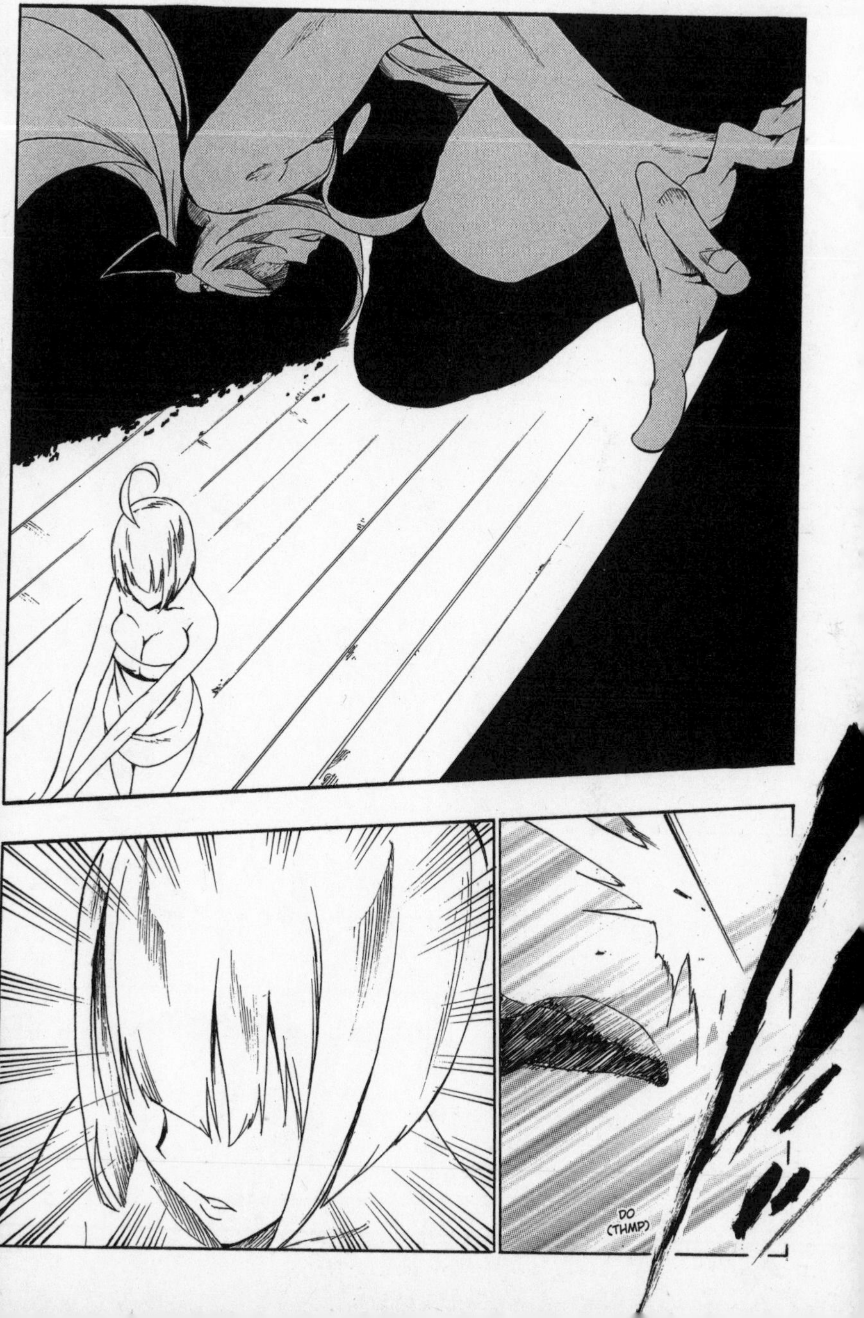
DO
(THMP)

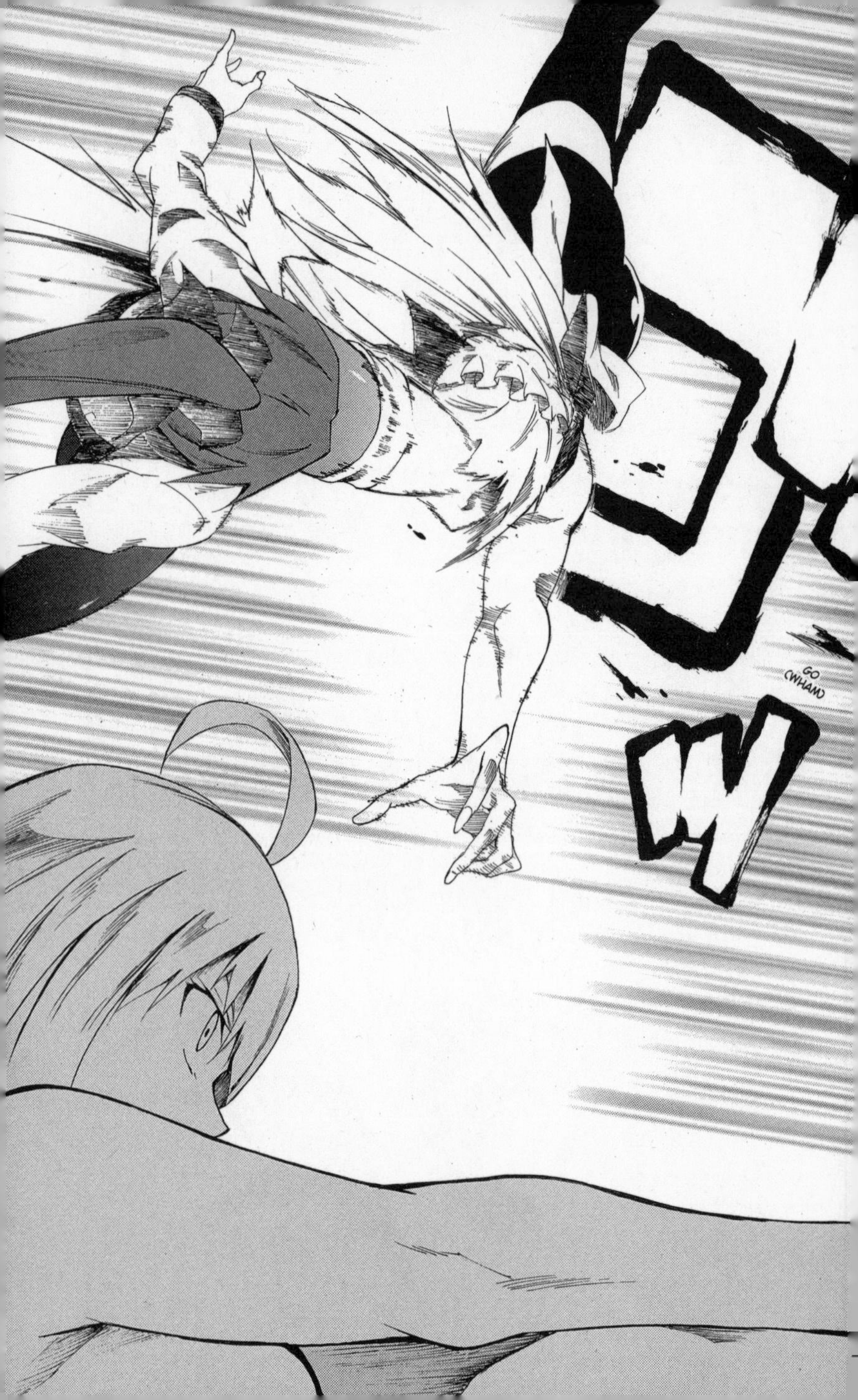
GO
(WHAM)

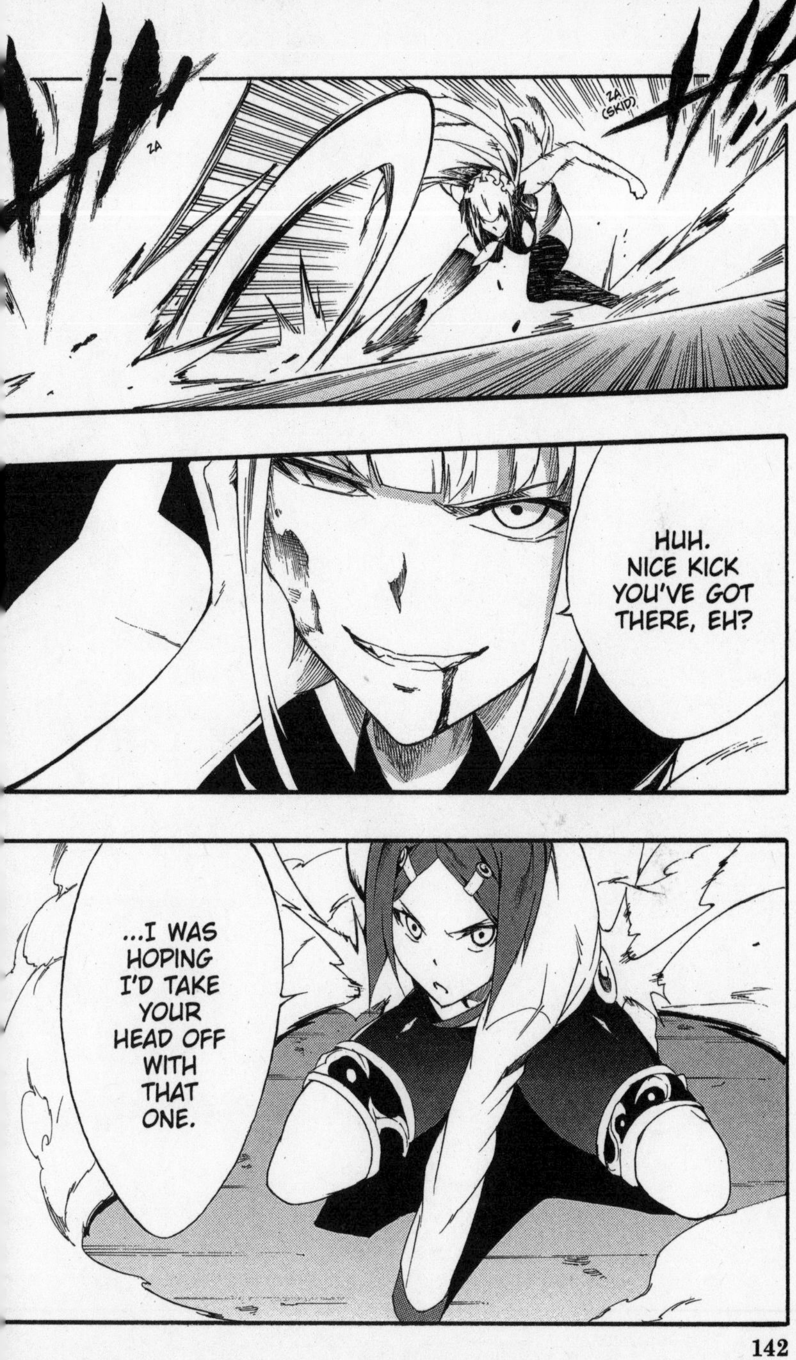
ZA (SKID)
ZA
HUH. NICE KICK YOU'VE GOT THERE, EH?
...I WAS HOPING I'D TAKE YOUR HEAD OFF WITH THAT ONE.

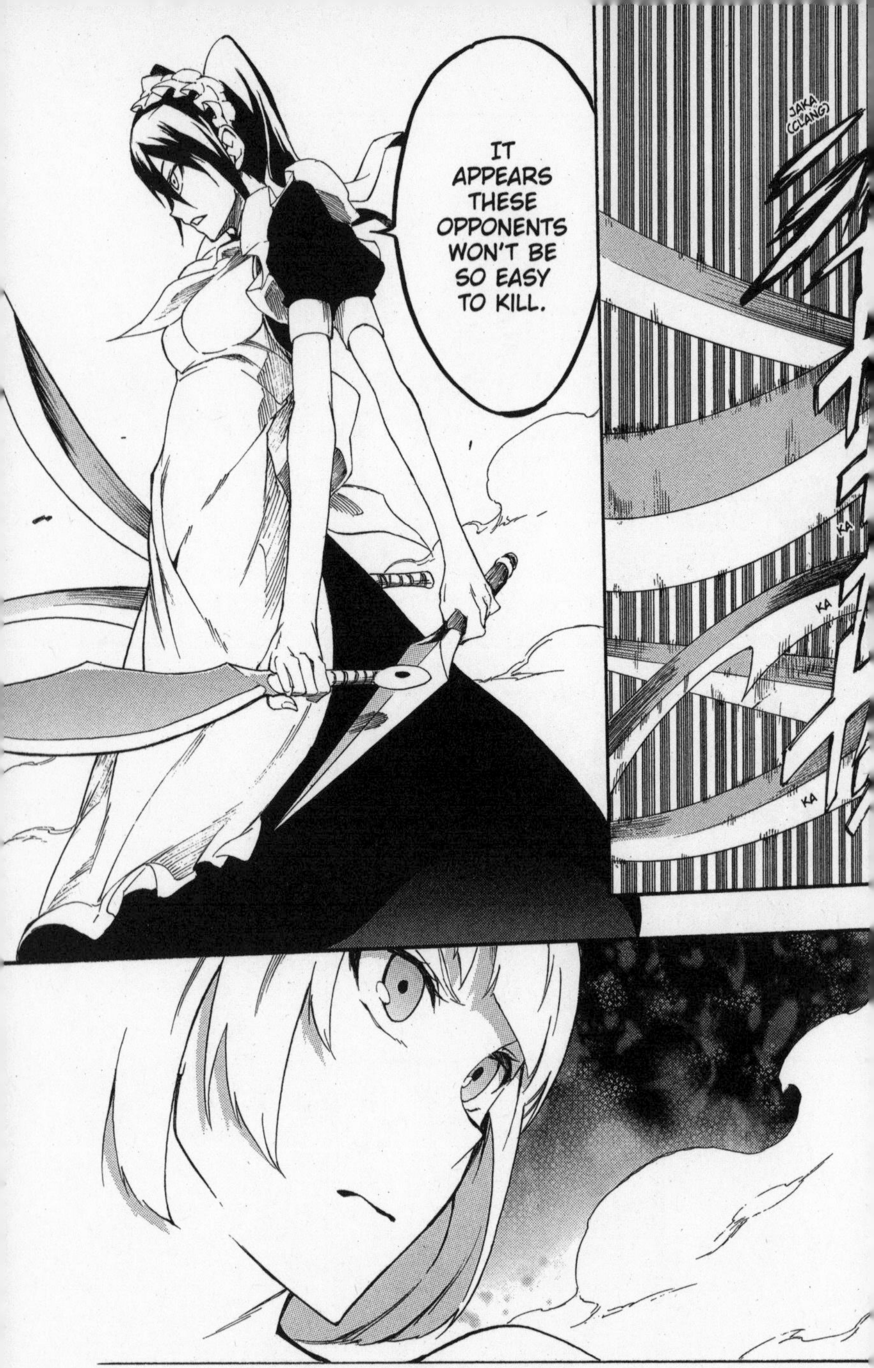
JAKA (CLANG)
KA
KA
KA
IT APPEARS THESE OPPONENTS WON'T BE SO EASY TO KILL.

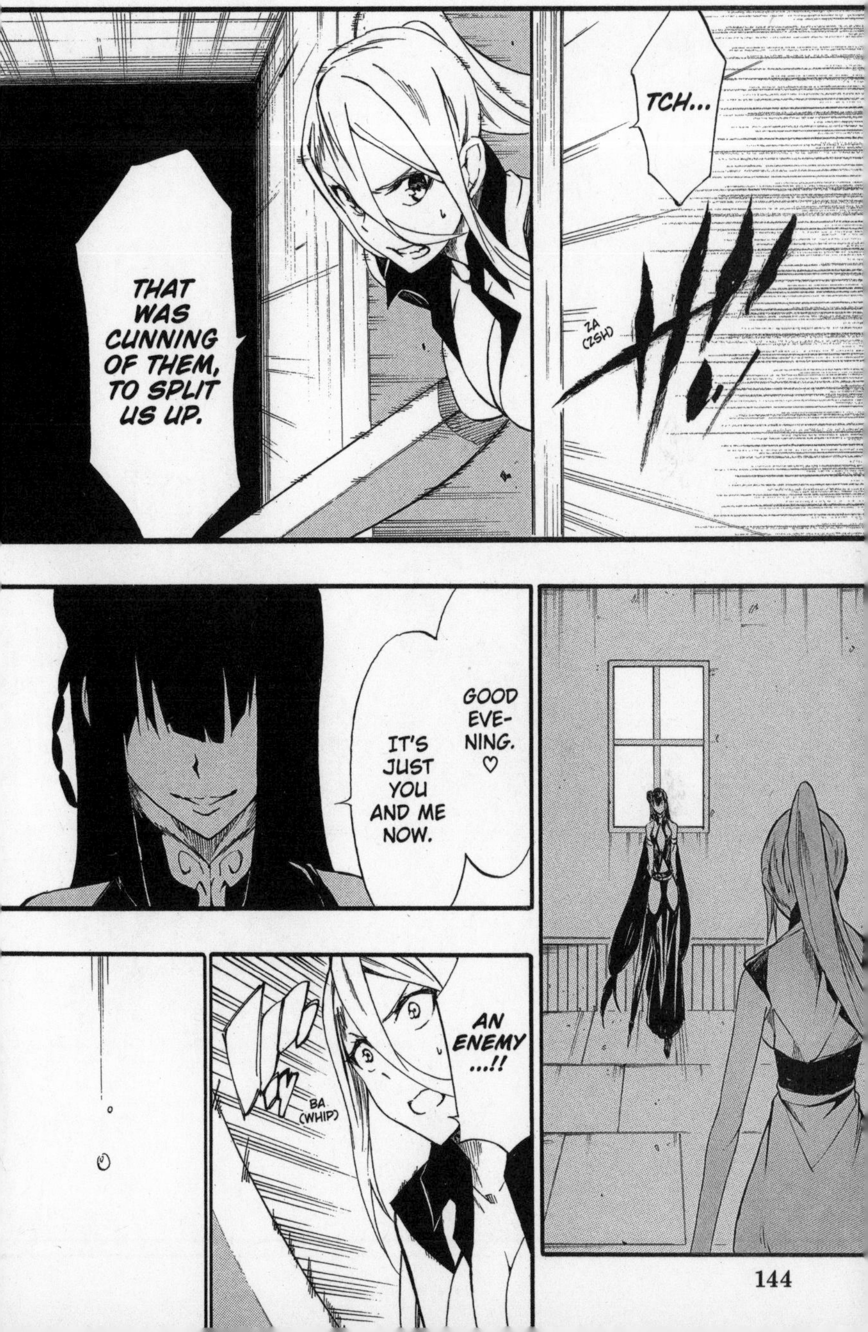
TCH...
ZA (ZSH)
THAT WAS CUNNING OF THEM, TO SPLIT US UP.
GOOD EVE- NING. ♡
IT'S JUST YOU AND ME NOW.
AN ENEMY ...!!
BA (WHIP)

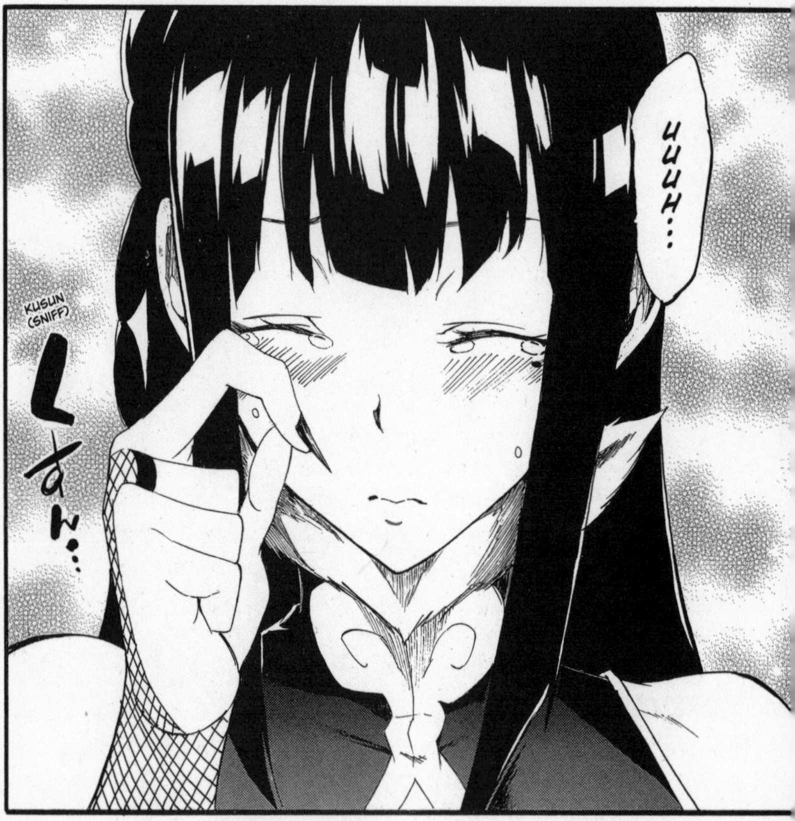
UUUH...
KUSUN (SNIFF)
くすん...

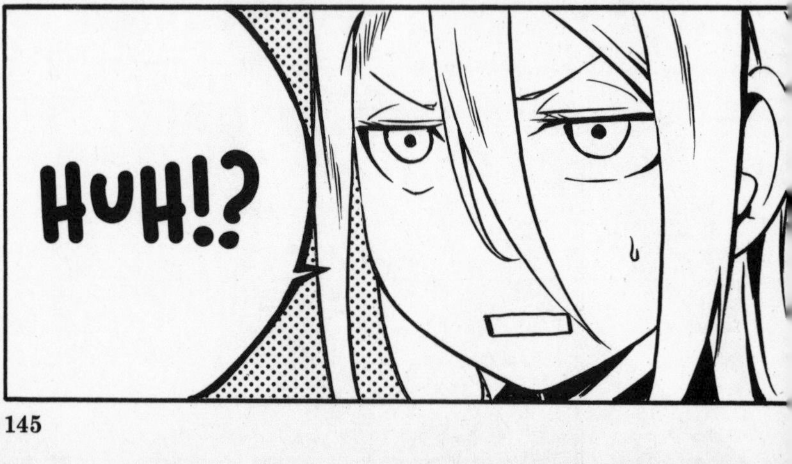
HUH!?

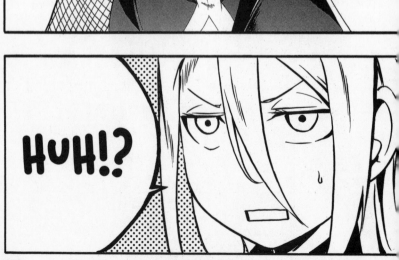

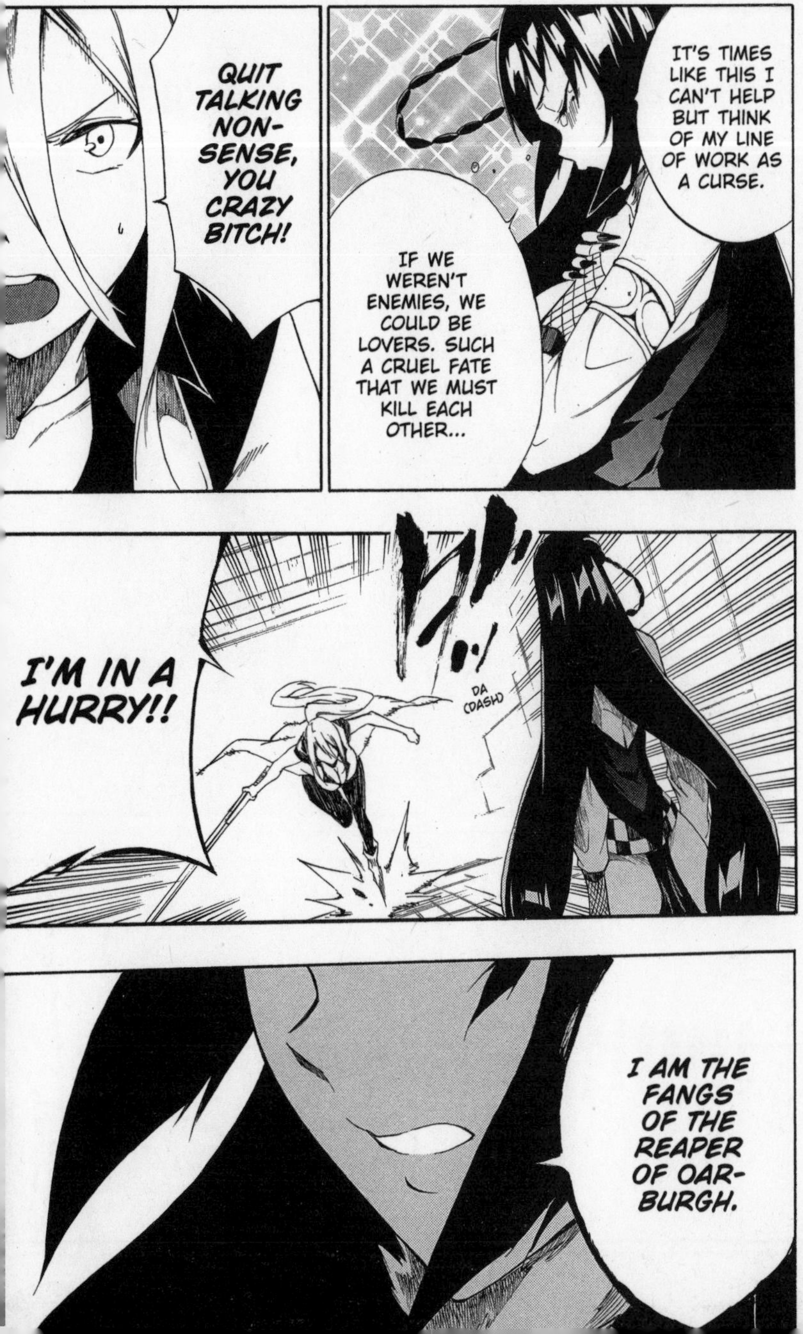
IT'S TIMES LIKE THIS I CAN'T HELP BUT THINK OF MY LINE OF WORK AS A CURSE.
IF WE WEREN'T ENEMIES, WE COULD BE LOVERS. SUCH A CRUEL FATE THAT WE MUST KILL EACH OTHER...
QUIT TALKING NON-SENSE, YOU CRAZY BITCH!
DA (DASH)
I'M IN A HURRY!!
I AM THE FANGS OF THE REAPER OF OAR-BURGH.

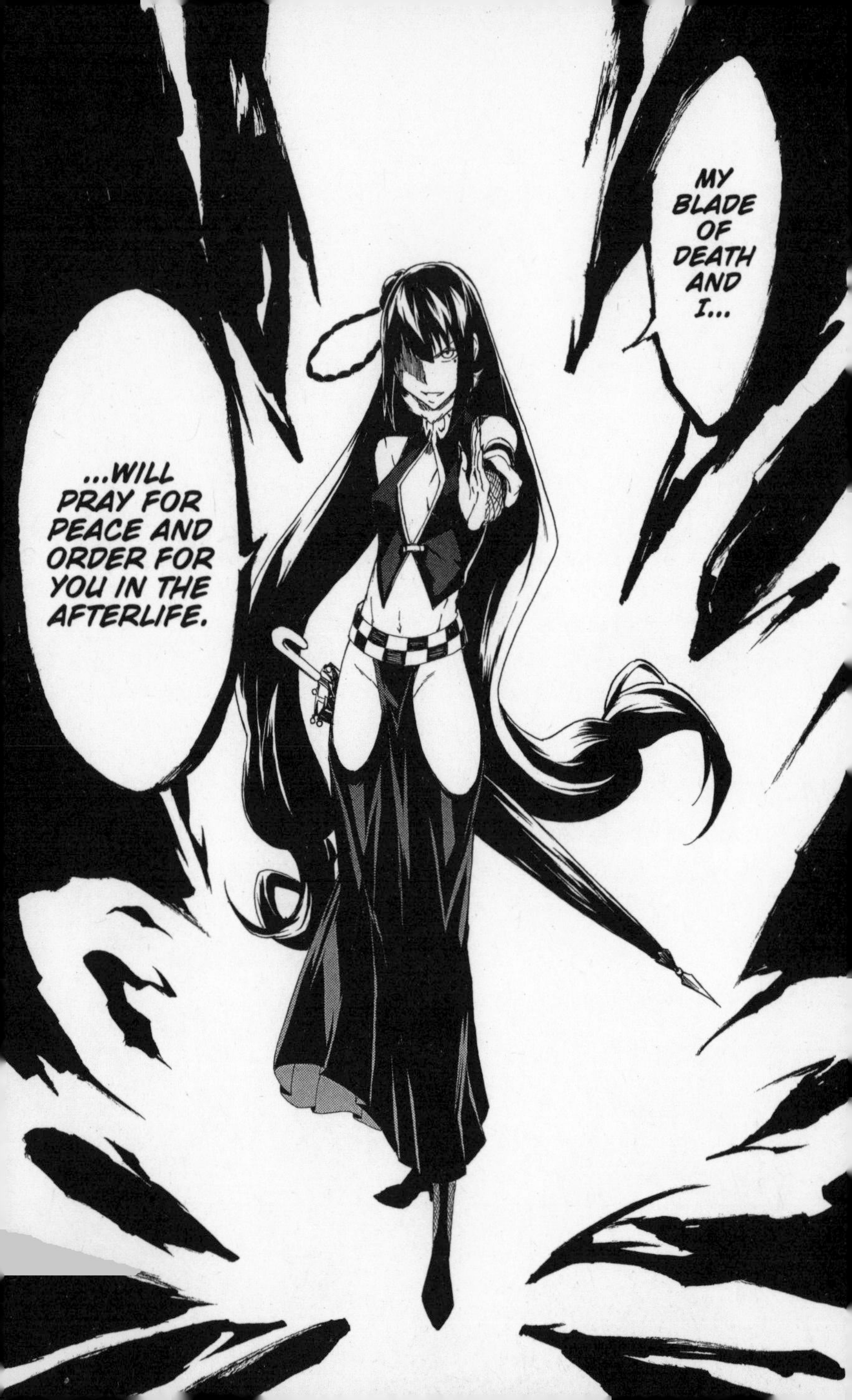
MY BLADE OF DEATH AND I...
...WILL PRAY FOR PEACE AND ORDER FOR YOU IN THE AFTERLIFE.

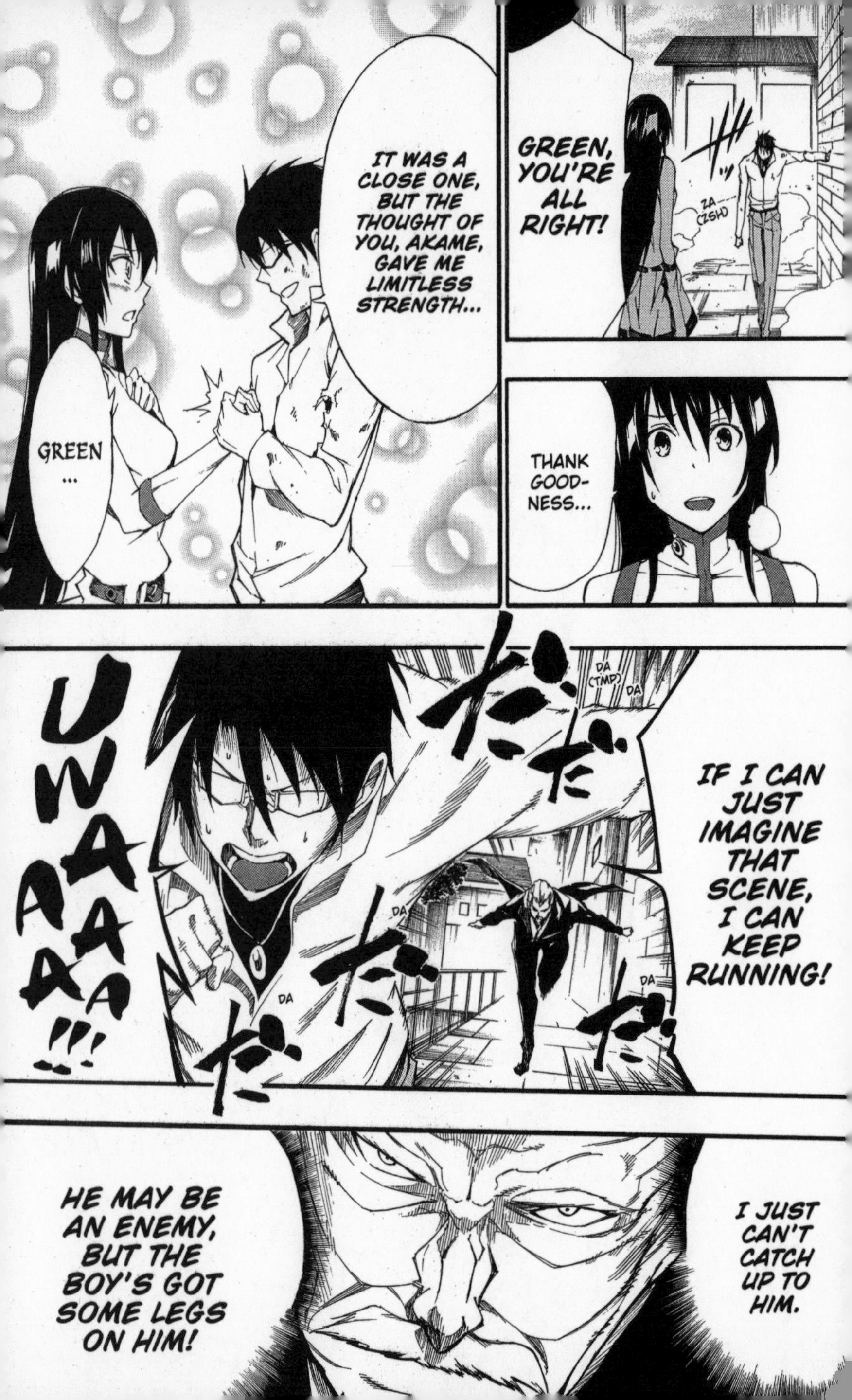

ZA (ZSH)
GREEN, YOU'RE ALL RIGHT!
THANK GOOD-NESS...
IT WAS A CLOSE ONE, BUT THE THOUGHT OF YOU, AKAME, GAVE ME LIMITLESS STRENGTH...
GREEN ...
IF I CAN JUST IMAGINE THAT SCENE, I CAN KEEP RUNNING!
DA (TMP) DA
DA
DA
DA
UWAAAAAA!!!
I JUST CAN'T CATCH UP TO HIM.
HE MAY BE AN ENEMY, BUT THE BOY'S GOT SOME LEGS ON HIM!

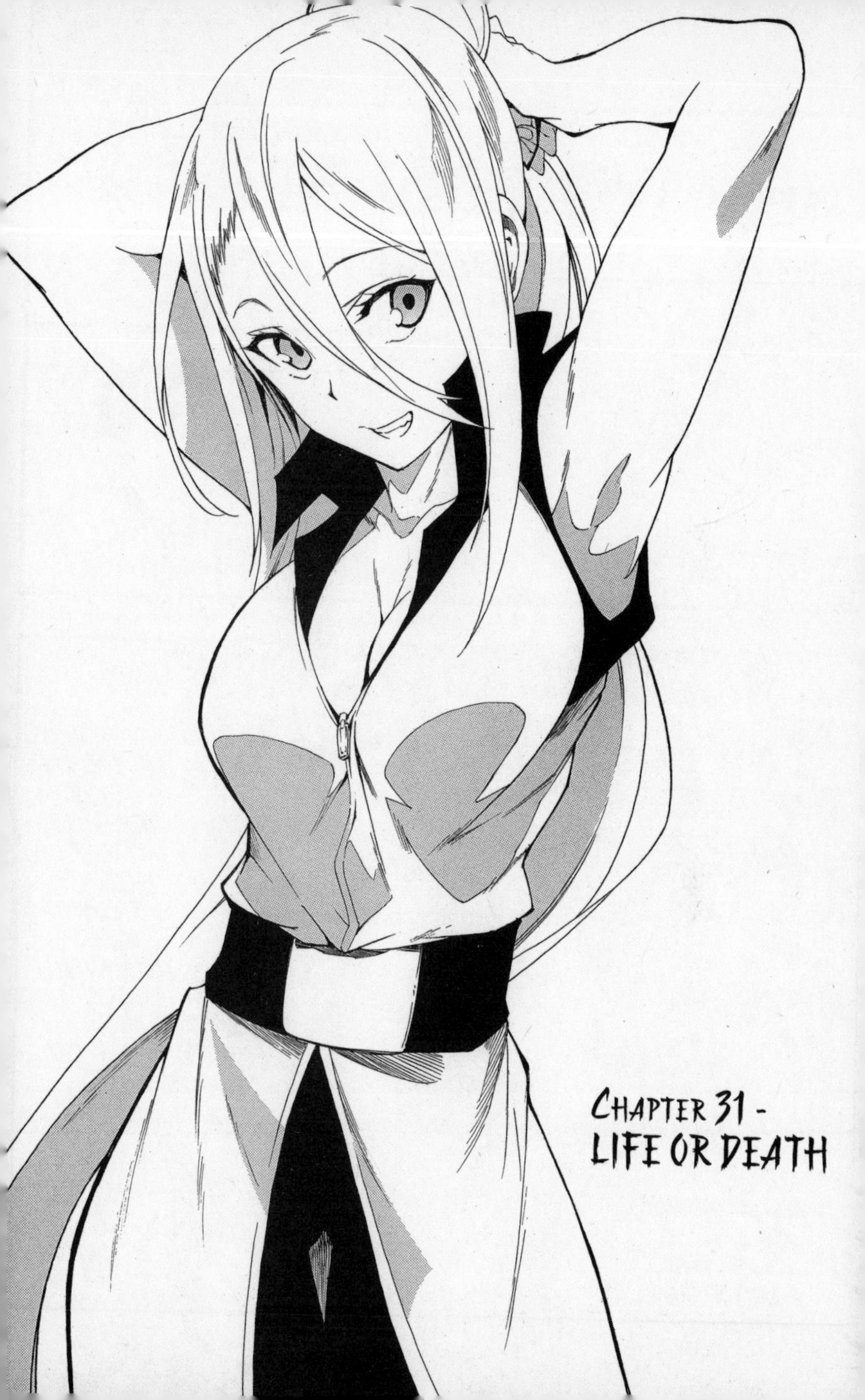
Chapter 31 -
Life or Death

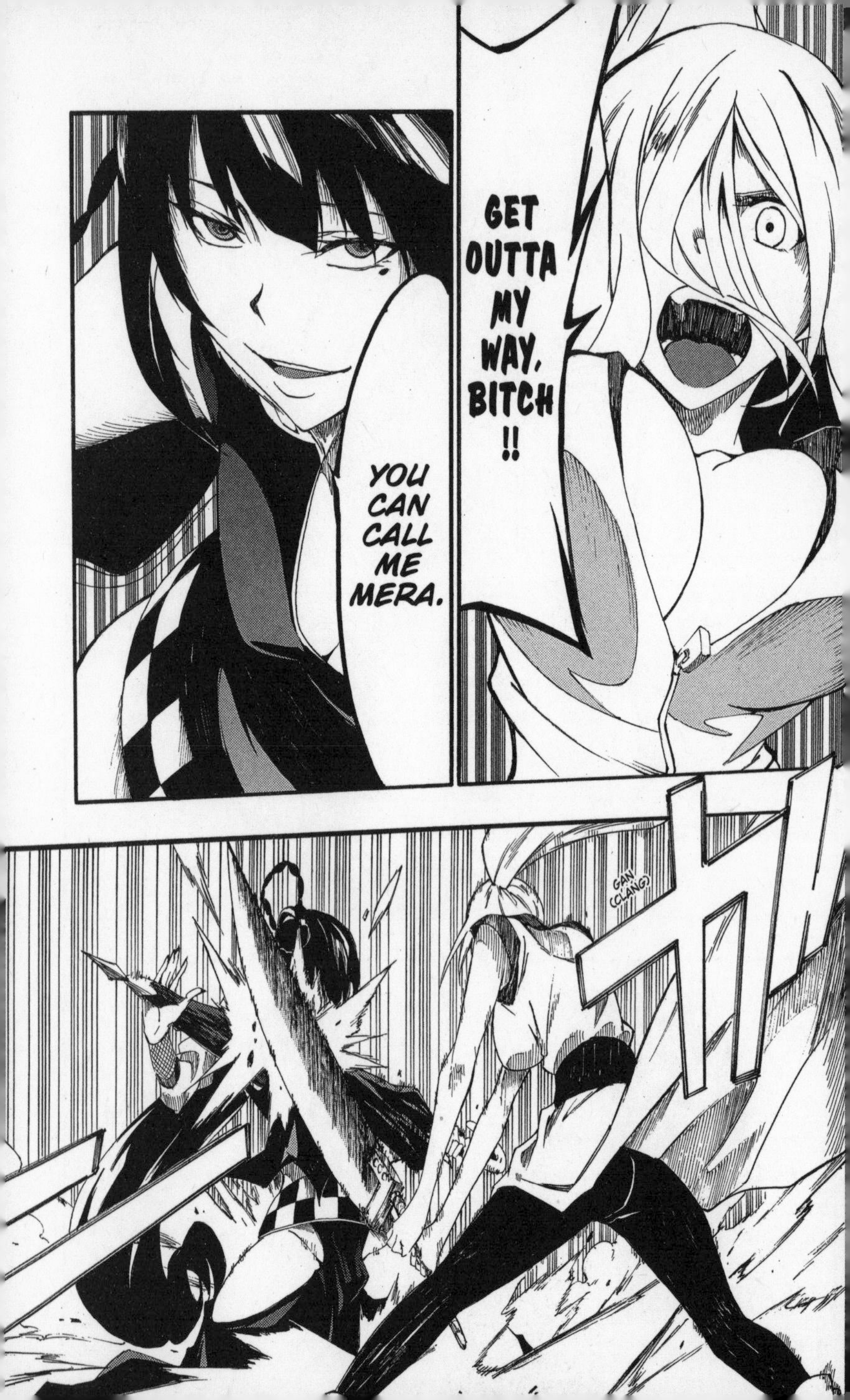
GET OUTTA MY WAY, BITCH!!
YOU CAN CALL ME MERA.
GAN (CLANG)

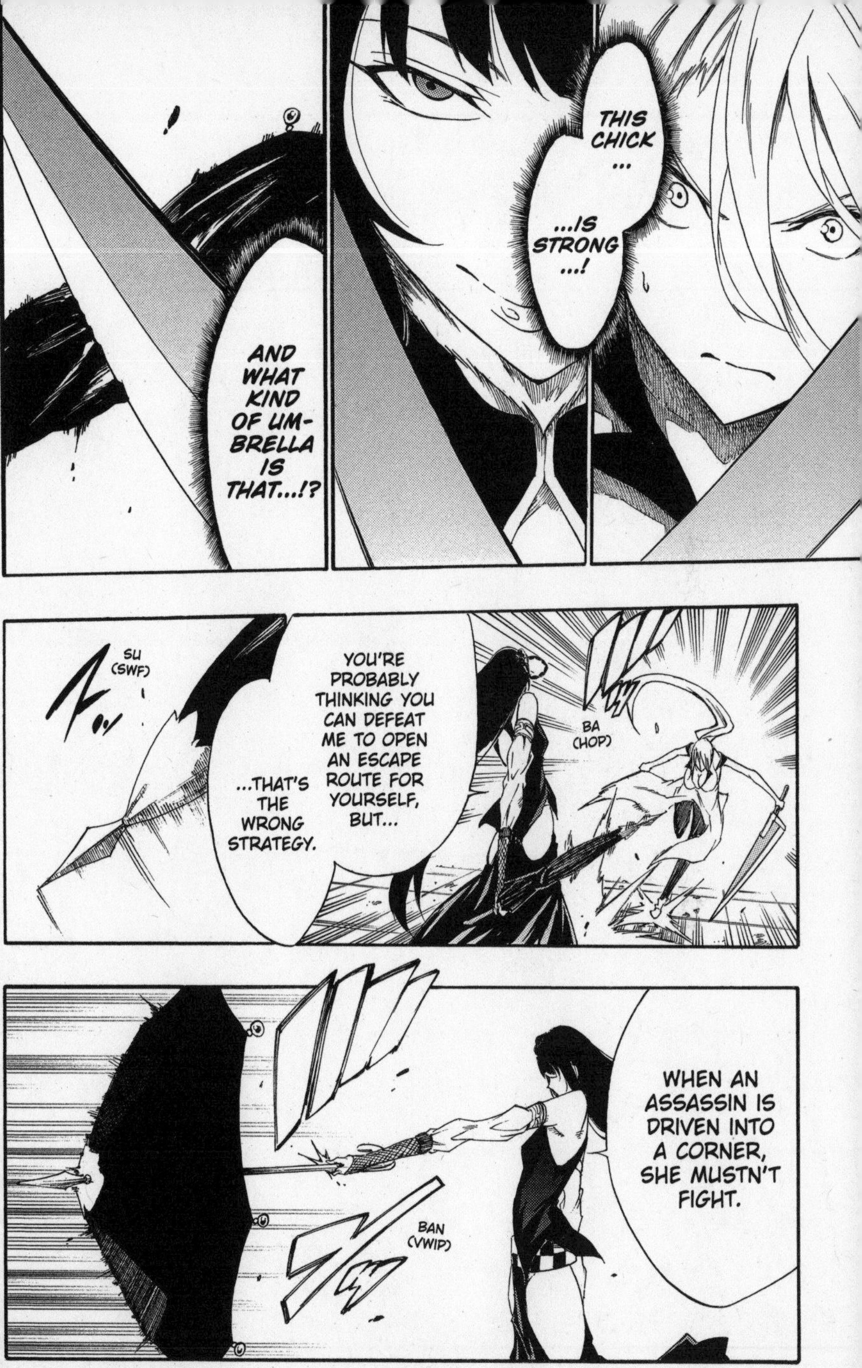
THIS CHICK ...
...IS STRONG ...!
AND WHAT KIND OF UM-BRELLA IS THAT...!?
BA (HOP)
YOU'RE PROBABLY THINKING YOU CAN DEFEAT ME TO OPEN AN ESCAPE ROUTE FOR YOURSELF, BUT...
...THAT'S THE WRONG STRATEGY.
SU (SWF)
WHEN AN ASSASSIN IS DRIVEN INTO A CORNER, SHE MUSTN'T FIGHT.
BAN (VWIP)

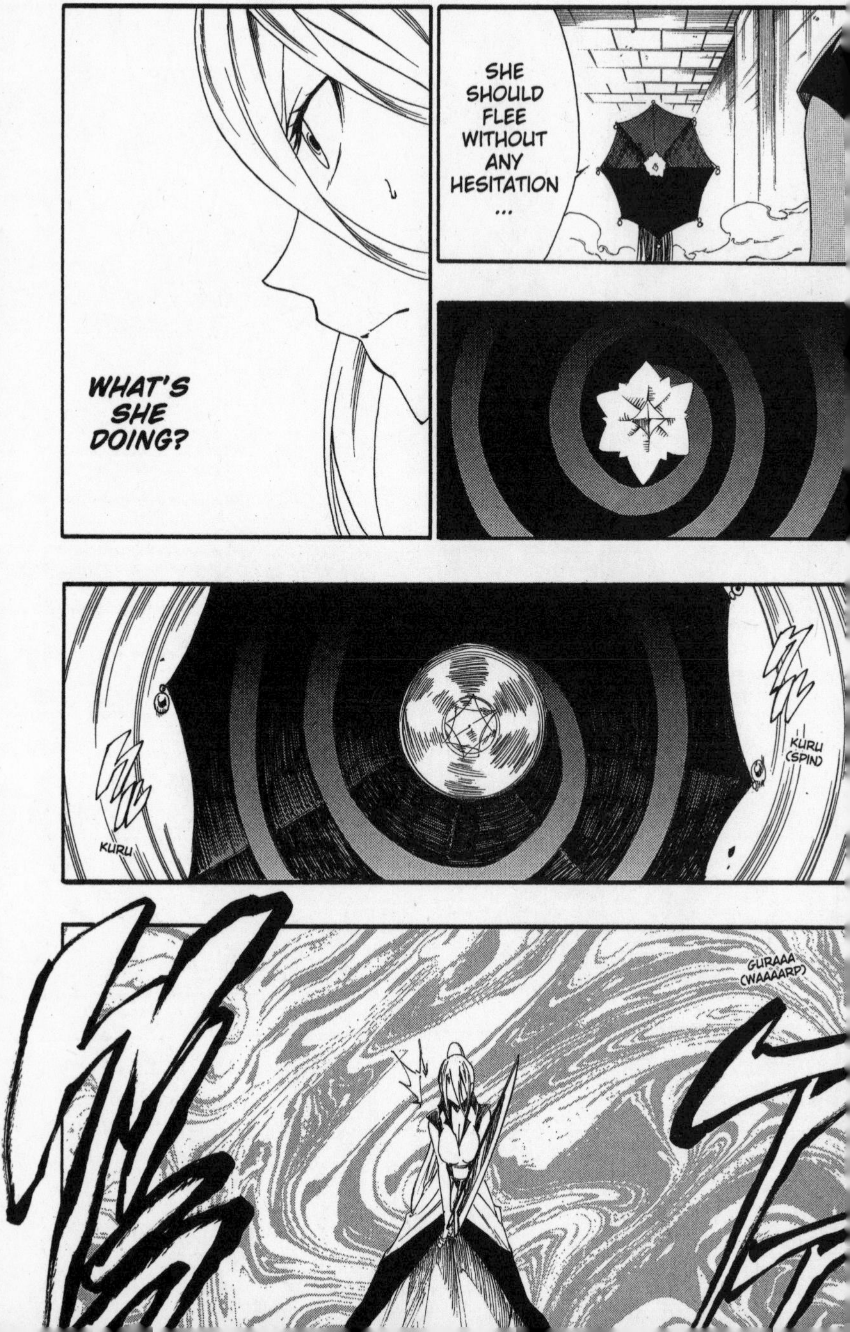
SHE SHOULD FLEE WITHOUT ANY HESITATION ...
WHAT'S SHE DOING?
KURU (SPIN)
KURU
GURAAA (WAAAARP)

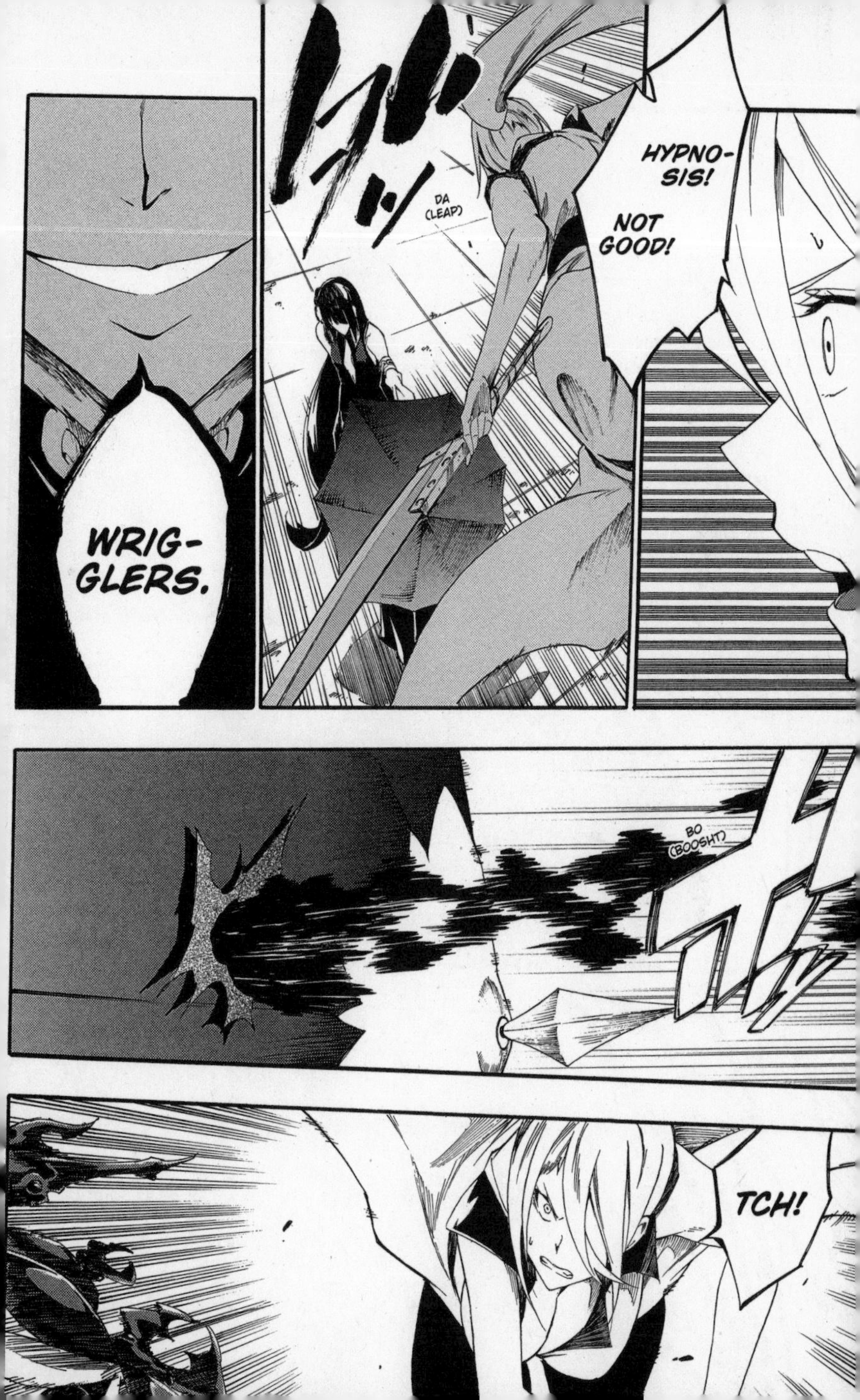
HYPNO-
SIS!
NOT
GOOD!
DA
(LEAP)
WRIG-
GLERS.
BO
(BOOSHT)
TCH!

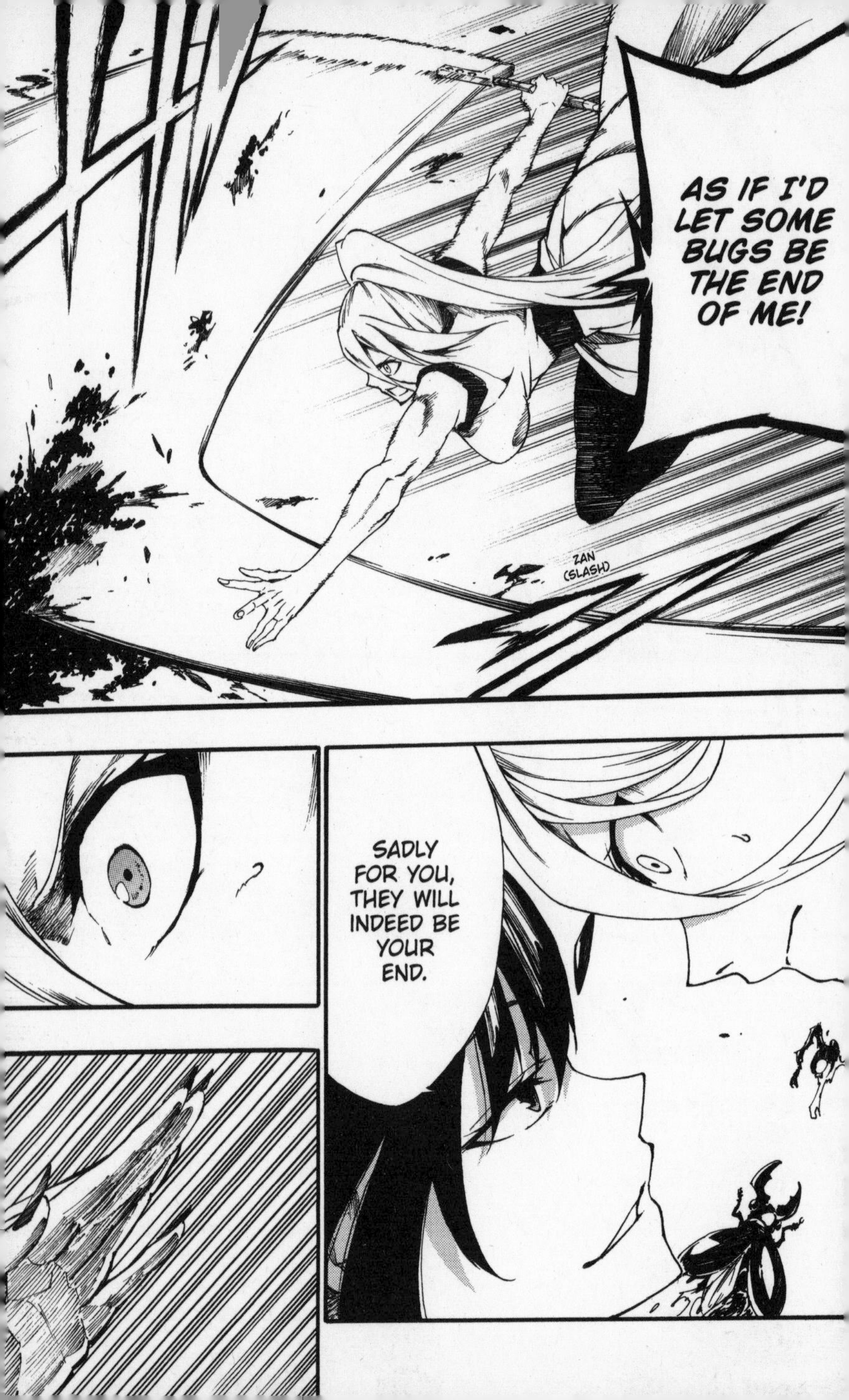
AS IF I'D LET SOME BUGS BE THE END OF ME!
ZAN (SLASH)
SADLY FOR YOU, THEY WILL INDEED BE YOUR END.

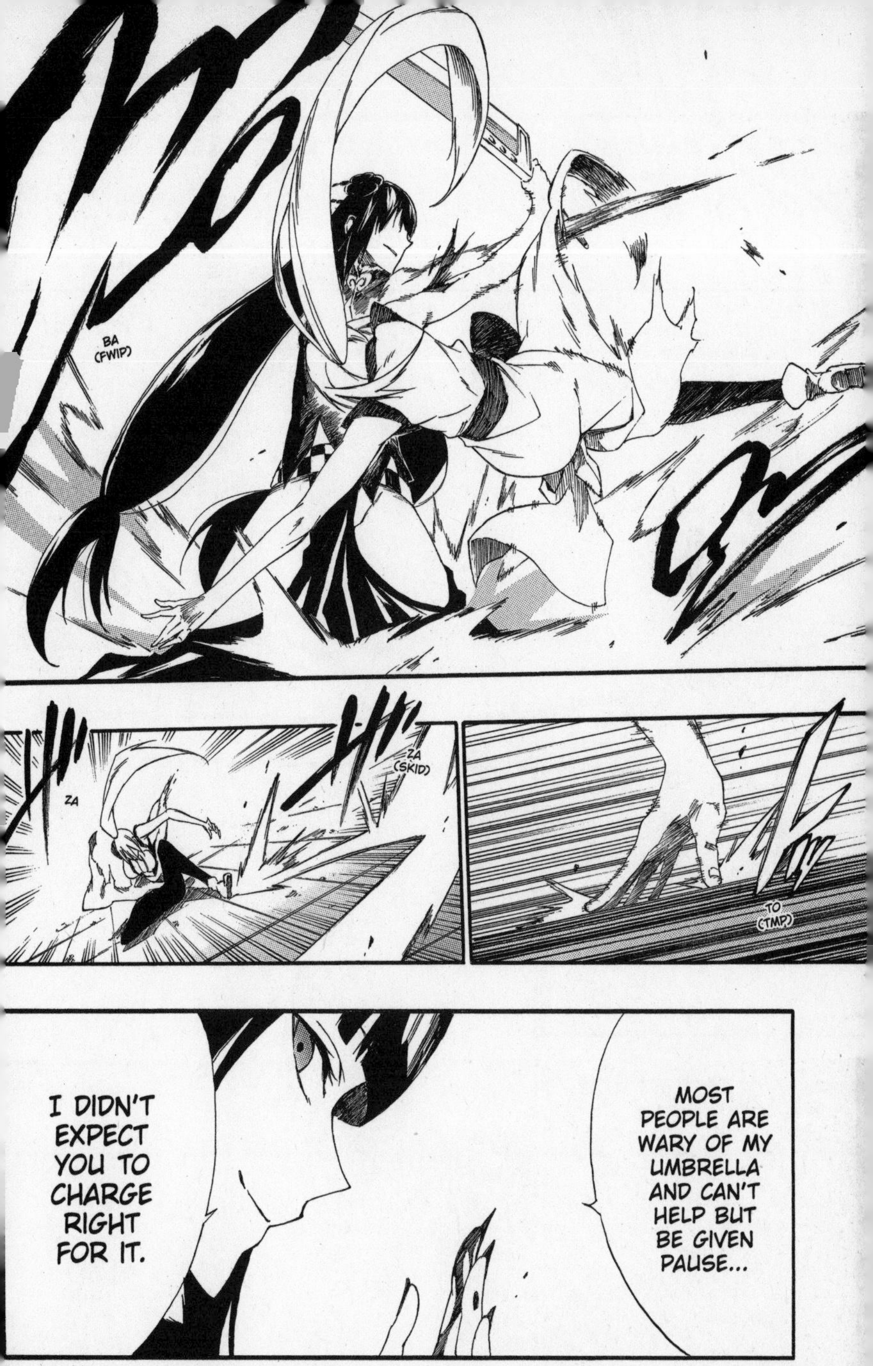
BA (FWIP)
TO (TMP)
ZA (SKID)
ZA
MOST PEOPLE ARE WARY OF MY UMBRELLA AND CAN'T HELP BUT BE GIVEN PAUSE...
I DIDN'T EXPECT YOU TO CHARGE RIGHT FOR IT.

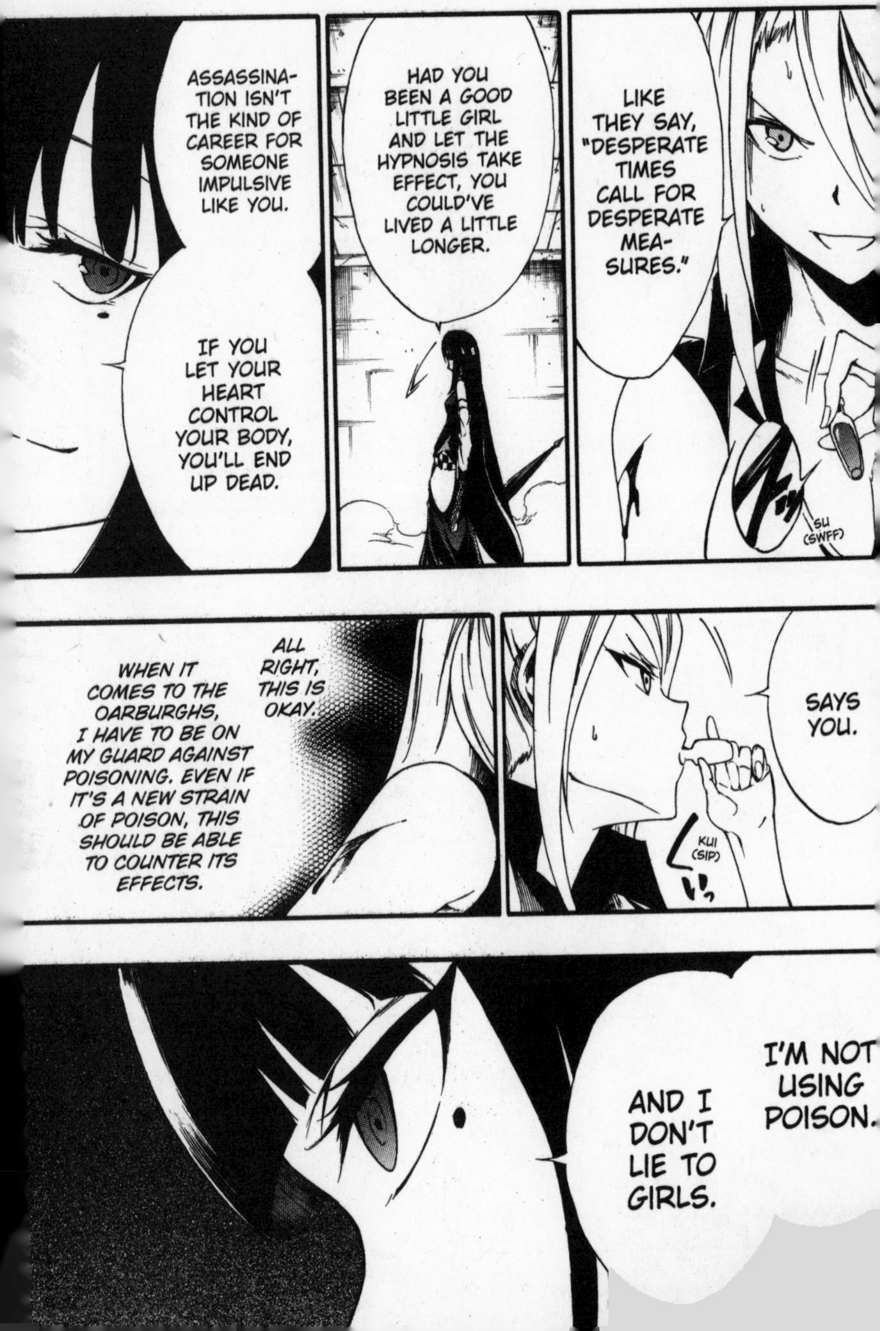
LIKE THEY SAY, "DESPERATE TIMES CALL FOR DESPERATE MEA-SURES."
SU (SWFF)
HAD YOU BEEN A GOOD LITTLE GIRL AND LET THE HYPNOSIS TAKE EFFECT, YOU COULD'VE LIVED A LITTLE LONGER.
ASSASSINA-TION ISN'T THE KIND OF CAREER FOR SOMEONE IMPULSIVE LIKE YOU.
IF YOU LET YOUR HEART CONTROL YOUR BODY, YOU'LL END UP DEAD.
SAYS YOU.
KUI (SIP)
ALL RIGHT, THIS IS OKAY.
WHEN IT COMES TO THE OARBURGHS, I HAVE TO BE ON MY GUARD AGAINST POISONING. EVEN IF IT'S A NEW STRAIN OF POISON, THIS SHOULD BE ABLE TO COUNTER ITS EFFECTS.
I'M NOT USING POISON.
AND I DON'T LIE TO GIRLS.

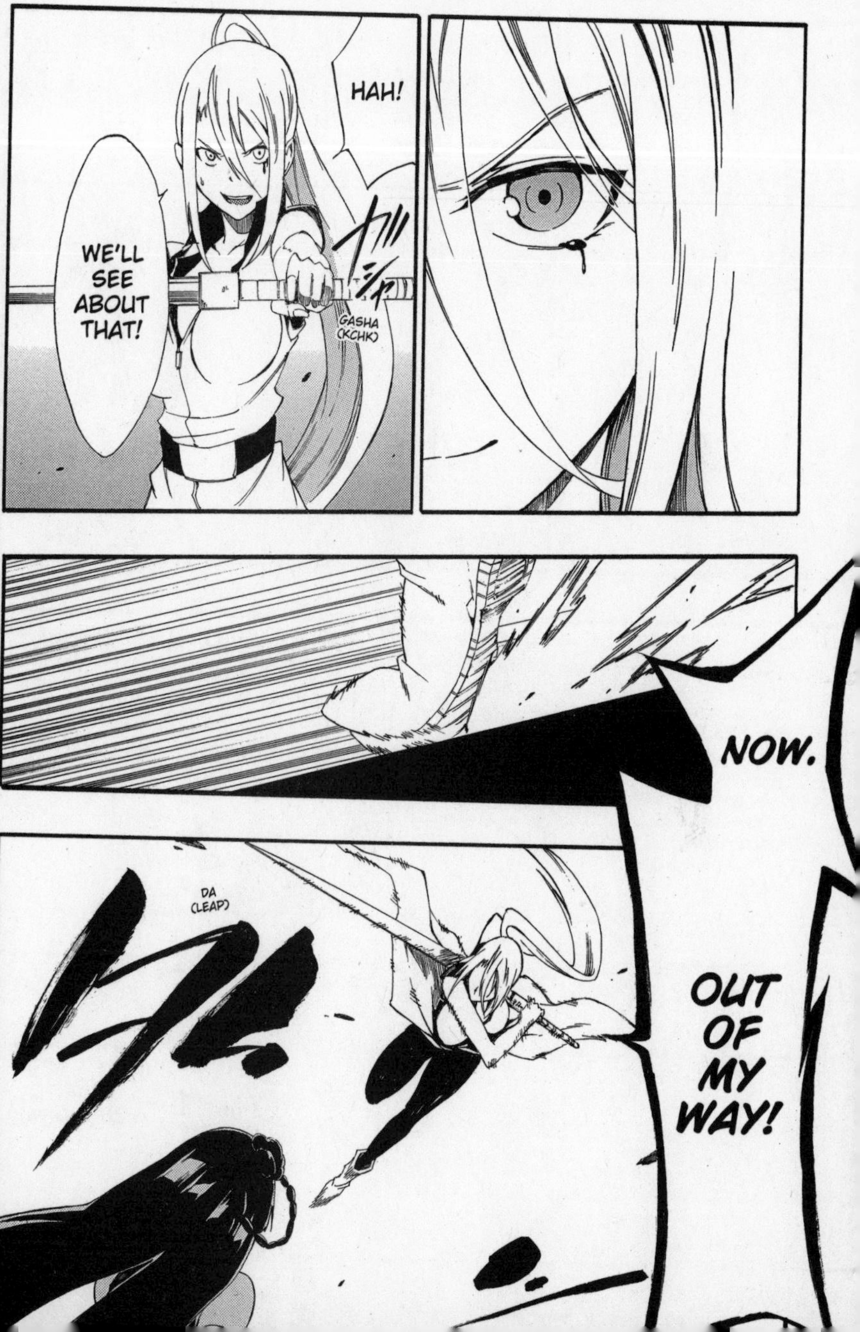
HAH!
WE'LL SEE ABOUT THAT!
GASHA (KCHK)
NOW.
OUT OF MY WAY!
DA (LEAP)

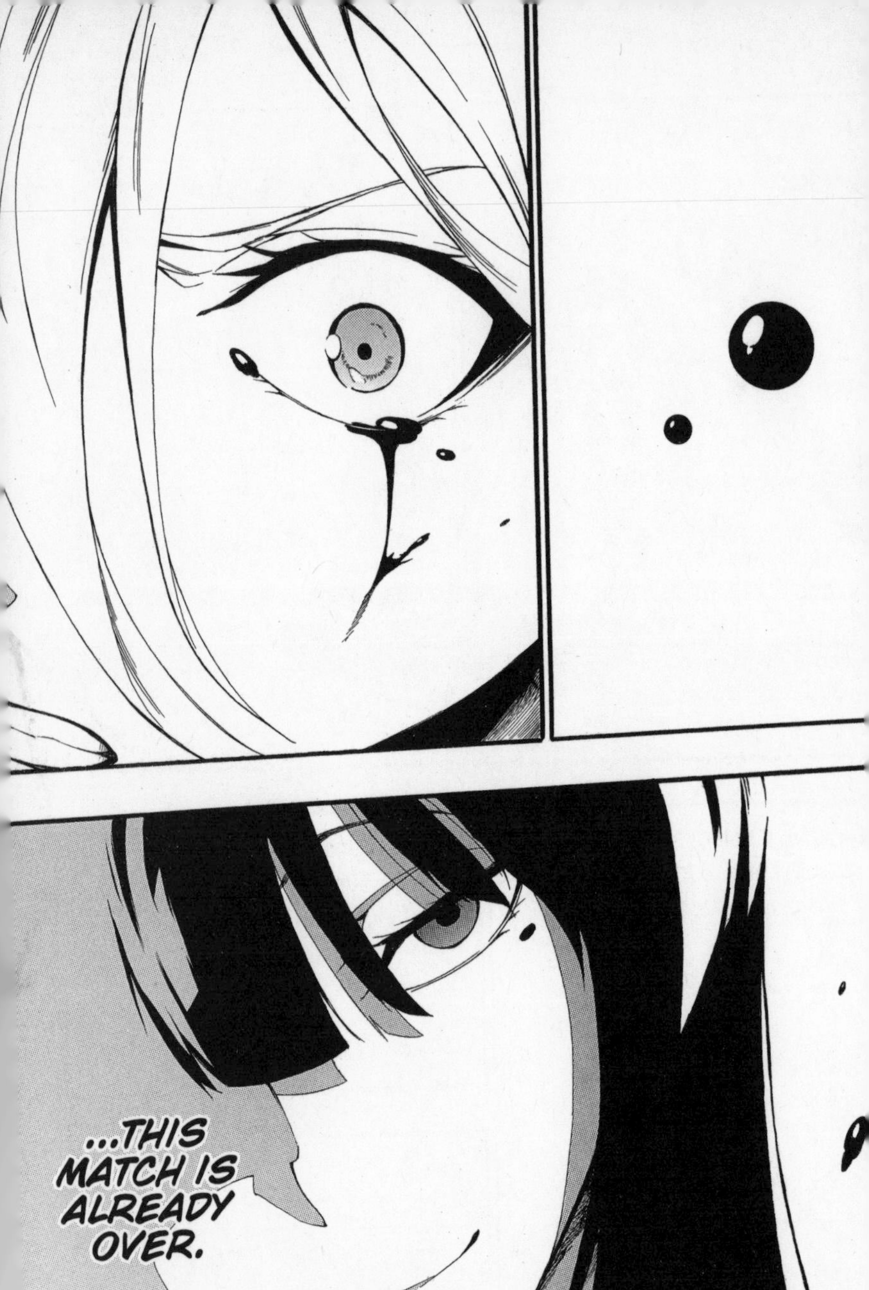
...THIS MATCH IS ALREADY OVER.

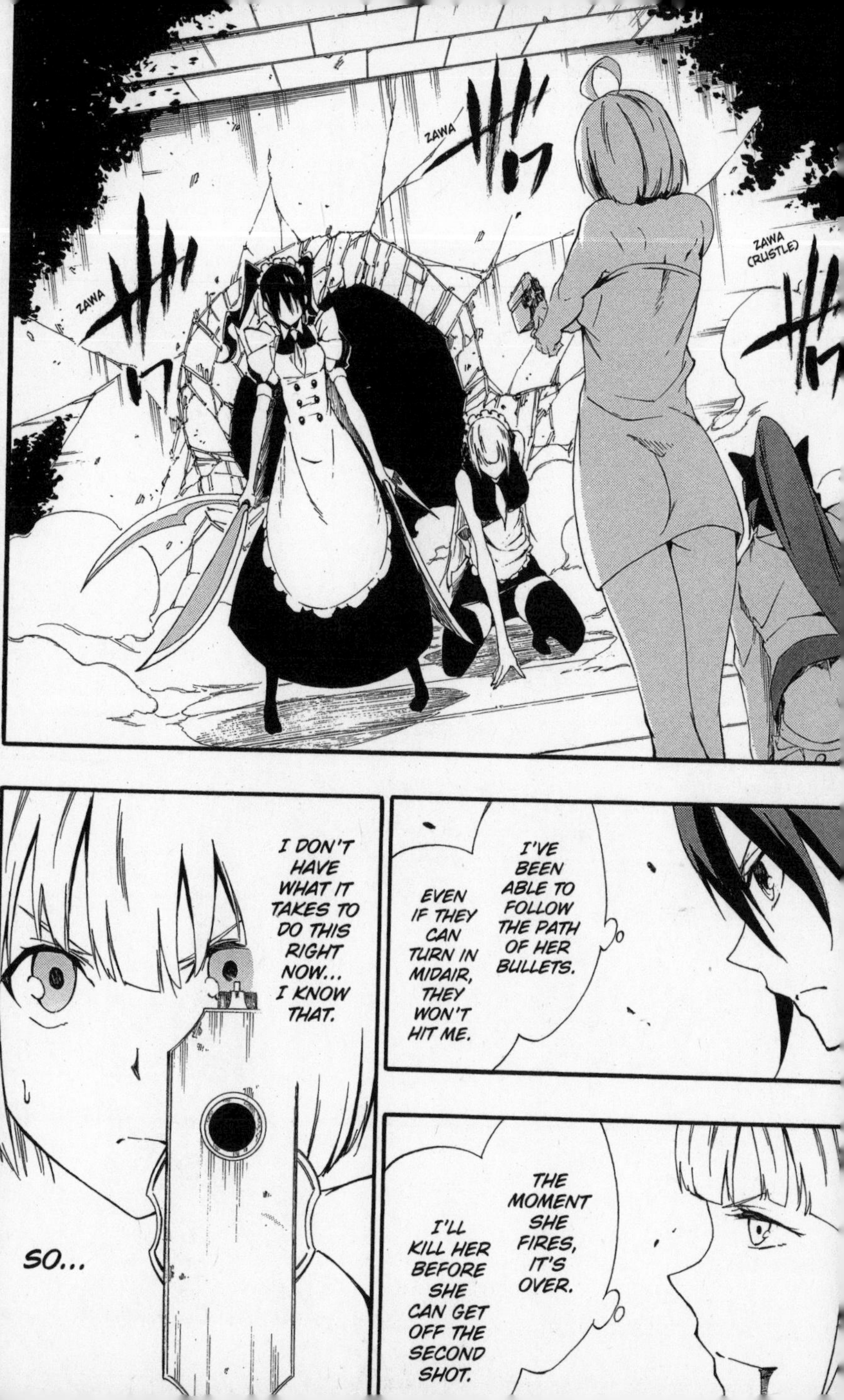
ZAWA (RUSTLE)
ZAWA
ZAWA
I'VE BEEN ABLE TO FOLLOW THE PATH OF HER BULLETS.
EVEN IF THEY CAN TURN IN MIDAIR, THEY WON'T HIT ME.
THE MOMENT SHE FIRES, IT'S OVER.
I'LL KILL HER BEFORE SHE CAN GET OFF THE SECOND SHOT.
I DON'T HAVE WHAT IT TAKES TO DO THIS RIGHT NOW... I KNOW THAT.
SO...

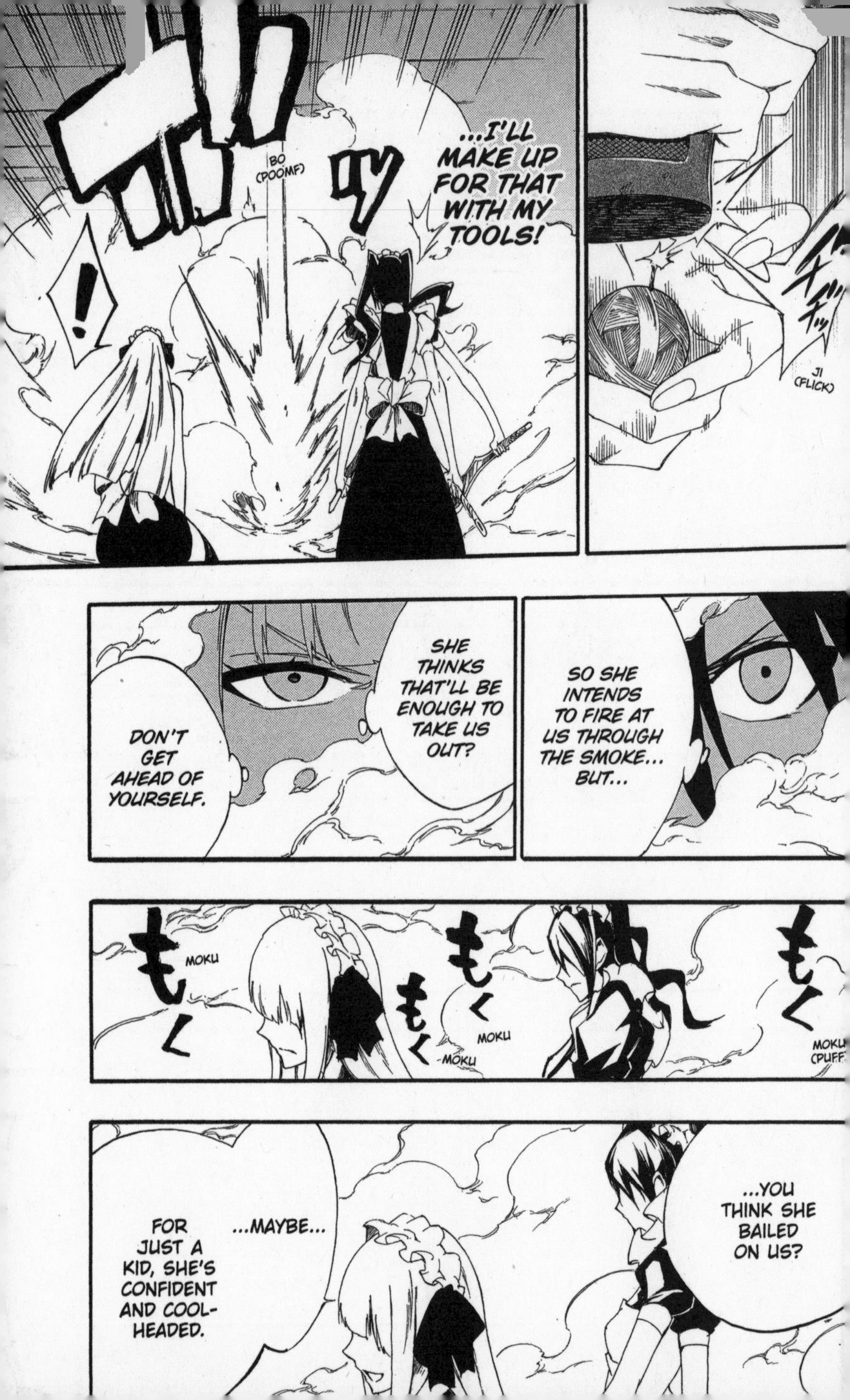
JI (FLICK)
BO (POOMF)
...I'LL MAKE UP FOR THAT WITH MY TOOLS!
!
SO SHE INTENDS TO FIRE AT US THROUGH THE SMOKE... BUT...
SHE THINKS THAT'LL BE ENOUGH TO TAKE US OUT?
DON'T GET AHEAD OF YOURSELF.
もく
MOKU (PUFF)
もく
MOKU
もく
MOKU
もく
MOKU
...YOU THINK SHE BAILED ON US?
...MAYBE...
FOR JUST A KID, SHE'S CONFIDENT AND COOL-HEADED.

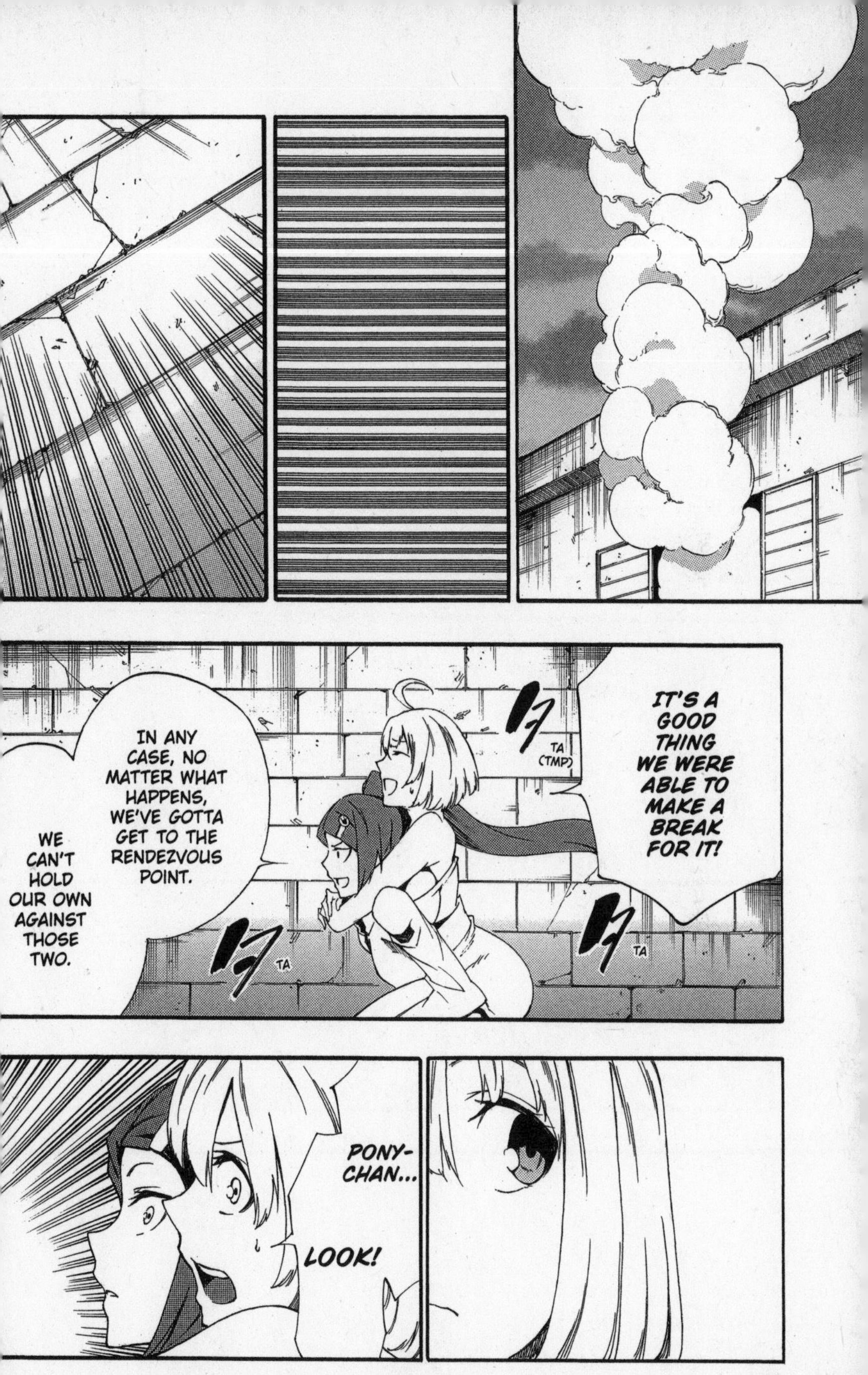
IT'S A GOOD THING WE WERE ABLE TO MAKE A BREAK FOR IT!
TA (TMP)
IN ANY CASE, NO MATTER WHAT HAPPENS, WE'VE GOTTA GET TO THE RENDEZVOUS POINT.
WE CAN'T HOLD OUR OWN AGAINST THOSE TWO.
TA
TA
PONY-CHAN...
LOOK!

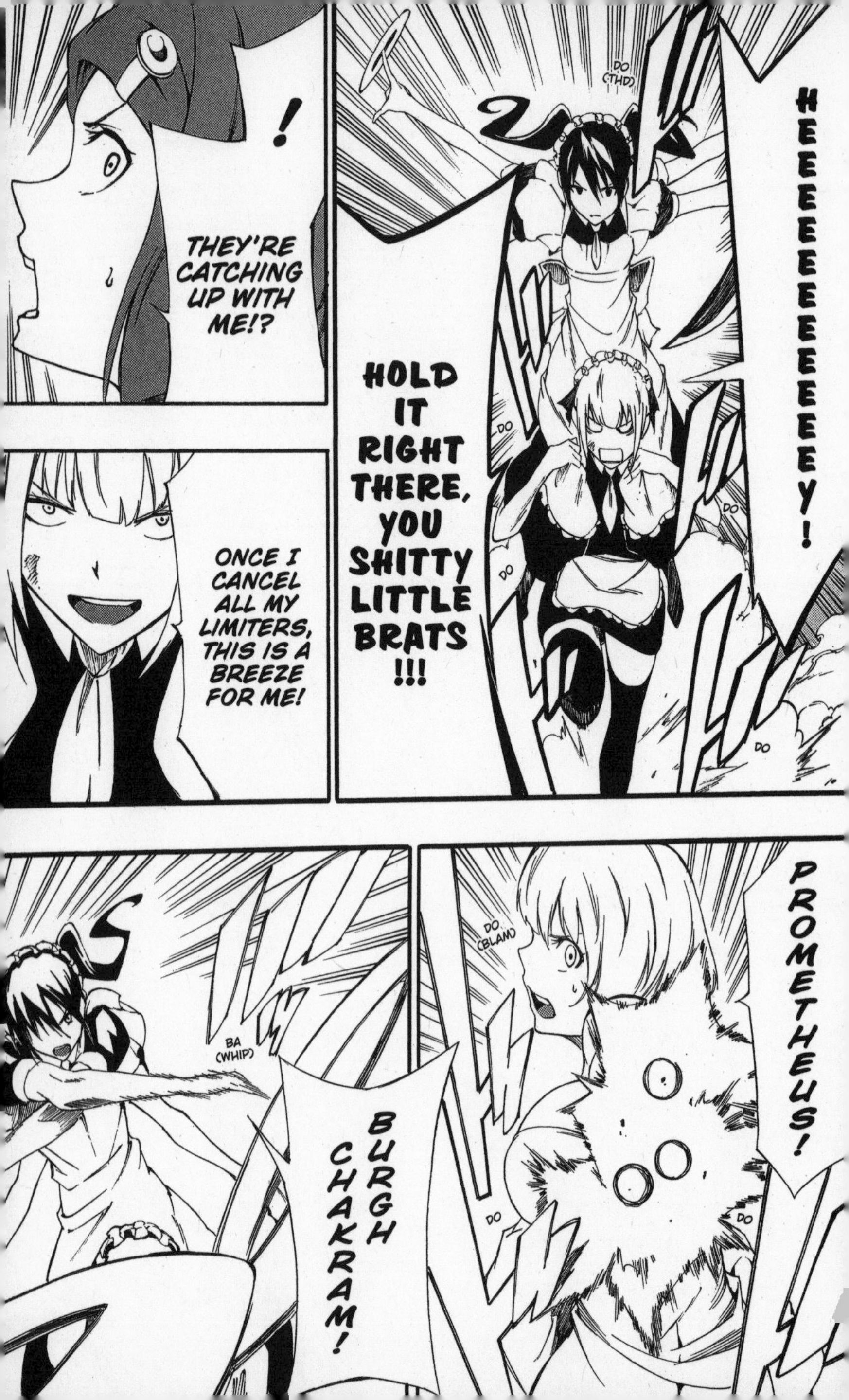
HEEEEEEEEEEEEEY!
DO (THD)
HOLD IT RIGHT THERE, YOU SHITTY LITTLE BRATS!!!
DO
DO
DO
DO
!
THEY'RE CATCHING UP WITH ME!?
ONCE I CANCEL ALL MY LIMITERS, THIS IS A BREEZE FOR ME!
PROMETHEUS!
DO (BLAM)
DO
DO
BA (WHIP)
BURGH CHAKRAM!

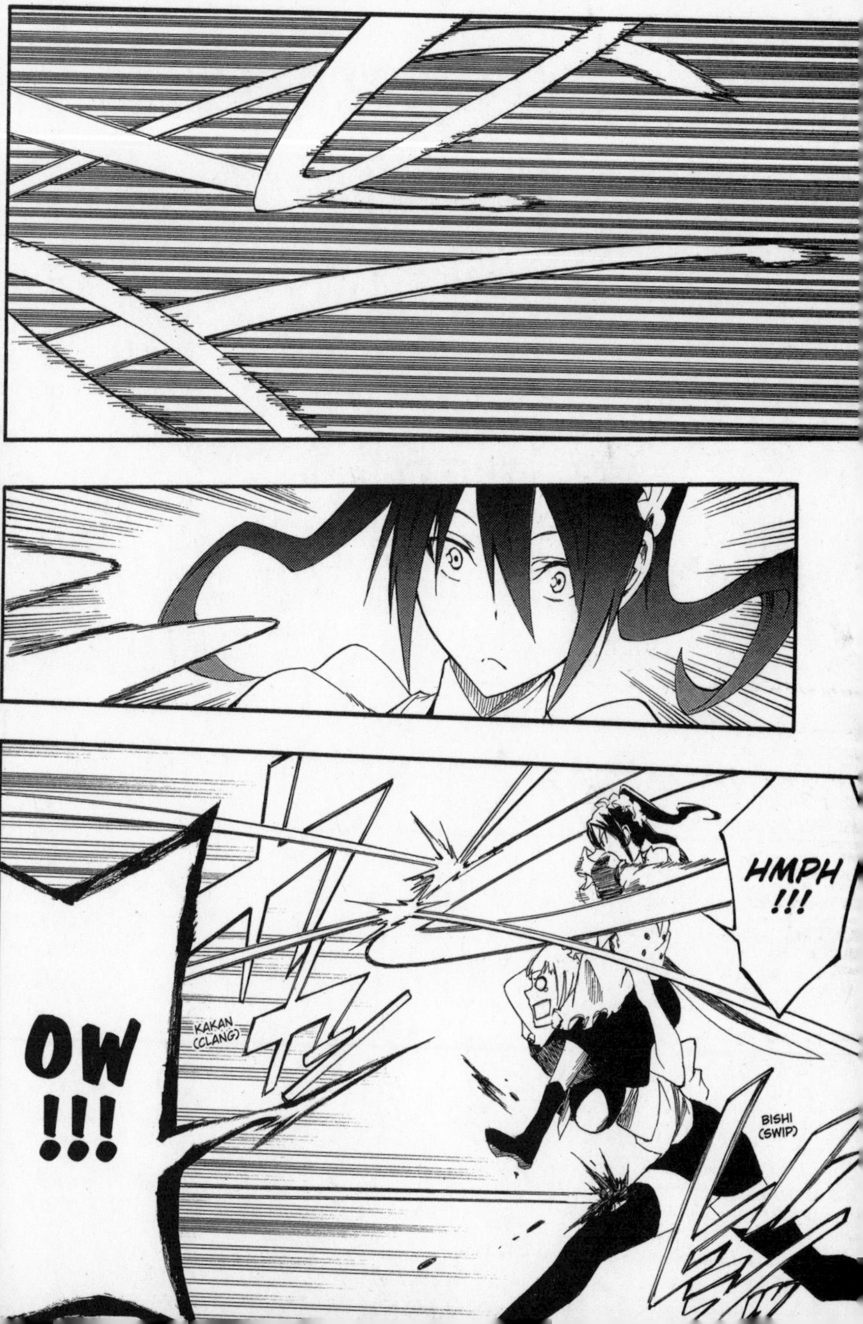
HMPH !!!
BISHI (SWIP)
KAKAN (CLANG)
OW !!!

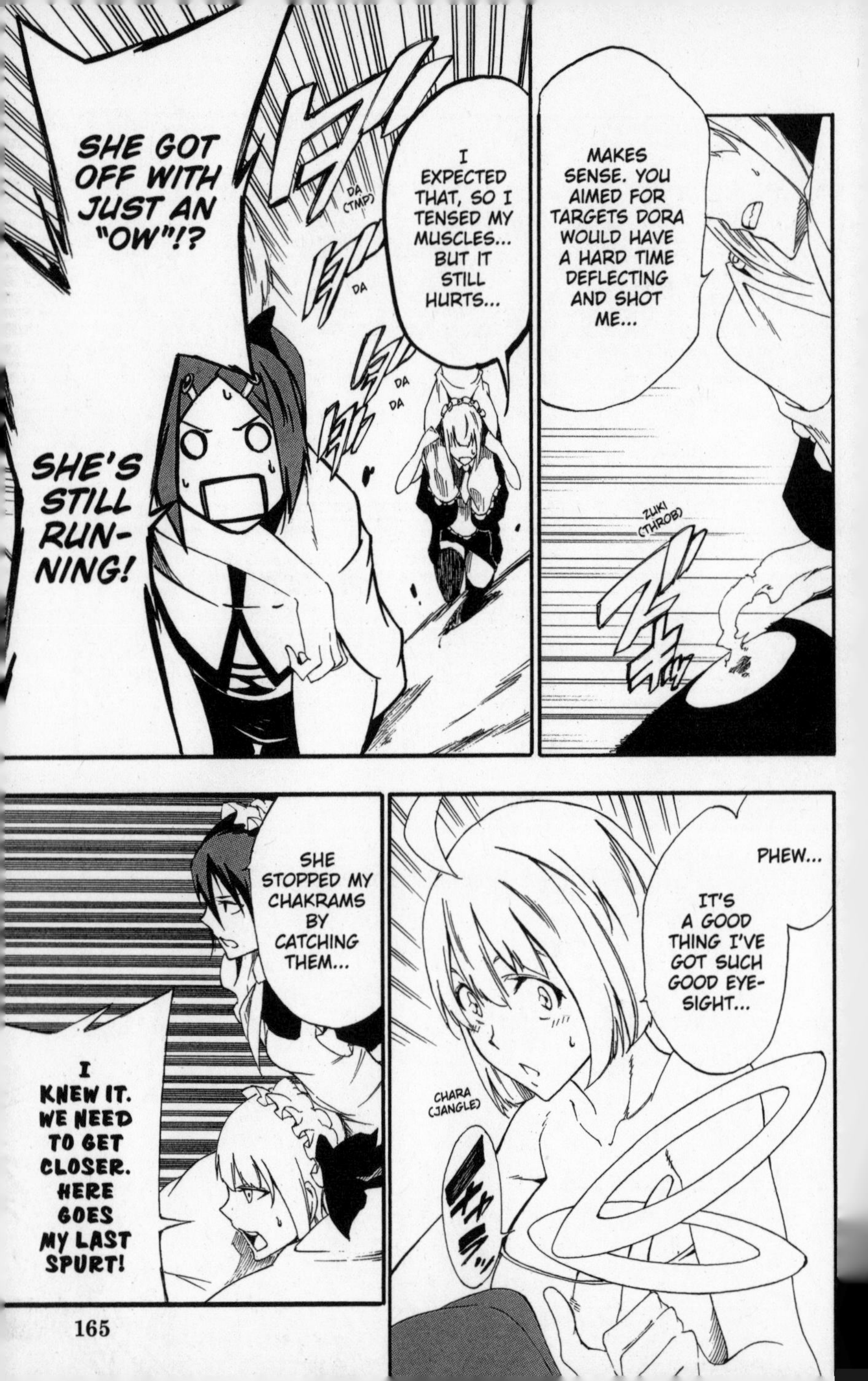
MAKES SENSE. YOU AIMED FOR TARGETS DORA WOULD HAVE A HARD TIME DEFLECTING AND SHOT ME...
ZUKI (THROB)
I EXPECTED THAT, SO I TENSED MY MUSCLES... BUT IT STILL HURTS...
DA (TMP)
DA
DA
DA
SHE GOT OFF WITH JUST AN "OW"!?
SHE'S STILL RUN-NING!
PHEW...
IT'S A GOOD THING I'VE GOT SUCH GOOD EYE-SIGHT...
CHARA (JANGLE)
SHE STOPPED MY CHAKRAMS BY CATCHING THEM...
I KNEW IT. WE NEED TO GET CLOSER. HERE GOES MY LAST SPURT!

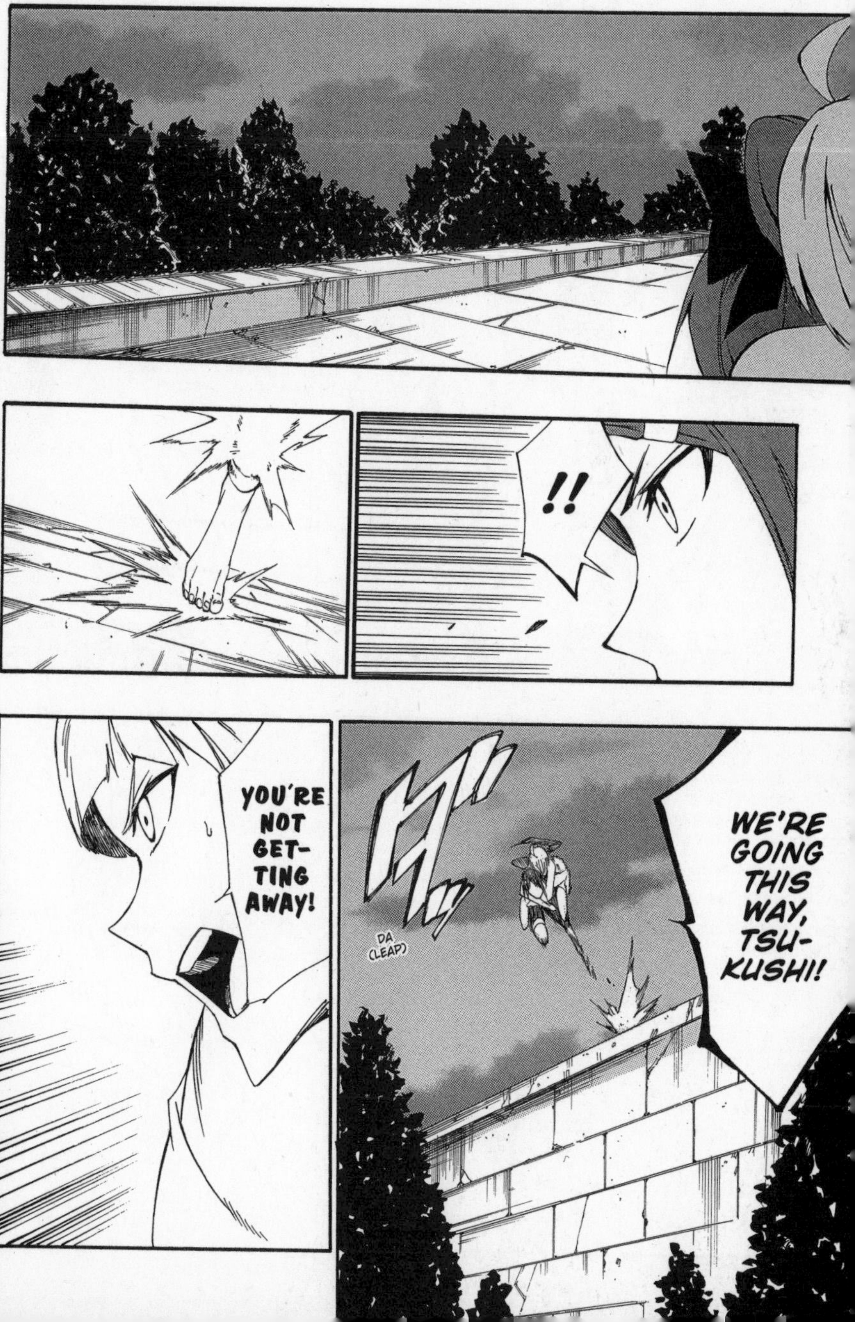
!!
WE'RE GOING THIS WAY, TSU-KUSHI!
DA (LEAP)
YOU'RE NOT GET-TING AWAY!

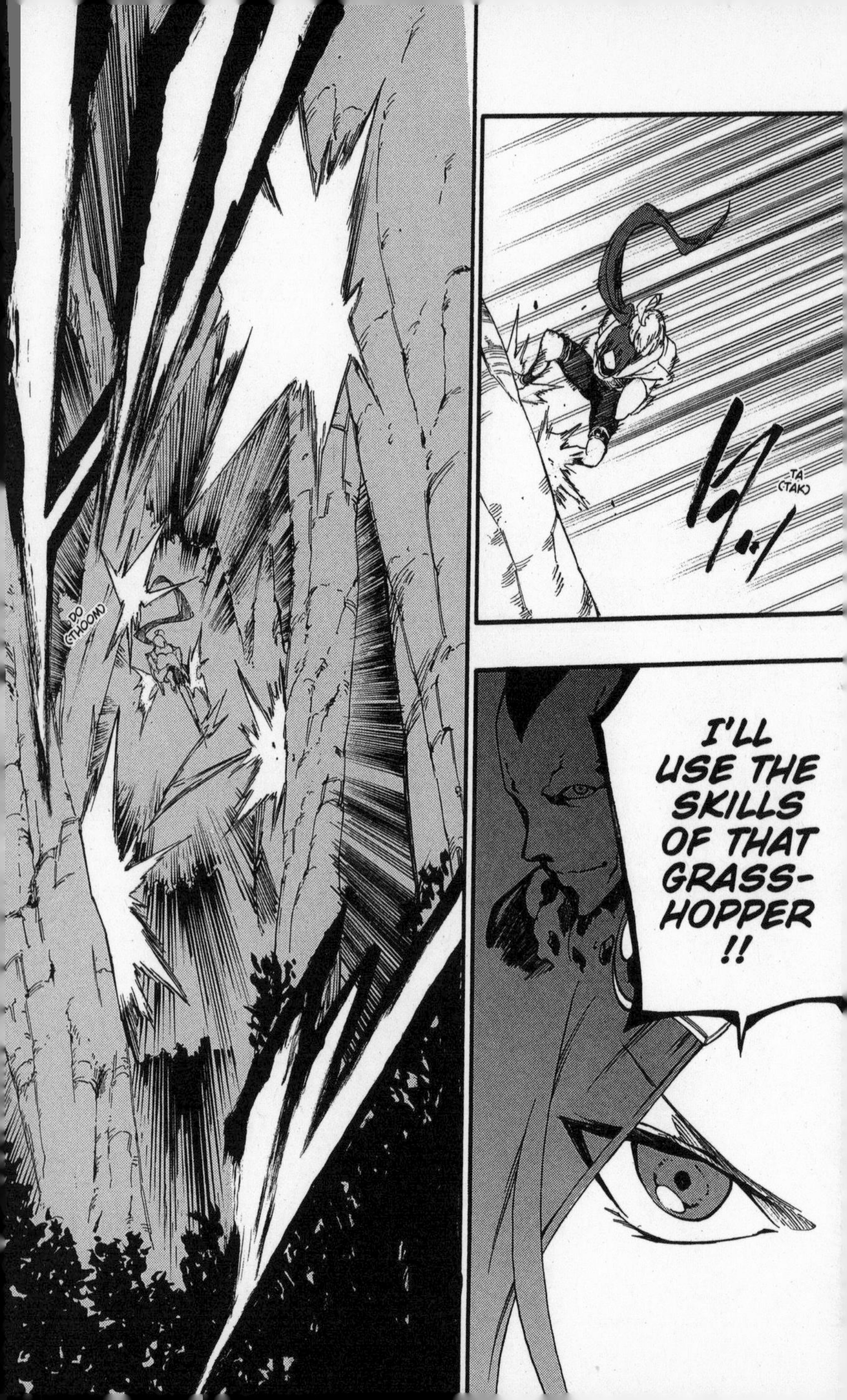
TA
(TAK)
I'LL USE THE SKILLS OF THAT GRASS-HOPPER !!
DO
(THOOM)

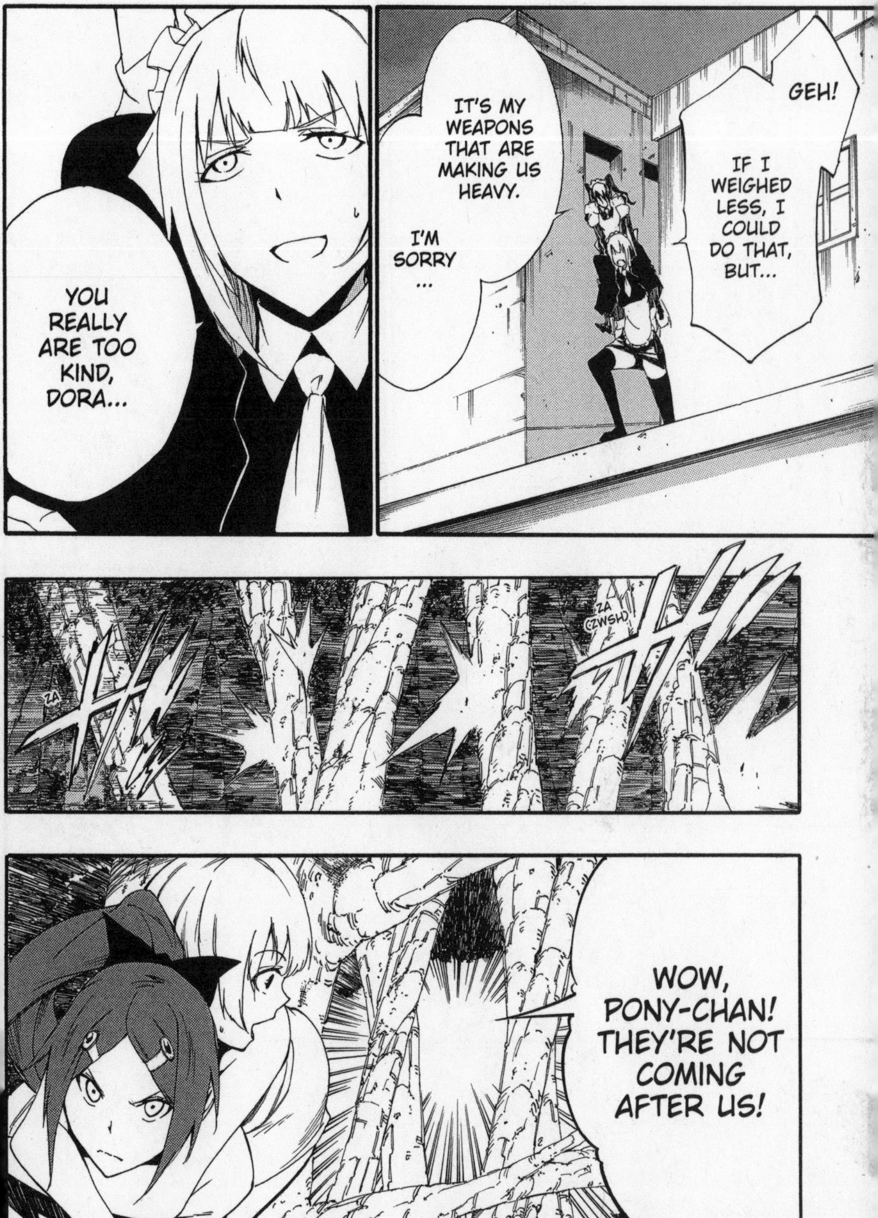
GEH!
IF I WEIGHED LESS, I COULD DO THAT, BUT...
IT'S MY WEAPONS THAT ARE MAKING US HEAVY.
I'M SORRY...
YOU REALLY ARE TOO KIND, DORA...
ZA (ZWSH)
ZA
WOW, PONY-CHAN! THEY'RE NOT COMING AFTER US!

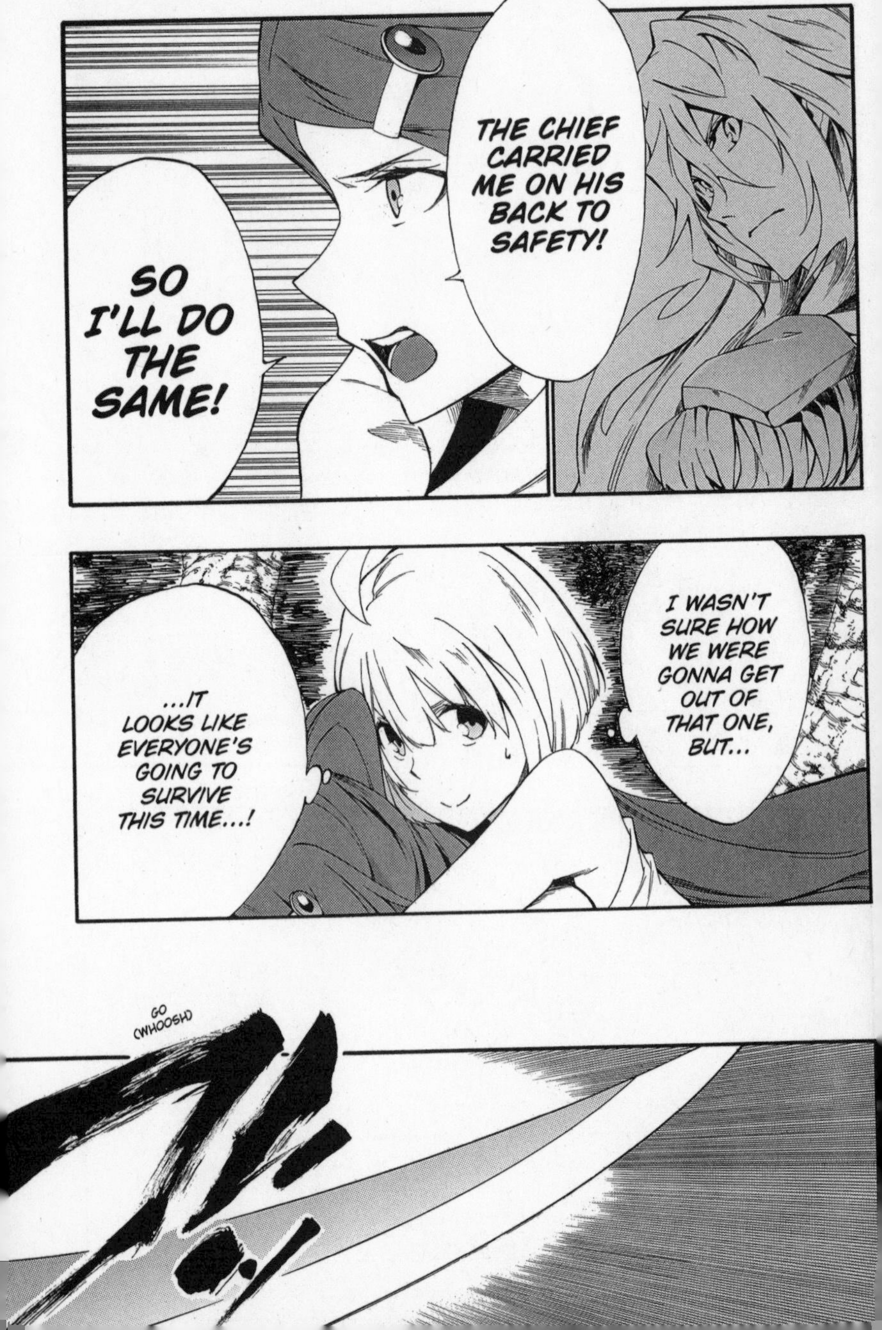
THE CHIEF CARRIED ME ON HIS BACK TO SAFETY!
SO I'LL DO THE SAME!
I WASN'T SURE HOW WE WERE GONNA GET OUT OF THAT ONE, BUT...
...IT LOOKS LIKE EVERYONE'S GOING TO SURVIVE THIS TIME...!
GO (WHOOSH)

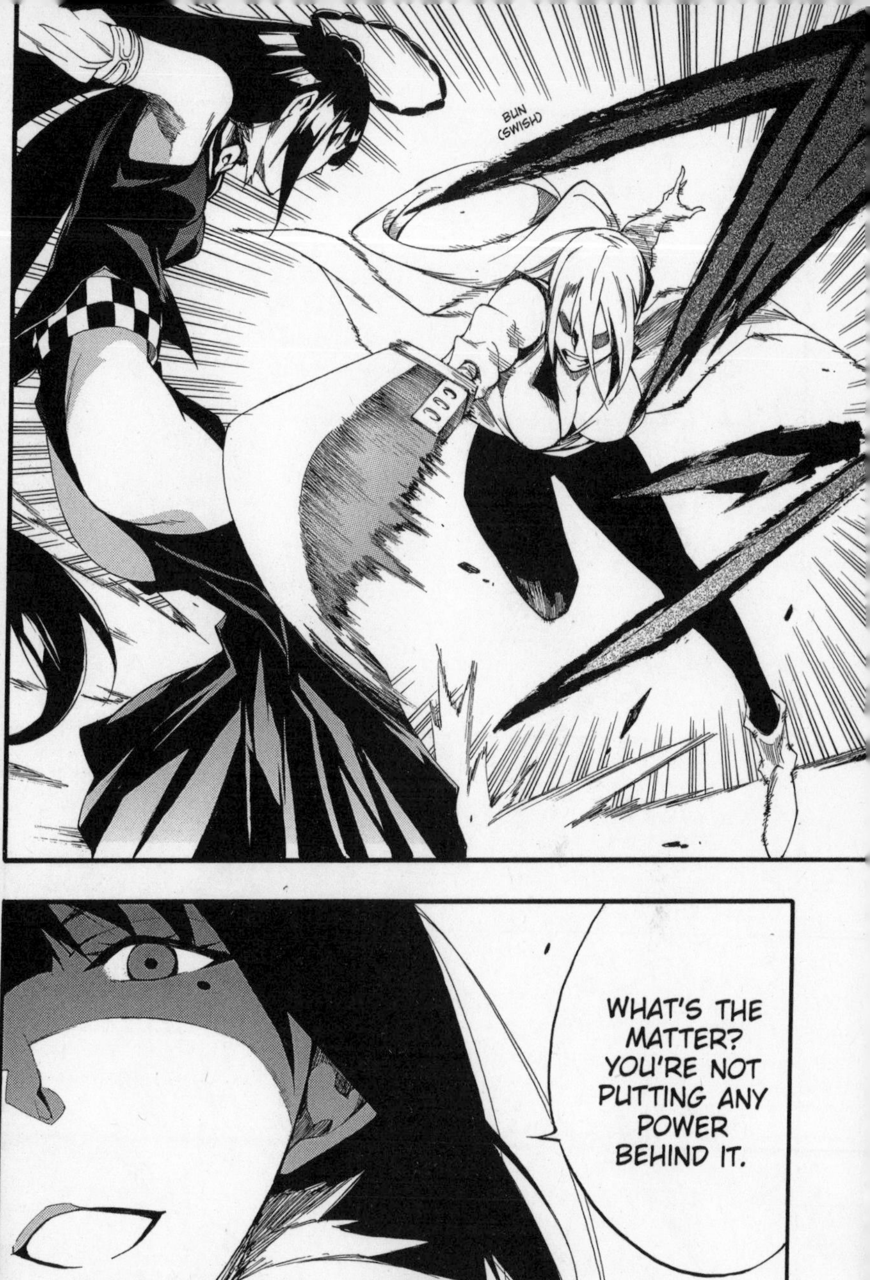
BUN
(SWISH)
WHAT'S THE MATTER? YOU'RE NOT PUTTING ANY POWER BEHIND IT.

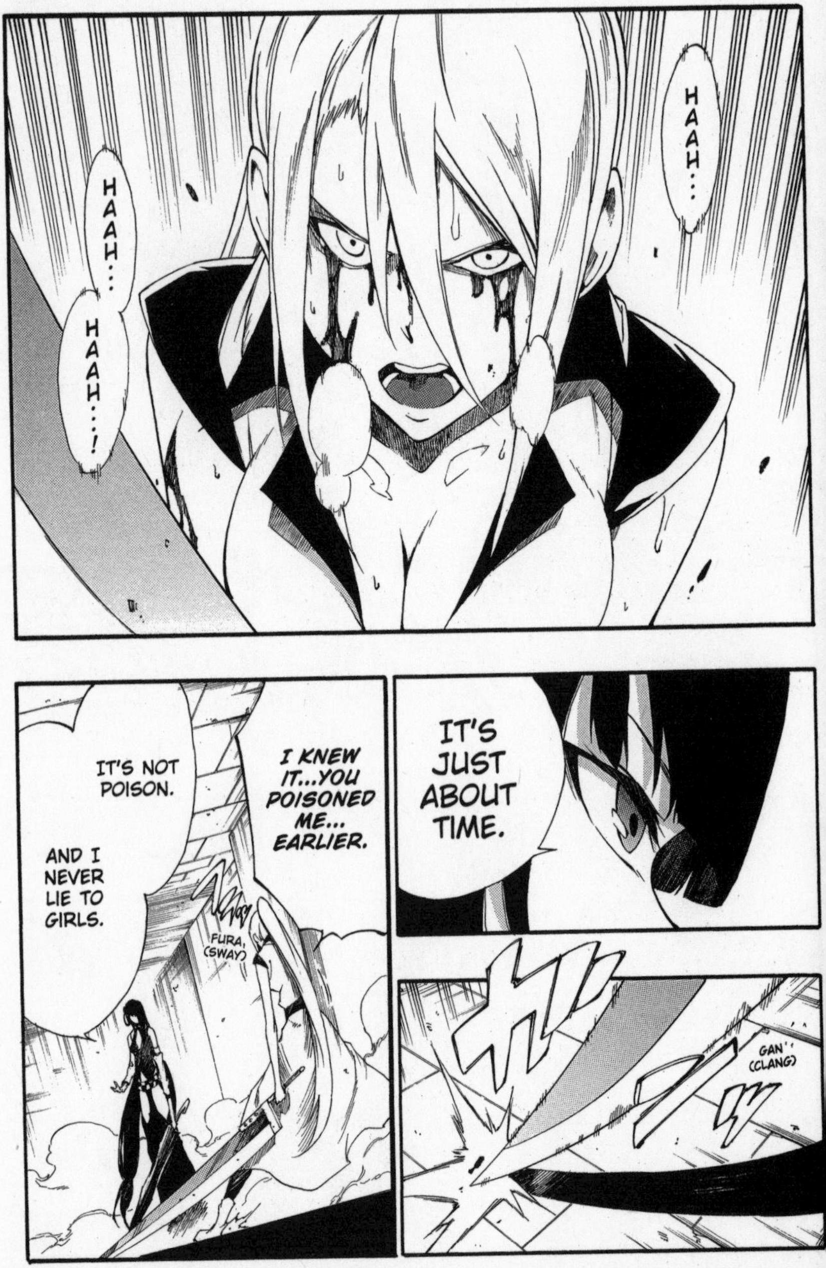
HAAH...
HAAH... HAAH...!
IT'S JUST ABOUT TIME.
GAN (CLANG)
I KNEW IT...YOU POISONED ME... EARLIER.
FURA (SWAY)
IT'S NOT POISON.
AND I NEVER LIE TO GIRLS.

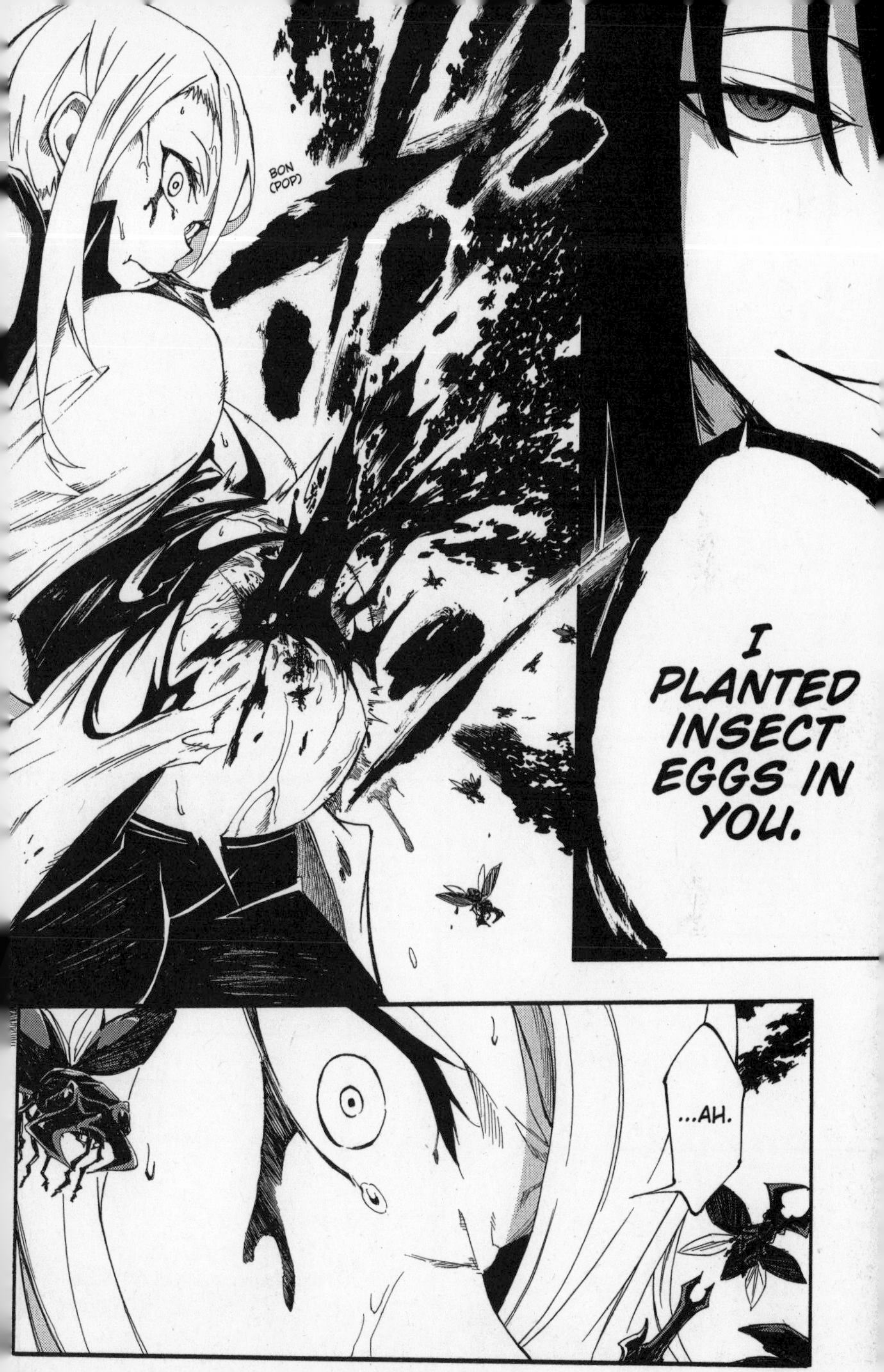
I PLANTED INSECT EGGS IN YOU.
BON (POP)
...AH.

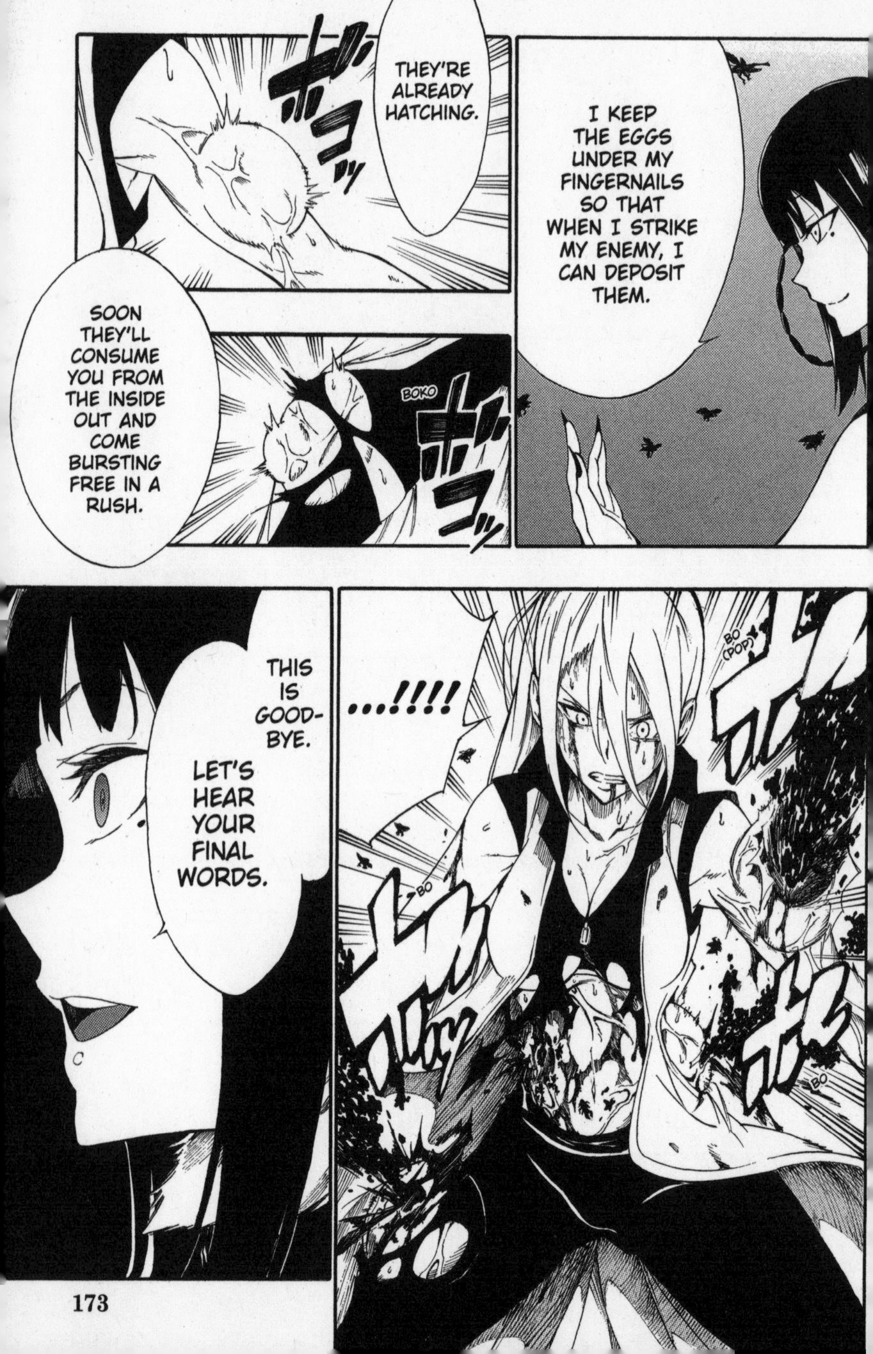

I KEEP THE EGGS UNDER MY FINGERNAILS SO THAT WHEN I STRIKE MY ENEMY, I CAN DEPOSIT THEM.
THEY'RE ALREADY HATCHING.
BOKO
SOON THEY'LL CONSUME YOU FROM THE INSIDE OUT AND COME BURSTING FREE IN A RUSH.
BO (POP)
...!!!!
BO
BO
THIS IS GOOD-BYE.
LET'S HEAR YOUR FINAL WORDS.

YES.

YOU'RE GOING TO DIE NOW.

FI... NAL?

VU (BZZ)

VU

VU

WITHOUT QUESTION.

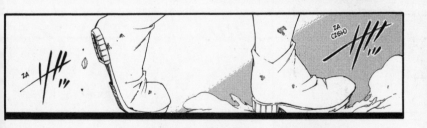

ZA (ZSH)

ZA

ZA

ZA

ZA

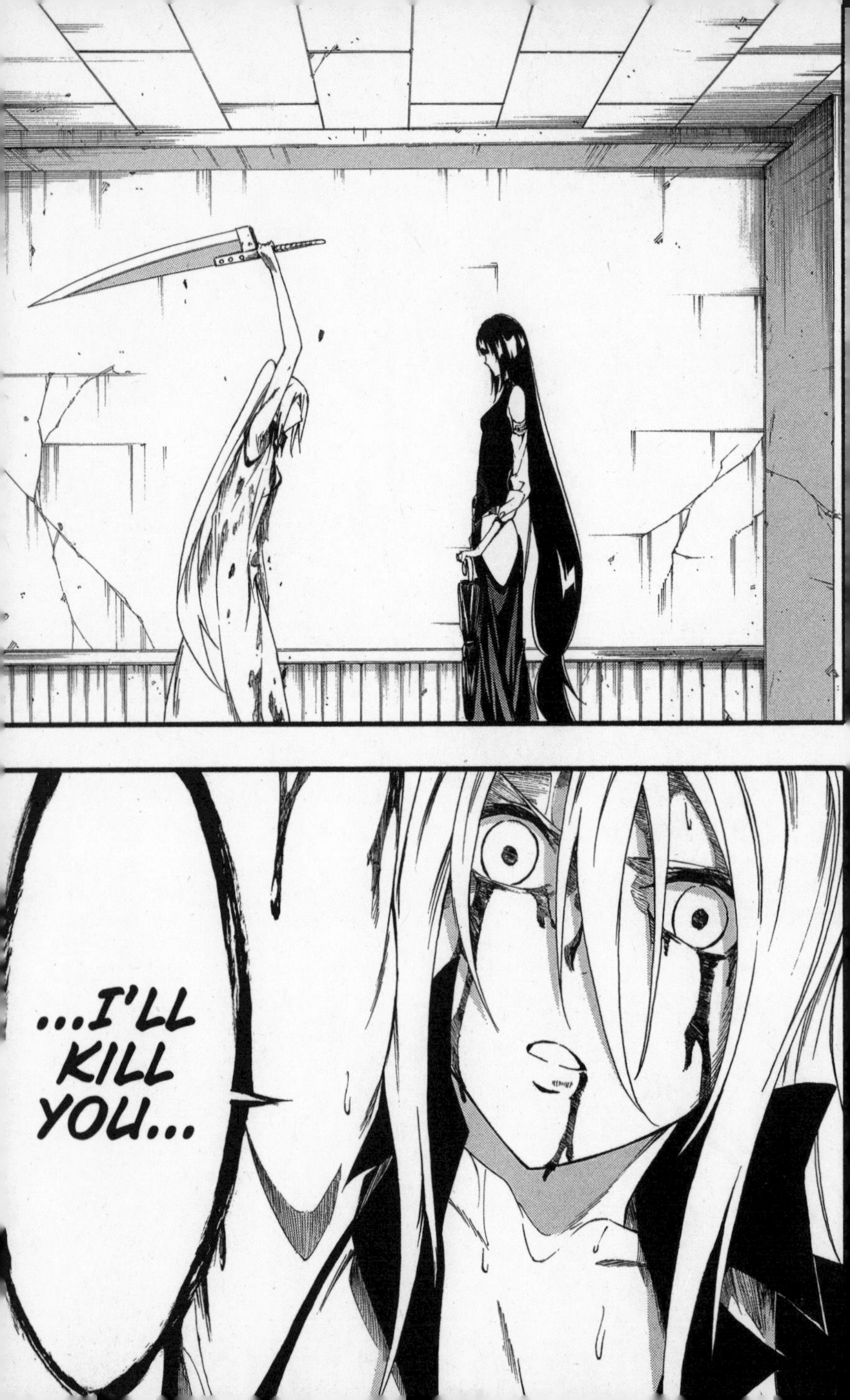
...I'LL KILL YOU...

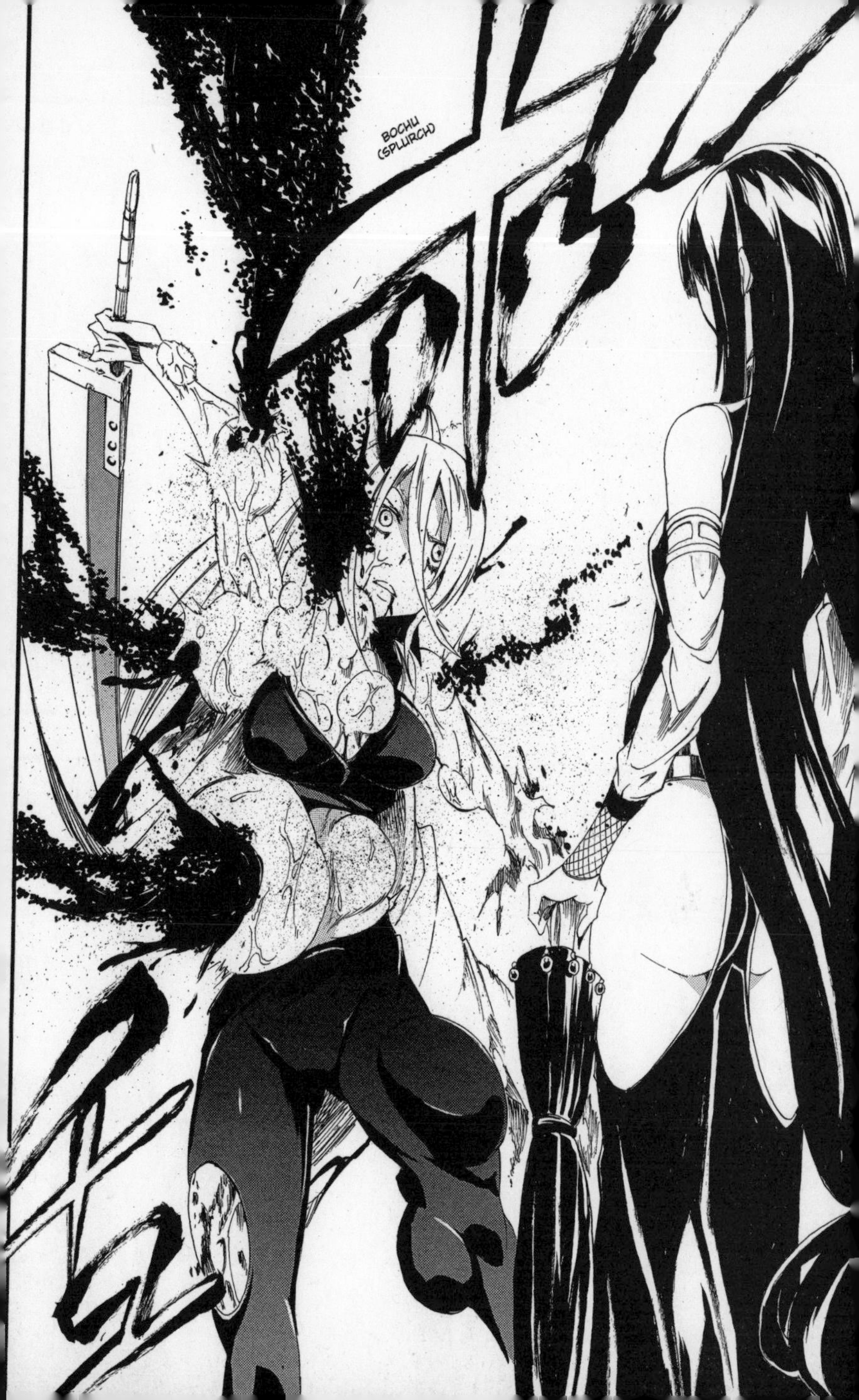
BOCHU
(SPLURCH)

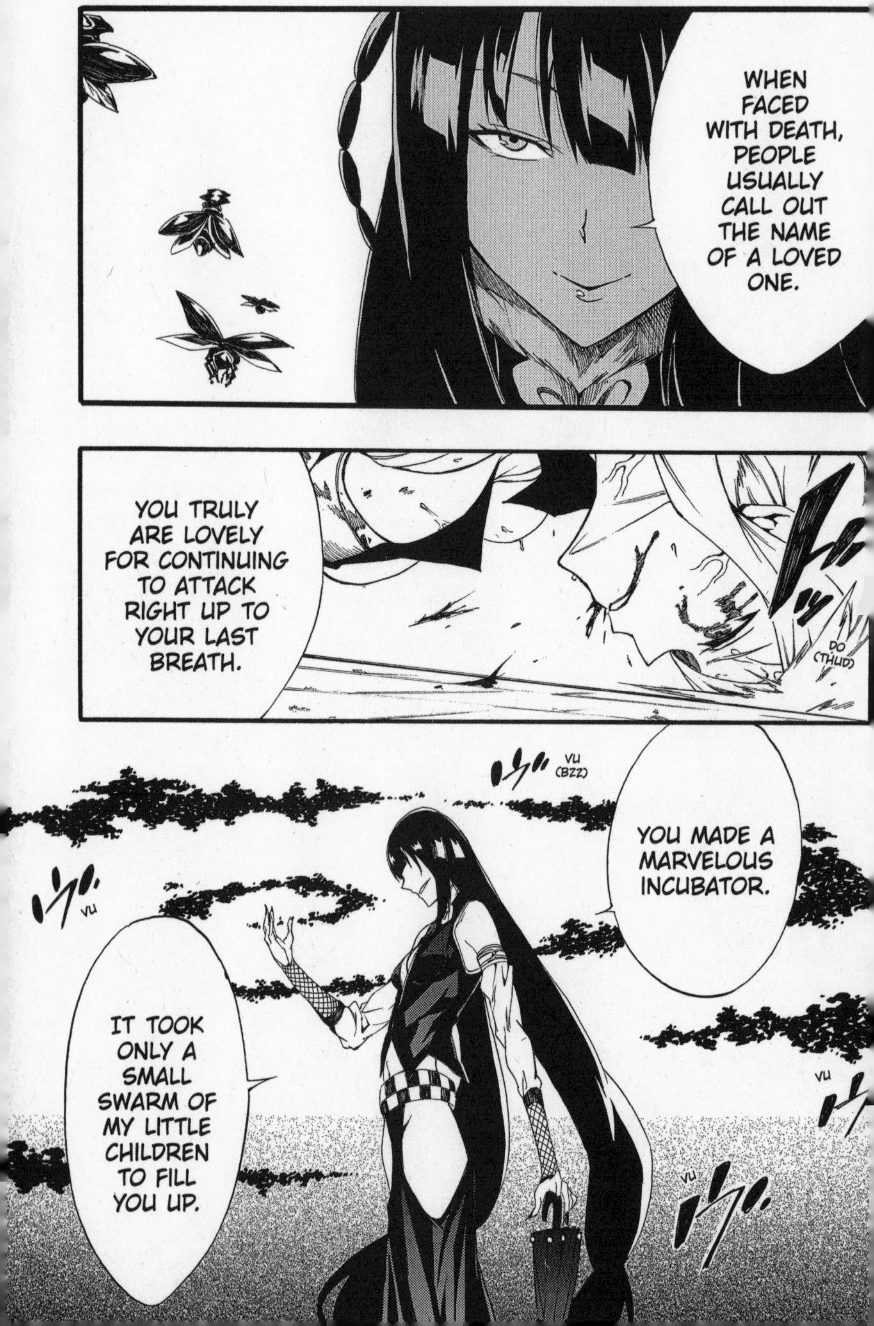
WHEN FACED WITH DEATH, PEOPLE USUALLY CALL OUT THE NAME OF A LOVED ONE.
DO (THUD)
YOU TRULY ARE LOVELY FOR CONTINUING TO ATTACK RIGHT UP TO YOUR LAST BREATH.
VU (BZZ)
YOU MADE A MARVELOUS INCUBATOR.
VU
VU
VU
IT TOOK ONLY A SMALL SWARM OF MY LITTLE CHILDREN TO FILL YOU UP.

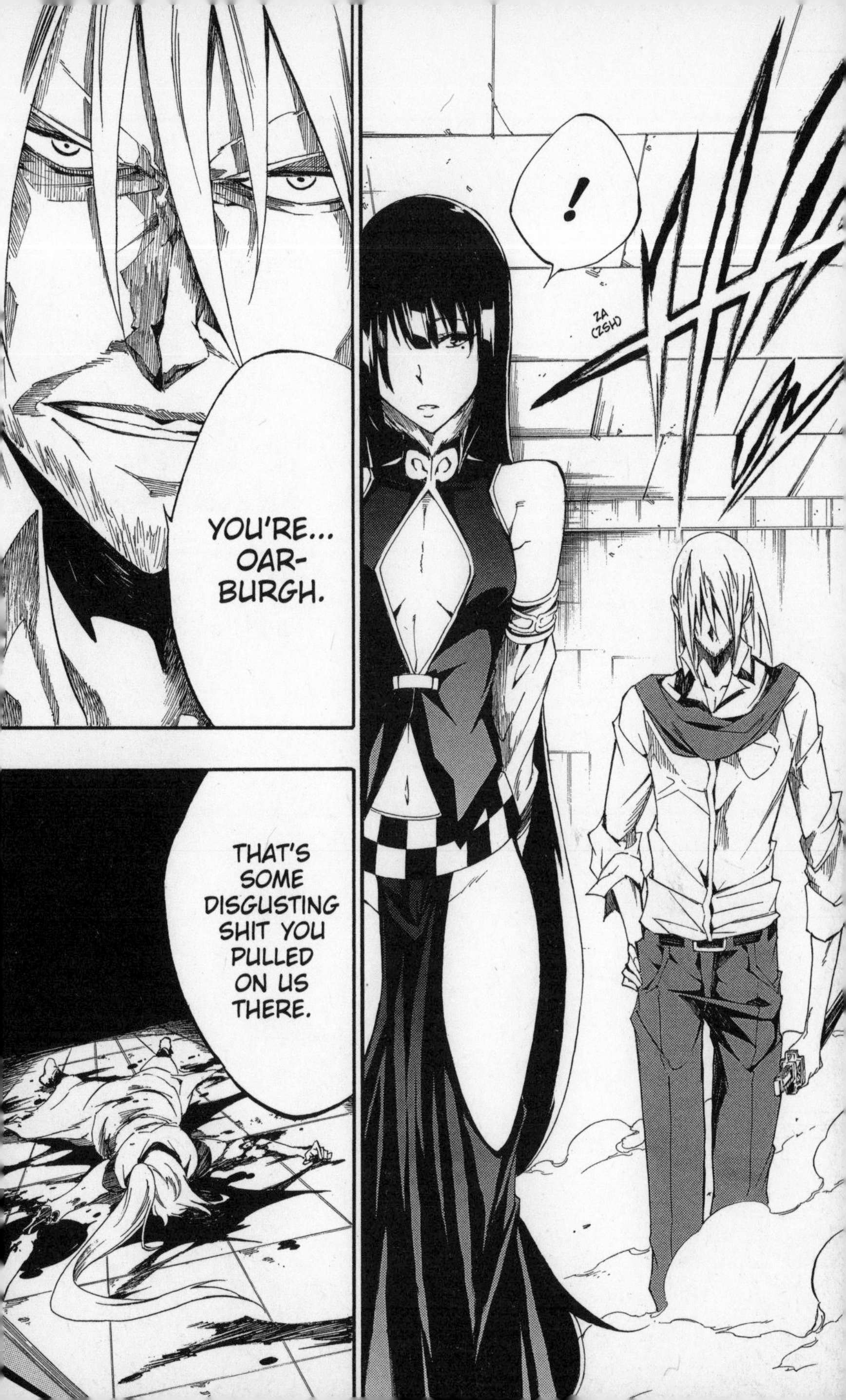
!
ZA (ZSH)
YOU'RE... OAR-BURGH.
THAT'S SOME DISGUSTING SHIT YOU PULLED ON US THERE.

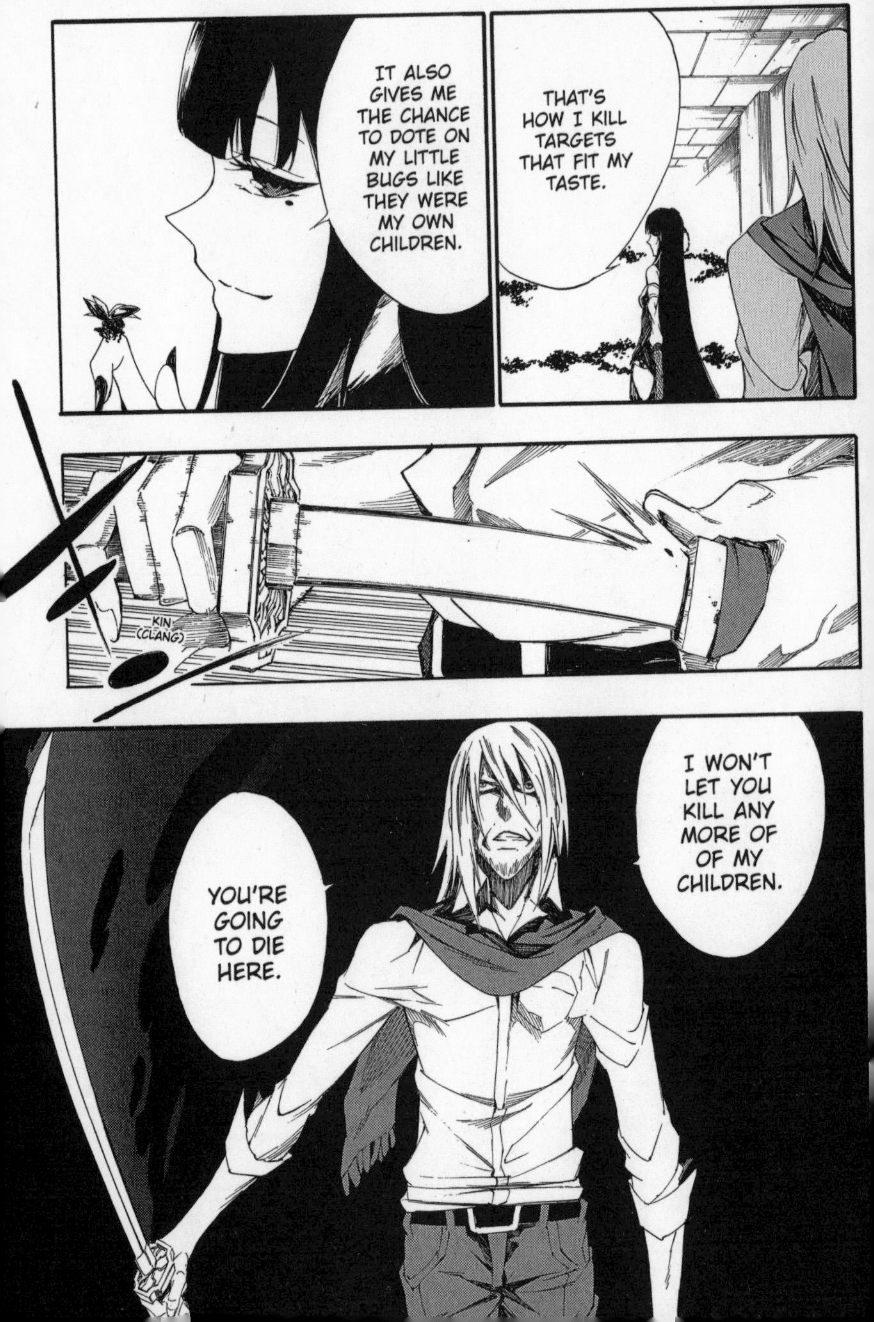
THAT'S HOW I KILL TARGETS THAT FIT MY TASTE.
IT ALSO GIVES ME THE CHANCE TO DOTE ON MY LITTLE BUGS LIKE THEY WERE MY OWN CHILDREN.
KIN (CLANG)
I WON'T LET YOU KILL ANY MORE OF OF MY CHILDREN.
YOU'RE GOING TO DIE HERE.

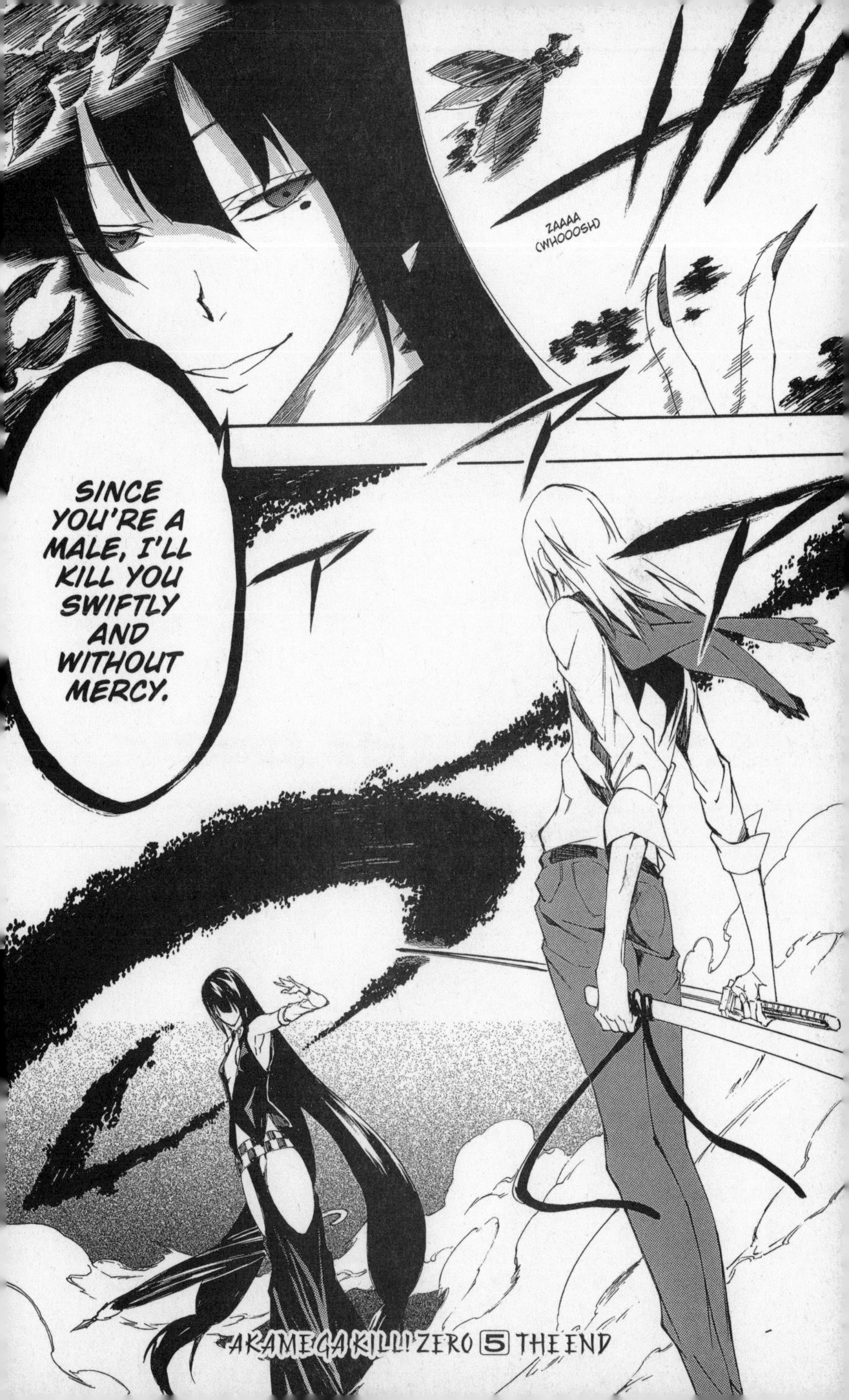
ZAAAA (WHOOOSH)
SINCE YOU'RE A MALE, I'LL KILL YOU SWIFTLY AND WITHOUT MERCY.
AKAME GA KILL! ZERO 5 THE END

Akame ga KILL! ZERO

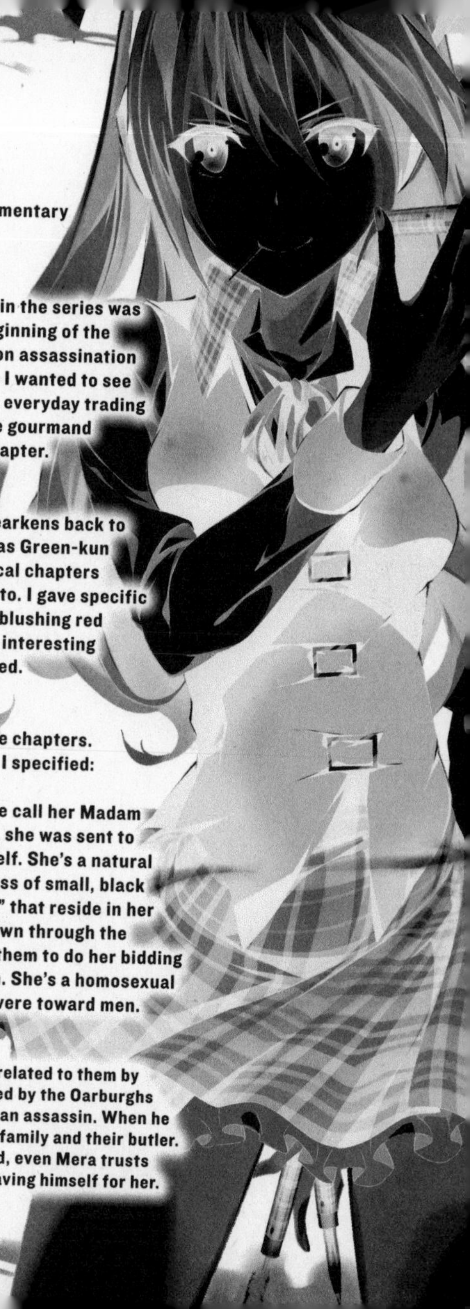

TAKAHIRO's PostScript

Hello, this is Takahiro with Minato Soft.
I'm going to provide some additional commentary on each chapter in Volume 5.

◆Chapter 26

Conveying the most heartwarming scene in the series was a must for the two-page spread at the beginning of the chapter. Akame and the gang are always on assassination missions, so I wrote this chapter because I wanted to see what life would be like if they took part in everyday trading and selling. And I got to add a touch of the gourmand to it too. It's basically a day-in-the-life chapter.

◆Chapter 27

The scene of Akame doing paper crafts hearkens back to something put into the original story. It was Green-kun who taught her. It's also one of those typical chapters where the main characters get confessed to. I gave specific instructions to not make Akame's face all blushing red with embarrassment, so it should be more interesting to see what it takes for her to really turn red.

◆Chapters 28–31

The Oarburghs show up and attack in these chapters. Below are the character design guidelines I specified:

①Merald Oarburgh

The youthful head of the Oarburghs, people call her Madam Mera. When Taeko and Babara were killed, she was sent to the front lines to take out the targets herself. She's a natural at assassination and commands a large mass of small, black insectoid Danger Beasts called "Wrigglers" that reside in her shadow. This is a technique only passed down through the leaders of the Oarburghs. She can control them to do her bidding for both assassinations and transportation. She's a homosexual who is very gentle toward girls and very severe toward men.

②Daniel

A butler employed by the Oarburghs. He's not related to them by blood, but since his childhood, he's been trained by the Oarburghs and sometimes takes part in their missions as an assassin. When he hit his sixties, he became the caretaker of the family and their butler. He's a man, but because he's so mild-mannered, even Mera trusts him. He's a virgin who loved Babara and was saving himself for her.

That's all. I'll continue the rest in the next volume. Thank you very much.

AKAME GA KILL! ZERO VOL. 5!

THANK YOU FOR YOUR PURCHASE!

EARLIER, I'D BEEN WARNED BY TAKAHIRO-SAN THAT "A REALLY DANGEROUS ENEMY IS GOING TO COME UP...(LOL)," BUT I WAS SHOCKED WHEN THEY TURNED OUT TO BE WICKED-STRONG ENEMIES CUT FROM A COMPLETELY DIFFERENT CLOTH THAN ESDEATH-SAMA FROM THE ORIGINAL STORY...I'M ALSO LOOKING FORWARD TO THE KILLING SPREE MERA-SAMA WILL SURELY GO ON AFTER THIS.

TO THE WRITER, TAKAHIRO-SAN; TASHIRO-SENSEI; OUR EDITOR, KOIZUMI-SAN; NAKAMURA-SAN, WHO HELPED WITH THE PICTURES; AND ALL THE READERS OUT THERE: THANK YOU VERY MUCH!

KEI TORU

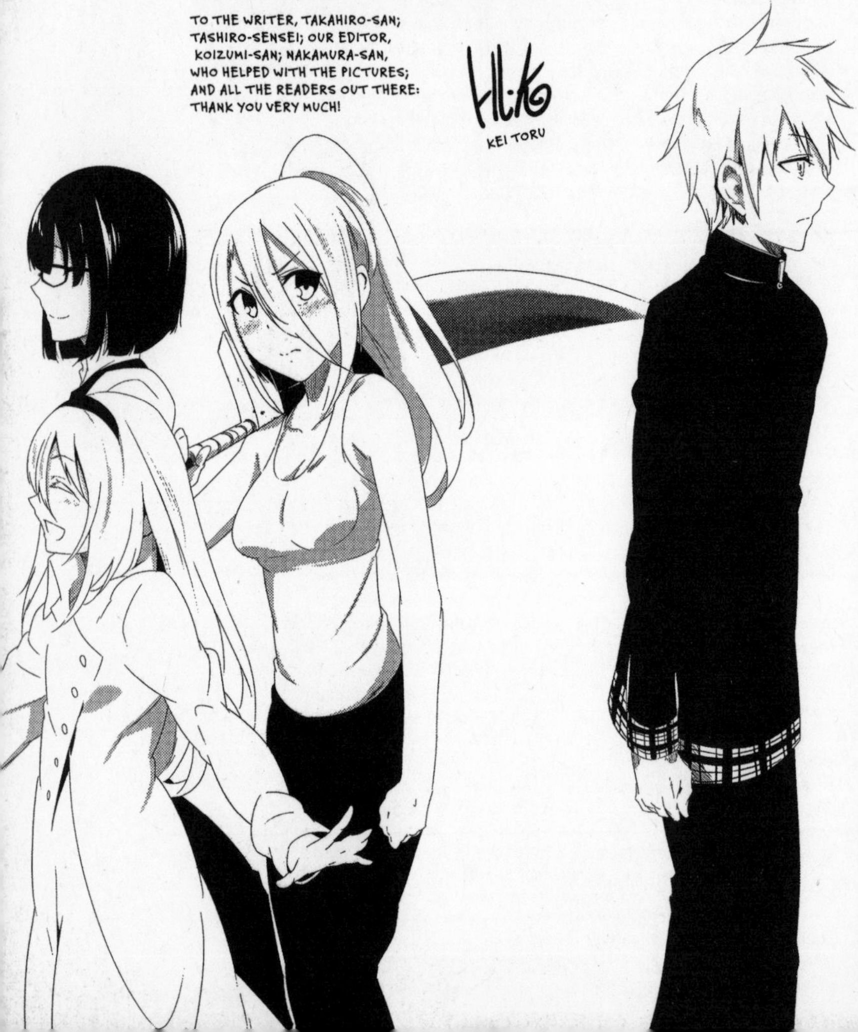

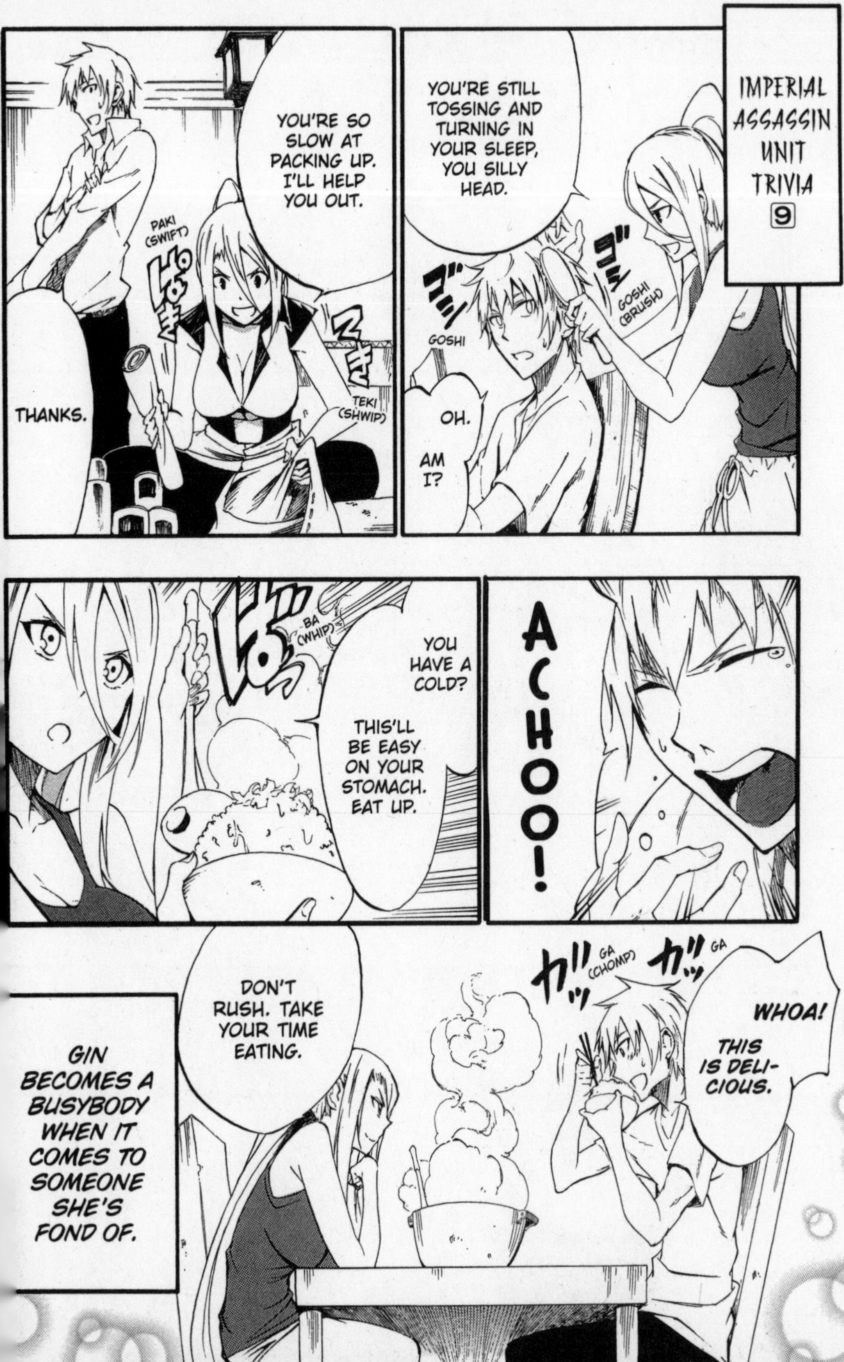
IMPERIAL ASSASSIN UNIT TRIVIA 9
YOU'RE STILL TOSSING AND TURNING IN YOUR SLEEP, YOU SILLY HEAD.
GOSHI (BRUSH)
GOSHI
OH.
AM I?
YOU'RE SO SLOW AT PACKING UP. I'LL HELP YOU OUT.
TEKI (SHWIP)
PAKI (SWIFT)
THANKS.
ACHOO!
BA (WHIP)
YOU HAVE A COLD?
THIS'LL BE EASY ON YOUR STOMACH. EAT UP.
GA
WHOA!
THIS IS DELICIOUS.
GA (CHOMP)
DON'T RUSH. TAKE YOUR TIME EATING.
GIN BECOMES A BUSYBODY WHEN IT COMES TO SOMEONE SHE'S FOND OF.

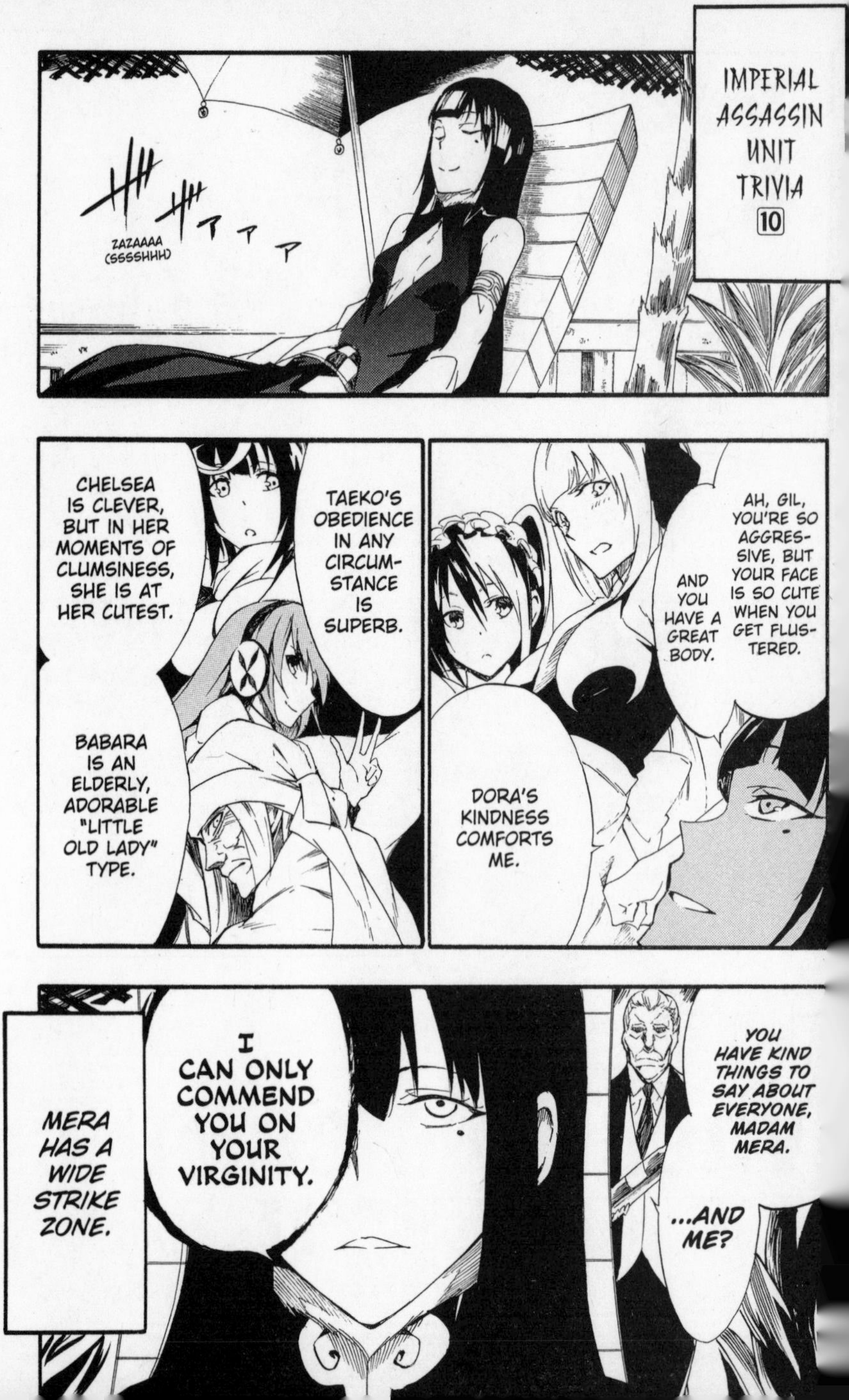
IMPERIAL ASSASSIN UNIT TRIVIA 10
ZAZAAAA (SSSSHHH)
AH, GIL, YOU'RE SO AGGRES-SIVE, BUT YOUR FACE IS SO CUTE WHEN YOU GET FLUS-TERED.
AND YOU HAVE A GREAT BODY.
DORA'S KINDNESS COMFORTS ME.
TAEKO'S OBEDIENCE IN ANY CIRCUM-STANCE IS SUPERB.
CHELSEA IS CLEVER, BUT IN HER MOMENTS OF CLUMSINESS, SHE IS AT HER CUTEST.
BABARA IS AN ELDERLY, ADORABLE "LITTLE OLD LADY" TYPE.
YOU HAVE KIND THINGS TO SAY ABOUT EVERYONE, MADAM MERA.
...AND ME?
I CAN ONLY COMMEND YOU ON YOUR VIRGINITY.
MERA HAS A WIDE STRIKE ZONE.

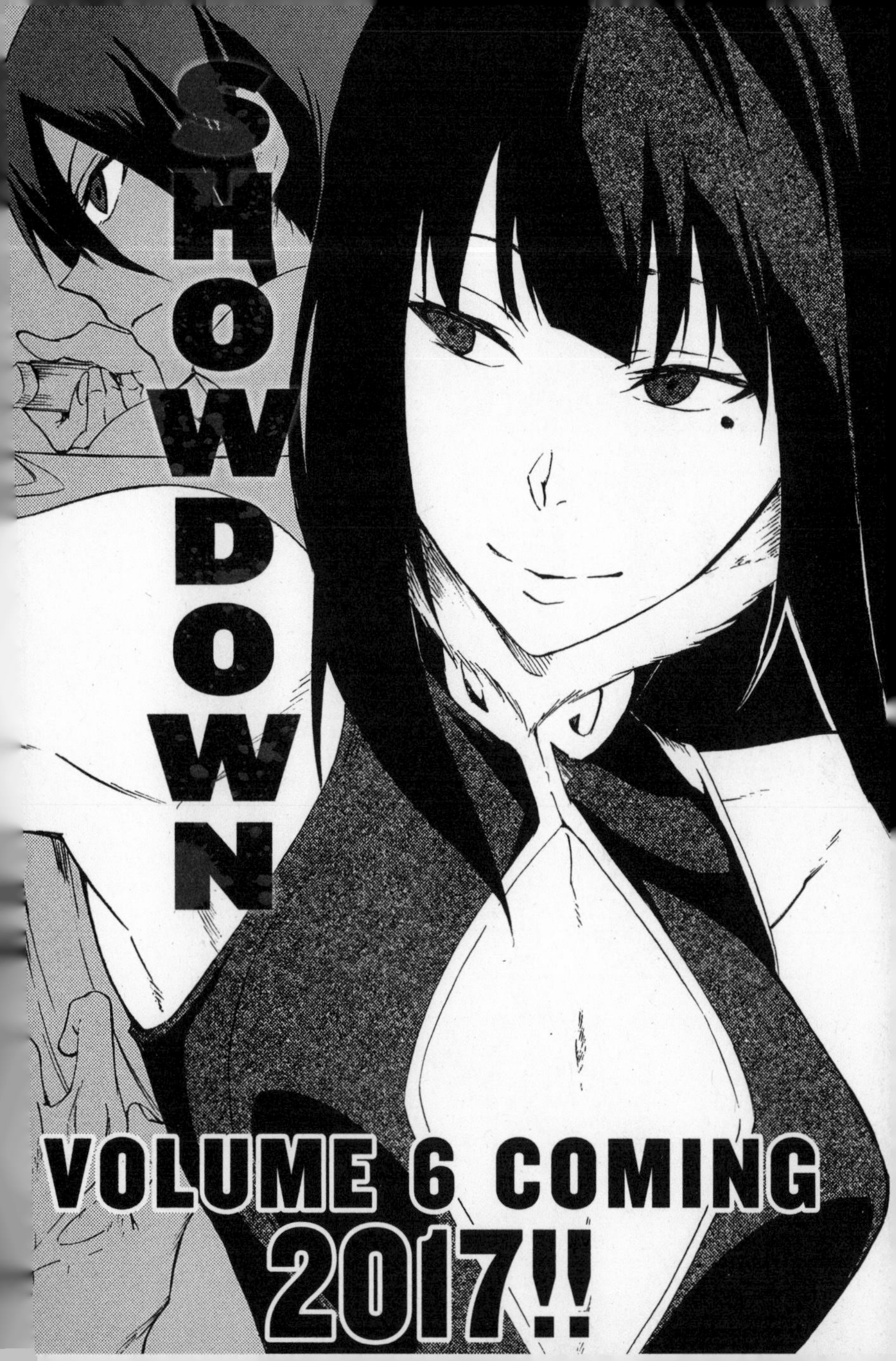
SHOWDOWN
VOLUME 6 COMING
2017!!

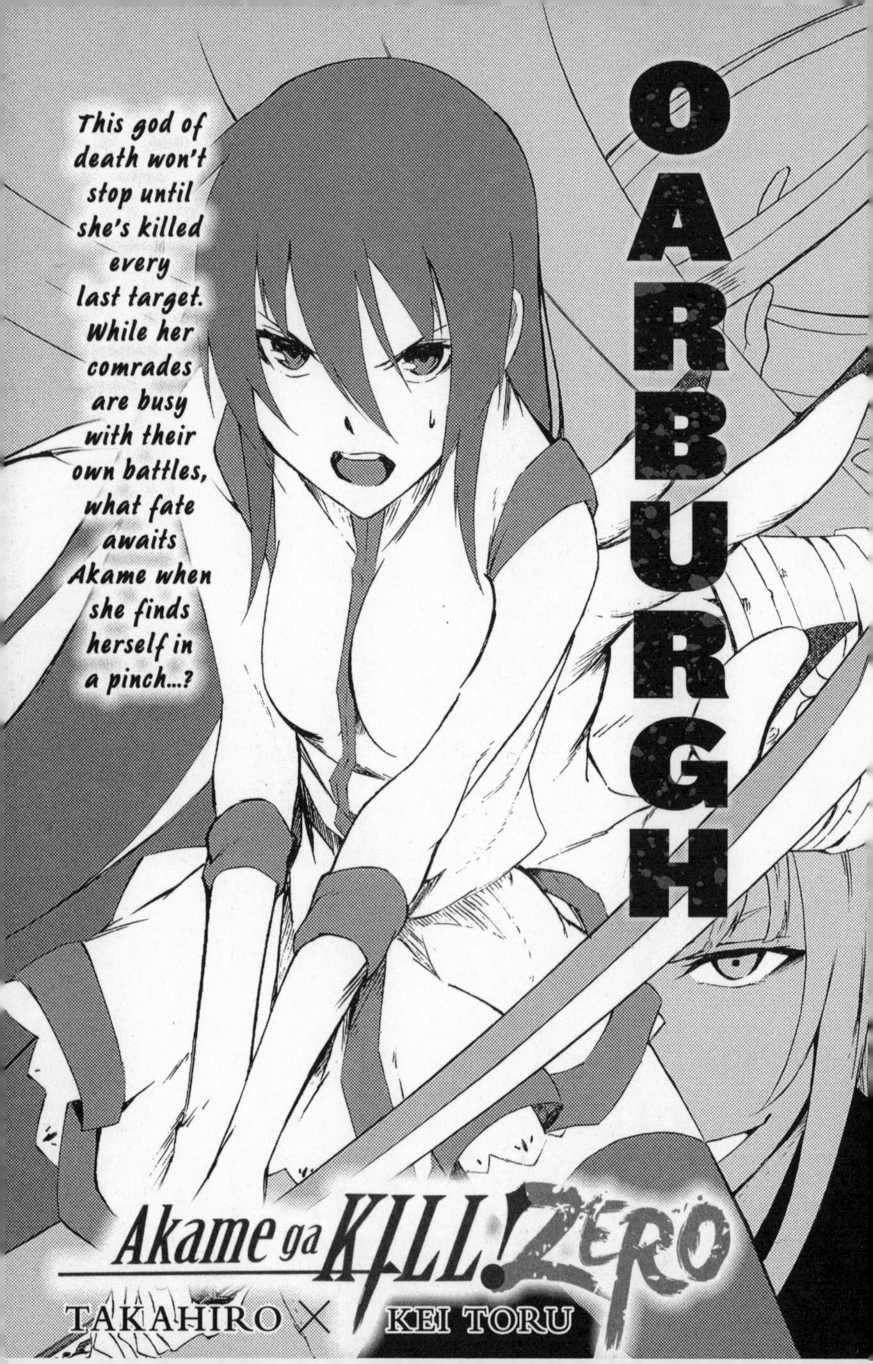
OARBURGH
This god of death won't stop until she's killed every last target. While her comrades are busy with their own battles, what fate awaits Akame when she finds herself in a pinch...?
Akame ga KILL! ZERO
TAKAHIRO × KEI TORU

Now read the latest chapters of *BLACK BUTLER* digitally at the same time as Japan and support the creator!

The Phantomhive family has a butler who's almost too good to be true...

...or maybe he's just too good to be human.

Black Butler

YANA TOBOSO

VOLUMES 1-23 IN STORES NOW!

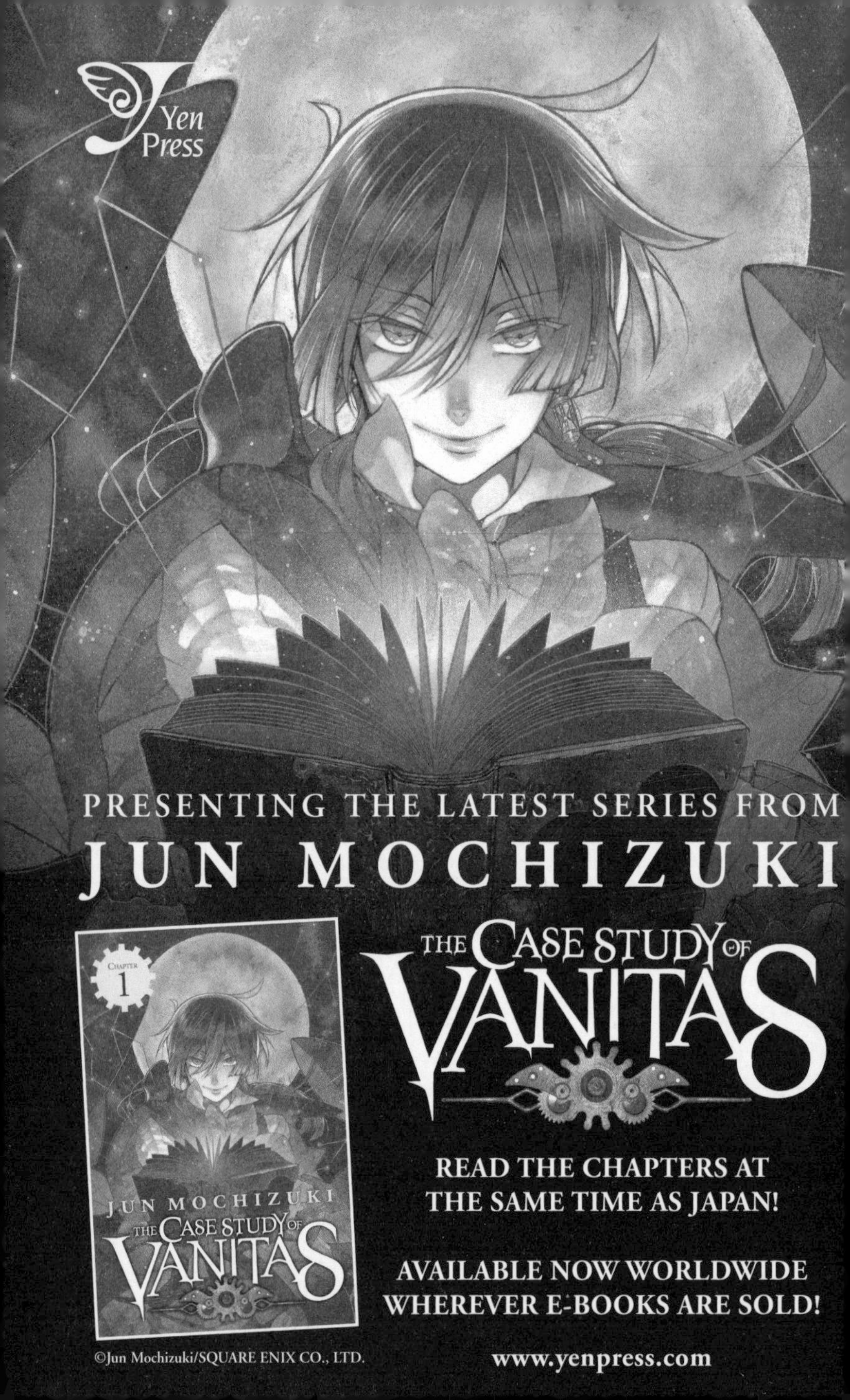
Yen Press
PRESENTING THE LATEST SERIES FROM
JUN MOCHIZUKI
CHAPTER 1
JUN MOCHIZUKI
THE CASE STUDY OF VANITAS
THE CASE STUDY OF VANITAS
READ THE CHAPTERS AT THE SAME TIME AS JAPAN!
AVAILABLE NOW WORLDWIDE WHEREVER E-BOOKS ARE SOLD!
©Jun Mochizuki/SQUARE ENIX CO., LTD.
www.yenpress.com

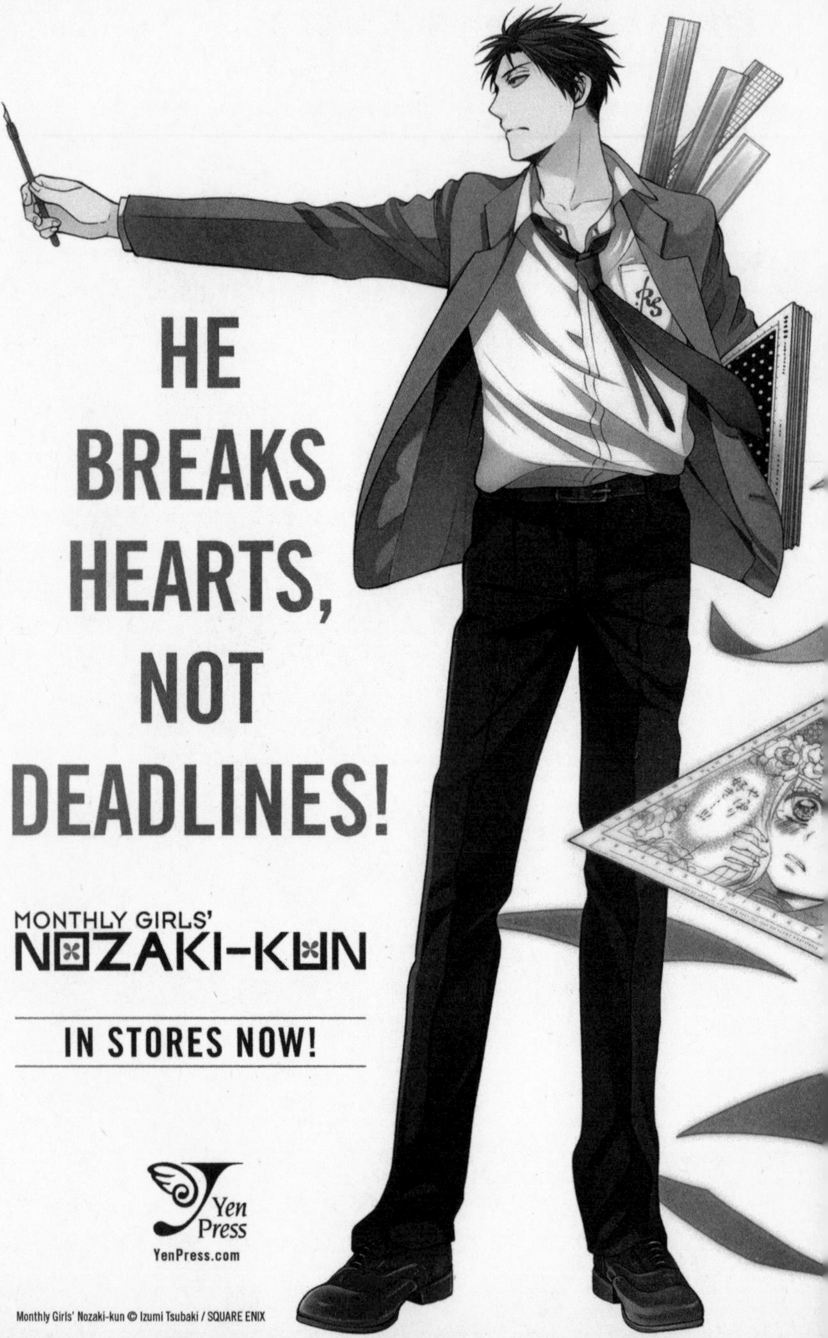
HE BREAKS HEARTS, NOT DEADLINES!
MONTHLY GIRLS'
NOZAKI-KUN
IN STORES NOW!
Yen Press
YenPress.com
Monthly Girls' Nozaki-kun © Izumi Tsubaki / SQUARE ENIX

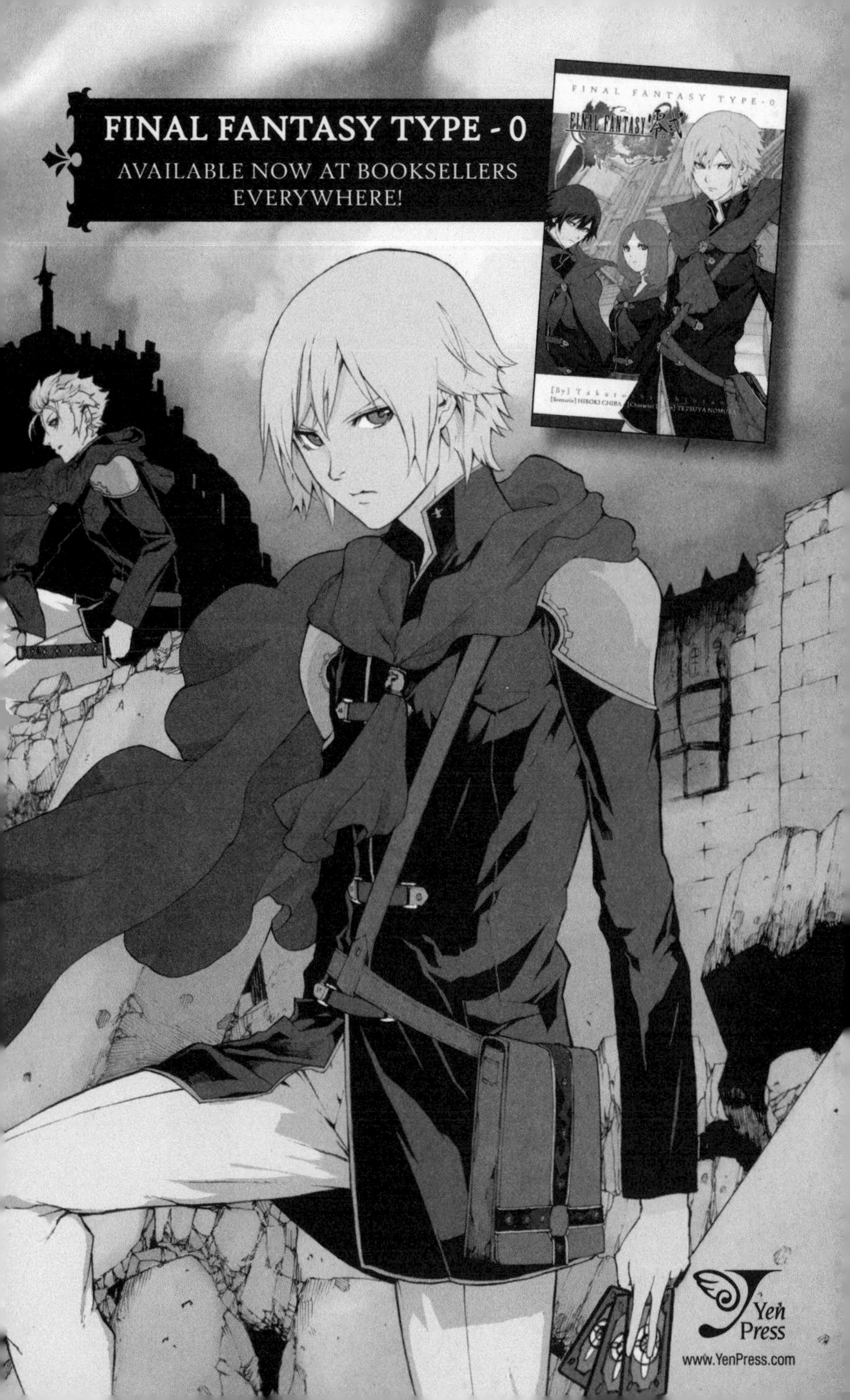
FINAL FANTASY TYPE - 0
AVAILABLE NOW AT BOOKSELLERS EVERYWHERE!
FINAL FANTASY TYPE-0
FINAL FANTASY 零式
[Scenario] HIROKI CHIBA
Yen Press
www.YenPress.com

FINAL FANTASY 零式 TYPE-0™

Art: TAKATOSHI SHIOZAWA
Character Design: TETSUYA NOMURA
Scenario: HIROKI CHIBA

The cadets of Akademeia's Class Zero are legends, with strength and magic unrivaled, and crimson capes symbolizing the great Vermilion Bird of the Dominion. But will their elite training be enough to keep them alive when a war breaks out and the Class Zero cadets find themselves at the front and center of a bloody political battlefield?!

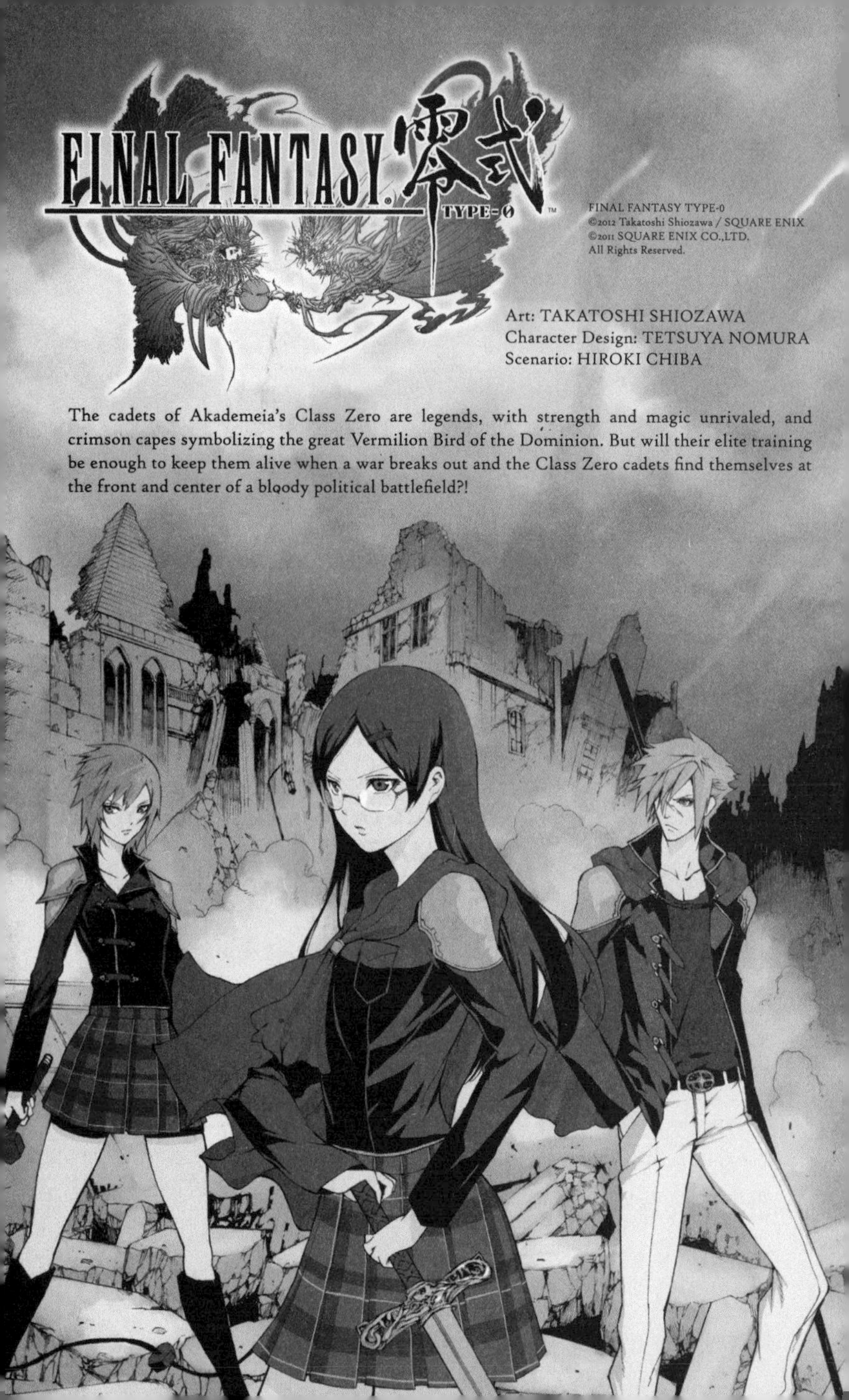

AKAME GA KILL! ZERO ⑤

Takahiro
Kei Toru

Translation: Christine Dashiell • **Lettering: Abigail Blackman**

AKAME GA KILL! ZERO 5
© 2016 Takahiro, Kei Toru / SQUARE ENIX CO., LTD. First published in Japan in 2016 by SQUARE ENIX CO., LTD. English translation rights arranged with SQUARE ENIX CO., LTD. and Yen Press, LLC through Tuttle-Mori Agency, Inc., Tokyo.

English translation © 2017 SQUARE ENIX CO., LTD.

Yen Press
1290 Avenue of the Americas
New York, NY 10104

Visit us at yenpress.com
facebook.com/yenpress
twitter.com/yenpress
yenpress.tumblr.com
instagram.com/yenpress

First Yen Press Edition: March 2017

Yen Press is an imprint of Yen Press, LLC.
The Yen Press name and logo are trademarks of Yen Press, LLC.

Library of Congress Control Number: 2015956843

ISBNs: 978-0-316-46921-0 (paperback)
       978-0-316-43917-6 (ebook)

10 9 8 7 6 5 4 3 2 1

BVG

Printed in the United States of America